Fifty years of the International Convention on the Elimination of All Forms of Racial Discrimination

MANCHESTER
1824
Manchester University Press

Fifty years of the International Convention on the Elimination of All Forms of Racial Discrimination

A living instrument

Edited by David Keane and Annapurna Waughray

Manchester University Press

Published by Manchester University Press
Altrincham Street, Manchester M1 7JA
www.manchesteruniversitypress.co.uk

British Library Cataloguing-in-Publication Data
A catalogue record for this book is available from the British Library

ISBN 978 1 7849 9304 7 hardback

First published 2017

Typeset by Out of House Publishing
Printed in Great Britain
by CPI Group (UK) Ltd, Croydon, CR0 4YY

Contents

Part III: Conflict and resolution

Part IV: Present and future of ICERD

Contributors

Michael Banton served as an elected member of the United Nations Committee on the Elimination of Racial Discrimination from 1986 to 2001, and as its chair from 1996 to 1998. He received his PhD from the University of Edinburgh, where he acted as Lecturer and Reader in Social Anthropology before becoming Professor of Sociology at the University of Bristol (1965–92). He was President of the Royal Anthropological Institute of Great Britain and Ireland (1987–89), and President of the Sociology section (1970–71), and the Anthropology section (1985–86), within the British Association for the Advancement of Science. He is the author of numerous scholarly works on race and racial theories, as well as the international fight against racial discrimination, such as *Racial Theories* (Cambridge University Press, 1987), *Racial Consciousness* (Longman, 1987) and *International Action against Racial Discrimination* (Oxford University Press, 1996), in addition to many journal articles. His latest work is *What We Know Now about Race and Ethnicity* (Berghahn, 2015).

Claude Cahn is Human Rights Adviser at the Office of the United Nations High Commissioner for Human Rights (OHCHR). From 2009 to 2015, he was based in the Office of the United Nations Resident Coordinator in the Republic of Moldova and in 2015 the position moved to Serbia. From 1996 to 2007, he worked for the European Roma Rights Centre (ERRC) in a number of capacities including Programmes Director and Acting Executive Director. He has been continuously involved in efforts to secure justice for Romani women coercively sterilised in the Czech Republic, Slovakia and Hungary, as well as in other aspects of the struggle to combat racism and discrimination against Roma, including school desegregation efforts in a number of countries.

Joshua Castellino is Professor of Law and Dean of the School of Law and the Business School at Middlesex University, London.

He worked as a journalist in Mumbai with the Indian Express Group, was awarded a Chevening Scholarship to pursue an MA in International Law and Politics, and completed his PhD in International Law in 1998. He has authored and edited eight books in international law and human rights law as well as a range of journal articles. He has completed the third in a five-book series published by Oxford University Press on global minority rights, the latest (with Kathleen Cavanaugh) entitled *Minority Rights in the Middle East: A Comparative Legal Analysis* (Oxford University Press, 2013). He serves on the Leadership Council of the UN Sustainable Development Solutions Network where he co-chairs the Thematic Group on Social Inclusion, Gender and Human Rights, and was appointed Chair by the OHCHR of the 8th Forum on Minority Issues, an inter-governmental dialogue with civil society under the auspices of the UN Human Rights Council.

Joshua Clark received his PhD in Anthropology from the University of California, Irvine, United States in December 2016. He is currently Managing Editor of the *Journal of Cultural Economy*. He has published a number of papers and essays on his site https://uci.academia.edu/JoshuaClark.

Ion Diaconu served as an elected member of the United Nations Committee on the Elimination of Racial Discrimination from 1991 to 2003 and 2008 to 2012, including chair of the Committee from 2002 to 2003 and rapporteur of the Committee from 2008 to 2012. He had previously acted as a member of the UN Sub-Commission on the Prevention of Discrimination and Protection of Minorities from 1988 to 1991, amongst many other regional and international positions. He holds a PhD in International Law from the University of Geneva, Switzerland (1971), and has acted as a Professor of International Law at a range of universities, from 2010 at Spiru Haret University, Bucharest, Romania. He has acted as Romanian ambassador to Denmark (1993–97), Iceland (1994–97) and the Russian Federation (1997–2001). He has published more than 100 studies and articles on different issues of international law and human rights in Romanian, English and French, including *Racial Discrimination* (Eleven International Publishing, 2010).

Cathal Doyle holds a PhD from Middlesex University London, School of Law, where he is currently employed as a Leverhulme Trust research fellow. He has published a range of books, articles, reports and other materials in the area of indigenous peoples' rights, as well as acting as an advocate on behalf of indigenous groups and a researcher with the Special Rapporteur on Indigenous Peoples, among other advocacy roles. His books include *Indigenous Peoples, Title to Territory, Rights and Resources: The Transformative Role of Free Prior and Informed Consent* (Routledge, 2014) and *Business and Human Rights: Indigenous Peoples' Experiences with Access to Remedy: Case Studies from Africa, Asia and Latin America* (International Work Group for Indigenous Affairs, 2015).

Jérémie Gilbert is Professor of Human Rights Law at the University of Roehampton, United Kingdom. He has published various books, articles and chapters on the rights of indigenous peoples and related minority rights questions, including *Indigenous Peoples' Land Rights under International Law: From Victims to Actors* (Brill, 2nd edn, 2016), and *Nomadic Peoples and Human Rights* (Routledge, 2014). He has served as a consultant for several international organisations including the Expert Mechanism on the Rights of Indigenous Peoples (2015). He regularly works with non-governmental organisations supporting indigenous peoples' rights such as the Forest Peoples' Programme, Minority Rights Group International and the Rainforest Foundation. He was the vice-chair of the International Work Group for Indigenous Affairs (IWGIA) international board (2009–15).

Nozipho January-Bardill completed her twelfth year as an elected member of the United Nations Committee on the Elimination of Racial Discrimination in January 2016. During this period she also served as South Africa's Ambassador to Switzerland, Lichtenstein and the Holy See and as Deputy Director General, Human Capital Management, in the South African Department of Foreign Affairs. She is currently an independent non-executive director on the boards of three companies and chairs the Social Ethics and Sustainability sub-committees of two of them, including oversight in human rights, the environment and sustainable development. After serving as Acting Chief of Staff for UN Women in 2014/15, she continues to act as Senior Advisor for the South Africa multi-country office of UNWomen. She was recently appointed to the Council of the Nelson Mandela Metropolitan University (NMMU) and Chairperson of the Advisory Committee of the United Nations Global Compact (UNGC) in South Africa. She remains committed to social justice and good governance and has published papers and articles analysing the international response to racism, xenophobia and related intolerance.

David Keane is Associate Professor in International Human Rights Law at Middlesex University, London, United Kingdom. He holds a BCL (Law and French) from University College Cork, and an LLM and

PhD from the Irish Centre for Human Rights, National University of Ireland, Galway, where he was awarded a Government of Ireland scholarship for his doctoral studies (2002–5). His book *Caste-based Discrimination in International Human Rights Law* (Ashgate-Routledge, 2007) was awarded the Hart Book Prize for early career scholars in 2008. He has published a further co-authored book, a co-edited collection, and over twenty-five journal articles and book chapters on issues of international human rights law, minority rights and racial discrimination. He is a co-author of the UK Equality and Human Rights Commission's Research Reports on Caste in Britain, as well as advising the United Nations on its forthcoming Guidance Tool on caste and descent-based discrimination.

Tarlach McGonagle is a senior researcher/lecturer at the Institute for Information Law (IViR) at the University of Amsterdam in the Netherlands. He specialises in and has published widely on a broad range of topics relating to international and European human rights law, media law and policy and journalism. He was awarded a PhD by the University of Amsterdam (2008) for his thesis examining the interface between freedom of expression and minority rights under international law. He regularly does expert work for various branches of the Council of Europe and the Organization for Security and Cooperation in Europe. He was Rapporteur of the Council of Europe's Committee of Experts on protection of journalism and safety of journalists (2014–15) and is currently a member of the Council of Europe's Committee of Experts on media pluralism and transparency of media ownership. He was an invited expert speaker at the Thematic Discussion on 'Racist Hate Speech' organised by the United Nations Committee on the Elimination of Racial Discrimination in 2012.

Pastor Murillo served as an elected member of the United Nations Committee on the Elimination of Racial Discrimination from 2008 to 2012 and 2016 to 2020. He acted as Deputy Director and Director of Negro, Race and Palenquera Community Affairs at the Ministry of the Interior and Justice in Colombia, with a permanent seat on the Council for Economic and Social Policy (CONPES), from where he coordinated the drawing-up of public policies for these groups. He worked as human rights adviser to Colombia's Ministry of Foreign Affairs and the Multilateral Economic, Social and Environmental Affairs Division. Additionally he acted as Alternate to the head of the Colombian delegation to the Third World Conference on Racism, Racial Discrimination, Xenophobia and other related forms of Intolerance, in Durban, South Africa. He was the author of the original draft resolution which led first to the adoption of the

International Year for People of African Descent in 2011 (GA Res. 64/169) and later the International Decade for People of African Descent 2015–24 (GA Res. 68/237).

Lydia A. Nkansah is Senior Lecturer and Dean at the Faculty of Law, Kwame Nkrumah University of Science and Technology, Ghana. She has served as the Head of Research Unit and Leader of Evidence at the Truth and Reconciliation Commission for Sierra Leone (2003), International Expert Advisor to the National Transitional Legislative Assembly of Liberia on its Reconciliation Bill (2005) and Senior Legal Officer at the Commission on Human Rights and Administrative Justice of Ghana (1994–2001). She has published a range of journal articles and papers on international criminal law, as well as truth and justice in post-conflict peacebuilding processes and related areas.

Esther Ojulari is a PhD candidate at the Institute for Commonwealth Studies, University of London, United Kingdom, where she is researching the human rights of Afro-descendant people in Colombia. She holds a Masters with distinction in human rights; and has particular knowledge of minority rights, children's rights and economic, social and cultural rights. She has eight years' work experience in international development and human rights with the United Nations and with UK-based NGOs, and is currently a consultant at the UN OHCHR in Geneva working on publications in the context of the International Decade for People of African Descent and related issues.

William Schabas is Professor of International Law at Middlesex University in London. He is also Professor of International Human Law and Human Rights at Leiden University, Emeritus Professor of Human Rights Law at the National University of Ireland Galway and Honorary Chairman of the Irish Centre for Human Rights, Invited Visiting Scholar at the Paris School of International Affairs (Sciences Politiques), Honorary Professor at the Chinese Academy of Social Sciences in Beijing, Visiting Fellow of Kellogg College of the University of Oxford, Visiting Fellow of Northumbria University, and professeur associé at the Université du Québec à Montréal. He is the author of more than twenty books dealing in whole or in part with international human rights law, including: *Introduction to the International Criminal Court* (Cambridge University Press, 2016, 5th edn), *The International Criminal Court: A Commentary on the Rome Statute* (Oxford University Press, 2016, 2nd edn), *The European Convention on Human Rights: A Commentary* (Oxford University Press, 2015); *The Universal Declaration of Human*

Rights: travaux préparatoires (Cambridge University Press, 2013); *Unimaginable Atrocities: Justice, Politics and Rights at the War Crimes Tribunals* (Oxford University Press, 2012), *Genocide in International Law* (Cambridge University Press, 2009, 2nd edn) and *The Abolition of the Death Penalty in International Law* (Cambridge University Press, 2003, 3rd edn). He has also published more than 350 articles in academic journals. From 2002 to 2004 he served as one of three international members of the Sierra Leone Truth and Reconciliation Commission. In 2014, he was appointed chair of the UN Commission of Inquiry into the Gaza Conflict. Professor Schabas has been awarded the Vespasian V. Pella Medal for International Criminal Justice of the Association internationale de droit pénal, and the Gold Medal in the Social Sciences of the Royal Irish Academy, and was named an Officer of the Order of Canada in 2006.

Patrick Thornberry served as an elected member of the United Nations Committee on the Elimination of Racial Discrimination from 2001 to 2014, acting as rapporteur of that Committee from 2002 to 2008. He is Emeritus Professor of International Law at Keele University, UK, a Visiting Fellow of Kellogg College, University of Oxford, an Honorary Professor of Law, Nottingham University. He is a former Chairman of Minority Rights Group International and has acted as consultant and adviser to a range of international organisations. Professor Thornberry is the author of numerous works in the field of minority rights, rights of indigenous peoples and racial discrimination, notably *International Law and the Rights of Minorities* (Clarendon Press, 1991) and *Indigenous Peoples and Human Rights* (Manchester University Press, 2002). He has recently published a commentary on ICERD, entitled *The International Convention on the Elimination of All Forms of Racial Discrimination: A Commentary* (Oxford University Press, 2016).

Annapurna Waughray is Reader in Human Rights Law at Manchester Metropolitan University, United Kingdom. She worked in the NGO and third sectors in women's rights and health rights before training as a lawyer, and was in practice as a civil litigation solicitor until moving into academia. She has published on human rights, minority rights and discrimination and equality issues, focusing on caste and the law in the UK, India, and in international human rights law. She is the author of a number of key articles on caste discrimination and the law, including the first article analysing caste discrimination in UK law, a co-author of the UK Equality and Human Rights Commission's Research Reports on Caste in Britain (2014), and has advised the United Nations on its forthcoming Guidance

Tool on caste and descent-based discrimination. She has a contract with Routledge for her book, *Capturing Caste in Law: The Legal Regulation of Caste-based Discrimination* (Routledge, forthcoming 2018). She holds a BA (Hons) from the University of Cambridge in Social and Political Sciences (having matriculated in French and German), an LLM in International and European Law from the University of Liverpool, and a PhD from the School of Law and Social Justice, University of Liverpool.

Foreword

The adoption by the General Assembly of the United Nations (UN) of the International Convention on the Elimination of All Forms of Racial Discrimination (ICERD/the Convention) on 21 December 1965 continues to stand as a signal moment in the history of international law on the rights of peoples and human rights, a landmark event.[1] The Convention stemmed from decades of agitation against the colonial possessions of, particularly, the Western powers, and the affront to humanity represented by apartheid, a system that purported to divide and rank human beings on the basis of their 'race', relegating some populations to the status of racial inferiors, whilst elevating the status of 'Europeans'. Apartheid and related practices built upon centuries of racial theorising, leading to predictable classifications of 'white' populations as representing the apex of civilisation, and further expressed through the grotesqueries of Nazism and its genocidal programmes of racial privilege and damnation.

Nineteenth-century international law imbibed the racist virus. The twentieth century attempted to find an escape through fundamental, principled restatements of the equality and dignity of human beings and the worth of the cultures of humanity in all their subtlety and variety. Intellectually, the escapology included the deconstruction of the category of 'race' by UNESCO. Institutionally, the statements of human rights in the UN Charter and the Universal Declaration of Human Rights (UDHR) laid the groundwork for a new synthesis of values. These values were further expressed through a raft of instruments expounding and clarifying the rights of individuals, groups and

1 See remarks of the representative of Italy (Bosco) on the adoption of the Convention: A/PV.1406, paras. 109–10. Surname references in brackets in this preface refer to contributors to the present volume.

categories of human beings, coupling statements of principle with practical methodologies designed to convert principle into practice.

Preceded by the Declaration on the Elimination of All Forms of Racial Discrimination in 1963, and converting its premises into legally binding standards, the Convention carried the hopes and aspirations of many in the international community for an international order of mutual respect and harmony among nations and peoples. The emerging document generated mixed emotions, and was regarded at the culmination of the drafting process as everything from merely an infant step in the progress of humanity,[2] to a triumph of diplomacy.[3] The focus on race, perceived as sharply distinguishable from problems associated with religious diversity and discrimination, was crucial to its adoption. The Convention rode on the crest of a wave of anti-colonial and anti-apartheid activism. It is not accidental that the Preamble makes explicit reference to the so-called Colonial Declaration of 1960 (UN General Assembly Resolution 1514(XV)), while apartheid is the only specific 'form' of discrimination identified by the operative text (Article 3). It was not perhaps so much the idea of race that incensed the experts and delegates involved in drafting the Convention as the suggestion of hierarchy (inferiority/superiority) applied to nations, peoples and individual worth.

It is also notable that many delegates approved the Convention on the assumption that doing so was in essence an act of international solidarity, since many of them claimed that racial discrimination did not manifest itself on their home territories, but was an aberration associated with (Western) colonialism and apartheid. Others, however, sensed the potential ubiquity of the phenomenon in light of the complex demographics of States worldwide and the melancholy archive of the historical suppression of ethnic minorities and indigenous peoples. Overall, the *travaux* of the Convention do not evidence great solicitude for ethnic minorities and non-citizens: the former go without specific mention in the Convention, while the latter were purportedly accounted for by the ostensibly ungenerous Article 1(2) of the Convention. The key ethic of the drafting majority was the building of strong, unified States and nations, with the development of sub-State identities treated at best as of secondary importance.

The setting up of the Committee on the Elimination of Racial Discrimination (CERD/the Committee), a committee of independent experts rather than representative of States, was an outstandingly important move in the drafting process. The Committee, the first of

2 Remarks of the representative of Ghana (Lamptey), *ibid.*, paras. 93–4.
3 'A resounding victory', comment by the representative of Colombia (Ospina), *ibid.*, para. 98.

the UN 'core' treaty bodies, has laboured since its inception to give sense and shape to the rapidly assembled text and complex intellectual inheritance of the Convention. Claims by States of 'no discrimination here' have been treated with increasing scepticism by the Committee. Insistent requests for disaggregated ethnic data (Clark) for the population as a whole as well as for the application of specific rights ride roughshod over counter-claims of ethnic homogeneity or interethnic harmony. The data requests are not innocent but presume complex ethnic realities, and insinuate demands to address the negative consequences thereof when expressed as racial discrimination. The Committee demands in effect an exercise in demographic truth-telling by the States parties, whatever their 'official' ideology on the recognition or otherwise of minorities (Castellino), indigenous peoples (Gilbert and Doyle), people of African descent (Murillo and Ojulari), caste groups (Waughray and Keane) and non-citizens.

The Committee pursues the quarry of racial discrimination through various procedural means set out explicitly in the Convention, or developed therefrom. The ostensibly anodyne reporting procedure under Article 9 is perhaps the most generally effective procedural device applied by the Committee, including the early warning and urgent action procedure for the most serious situations of actual or potential violations of human rights developed under its auspices (Doyle, Schabas). Examining State reports under Article 9 allows the Committee to gain a holistic view of country situations, and is geared to constructive dialogue rather than the condemnation of violations, though Concluding Observations have also been highly critical of State performance, expressed in terms of 'concern' or 'serious concern' by the Committee.

By contrast, the communications procedure under Article 14 has not fulfilled the hopes of its progenitors, though it has made important determinations, including in the field of hate speech (McGonagle), and on sundry forms of discrimination against Roma (Cahn). The Committee has engaged in inconclusive heart-searching as to why the Article 14 procedure has not proved more attractive to States parties.[4] Perhaps there are simply too many such international procedures around, even if they do not have a specific 'racial' focus. It is in any case arguable that the vocation of the Convention is well served by the broader procedures that address the rights of populations as a whole. The inter-State procedure under Articles 11–13 has also not been formally applied, though remains open as a possibility; in this respect the situation is similar to that of other UN treaty bodies.

4 57 States parties have made the 'optional declaration' under Article 14, out of 178 States parties to the Convention.

The major inter-State 'case' on the Convention (*Georgia* v. *Russian Federation*) took place before the International Court of Justice and outside the confines of the Committee (Nkansah). The interpretation of the Convention by the Committee is principally expressed through the constantly growing body of Concluding Observations on State party reports, and through general recommendations (GRs), the last of which, GR 35, distilled the opinion of the Committee on the vexed issue of racist hate speech,[5] aligning the Article 4 prohibition of racial incitement and dissemination of ideas of racial superiority more closely with contemporary currents on freedom of speech.

The Committee has made some outstanding determinations and has engaged in discussion of many if not all the key issues in the Convention. The ground of 'race' continues to trouble some States parties, concerned in case their legislation appears to endorse the theory of separate human races. The Committee has still to address the issue fully and concretely, though its main concerns in Concluding Observations to States parties are practical rather than philosophical, in that the absence of a prohibition of discrimination based on 'race' may result in legal lacunae, to the potential detriment of victims. The Committee's approach to addressing caste among the grounds of discrimination under 'descent' is strongly challenged by India, and less stridently by Japan. The 'grounds' of discrimination (race, colour, descent; national origin, ethnic origin) have been 'stretched' through utilisation of the concept of 'intersectionality', especially in the area of gender, where the Committee has developed a solid and innovative practice (January-Bardill). The Committee has nonetheless been cautious on the intersectionality front more widely, lest too many claimed associations between racial discrimination and other factors deflect attention from the primary focus of the Convention.[6]

The rights in the Convention, as expressed in, for example, Article 5, are set out schematically and without great detail, without qualifications and 'clawbacks', and in an incomplete listing. The open, porous nature of rights to be protected from discrimination allows the Committee to make sense of the Convention as a 'living instrument', and draw upon developments in sister instruments under the broad rubric of the interdependence and indivisibility of human rights.[7] As

5 See in particular *TBB Turkish Union in Berlin/Brandenburg* v. *Germany*, CERD/C/82/D/48/2010 (2013), including the dissenting opinion by CERD member Vázquez.

6 For a recent critique of the intersectionality concept, see report of the Holy See, CERD/C/VAT/16–23, para. 5; the Committee's response is elaborated in CERD/C/VAT/CO/16–23, paras. 6 and 7.

7 Sundry chapters in the present volume, including those by the editors, address the concept of the Convention as a 'living instrument'; see also *Hagan* v. *Australia*, CERD/C/62/D/26/2002 (2003).

amply testified in the present volume, the living instrument notion affects all areas of the Convention. Committee practice on hate speech has been enriched by drawing upon developments in the Human Rights Committee (General Comment 34) and elsewhere. The adaptation of Article 3 on segregation and apartheid to the disappearance of 'formal' apartheid and the prevalence of 'informal' segregation practices in a variety of social fields, is another example of movement and adaptation.

A further notable development in the 'aggiornamento' of the Convention is the increased respect paid to collective rights, whether of indigenous peoples, Afro-descendant populations or other groups. Cultural aspects of the enjoyment of human rights have also been accorded significant prominence by the Committee, following similar patterns of 'culturalization' in practice under sister human rights instruments.[8] The Convention is not, as might have been feared at its adoption, an assimilationist instrument; on the contrary, the Committee has interpreted the Convention as validating human rights, individual and collective, as appropriate to the realities of the populations concerned. This validation extends to the endorsement of the right of self-determination for indigenous peoples as expressed in the UN Declaration of their rights (UNDRIP). The Committee's interpretative approach may be broadly described as teleological – the marshalling of standards towards the achievement of the essential aims and objectives of the Convention; literalist interpretations have foundered on the rocks of textual ambiguity.

The prohibition of racial discrimination, the primary international expression of which remains the Convention, has continuing relevance. The movement from nineteenth-century forms of racial discrimination based on an assumed hierarchy of 'races' towards 'cultural difference racism' has not diminished the importance of the Convention and allied contemporary anti-discrimination principles and instruments (Diaconu); on the contrary it enlarges the necessary fields of action to combat discrimination. Racial discrimination is constantly restated new through forms, new modalities, and finds new victims. The current international ferment over migration, the resurgence of interlinked racist and nationalist ideologies, the continuance of internal, even genocidal, oppression based on 'race' and ethnicity, including when mixed with issues of religion, are currently prominent cases in point. The Committee has amply demonstrated the reality of racial oppression and its potential ubiquity. The abstract 'grounds' of discrimination have been humanised through the Committee's unrelenting work

8 Federico Lenzerini, *The Culturalization of Human Rights Law* (Oxford: Oxford University Press, 2014).

in recognising and highlighting the plight of the racially oppressed, the parlous conditions of the ethnic 'others' of the contemporary imaginary.

The chapters in the present volume present ample testimony to the achievements of the Committee, and to the quality of the international community's ongoing struggle against racial discrimination, to what has been done, and what remains to be done (Banton and Diaconu). If racial discrimination is unlikely to be eliminated for all and in 'all forms', it can be eliminated for some, in at least some forms. Principled action against racial discrimination makes a vital difference in reaching down to the capillaries of existence in society, recognising and restoring individual and collective dignity, helping to repair damaged individuals and their communities. The test of the work of the Committee and other bodies engaged in combating racial discrimination is whether, in the grand scheme of things, they 'make a difference' – to the lived realities of human beings. The present volume supplies some of the answers to this fundamental question, as well as opening up new questions and suggesting pathways to a better ordering of human affairs for the common good.

Patrick Thornberry

Acknowledgements

There are a number of persons who the editors would like to thank. We are grateful to the excellent staff at Manchester University Press for their patience and professionalism in ensuring the final manuscript is to the highest standard, as well as to all of our contributors for the time they dedicated to enriching the collection. We would like to thank Patrick Thornberry, who has acted as a mentor as well as a guide on the evolution of CERD's work. The editors also thank Michael Banton for his historical and contemporary insights on CERD, and the visit to his home in Orpington, Kent, which helped shape the title and direction of the collection. David would like to thank Michaela and Séamus for the warm support and encouragement throughout the process, as well as the wider Keane family. Annapurna would like to thank Julian, Indra, Silas and Beatrix for their constant encouragement, support and patience. Finally, thank you to the many colleagues and friends too numerous to name individually who have listened to months of discussions on ICERD and its meaning. We hope the collection does this justice.

Abbreviations

CEDAW	Committee on the Elimination of Discrimination against Women
CERD	Committee on the Elimination of Racial Discrimination
CESCR	Committee on Economic, Social and Cultural Rights
CRC	Committee on the Rights of the Child
CO	Concluding Observations
ECHR	European Convention on Human Rights
ECtHR	European Court of Human Rights
FPIC	free, prior and informed consent
GC	General Comment
GR	General Recommendation
ICC	International Criminal Court
ICCPR	International Covenant on Civil and Political Rights
ICERD	International Convention on the Elimination of All Forms of Racial Discrimination
ICESCR	International Covenant on Economic, Social and Cultural Rights
ICJ	International Court of Justice
NGO	non-governmental organisation
OHCHR	Office of the High Commissioner for Human Rights
UN	United Nations
UNDRIP	UN Declaration on the Rights of Indigenous Peoples
UDHR	Universal Declaration of Human Rights
UPR	Universal Periodic Review
WCAR	UN World Conference Against Racism, Racial Discrimination, Xenophobia and related Intolerance
WGIP	UN Working Group on Indigenous Peoples

Introduction

David Keane and Annapurna Waughray

> The United Nations exists not merely to preserve the peace but also to make change – even radical change – possible.
>
> – Ralph Bunche, Nobel Lecture (1950)[1]

The origins of ICERD

On 21 December 1965, the International Convention on the Elimination of All Forms of Racial Discrimination (ICERD)[2] was adopted in the United Nations General Assembly in plenary session by 106 votes to none.[3] ICERD was the first international human rights treaty, and the first major piece of international law in the drafting of which the then newly independent States participated and played a leading and decisive role.[4] The Committee on the Elimination of Racial Discrimination (CERD/the Committee), established under Article 8 from 1970 once the treaty had entered into force, was the first international treaty-monitoring body of its kind.[5] The provisions governing its establishment and functions were even approved by the Soviet Union and its allies, which

---

1 Ralph Bunche, 'Some Reflections on Peace in Our Time', Nobel Lecture, 11 December 1950, available at: www.nobelprize.org/nobel_prizes/peace/laureates/1950/bunche-lecture.html.

2 International Convention on the Elimination of All Forms of Racial Discrimination, GA Res. 2106 (XX), Annex, 20 UN GAOR Supp. (No. 14) at 47, UN Doc. A/6014 (1966), 660 UNT.S. 195, entered into force 4 January 1969.

3 UN Doc. A/PV.1406, GA Res. 2106 A (XX). One State, Mexico, abstained from the vote on the grounds that it objected to the reservations clause in the treaty. It subsequently announced that it was giving its affirmative vote to the Convention.

4 Egon Schwelb, 'The International Convention on the Elimination of All Forms of Racial Discrimination', *International and Comparative Law Quarterly*, 15:4 (1966), 1057.

5 Thomas Buergenthal, 'The UN Human Rights Committee', *Max Planck Yearbook of United Nations Law*, 5 (2001), 341.

had maintained for two decades that machinery of this kind infringed national sovereignty and was contrary to the UN Charter.[6] Banton notes that it was important to call the monitoring body a 'committee', which made it sound 'less novel and less threatening',[7] nomenclature adopted by all subsequent UN treaty-monitoring bodies. As observed by the French delegate at the conclusion of the drafting process, no treaty of equal scope or significance had ever been adopted before.[8]

From its inception, one of the purposes of the United Nations as articulated in Article 1(3) of the 1945 UN Charter was to achieve international cooperation in promoting and encouraging respect for human rights for all 'without distinction as to race',[9] reiterated in Article 2 of the 1948 Universal Declaration of Human Rights (UDHR).[10] The word 'race' had not appeared at all in the Covenant of the League of Nations signed in 1919. But the language of racism pervaded this first attempt at internationalism nearly a century ago, with its mandate system operationalised by the Article 22 'sacred trust of civilization' over 'peoples not yet able to stand by themselves under the strenuous conditions of the modern world', with 'the tutelage of such peoples … entrusted to advanced nations'.[11] The UN swept away this rhetoric, 'the explicit endorsement of racial equality in sharp contrast with the racial underpinnings of the League system'.[12] However the legacy of the League of Nations is not entirely absent from the UN system, and the subsequent ICERD regime. The monitoring mechanisms that CERD would pioneer for the UN treaty system, in particular State reports and a petition process, were core procedures of the League of Nations mandates regime, as well as the apparatus of 'internationalisation' centred in Geneva with its 'interrogations … often with experts briefed by humanitarian lobbies'.[13]

The UN General Assembly expressed concern about racial discrimination from its earliest sessions, often grouped with religious intolerance, declaring in a 1946 resolution that it is 'in the higher interests of humanity to put an immediate end to religious and so-called racial

6 Schwelb, 'The International Convention on the Elimination of All Forms of Racial Discrimination', 1058.
7 Michael Banton, *The International Politics of Race* (Oxford: Blackwell, 2002), p. 67.
8 UN Doc. A/C.3/SR.1345 (France).
9 Charter of the United Nations, 26 June 1945, 59 Stat. 1031, T.S. 993, 3 Bevans 1153, entered into force 24 October 1945.
10 Universal Declaration of Human Rights, GA Res. 217A (III), UN Doc. A/810 at 71 (1948).
11 Covenant of the League of Nations, [1919] UKTS 4 (Cmd. 153)/[1920] ATS 1/[1920] ATS 3.
12 Susan Pedersen, *The Guardians: The League of Nations and the Crisis of Empire* (Oxford: Oxford University Press, 2015), p. 399.
13 Pedersen, *The Guardians*, p. 398 and p. 4.

persecution and discrimination'.[14] The movement towards a specific body of international rules began as a response to a global outbreak of anti-Semitic incidents that took place in the winter of 1959–60, known as the 'swastika epidemic'. It resulted in a resolution from the UN Sub-Commission on the Prevention of Discrimination and Protection of Minorities on 'manifestations of … religious and racial prejudices',[15] and an instrument was proposed in debates that followed. However, in 1962, the Third Committee of the General Assembly decided to split the issues of racial and religious discrimination, resulting in two separate Resolutions calling for the preparation of draft declarations and conventions dealing separately with racial discrimination and religious intolerance.[16] The rationale was driven by political opposition to the inclusion of anti-Semitism as legal recognition of the State of Israel,[17] although Soviet and Eastern European countries also viewed racial discrimination as being significantly more important than religious intolerance.[18] With the decision to separate the instruments, it was understood that the Draft Declaration and Convention on Racial Discrimination would receive priority. The 1963 Declaration on the Elimination of All Forms of Racial Discrimination, which contained eleven articles but no definition of 'racial discrimination', was proclaimed on 20 November 1963.[19] It was followed by the preparation of a Convention of ten articles and a Preamble by the Sub-Commission in January 1964, submitted to the Commission on Human Rights, who adopted the substantive articles. This was in turn submitted to the General Assembly in July 1964, along with a draft article on implementation and the text of an additional article on anti-Semitism

14 United Nations General Assembly, 'Persecution and discrimination', GA res. 103(I) (1946), cited in William A. Schabas, 'Genocide and the International Convention on the Elimination of All Forms of Racial Discrimination', in David Keane and Annapurna Waughray (eds), *50 Years of ICERD: A Living Instrument* (Manchester: Manchester University Press, 2016), Ch. 8.

15 UN Econ. & Soc. Council, Sub-Comm. on the Protection and Promotion of Human Rights, UN Doc. E/CN.4/Sub.2/206 (1960).

16 Preparation of a Draft Declaration and a Draft Convention on the Elimination of All Forms of Racial Discrimination, GA Res. 1780 (XVII), at 32, UN Doc. A/5217 (7 December 1962) and Preparation of a Draft Declaration and a Draft Convention on the Elimination of All Forms of Religious Intolerance, GA res. 1781, at 33, UN Doc. A/5217 (7 December 1962).

17 Natan Lerner, *The UN Convention on the Elimination of All Forms of Racial Discrimination: A Commentary* (Leiden: A.W. Sijthoff, 1970), p. 82.

18 Schwelb, 'The International Convention on the Elimination of All Forms of Racial Discrimination', 999.

19 GA Res. 1904 (XVIII), at 35 (20 November 1963). The Declaration was adopted in the Third Committee by eighty-nine votes to zero, with seventeen abstentions, which were all the result of objections on the basis of the Declaration's conflict with the right to freedom of expression.

proposed by the United States, and shadowed by a sub-amendment submitted by the USSR.[20]

The proposed article on anti-Semitism did not enjoy broad support in the Third Committee. Delegates expressed the view that the Convention should be a timeless one, applicable without any qualification to every kind of racial discrimination.[21] Most believed that it would be inappropriate to single out certain forms of racial discrimination to the exclusion of others.[22] A proposal by Greece and Hungary to avoid reference to specific forms of racial discrimination in the draft convention was approved by a large majority and the proposed article on anti-Semitism was excluded.[23] The final text was subsequently adopted in December 1965. By contrast the parallel instrument on religious intolerance was never achieved, with almost twenty years of debates resulting in a non-binding declaration in 1981.[24]

While the impetus for ICERD may lie in anti-Semitism and the swastika epidemic, its realisation came from the support of many African and Asian States for what was seen as an international statement against apartheid and colonialism.[25] This political factor saw a clear connection between racism, and apartheid and colonialism, and it is this aspect that emerged most forcefully from the 1962 decision to split the issues of racial discrimination and religious intolerance. The text of the treaty itself reflects this, and despite the decision taken in the Third Committee not to include in the ICERD any reference to specific forms of racial discrimination, it retained a specific reference to apartheid in Article 3 on the basis that: 'it differed from other forms in that it was the official policy of a State Member of the United Nations'.[26] In relation to colonialism, the right of petition was considered an important device in the international trusteeship

20 David Keane, 'Addressing the aggravated meeting points of race and religion', *University of Maryland Law Journal of Race, Religion, Gender and Class*, 6 (2006), 360.
21 UN Gen. Assembly, Third Committee, Summary, UN Doc. A/C.3/SR.1313 (New Zealand).
22 UN Gen. Assembly, Third Committee, Summary, UN Doc. A/C.3/SR.1311 (Ireland).
23 UN Gen. Assembly, Third Committee, Summary, UN Doc. A/C.3/SR.1312.
24 United Nations Declaration on the Elimination of All Forms of Intolerance and of Discrimination Based on Religion or Belief, GA res. 36/55, UN Doc. A/RES/36/55 (15 November 1981).
25 Theo Van Boven, 'The petition system under the International Convention on the Elimination of All Forms of Racial Discrimination: A sobering balance sheet', *Max Planck Yearbook of United Nations Law*, 4 (2000), 273.
26 UN Gen. Assembly, Third Committee, Summary, UN Doc. A/C.3/SR.1313. Article 3 reads: 'States Parties particularly condemn racial segregation and apartheid and undertake to prevent, prohibit and eradicate all practices of this nature in territories under their jurisdiction.'

system and its decolonisation procedures, leading to the inclusion of Article 15 ICERD dealing with petitions from the inhabitants of Trust and Non-Self-Governing Territories and all other territories to which the 1960 Declaration on the Granting of Independence to Colonial Countries and Peoples applies.[27] While today Article 15 has lost most of its significance since only a few non-self-governing territories are left, ICERD as a statement against colonialism is still considered the 'logical place' for this right of petition.[28] The Preamble to the treaty reads as a combined statement against apartheid and colonialism in its articulation that 'the United Nations has condemned colonialism and all practices of segregation', as well as 'governmental policies based on racial superiority or hatred, such as policies of apartheid'.

Apartheid and colonialism were not the only forces influencing the treaty's drafting. For example, Lovelace Jr. investigates the fourteen-member UN Sub-Commission's January 1964 visit to Atlanta, Georgia, in the United States, suggested by the US member Morris Abram in part in order to persuade the drafters that the city's transition away from Jim Crow laws was possible under a juridical framework which protected the freedom of speech of hate groups as well as civil rights organisations.[29] In documenting the visit through a range of sources including local media, and charting the impact of demonstrations by the Student Nonviolent Coordinating Committee, among other civil rights groups, on the Sub-Commission members, Lovelace Jr. argues persuasively that historians of ICERD need to employ a more diverse range of primary and secondary sources to reconstruct the treaty's rich drafting history.[30] Additionally the Atlanta experience should have underlined for the Sub-Commission 'the importance of expanding the formal drafting process to include more critical, non-state actors of color … in understanding how law might be used in diverse areas of the world to end manifestations of racial discrimination'.[31] This did not occur; Lovelace Jr. points out that the Sub-Commission 'experts' were an all-male body largely representative of the global North, with half of its composition from Europe alone and its agenda dictated by State actors or elite NGOs.[32] For example, despite its preoccupation with apartheid, 'the Sub-Commission failed to

---

27 Declaration on the Granting of Independence to Colonial Countries and Peoples, GA Res. 1514 (XV), 15 UN GAOR Supp. (No. 16) at 66, UN Doc. A/4684 (1961).

28 Van Boven, 'The petition system', 274.

29 Timothy Lovelace Jr., 'Making the world in Atlanta's image: The Student Nonviolent Coordinating Committee, Morris Abram, and the legislative history of the United Nations Race Convention', *Law and History Review*, 32:2 (2014), 401.

30 *Ibid.*, 421.

31 *Ibid.*, 422–3.

32 *Ibid.*, 425.

invite any South African freedom fighters to inform and enrich its discussions of the proposed Convention'.[33] Hence the influence of the global South or black internationalism on the treaty can only be traced by moving beyond the dominant methodological approach of tracking Convention debates in various UN organs, represented in 'internalist' accounts of the treaty's origins.[34]

In the UN General Assembly, the early perception of ICERD as a cornerstone in the anti-apartheid and anti-colonial struggle led the representative of Ghana, the first former British colony in Africa to achieve independence, to comment following the vote to approve the treaty: 'this was its finest hour'.[35] The momentum that turned a resolution on anti-Semitism in 1960 into a binding instrument on racial discrimination in 1965 was driven by the belief that it was a statement to put an immediate end to apartheid, colonialism, and more generally discrimination against 'black' and other 'non-white' persons.[36] The initial and to some extent continuing task of CERD would be to convince States parties that the treaty was not only a condemnation of these practices but applied equally to all States parties in their internal affairs, as well as to forms of racial discrimination that were not necessarily based on paradigmatic skin colour prejudices and its manifestations.

To date, the Convention has been ratified by 177 States parties,[37] with a further six States signatories. Just fourteen States have failed to engage with the treaty – Brunei Darussalam, the Democratic People's Republic of ['North'] Korea, Malaysia, Myanmar and South Sudan, plus eight Pacific Island Countries, and the Caribbean island of Dominica.[38] Of these, the only State that has not signed or ratified ICERD to some extent attributable to a lack of capacity due to size or geography, an isolationist civil and political climate hostile to international engagement, or relative youth, is Malaysia. Indeed, a call from the Human Rights Commission of Malaysia to ratify the instrument highlights how ICERD is 'nearing universal

33 *Ibid.*, 427.

34 *Ibid.*, 388. Lovelace Jr. cites Natan Lerner's 1970 book as an example of such an 'internalist' account, relying solely on debates in UN organs.

35 UN Doc. A/PV.1406, quoted in Schwelb, 'The International Convention on the Elimination of All Forms of Racial Discrimination', 1003.

36 Kevin Boyle and Annaliese Baldaccini, 'International human rights approaches to racism', in S. Fredman (ed.), *Discrimination and Human Rights* (Oxford: Oxford University Press (Academy of European Law), 2001), p. 153.

37 Office of the High Commissioner for Human Rights, 'Status of ratification', available at: http://indicators.ohchr.org.

38 The eight Pacific Island countries are Cook Islands, Kiribati, Marshall Islands, Micronesia (Federated States of), Niue, Samoa, Tuvalu and Vanuatu.

acceptance'.[39] Thus the first achievement of ICERD in its fifty years must be its current 'near universal' status in terms of States parties, covering approximately 95 per cent of the world's population. As described by CERD, it represents: 'the international community's only tool for combating racial discrimination which is at one and the same time universal in reach, comprehensive in scope, legally binding in character, and equipped with built-in measures of implementation.'[40]

ICERD and CERD

ICERD is a concise instrument by contemporary standards with a relatively small number of operative provisions. Meron highlights deficiencies in the drafting, noting that '[t]he speed with which the Convention was considered and adopted, the robustness of the political forces that pushed its formulation and adoption, and perhaps a certain impatience with the niceties of legal drafting are among the factors that underlie some of the problems'.[41] Yet, while in parts a flawed text, it has proven remarkably effective in realising a shift from a narrow understanding of its scope to a much wider reach and relevance. In the early days, many States simply emphatically denied that any form of racial discrimination existed in their territories.[42] Of the first forty-five State party reports, only five States admitted there was any racial discrimination occurring, with two of these explaining it was being practised by another State.[43] It was also common for States to refer to racial discrimination only as part of their inheritance from the colonial era. CERD issued General Recommendation (GR) 2 in 1972 as a response to the 'express or implied' belief from States that 'racial discrimination does not exist' on their territories, requiring all States parties to submit reports on the measures adopted that give effect to

39 Human Rights Commission of Malaysia (SUHAKAM), 'The Human Rights Commission of Malaysia calls on the Government to accede to the International Convention on the Elimination of All Forms of Racial Discrimination 1969', 21 March 2015, available at: www.suhakam.org.my/wp-content/uploads/2015/04/Press-Release-ICERD-2015-.pdf.

40 33 UN GAOR Supp. (No. 18) at 108, 109, UN Doc. A/33/18 (1978) (statement by the Committee on the Elimination of Racial Discrimination at the World Conference to Combat Racism and Racial Discrimination), quoted in Theodor Meron, 'The meaning and reach of the International Convention on the Elimination of All Forms of Racist Discrimination', *American Journal of International Law*, 79 (1985), 283.

41 *Ibid.*, 309 and 291.

42 Michael Banton, *International Action against Racial Discrimination* (Oxford: Oxford University Press, 1996), p. 106.

43 Banton, *The International Politics of Race*, p. 69.

the provisions of the Convention.[44] The fulcrum in counteracting this outlook and opening up the treaty to a wide range of groups is the definition of 'racial discrimination' in Article 1(1), as:

> any distinction, exclusion, restriction or preference based on race, colour, descent, or national or ethnic origin which has the purpose or effect of nullifying or impairing the recognition, enjoyment or exercise, on an equal footing, of human rights and fundamental freedoms in the political, economic, social, cultural and any other field of public life.

The five grounds, 'race, colour, descent, or national or ethnic origin', serve to distinguish 'race' from the broader concept of 'racial discrimination'. Furthermore the treaty makes no comment on the meaning of 'race' itself, an exercise that UNESCO attempted in a series of ultimately contradictory statements on race from 1950 to 1967.[45] Instead, ICERD contains a legal definition of racial discrimination that does not further define its constituent elements. As Thornberry notes:

> it is an obvious point – but easily missed – that the umbrella term for the Convention is 'racial discrimination', not race. Thus, racial discrimination is given a stipulative meaning by the Convention: as precisely the five terms set out in Article 1, which means 'race' but four other terms as well. It is thus clear that the scope of the Convention is broader than ... notions of race, which in any case may express many usages.[46]

The five terms are a closed group, with no indicative phrase (e.g. 'such as') preceding their enumeration. Thus in principle any group that falls under the aegis of the treaty must come under one (or a combination) of the five grounds, although the practice of the Committee is not necessarily to articulate which one. For example its GR 27 on the Roma does not specify where this group fits in the definition of Article 1(1).[47] In a contemporary setting, certain groups, such as indigenous peoples,[48] non-citizens including migrants and refugees,[49]

---

44 CERD, 'General Recommendation 2 on States' parties obligations', UN Doc. A/8718 at 38 (1972).

45 UNESCO, 'Four Statements on the Race Question', Com.69/II.27/A (Paris: UNESCO, 1969).

46 Patrick Thornberry, 'The Convention on the Elimination of Racial Discrimination, indigenous peoples, and caste/descent-based discrimination', in J. Castellino and N. Walsh (eds), *International Law and Indigenous Peoples* (Leiden: Martinus Nijhoff, 2005), pp. 17–53, at 19.

47 CERD, 'General Recommendation 27 on Discrimination against Roma', UN Doc. A/55/18, Annex V at 154 (2000).

48 CERD, 'General Recommendation 23 on Rights of indigenous peoples', UN Doc. A/52/18, Annex V at 122 (1997). See also Thornberry, 'The Convention on the Elimination of Racial Discrimination'.

49 CERD, 'General Recommendation 30 on Discrimination against non-citizens', UN Doc. CERD/C/64/Misc.11/rev.3 (2004).

minorities,[50] or caste groups,[51] none of which may appear obviously to fall under an existing ground or grounds, have been interpreted as coming under the 'umbrella term' of racial discrimination. The Committee will at times pinpoint exactly where they fall, as it did in relation to caste groups and the third ground 'descent',[52] but generally prefers simply to treat them as coming within the purview of the treaty without specifying exactly where. The principle of self-identification, expressed in GR 8, means that membership of a particular group for the purposes of Article 1(1) 'shall, if no justification exists to the contrary, be based upon self-identification',[53] leaving the question to the individual or group themselves (with an option of contestation by the State party concerned, the 'justification … to the contrary').

The difficulty with this approach is that for certain groups it may not be clear whether they do come under the treaty, for example religious groups;[54] while for others, States parties may oppose their inclusion via CERD interpretation, such as India in relation to caste groups, or Ireland in relation to Travellers.[55] While there are examples of conflicting views, for the most part States parties do not contest the treaty body's understanding of which groups form part of their reporting remit. The definition of racial discrimination in Article 1 has been instrumental in furthering the object and purpose of the treaty, namely the elimination of *all forms of* racial discrimination, and its adaptability has been a key aspect in ensuring that ICERD is a 'living instrument' continually identifying groups previously excluded, marginalised, or insufficiently protected within the international system.

---

50 There is no CERD GR on minorities, but for an analysis of the many minority rights aspects to CERD's work, see David Keane and Joshua Castellino, 'Is ICERD the de facto minority rights treaty?' in C. Buckley, A. Donald and P. Leach (eds), *Towards Convergence in International Human Rights Law: Approaches of Regional and International Systems* (Leiden: Martinus Nijhoff, 2016), pp. 275–95.

51 CERD, 'General Recommendation 29 on Discrimination based on descent', UN Doc. A/57/18 at 111 (2002). See also David Keane, *Caste-based Discrimination in International Human Rights Law* (Surrey: Ashgate/Routledge, 2007) and Annapurna Waughray, *Capturing Caste in Law: The Legal Regulation of Caste Discrimination* (Routledge, 2018, forthcoming).

52 GR 29, *ibid.*

53 CERD, 'General Recommendation 8 on Membership of racial or ethnic groups based on self-identification', UN Doc. A/45/18 at 79 (1991).

54 See further Jose A. Lindgren Alves, 'Race and religion in the United Nations Committee on the Elimination of Racial Discrimination', *University of San Francisco Law Review*, 42 (2007–8), 941–82.

55 For an account of Ireland's refusal to recognise Irish Travellers as an ethnic group for the purposes of ICERD, see Robbie McVeigh, '"Ethnicity denial" and racism: The case of the Government of Ireland against Irish Travellers', *Translocations*, 2:1 (2007), 90–133.

While the text of the treaty remains static (with no additions via protocols), CERD has been the vehicle for evolution in terms of procedural innovations and interpretation of key terms. Initially from 1970, there was a heavy representation of diplomats on CERD. This assisted in gaining support for the novelty of the State reporting process including examination of reports, but created an environment whereby Committee membership was seen 'as simply one diplomatic duty among others'.[56] The Cold War impeded the Committee's work in the 1980s, but after the Committee elections in 1988 the atmosphere began to change and '[m]embers could trust one another more'.[57] From the late 1980s States parties began to see treaty-body membership as calling for persons independent from governments, and the Committee started to succeed in improving many of its procedures. It is also apparent that the Committee benefited from more legal expertise among its membership. The examination of States' reports became more searching, with major advances including the appointment of country rapporteurs, and the issuing of a collective view on a report instead of a summary of what different members had said, which would become known as Concluding Observations (COs).[58]

From 1991, CERD formally decided that while the base for its examination was State reports, members must have access as independent experts to all other available sources of information, including non-governmental sources. CERD also decided it would review implementation of the treaty in the absence of a State report where that report was overdue by five years or more, later extended to a five-year absence or more of an initial report, enabling the Committee to 'take charge of the reporting process instead of simply reacting to incoming reports'.[59] From 1992, it evolved new early warning and urgent action procedures for more critical instances or patterns of discrimination with the potential for widespread and systematic violations or targeting of groups.[60] New follow-up procedures from 2005 saw the appointment of rapporteurs for the purpose of ascertaining measures taken by States parties to give effect to the Committee's suggestions and recommendations.[61]

56 Banton, *The International Politics of Race*, p. 69.

57 *Ibid.*, p. 71.

58 *Ibid.*

59 *Ibid.*, p. 72.

60 CERD, 'Prevention of Racial Discrimination, including Early Warning and Urgent Procedures', UN Doc. A/48/18 (1993), Annex III and CERD, 'Guidelines for the Early Warning and Urgent Action Procedure', UN Doc. A/62/18 (2007), Annex III.

61 Nathalie Prouvez, 'Committee on the Elimination of Racial Discrimination: Confronting racial discrimination and inequality in the enjoyment of economic, social and cultural rights', in M. Langford (ed.), *Social Rights Jurisprudence:*

Under Article 9(2), CERD may 'make suggestions and general recommendations based on the examination of the reports', a phrase that authorises both the COs and GRs of today and additional to the main dialogues, CERD GRs now number thirty-five. These 'cover a wide area of practical, exegetical and group-oriented themes, integrated into the work of the Committee as it interfaces with States Parties'.[62]

Alston, in tracing the history of GRs/comments, highlights how they have evolved from a concept of unclear and contested meaning to a tool of fundamental importance in the armoury of international human rights law.[63] CERD was the first treaty body to issue GRs, from 1972. These were initially focused on treaty provisions and more technical reporting requirements, but have more recently facilitated the Committee in turning its attention to groups that had received a low priority within the structures of the UN, or were suffering continued marginalisation, such as indigenous peoples, the Roma, caste/descent-based groups, migrants, refugees and other non-citizens, and people of African descent, all of whom have been the subject of a GR. The gender-based dimensions of all aspects of the Committee's work were recognised in GR 25, marking a more systematic and consistent approach in this cross-cutting area.[64] The practice of holding 'thematic discussions' to inform GRs began in relation to GR 27 and the Roma in 2000, and continued in GR 29 and caste/descent in 2002, and GR 34 and people of African descent in 2011.[65] It moved away from its group focus in relation to the most recent thematic discussion held on combating racist hate speech, resulting in GR 35 in 2013.[66]

The communications procedure contained in Article 14 has been operative since 1984 but attracted few cases in its first years. It has

---

Emerging Trends in International and Comparative Law (Cambridge: Cambridge University Press, 2008), p. 538.

62 Patrick Thornberry, 'Confronting racial discrimination: A CERD perspective', *Human Rights Law Review*, 5:2 (2005), 246.

63 Philip Alston, 'The historical origins of "General Comments" in human rights law', in L. Boisson de Chazournes and V. Gowlland-Debbas (eds), *The International Legal System in Quest of Equity and Universality* (The Hague: Martinus Nijhoff, 2001), 776. The chapter outlines how General Comments have their source in short-lived arrangements for a periodic reporting procedure under the UDHR made in the Commission on Human Rights in the 1950s, re-shaped in a Human Rights Committee debate in 1980 that established a formal framework more attuned to their current understanding (at 769–75).

64 CERD, 'General Recommendation 25 on Gender-related dimensions of racial discrimination', UN Doc. A/55/18, Annex V at 152 (2000).

65 CERD, 'General Recommendation 34 on Racial discrimination against people of African descent', UN Doc. CERD/C/GC/34 (2011).

66 CERD, 'General Recommendation 35 on Combating racist hate speech', UN Doc. CERD/C/GC/35 (2013).

potential for more significant impact as more States parties accept the Committee's competence to receive such communications – currently numbering fifty-four – and the procedure becomes better known. Van Boven, writing in 2000, found that 'Article 14 did more to serve as a break-through and a precedent in connection with other international legal instruments than as an international recourse procedure for victims of racial discrimination'.[67] In other words its principal impact was in opening the way to more successful communication procedures for other UN treaty bodies. Since then, the increased number of declarations and resulting communications or 'cases' may be changing the overall perception of its efficacy. It has unique features, including the fact that Article 14 explicitly provides for the possibility that groups as well as individuals may initiate a procedure alleging a violation of any of the rights of the Convention.[68] A second distinct aspect is that CERD is not prevented from considering communications that are being or have been examined under another procedure of international investigation or settlement. It is apparent that more analysis is needed on the communications procedure as it grows in importance, although the OHCHR recently published a first volume of 'selected decisions' of the Committee, presenting thirty-two of the most significant decisions on admissibility and merits.[69] The inter-State procedure that can be triggered under Article 11 has not been effectively used, in common with other treaties. There have been a number of what Buergenthal terms 'disguised inter-state disputes', in which States complain about other States in their reports under Article 9, but decline to formally access the Article 11 inter-State complaints procedure.[70]

CERD for the most part focuses on building a 'dialogue' with States parties over reporting cycles that have a range of technical requirements. The obligations in the Convention are found in general in Article 2(1), and in more detail in Articles 3 to 7, and the reporting State must detail how it is implementing these provisions. The process is premised on the need for the State party to identify through disaggregated data who the groups are on its territory that fall under the purview of the Convention definition and their position in relation to the enjoyment of the full range of rights. Each dialogue is followed by a set of COs by the Committee that contain elements of praise, statements of concern

67 Van Boven, 'The petition system', 272.

68 *Ibid.*, 274.

69 OHCHR, 'Selected decisions of the Committee on the Elimination of Racial Discrimination: Vol.1' (New York and Geneva: United Nations, 2012), available at: www.ohchr.org/Documents/Publications/CERDSelectedDecisionsVolume1.pdf.

70 Thomas Buergenthal, 'Implementing the UN racial convention', *Texas International Law Journal*, 12 (1977), 211.

and recommendations for further action.[71] These will be informed and supported by reference to relevant GRs which lend authority to Committee pronouncements and guide States in the implementation of the relatively terse COs.

Although a 1960s document, ICERD did not suffer the Cold War bifurcation between civil and political, and economic, social and cultural rights, with its Article 5 containing a non-exhaustive list of civil, political, economic, social and cultural rights comparable in its scope to the 'International Bill of Human Rights'.[72] The equal status of economic, social and cultural rights is explained by the fact that the obligations of the States parties do not refer to the granting of these rights, but only to admitting no racial discrimination in their enjoyment to the extent that they were guaranteed in the domestic law of the States parties.[73] If the elimination of racial discrimination is generally viewed as a civil and political right, which it almost certainly was at the time, the economic, social and cultural rights recognised in the treaty provisions are granted only in the furtherance of that object and purpose. Nevertheless, ICERD is the first international treaty not to separate these 'generations' of rights. In GR 20, CERD noted that Article 5 'assumes the existence and recognition of these rights', and in addition to its civil and political emphases,[74] it has more recently advanced the understanding of the elimination of racial discrimination in the economic, social and cultural spheres. Prouvez highlights how under Article 5 'the equal enjoyment of economic, social and cultural rights has been a matter of continuing and major concern for the Committee', including labour, housing, health, education, land, language and culture rights, with the 'deplorable socio-economic situation in which many members of these vulnerable groups live', together with the lack of effective remedies for violations of these rights, 'relentlessly stressed by the Committee'.[75]

Overall the priority for CERD in eliminating racial discrimination in the enjoyment of the full range of civil, political, economic, social and cultural rights, is to devise new ways to ensure recommendations have a practical impact, meaning recommendations are increasingly concrete and specific with established procedures for follow-up that require reports on implementation.[76] This is allied with the Article 6

71 Thornberry, 'Confronting racial discrimination', 244.

72 Buergenthal, 'Implementing the UN racial convention', 209.

73 Boyle and Baldaccini, 'International human rights approaches to racism', p. 153.

74 See Karl Josef Partsch, 'Elimination of racial discrimination in the enjoyment of civil and political rights: A study of Article 5, subparagraphs (a) to (d), of the International Convention on the Elimination of All Forms of Racial Discrimination', *Texas International Law Journal*, 14 (1979), 191.

75 Prouvez, 'Committee on the Elimination of Racial Discrimination', pp. 525–37.

76 *Ibid.*, 537.

direction to assure 'effective protection and remedies', supported by GR 26.[77] Furthermore GR 32 has set out the meaning and scope of special measures under the treaty, governed by Articles 1(4) and 2(2).[78] It emphasises that special measures for the purposes of ICERD has an 'autonomous meaning' to be interpreted in the light of the Convention as a whole, which may differ from domestic usage of the concept in particular States parties.[79]

Understanding CERD's impact to a given situation or group requires close examination of the dialogue process with an individual State party. In effect, the 'dialogue' that CERD advocates is a misnomer, since non-governmental organisations (NGOs) and civil society have become a key third party in its efficacy, with further input and participation from other international bodies and experts in line with wider UN mainstreaming and collaboration. Particularly since the turn of the new millennium, CERD has understood that 'examination necessitates an active civil society input in order to make a reality of the notion of a "constructive" dialogue: otherwise the "dialogue" could be reduced to a mere page-turning exercise'.[80] The idea is to 'encourage civil society to activate this important safety valve for victims of racial discrimination'.[81] In practice it means that all sources of information, including civil society information, are critically and professionally appraised by the Committee before the adoption of COs. In addition to the larger or international NGOs, small or grassroots organisations are encouraged and have made a visible contribution to the Committee's work, bringing the treaty closer to local activists and issues. Drawing increased NGO participation into the Committee's work is reflective of the enlargement of CERD's concerns since its inception in the 1970s, notably in the recognition of new categories of rights-holders, and it has in turn 'served to provide a legal cutting edge to defend their rights'.[82]

A living instrument

The notion of an evolutionary or dynamic interpretation of treaties has been applied in international jurisprudence predating the UN human

77 CERD, 'General Recommendation 26 on The right to seek just and adequate reparation or satisfaction', UN Doc. A/55/18, Annex V at 153 (2000).

78 CERD, 'General Recommendation 32 on The meaning and scope of special measures in the ICERD', UN Doc. CERD/C/GC/32 (2009).

79 *Ibid.*, para. 12.

80 Patrick Thornberry, 'Preface', in *ICERD and CERD: A Guide for Civil Society Actors* (Geneva: IMADR, 2011), available at: www.ohchr.org/Documents/HRBodies/CERD/ICERDManual.pdf.

81 *Ibid.*

82 *Ibid.*

rights system,[83] but regional and international human rights bodies have formulated this idea through the concept of the human rights treaty as a 'living instrument'. The origin of the phrase is commonly attributed to the European Court of Human Rights (ECtHR), which held in *Tyrer* v. *United Kingdom* (1978) that the European Convention on Human Rights (ECHR) is a 'living instrument ... [to be] interpreted in the light of present-day conditions'.[84] Bjorge believes that the phrase was coined by Judge Max Sorenson, in a 1975 report,[85] three years before the ECtHR first employed it in *Tyrer*.[86] The concept has been criticised particularly in an ECtHR context, seen in a dissenting opinion in the original *Tyrer* decision up to current accusations of excessive judicial activism or creativity, inconsistent with established principles of treaty interpretation.[87]

Nicolas Bratza, the former President of the ECtHR, observes that Article 31 of the Vienna Convention on the Law of Treaties[88] requires that treaties be interpreted in good faith and in accordance with the ordinary meaning to be given to its terms, but that those terms are also required to be read 'in their context' which includes the Preamble, and in the light of the treaty's 'object and purpose'. This requires making safeguards practical and effective and of continuing relevance, which led the ECtHR 'to adopt an evolutive and purposive approach to the interpretation of the Convention and thereby breathe life into the words of the instrument so as to make it relevant to contemporary European society'.[89] This is balanced by ensuring that 'the application of the "living instrument" doctrine is confined within reasonable bounds',[90] leading to his characterisation of the Court's approach as

---

83 Eirik Bjorge, *The Evolutionary Interpretation of Treaties* (Oxford: Oxford University Press, 2014), p. 10. Bjorge cites the *Spanish Zone of Morocco Claims* arbitral decision from 1925 as one example of evolutionary treaty interpretation outside of, and indeed predating, the international human rights law realm.

84 *Tyrer* v. *United Kingdom* (1978), 58 ILR 339, 353.

85 Max Sorenson, 'Do the rights set forth in the ECHR in 1950 have the same significance in 1975?', reprinted in *Max Sorenson: A Bibliography* (Aarhus: Aarhus University Press, 1988), p. 23 and pp. 54–5, cited in Bjorge, *The Evolutionary Interpretation of Treaties*, p. 12.

86 Nicolas Bratza writes that while *Tyrer* was the first case in which express reference was made to the phrase, it has its source in the 1958 US Supreme Court decision *Trop* v. *Dulles* 356 US 86 (1958), which held that: 'the provisions of the [US] Constitution are not time-worn adages or hollow shibboleths. They are vital living principles'. See Nicolas Brazta, 'Living instrument or dead letter: The future of the European Convention on Human Rights', *European Human Rights Law Review*, 2 (2014), 117.

87 See further *ibid.*

88 Vienna Convention on the Law of Treaties, 1155 UNT.S. 331, 8 I.L.M. 679, entered into force 27 January 1980.

89 Bratza, 'Living instrument or dead letter', 118.

90 *Ibid.*, 123.

'incremental and evolutionary, rather than revolutionary'.[91] Letsas similarly understands evolutionary interpretation under the ECtHR as 'a process of moral discovery', where 'the Court is not expanding or inflating the scope of the ECHR rights by treating the Convention as a living instrument; rather it *discovers* what these human rights always meant to protect'.[92]

In the regional systems outside Europe, the doctrine has been invoked by the Inter-American Court of Human Rights in a number of decisions, such as *The Mayagna (Sumo) Awas Tingni Community* v. *Nicaragua* (2001) which held that: 'human rights treaties are live instruments whose interpretation must adapt to the evolution of the times and, specifically, to current living conditions'.[93] The African Commission on Human and Peoples' Rights recently adopted the living instrument approach to interpret the term 'peoples' in the African Charter on Human and People's Rights to include indigenous peoples, in *Centre for Minority Rights Development (Kenya) and Minority Rights Group (on behalf of Endorois Welfare Council)* v. *Kenya* (2009).[94]

Internationally, Schlutter notes that the principle of what she terms 'dynamic interpretation' has been adopted by all of the UN treaty bodies.[95] For example, in *Judge* v. *Canada* (2003) the Human Rights Committee noted in relation to the International Covenant on Civil and Political Rights: 'the Covenant should be interpreted as a living instrument and the rights protected under it should be applied in context and in the light of present-day conditions.'[96] In *V.X.N. and H.N.* v. *Sweden* (2000), the Committee Against Torture considered that the Convention Against Torture 'as a living instrument, must be interpreted and applied taking into account the circumstances of contemporary society'.[97] The Chairperson of the Committee on the

91 *Ibid.*

92 George Letsas, 'The ECHR as a living instrument: Its meaning and legitimacy', in A. Follesdahl, B. Peters and G. Ulfstein (eds), *Constituting Europe: The European Court of Human Rights in a National, European and Global Context* (Cambridge: Cambridge University Press, 2013), 125.

93 *The Mayagna (Sumo) Awas Tingni Community* v. *Nicaragua*, Judgment of 31 August 2001, Inter-Am. Ct. H.R. (Ser. C) No. 79 (2001), para. 146.

94 *Centre for Minority Rights Development (Kenya) and Minority Rights Group (on behalf of Endorois Welfare Council)* v. *Kenya*, 276/03 (2009), n.115.

95 Birgit Schlutter, 'Aspects of human rights interpretation by the UN Treaty bodies', in H. Keller and G. Ulfstein (eds), *UN Human Rights Treaty Bodies: Law and Legitimacy* (Cambridge: Cambridge University Press, 2015), p. 296.

96 *Roger Judge* v. *Canada*, Communication No. 829/1998, UN Doc. CCPR/C/78/D/829/1998 (2003), para. 10.3, cited in Schlutter, 'Aspects of human rights interpretation'.

97 V.*X.N. and H.N.* v. *Sweden*, Communications Nos. 130/1999 and 131/1999, UN Doc. CAT/C/24/D/130 and 131/1999 (2000), para. 7.3, cited in Schlutter, 'Aspects of human rights interpretation', pp. 296–7.

Elimination of Discrimination Against Women (CEDAW) has written that: 'CEDAW has ensured that the Convention is a living instrument both in substance and procedures',[98] while CEDAW's GR 25 on special measures states: '[t]he Convention is a dynamic instrument'.[99] The Committee on the Rights of the Child captures the pan-treaty character of the living instrument doctrine in its General Comment 8, which highlights: 'the Convention, like all human rights instruments, must be regarded as a living instrument, whose interpretation develops over time'.[100]

The confluence of the adoption of the living instrument doctrine in regional and international human rights treaties is a result of the special character of human rights instruments, designed to protect the rights of individuals within States parties rather than to create reciprocal rights for the States parties themselves.[101] While the UN treaty bodies have expressed their common adherence to this approach, their activation of the doctrine may differ, broadly as a feature of the contrast between the international and regional systems, and more specifically between individual treaty bodies.

Broadly, a clear differentiating feature between the international and regional human rights systems is the preponderance of caselaw within the regional systems. Since the living instrument doctrine has its origins in the judge-made caselaw of the regional systems, specifically Europe, this has been initially mirrored by the international mechanisms in articulating the living instrument doctrine in individual communications. However within international human rights treaty law, the State reporting procedure rather than individual communications is the heart of the monitoring process, and the general recommendations/comments form the doctrinal basis for the State reporting system. Hence it is the Concluding Observations and general recommendations/comments that better reflect the emergence and practice of the living instrument doctrine within international human rights law. Specifically, certain treaty bodies may point more readily to the

98 Dubravka Simonovic, 'Convention on the Elimination of All Forms of Discrimination against Women: Introductory note', Audiovisual Library of International Law, available at: http://legal.un.org/avl/ha/cedaw/cedaw.html.

99 CEDAW, 'General Recommendation No. 25 on Article 4, paragraph 1, on temporary special measures', reprinted in *Compilation of General Comments and General Recommendations, adopted by Human Rights Treaty Bodies*, UN Doc. HRI/GEN/1/Rev.7 at 282 (2004), para. 3.

100 CRC, 'General Comment No. 8 on The right of the child to protection from corporal punishment and other cruel or degrading forms of punishment', UN Doc. CRC/C/GC/8 (2006), para. 20.

101 See further Magdalena Sepulveda Carmona, *Nature of the Obligations under the International Covenant on Economic, Social and Cultural Rights* (Cambridge: Intersentia, 2003), pp. 77–8.

individual communications procedure as an expression of the living instrument doctrine, in particular the Human Rights Committee with its advanced and substantive jurisprudence.[102] But in general for the treaty bodies, the optional character of individual communications means they are not recognised by the majority of States parties, and have a distinctly lesser relevance compared to the State reporting procedure. Hence an idea that has become as central to the treaty bodies' work as the living instrument doctrine should not be located primarily within an under-representative individual communications procedure.

In relation to CERD, the living instrument doctrine has been expressly invoked in an individual communication, *Hagan* v. *Australia* (2003), in which the Committee noted that: 'the Convention, as a living instrument, must be interpreted and applied taking into [account] the circumstances of contemporary society.'[103] This echoes the origins of the living instrument doctrine in regional human rights caselaw, and the communication is cited by commentators as the 'source' or authority for the living instrument doctrine in ICERD.[104] The facts in *Hagan* relate to a sports stand in Australia, named in the 1960s after a sports personality whose nickname was a racial epithet (although he was neither black nor of aboriginal descent), which the petitioner as an aborigine found objectionable and offensive. The Committee did not find a violation of the treaty, but instead recommended that the offending term be removed from the sign, on the basis that in contemporary society the term was offensive:

> [T]he Committee considers that that use and maintenance of the offending term can at the present time be considered offensive and insulting, even if for an extended period it may not have necessarily been so regarded. The Committee considers, in fact, that the Convention, as a living instrument, must be interpreted and applied taking into [account] the circumstances of contemporary society. In this context, the Committee considers it to be

102 See Jakob Moller and Alfred de Zayas, *The United Nations Human Rights Committee Case Law 1977–2008* (Kehl/Strasbourg: N.P. Engel, 2009).

103 *Stephen Hagan* v. *Australia* (2003), CERD Communication No. 26/2002, UN Doc. CERD/C/62/D/26/2002, para. 7.3. This sentence contains a typographical error, the missing word 'account', which has to be filled in by commentators using square brackets every time they recall this key phrase as a direct quotation.

104 See Thornberry, 'Confronting racial discrimination', 266, and Bjorge, *The Evolutionary Interpretation of Treaties*, p. 11, both of whom cite *Hagan* when referencing the living instrument doctrine in ICERD. See also Special Representative of the Secretary-General on Human Rights and Transnational Corporations and Other Business Enterprises, 'Mapping State Obligations for Corporate Acts: An Examination of the UN Human Rights Treaty System Report No. 1, ICERD' (United Nations, 2006), which has four paragraphs discussing ICERD as a living instrument and cites *Hagan* as the authority (paras. 102–5).

> its duty to recall the increased sensitivities in respect of words such as the offending term appertaining today.[105]

This opinion appears to be a misreading of the meaning of the Convention as a living instrument. The decision is not about a term, phrase or provision in the Convention itself; it is about a racial epithet, whose supposed offensiveness may have changed over time. Additionally the term itself was clearly racist and offensive in the 1960s as well as today and it seems strange that the Committee required invoking the living instrument doctrine to justify a contemporary recommendation to have it removed.[106] The doctrine is not about external words that may change over time, but rather the terms or provisions of the instruments themselves that may evolve and find new applications. Nowhere in *Hagan* is there a point about ICERD terms or provisions changing over time, requiring dynamic or evolutive interpretation to render them applicable to the contemporary circumstances in the communication.

The idea of a living instrument has its origins in regional human rights caselaw and so it may seem logical to locate the idea in international human rights law in individual communications, but these may not be reflective of the evolutive approach to international treaty interpretation. More generally in relation to international human rights treaties, and certainly specifically in relation to ICERD, it is the Concluding Observations and general recommendations, rather than the individual communications, that better capture the idea of the treaties as living instruments. While the Concluding Observations are State-specific, the general recommendations provide a treaty-wide and pan-State party overview of its operation and effects and are key to understanding CERD's practice of the living instrument doctrine. CERD has 'shown over time its ability to adapt to and address issues and actors relevant to the contemporary global context',[107] and this may be briefly illustrated by looking at three general recommendations: GR 19 on apartheid; GR 29 on descent; and GR 30 on non-citizens. These evoke different facets of the living instrument doctrine in CERD's workings, through what may be termed affirmative, purposive and contextual readings of ICERD provisions.

---

105 *Stephen Hagan* v. *Australia* (2003), para. 7.3.

106 The idea articulated by CERD that the term may not necessarily have been considered offensive and insulting 'for an extended period' in the past begs the question – by whom? In addition to its poor reasoning, the ambiguity of the Committee's decision despite finding in Hagan's favour did not assist the fact that it was not complied with. See Remedy Australia, 'Hagan v Australia (CERD, 2003)', available at: http://remedy.org.au/cases/15/.

107 Special Representative of the Secretary-General on Human Rights and Transnational Corporations and Other Business Enterprises, para. 102

Under Article 3 ICERD, 'States Parties particularly condemn racial segregation and apartheid and undertake to prevent, prohibit and eradicate all practices of this nature in territories under their jurisdiction'. GR 19 on Article 3 reads: 'The reference to apartheid may have been directed exclusively to South Africa, but the article as adopted prohibits all forms of racial segregation in all countries.'[108] Issued in 1995, it may be read as a reaction to the ending of apartheid in South Africa and a re-interpretation of Article 3, with its primary purpose now achieved, as being of relevance to other situations of racial segregation engaging all States parties. The acknowledgement of the narrow drafting intention behind Article 3 is juxtaposed with an interpretive statement that the Committee intends to apply the provisions beyond the parameters of (now defunct) apartheid South Africa. Yet GR 19 does nothing new to the words of Article 3; it simply restates them. This is present in the phrase 'as adopted', in other words, that an ordinary reading of Article 3 'as adopted' clearly indicates that it is a provision that applies to all States parties engaging in practices of this nature. While there may be debate as to whether apartheid is a term of relevance outside South Africa, there can be no disagreement that situations of racial segregation can be global. Nowhere in Article 3 are the words 'South Africa' found, and it involves the composite term 'racial segregation and apartheid', hence GR 19 is not so much an interpretation as an affirmation that a *sui generis* South African interpretation of the meaning of Article 3 is too narrow and not in line with the text itself. This is one expression of the living instrument doctrine; an affirmation of existing terms in reaction to contemporary events or as a statement of renewed Committee intent on a provision.

GR 29 on discrimination based on descent takes a term that did not have any clear meaning at the drafting stage and imbues it with a purpose. Its Preamble reads that 'descent' includes discrimination against members of communities based on forms of social stratification such as caste and analogous systems of inherited status, thus locating the issue of caste and analogous systems under the rubric of descent-based discrimination. The Preamble to GR 29 references the State reporting process, '[n]oting that the existence of such discrimination has become evident from the Committee's examination of reports of a number of States parties to the Convention'. In this way the challenge faced by the Committee – where to fit caste and analogous systems within the closed definitional grounds in Article 1(1) – is resolved by locating it within the wider and relatively open category of descent. The term

108 CERD, 'General Recommendation 19 on The prevention, prohibition and eradication of racial segregation and apartheid', UN Doc. A/50/18 at 140 (1995), para. 1.

'descent' was largely dormant up until this point and thus GR 29 is a reflection of a purposive living instrument doctrine whose task it is, to quote the ECtHR in *Tyrer*, to 'breathe life into the words of the instrument'.

GR 30 on non-citizens has been referenced in a UN Special Representative report as a specific example under the heading 'CERD as a Living Instrument':

> CERD considers it crucial to reflect the actual development of international standards in its interpretation of the Convention, as reflected also by General Recommendation 30 regarding non-citizens. By outlining a wide range of obligations that States have in relation to non-citizens, General Recommendation 30 arguably transcends to a significant extent the limitations contained in Article 1(2).[109]

The quote reflects the problem that Article 1(2) ICERD appears to specifically exclude non-citizens from the ambit of the treaty. It reads: 'This Convention shall not apply to distinctions, exclusions, restrictions or preferences made by a State Party to this Convention between citizens and non-citizens.' GR 30 notes in its Preamble that it has become evident from the examination of the reports of States parties to the Convention that groups, including migrants, refugees, asylum-seekers and undocumented non-citizens, 'constitutes one of the main sources of contemporary racism and that human rights violations against members of such groups occur widely', and as a result:

> Article 1, paragraph 2, must be construed so as to avoid undermining the basic prohibition of discrimination; hence, it should not be interpreted to detract in any way from the rights and freedoms recognized and enunciated in particular in the Universal Declaration of Human Rights, the International Covenant on Economic, Social and Cultural Rights and the International Covenant on Civil and Political Rights.[110]

Thus GR 30 is not so much an interpretation as a re-reading of one its provisions, Article 1(2), by reference to the full range of provisions in ICERD and the wider international legal context. It is triggered by reference to information from States parties through the reporting procedure that non-citizens such as the undocumented are clearly a group of concern, with the wider justification of the growing recognition of their rights under the 'International Bill of Rights'. GR 30 does not employ the phrase 'living instrument', but it is a clear reflection of the doctrine in the sense of adopting an evolutive approach to

109 Special Representative of the Secretary-General on Human Rights and Transnational Corporations and Other Business Enterprises, para. 104.

110 CERD, GR 30, Preamble and para. 2.

the treaty's provisions congruent to the context of related provisions within the treaty, and the wider recognition of non-citizens' rights in international human rights law. It affirms that no provision of ICERD can be viewed in isolation.

In fact none of GR 19, GR 29 or GR 30 employ the phrase 'living instrument', although all can be seen as reflecting different expressions of CERD's employment of the doctrine, triggered or justified by information gathered in the State reporting process. Later general recommendations have made such an express reference to the doctrine. Thus GR 32 on special measures reads:

> The Convention, as the Committee has observed on many occasions, is a living instrument that must be interpreted and applied taking into account the circumstances of contemporary society. This approach makes it imperative to read its text in a context-sensitive manner. The context ... includes, in addition to the full text of the Convention including its title, preamble and operative articles, the range of universal human rights standards on the principles of non-discrimination and special measures. Context-sensitive interpretation also includes taking into account the particular circumstances of States parties without prejudice to the universal quality of the norms of the Convention. The nature of the Convention and the broad scope of its provisions imply that, while the conscientious application of Convention principles will produce variations in outcome among States parties, such variations must be fully justifiable in the light of the principles of the Convention.[111]

The passage underlines the idea that ICERD as a 'living instrument' permeates the Committee's current thinking and is finding more overt expression. Of the different approaches outlined above, the first two, the affirmative and purposive, can be seen as early incarnations of the doctrine, with the contextual approach, implicit in GR 30 and articulated expressly in GR 32, capturing the particular CERD living instrument identity. The '[c]ontext-sensitive interpretation' of GR 32 situates CERD's dialogue with States parties within: (1) the full text of the Convention, including its title, preamble and operative articles; (2) wider international human rights law standards, both treaty-based and Charter-based; and (3) the changing history, politics and experience of the State itself in terms of its Convention groups. The living instrument doctrine also serves to bring the treaty closer to the victims of all forms of racial discrimination, in particular as represented by NGOs. This link is emphasised in the most recent GR 35 (2013): 'By virtue of its work in implementing the

---

111 CERD, 'General Recommendation 32 on The meaning and scope of special measures in the International Convention on the Elimination of All Forms Racial Discrimination', UN Doc. CERD/C/GC/32 (2009), para. 5.

Convention as a living instrument, the Committee engages with the wider human rights environment, awareness of which suffuses the Convention.'[112]

Nathalie Prouvez, former Secretary of CERD, notes: 'the Committee views the Convention as a living instrument', and continues: 'The general approach of the Committee to the interpretation of the Convention has been increasingly creative, as can be seen through the … General Recommendations.'[113] She highlights how the Committee also provides its interpretation of the Convention in the COs, as well as early warning and urgent action procedures, and individual communications,[114] and all of these reflect the workings of the doctrine. ICERD is a living instrument in the combination of its mechanisms and work, but this 'creative' aspect is perhaps best captured '[t]hrough its General Recommendations and Concluding Observations, [where] CERD has elaborated upon the scope of protection of the Convention and demonstrated its continuing relevance and application to contemporary forms of racism suffered by specific groups'.[115] It is also reflected in the autonomous meaning and nature of the special measures recommended by CERD.

Through its interpretive approach, CERD, in the past fifty years, has become a node within the UN for minorities, indigenous peoples, and many other groups including those who were previously not covered by any understanding. It is not the only source of regional and international rights for these groups, but it offers a coherent 'umbrella' to advance the dialogue between these groups and States parties. It views NGOs and civil society, small and large, as essential to this process. The idea of ICERD as a living instrument drives its evolution. The doctrine was specifically highlighted in the short document marking the treaty's fiftieth anniversary: 'Indeed, even after half a decade since its adoption, ICERD continues to remain relevant to the issues that we face today … The Convention, as a living instrument, must be interpreted and applied taking into account the circumstances of contemporary society.'[116] Although certain aspects of a particular CERD understanding of the living instrument doctrine can now be discerned, it continues to evolve.

---

112 CERD, 'General Recommendation 35 on Combating racist hate speech', UN Doc. CERD/C/GC/35 (2013), para. 4.

113 Prouvez, 'Committee on the Elimination of Racial Discrimination', p. 517.

114 *Ibid.*, pp. 517–18.

115 *Ibid.*, p. 520.

116 OHCHR, 'International Convention on the Elimination of All Forms of Racial Discrimination: 50 years of fighting racism', 26 November 2015, available at: www.ohchr.org/EN/HRBODIES/CERD/50/Pages/Icerd50.aspx.

Chapters summary

Thornberry observes: 'There is perhaps less written about ICERD than about other "core" UN human rights conventions.'[117] This was acknowledged in presentations at the event held in Geneva in November 2015 to mark the fiftieth anniversary, in which Gay McDougall, a former CERD member re-taking a place on the Committee in 2016, stated that CERD needs to be more visible, and speak loudly in corridors where it has not had its voice heard sufficiently thus far. She referred to the need to influence decision-making on development, poverty, and peace and security, and having a voice in New York as well as in Geneva. Through the living instrument doctrine, the instrument has achieved great relevance to a range of groups and this needs to be better communicated. In this vein the current collection seeks to make a contribution to this process in terms of providing a range of contributors and themes, combining current and former CERD members with academics and commentators to provide an overview of the treaty and its contemporary meaning and importance.

Part I: ICERD: cross-cutting themes

Chapter 1, Michael Banton, 'Extending the Rule of Law', opens the collection with a *tour d'horizon* of the origins, lifetime and experience of implementing the treaty from the perspective of a CERD member. It argues that the treaty ought to be considered a significant step forward in the extension of the rule of law. The innovations that have been realised by CERD are recognised, documented and placed in their historical and legal contexts, with assessments as to their efficacy. Practical impediments to the realisation of the treaty's aims, both past and present, inform the discussion, such as past state evasions in budgetary responsibilities. The character of the dialogue that is central to CERD's operations, and the factors around its emergence and influence on the wider treaty body system, are explored. This chapter, with its bird's-eye view of CERD both in terms of its legal meaning and scope, and history of operation in time, as well as appreciation of the nuance and practicalities of realising its object and purpose, will serve to bring much needed illumination to the study of CERD and the wider UN treaty bodies. It provides an essential keynote to the collection.

---

117 Thornberry, 'Preface'. Thornberry's book-length commentary on the treaty was published in 2016. See Patrick Thornberry, *The International Convention on the Elimination of All Forms of Racial Discrimination: A Commentary* (Oxford: Oxford University Press, 2016).

Chapter 2, Joshua Clark, 'Knowing and Doing with Numbers: Disaggregated Data in the Work of the Committee on the Elimination of Racial Discrimination', is a lynchpin of the collection and a crucial contribution to the understanding of ICERD on its fiftieth anniversary. Through the issue of disaggregated data collection, Clark tracks the changes in CERD's approach from its early days to contemporary questions, capturing shifts in the Committee's priorities and engagement with States parties. The focus is on the centrality of data to CERD's task in eliminating racial discrimination, but the history of the treaty is also highlighted through this question. At present CERD receives disaggregated data from the vast majority of States, linked to the key concept of special measures, with few exempted from this obligation. However some Committee members' apprehension ensures that CERD does not automatically press for ethno-racial data from every reporting state. It is worthwhile to push States to produce their own indicators if doing so sparks a wider state process, that is, quantification is valuable inasmuch as it mobilizes state action. The burden rests on States to show that producing disaggregated data does more harm than good. Overall the chapter is at once a legal, historical and sociological investigation of the Committee's work, with an eye on the technical nature of realising its mandate.

Chapter 3, Nozipho January-Bardill, 'Racial Dicrimination and Gender Justice', represents a CERD member discussion of racial discrimination and gender justice, or the link between the elimination of all forms of racial discrimination and the furtherance of gender justice via the UN treaty system. It does not assume a correlation between the standards of the treaty and practice of CERD, and the protection and promotion of women's rights as members of groups based on race, colour, descent and national or ethnic origin. Indeed, specific initiatives in the region of women's rights which highlighted the intersectional nature of discrimination, specifically world conferences on racism and women in Durban and Beijing respectively that brought together voices from the NGO and activist community as well as professionals, experts and others, have most effectively sought to expose the power relations that underpin the continuing marginalisation of women's voices in a range of spheres. While CERD initially struggled to identify structural discrimination in a similarly effective manner, it has made inroads more recently in aligning itself with identifiable aims of gender justice. The chapter highlights the gains made in GR 25, which mainstreams gender into all aspects of CERD's work and marks a breakthrough for the mandatory inclusion of gender in the State reporting process including disaggregated data requirements. GR 25 further cements a position in the treaty for all women of African descent, women from national and ethnic minority groups, Roma women, indigenous and migrant women, and women who are non-citizens, among others, with many aspects of the gender dimensions of ICERD still to emerge. Significantly, GR 25 also represents a gain for women on the Committee itself, including black and other non-white voices, and the chapter details some internal struggles in achieving consensus within CERD as to the importance of certain initiatives supporting or realising gender rights. The chapter concludes with the author's shared experience of South Africa and the struggles in moving from a society with deep subordinations on the basis of race and gender to a more inclusive one, both in law and in fact.

Part II: groups and general recommendations

Chapter 4, Jérémie Gilbert, 'CERD's Contribution to the Development of the Rights of Indigenous Peoples under International Law', reviews CERD's engagement with and contribution to indigenous peoples' rights under international law. CERD has been at the forefront of the development of the rights of indigenous peoples and was the first human rights treaty monitoring body to adopt a specific general recommendation on the rights of indigenous peoples, GR 23. The chapter focuses on four aspects of CERD's work on indigenous peoples' rights: tackling structural discrimination; protection of their rights to land and territories; ensuring their access to and control over their natural resources; and the application of the urgent action and early warning procedures. The question of definition is addressed, with many States rejecting CERD's concern with indigenous peoples. In GR 23, CERD affirmed that discrimination against indigenous peoples is racial discrimination falling under the scope of the Convention, and its interpretation and extension of non-discrimination norms from individual to collective rights, treating indigenous peoples as specific category of rights-holders, is innovative. The chapter identifies the early warning and urgent action procedures as one of the most relevant procedural developments for indigenous peoples, particularly in relation to proposed legislation that negatively affects indigenous peoples' rights.

Chapter 5, Claude Cahn, 'CERD and Discrimination Against Roma', provides a chronological account of CERD's engagement with discrimination against Roma and its central contribution to developments which have brought about a fundamentally changed understanding of the Roma as a heterodox set of ethnic groups. The chapter provides a detailed analysis of CERD's GR 27 on discrimination against Roma. In the years since 2000, CERD's approach to discrimination against Roma has been enriched both by its own deepening expertise in the factual matters of Roma exclusion, as well as by the broadening nature of civil society interventions, and by the growth of State policies and expertise in this area. COs have become more detailed and concrete, as well as in some cases more bold in the expression of discontent with States' actions. In addition, new issues have emerged in the review of States. Also, the Committee has found States in violation of the ICERD treaty within the complaints procedure set out under Article 14. Finally, the Committee has expanded the geographic range of its concerns on Roma beyond Europe. The chapter concludes by noting that CERD has played a key role in moving forward the understanding that anti-Romani sentiment is racism and anti-Romani action is racial discrimination in the sense of ICERD.

Chapter 6, Annapurna Waughray and David Keane, 'CERD and Caste-based Discrimination', examines the emergence of the issue of caste-discrimination in international human rights law, in particular in the 1990s through application of the descent limb in Article 1(1) to caste groups in the context of India's 1996 state report. It charts the emergence of GR 29 (2002) on Article 1(1) (Descent), in which the scope and meaning of descent is examined in greater detail, with a definition of descent-based discrimination as including caste and analogous systems of inherited status. In addition to examining the meaning of caste and the nature of rights violations that occur, the chapter engages with State opposition to CERD's interpretation, in particular from India, which contests the categorisation of caste as a form of descent-based discrimination and therefore a form of racial discrimination. The chapter illustrates that while the Committee considers the treaty to be a living instrument, and may invest meaning in key terms to bring in previously marginalised groups such as those based on caste and descent, States parties may not accept these interpretations. The chapter outlines the importance of the Committee's pioneering work on caste, and argues that despite the CERD–India stalemate, its crucial work on caste will continue given the crucial role of NGOs in the process and the need for a global response for victims of caste discrimination.

Chapter 7, Pastor Murillo and Esther Ojulari, 'General Recommendation 34: A Contribution to the Visibility and Inclusion of Afro-descendants in Latin America', provides an overview of the role of CERD in highlighting and addressing the discrimination suffered by Afro-descendants in Latin America, in a combined CERD member-academic piece. It examines the history of discourses on race in the region which served to hide the particular racial discrimination faced by Afro-descendants. Afro-descendants are a relatively new group in terms of human rights protections; it was the UN World Conference on Racism in Durban Conference in 2001 which served as a catalyst for the emergence of a framework focusing on the rights of Afro-descendants, contributing to both their greater visibility and protection. During the Durban Review Conference in 2009, CERD proposed the adoption of an international decade on people of African descent. This led first to the proclamation of 2011 as the UN International Year for People of African Descent and later to the UN International Decade for People of African Descent (2015–2024). However CERD has been engaged with Afro-descendants since the 1980s, using Concluding Observations and recommendations to address issues such as structural discrimination, violence, and the importance of collecting statistical data, among others, in relation to Afro-descendants in Latin America. CERD GR 34 (2011) on people of African descent is detailed, including its potential as a stepping-stone towards an International Declaration on the Rights of Afro-descendants.

Part III: conflict and resolution

Chapter 8, William Schabas, 'Genocide and the ICERD', investigates CERD's engagement with the subject of genocide. Although there is no reference to genocide in ICERD, in 1994 CERD raised the problem of ethnic violence in response to Rwanda's periodic report, examined just ahead of the outbreak of the genocide in that country and prompting the adoption of a Decision expressing concern and alarm over the genocidal loss of life in Rwanda. In 2005 CERD adopted a Declaration on the Prevention of Genocide, and developed a list of indicators relevant to the prevention of genocide, termed 'indicators of patterns of systematic and massive racial discrimination'. Since then, CERD has focused less on genocide specifically, instead referring to genocide in its outputs on other issues. An exception was in 2014 when it invoked its early warning and urgent action procedures as well as its Declaration on Genocide, in relation to Darfur. The chapter asks why the promise of much greater attention to genocide by CERD that seemed to emerge in 2005 has not been borne out and a number of reasons are suggested. Conclusions are reached on the common thread linking ICERD and the Genocide Convention.

Chapter 9, Cathal Doyle, 'CERD, the State, Mining Corporations and Indigenous Peoples' Rights: The Experience of the Subanon in the Philippines', offers a compelling case study on the operationalization of CERD's early warning and urgent action procedure in the case of the Subanon community located at the foot of Mt Canatuan in the Philippines, and provides a close-up of the relevance of the treaty on the ground. It constructs the events and the legal consequences of the infringement of an external mining company on the ancestral and sacred lands, and documents the tangle of domestic legal provisions triggered as the Subanon community sought to assert its rights in the absence of its free, prior and informed consent to the operations. The effectiveness of the CERD procedures form the axle of the piece, as it assesses the necessity for international intervention, why CERD became the focal point for this, and the positive and negative consequences of the Committee's reactions. It further charts the wider relevance of the community's triggering of the CERD procedures, including the creation of networks that are accessing other mechanisms of international human rights law, while not shying from the practical failures to prevent the ultimate destruction of the site. The chapter marks both an illustration of the importance of CERD in highlighting and actioning critical causes for peoples, and the limits to its remedial powers in light of concerted private–public collaboration in subordinating peoples' rights. It ultimately represents a marker of how peoples themselves are contributing to the elaboration of the treaty, and that the old CERD–State party model has given way to a situation where the groups addressed and protected by the treaty are providing the greatest legal analysis of its meaning and reach, often compelled to do so by the critical erosion of their rights.

Chapter 10, Lydia A. Nkansah, 'ICERD in the Post-Conflict Landscape: Towards a Transitional Justice Role', highlights the potential of ICERD to contribute to the process of transitional justice in post-conflict societies. It argues that to date, ICERD has not featured in the range of international and national mechanisms that follow conflict often wrought by ethnic tensions. The treaty has been triggered in a number of relevant situations, including before the ICJ in the Russia–Georgia and DRC–Rwanda cases that involved armed conflict, but the opportunity to assert a role for the treaty was not realised. The analysis engages with what the best role for ICERD might be, including its potential as a contextual element in understanding certain international crimes. In particular it identifies truth commissions as having largely ignored the potential for ICERD as a transitional tool, and calls on CERD, States parties and other actors to better understand and carve out a role for ICERD in the truth and reconciliation process. Through its potential use in truth commissions and beyond, the chapter highlights ICERD's major potential as a post-conflict, transitional justice tool. It offers a vision for the treaty as an important component in rebuilding post-conflict societies, arguing that this role has been overlooked in the discussion on CERD and conflict, suggesting the potential for a general recommendation in this sphere.

Part IV: present and future of ICERD

Chapter 11, Joshua Castellino, 'How Effective has CERD been in Protecting Minorities?', articulates the relationship between the minority rights discourse and ICERD, and looks forward to a greater understanding of its relevance to minority rights. The author traces the emergence within the UN human rights bodies of a concern with groups and group rights to the work of the Committee in carving out its scope and operations. The argument is that CERD was pioneering in the process of unravelling the rhetoric of general human rights articulated by the emergent United Nations human rights system, setting a trend subsequently replicated by later mechanisms and bodies in the need for *lex specialis* regimes to protect specific categories of individuals who are classifiable as members of a definitive group. The chapter subsequently engages the work of the Committee in a number of areas of importance to minority and indigenous rights. The limits of CERD are also understood, in particular as an instrument that was not oriented initially at minorities or indigenous peoples and the consequent textual checks on its ability to realise these aims, as well as the nature of the process of dialogue undertaken by the Committee. Overall the chapter paints ICERD as a key custodian of minority rights within the UN system, a role which has been under-represented in the literature. It is expected that in the next years and decades, the contribution of CERD to minority rights will become more generally understood.

Chapter 12, Tarlach McGonagle, 'General Recommendation 35 on Combating Racist Hate Speech', outlines how ICERD has traditionally had an outlier status among international human rights treaties in respect of racist hate speech due to its heavy reliance on the criminalisation of certain types of expression in order to combat racism. The recent GR 35 (2013) recognises that ICERD as a living instrument must be better synchronised and informed by contemporary understandings of racist hate speech, its causes, manifestations and impact. The chapter provides an expert assessment of the significance of GR 35, noting that it aligns CERD's approach more closely with those of other international bodies and standards. It furthermore removes the treatment of racist hate speech from the relatively narrow confines of Article 4 ICERD to a more relational approach engaging a range of relevant provisions in the treaty itself, in particular Articles 5 and 7. Hence the chapter emphasises the evolution of the Committee's approach, internally by drawing in a wider range of ICERD provisions, and externally by reflecting and growing interpretations from other treaty bodies. Since GR 35 is both the latest in a series of general recommendations on racist hate speech going back in time, and the most recent of the general recommendations, it very much tracks and represents the changing face of the Committee. The chapter marks a detailed and thought-provoking analysis of a document that reflects the CERD approach today and looking forward.

Chapter 13, Ion Diaconu, 'ICERD: The Next Fifty Years', closes the collection with the views of CERD member Diaconu on the continued and future relevance of ICERD. While racism as an official State policy no longer exists, racial discrimination remains a reality, taking new forms, and in some cases affecting large segments of the population. The constructive dialogue between States parties and CERD has enabled the continued application of the treaty to new and emerging situations and to new forms of racial discrimination. Thus CERD's evolving concerns have emerged as a result of its engagement with States parties and other bodies, notably NGOs, and a number of areas are highlighted as being of particular importance for the future: ensuring the extended application by States of the provision on special measures; insisting that policies and practices adopted by States for the elimination of racial discrimination include the activities of private actors; the dissemination of racist ideas, bearing in mind that CERD has made it clear that criminalization of racist should be reserved for the most serious cases; and Article 5 and the promotion of the full range of civil, political, economic, social and cultural rights without racial discrimination, focusing in particular on vulnerable groups. The Committee should remain alert to new trends and problems, for example the increased significance of cultural identities, and in this it will be assisted by developments in other human rights treaty bodies and UN organisations. The chapter concludes by noting that while the prohibition of racial discrimination will remain as a generally accepted norm of international law, ICERD and the system developed around it provide the detail on how the norm is to be realised on the ground.

In a very brief Conclusion, the editors reflect on the growth in the meaning and reach of ICERD since 1965. CERD has taken what was perceived to be a narrow mandate on apartheid and colonialism and created a near-universal system of innovative protection for a wide range of groups. What emerges in the collected writings is that ICERD is a node for group rights within the UN human rights system, as well as a technical instrument that through its dialogue is acting as a pilot light for States parties to align domestic laws and policies towards the equalisation of the enjoyment of the full range of civil, political, economic, social and cultural rights.

Part I
ICERD: cross-cutting themes

Chapter 1

Extending the rule of law

Michael Banton

Adoption of the International Convention on the Elimination of All Forms of Racial Discrimination (ICERD/the Convention) was a significant forward step in the extension of the rule of law. That process had begun in classical antiquity with the recognition of *ius gentium*, the law of peoples, as a step above the laws of particular peoples. It also featured in the conception of natural law, according to which the State must respect a lawfulness that is not of its own creation. So the story of human rights law is a story of how issues that could be made subject to legal regulation were identified, and how States were persuaded to make this possible by ceding some of their authority.

After the Second World War, new opportunities opened with the adoption in 1945 of the Charter of the United Nations. The Statute of the International Court of Justice is an integral part of the Charter. UN actions have been divided between those that are based on the Charter (mainly political) and those that are treaty-based (where legal remedies have been developed). So UN action to combat racial discrimination has followed a twin-track approach. The Committee on the Elimination of Racial Discrimination (CERD/the Committee) was the first human rights treaty monitoring body. ICERD provided, in Article 22, that if two or more States parties disputed the interpretation of the Convention, the matter might be referred to the International Court of Justice.

Fifty years after the adoption of the Convention another nine similar treaty bodies had started work. These bodies and the dates of their first meeting or, in the later cases, the date when they came into operation, are listed in Table 1.1.

In addition, it is necessary to take account of the monitoring by the Committee on the Rights of the Child (CRC) of optional protocols on the involvement of children in armed conflict (OPAC) and that on the sale of children, child prostitution and child pornography (OPSC).

Table 1.1 UN treaty bodies: year of first meeting

CERD	Committee on the Elimination of Racial Discrimination	1970
HRC	Human Rights Committee	1977
CEDAW	Committee on the Elimination of Discrimination Against Women	1982
CESCR	Committee on Economic, Social and Cultural Rights	1987
CAT	Committee Against Torture	1988
CRC	Committee on the Rights of the Child	1991
CMW	Committee on the Rights of Migrant Workers	2004
SPT	Subcommittee on Prevention of Torture	2007
CRPD	Committee on the Rights of Persons with Disabilities	2009
CED	Committee on Enforced Disappearances	2010

The treaty bodies operate in a political and legal environment recently dramatised by the establishment of an International Criminal Court, by war crimes trials and by the indictment of heads or former heads of state. The work of the European Court of Human Rights and that of the Inter-American Court of Human Rights has become more prominent. The African Court on Human and Peoples' Rights came into being in 2004 though there has been little progress towards the adoption of a corresponding human rights convention for the Asia-Pacific region. All these moves come together in the struggle to extend the rule of law.

The treaty body system is now complex and difficult for anyone but a specialist to grasp its nature and potentialities. The contention of this chapter is that the system can best be understood as part of the history of the extension of the rule of law. It is a story of struggle.

The origins of the Convention

ICERD was the pioneer in showing what might be possible. The initiative that made it possible started at the end of the 1950s in the fear of a revival of Nazism in western Germany. It was first expressed by a Charter-based body, the Sub-Commission for the Prevention of Discrimination and the Protection of Minorities. Since Jews were thought to be differentiated both by their race and by their religion, the Sub-Commission coupled the two. It drew attention to 'manifestations of anti-Semitism and other religious or so-called racial prejudices'. Its report attracted widespread notice because of the Arab–Israeli dispute and because of opposition to apartheid.

The prospect of UN action along the legal track gathered support in the General Assembly because, amid the tensions of the so-called Cold War, States within the UN's East European group saw in it opportunities to attack the colonial powers, Belgium, France, Portugal and the United Kingdom, and to put themselves forward as the protectors of the new States created by decolonisation. In the General Assembly debate the delegate of the United Arab Republic claimed that it was noteworthy that colonialism was responsible for all the cases of racial discrimination that he had mentioned, except that of the United States. The delegate of the Soviet Union averred that racism and racial discrimination were 'shameful and odious products of imperialism and colonialism', and that in 1917 the Soviet people were the first 'to put an end to discrimination'. For him, as for others, it could be completely eliminated. The Arab States saw it as a weapon to use against Israel. The size of the African group of States increased dramatically; one priority they shared was the desire for action against the apartheid policies of the then Government of South Africa. In the General Assembly, the campaign for a convention was led by the Ghanaian ambassador, Mr George Lamptey. As black Africans were widely perceived to be the main victims of racial discrimination, leadership in UN action to combat action against it came to be seen as the prerogative of the African group.[1] The perception of racial discrimination as an African interest led some diplomats to regard it as regional issue that bore solely upon their foreign policies. Some of their governments later said that they had ratified the Convention out of 'solidarity'; they had not appreciated that they were assuming onerous domestic obligations. The publication at an early stage of Guidelines for the Preparation of Reports helped clear some of these misconceptions.

Why an increasing number of States chose to ratify the Convention is an interesting question. The United States was a relative latecomer; there, the Senate was told in 1994:

> First, by ratifying the Convention, we will be better able to hold other signatories to their commitments ... Second, we could be a more effective part of the discussion now taking place over evolving international norms in the world ... Third, this would be part of our effort to inject new American energy into the UN human rights system.[2]

Today, 177 States (including the Holy See) have become parties to the ICERD.

---

1 In the drafting process, the Third Committee voted against mentioning specific forms of racial discrimination, but just two days beforehand the African States had secured mention of the specific form that chiefly concerned them, for Article 3 condemned segregation and *apartheid*.

2 Michael Banton, *The International Politics of Race* (Cambridge: Polity, 2002), p. 100.

Innovations

ICERD followed a familiar form in being divided into preambular and operative paragraphs. The former linked the Convention to the political track by explaining why it had been prepared; the latter detailed the legal obligations.

Article 9 marked a major advance upon the Convention on the Crime and Punishment of Genocide, in that by accession to ICERD, States accepted an obligation to report to the UN on their implementation of the Convention's provisions, and that a monitoring body (composed of experts elected by the States themselves) was to report to the General Assembly the results of their examination of these reports. CERD was to report to the General Assembly rather than to the States parties because racial discrimination was seen as a worldwide problem, not only for those States (which might be few in number) that might choose to ratify the treaty.

Article 8 provided that CERD should consist of eighteen experts. That States in the General Assembly saw racial discrimination as posing a political problem may explain why, when specifying the qualifications necessary for election to the committee of experts, they did not refer to 'the usefulness of the participation of some persons having legal experience', as they did when constituting the committee to monitor implementation of obligations under the International Covenant on Civil and Political Rights. The legal expertise of that body, the Human Rights Committee, enabled it to acquire an especial authority.

Another innovation was the provision in Article 14 of what later became the Optional Protocol procedure, whereby a state party could declare that it recognized the competence of the Committee to receive and issue opinions on complaints from individuals or groups within their jurisdiction claiming that the State party had violated any of their rights as detailed in the Convention.

When CERD first assembled, some members thought it should work like the UN Trusteeship Council. It was proposed that States parties should be invited to send representatives to present their reports. The following year, the delegation of Pakistan to the UN in New York made a similar request that was also denied. It was objected that the Convention gave the Committee no right to ask questions of a State representative. After the same proposal was made in the General Assembly, however, the objections were set aside; soon afterwards it was celebrated as 'perhaps the greatest success of the Committee'.[3]

---

3 CERD, 'The first twenty years: Progress report of the Committee on the Elimination of Racial Discrimination', UN Doc. HR/PUB/91/4 (1991), 28–9.

The establishment of a treaty monitoring body was itself a remarkable innovation, viewed with suspicion by States that wanted no oversight of their policies and actions. It was not to be a court. So, calling it a 'committee' made its very limited powers appear less threatening to the independence of States.

Dialogue

Though a treaty body is not a court, it may exercise a judicial function, particularly if, like CERD, it is empowered to publish legal opinions in response to individual complaints. Only recently has it begun to create a jurisprudence built up from this response. For its first fifty years CERD's main function was one nowhere identified in the drafting process or named in the Convention. It is exemplified in dialogue. In a two-way exchange with a reporting State, CERD has elaborated on the obligations incurred by accession to the Convention. At the same time, CERD members have also learned much from studying State party reports and from the replies of State representatives to their questions. A reading of the records suggests that the approach of Committee members changed greatly once State delegations attended to present reports. Through dialogue, both the States parties and the Committee members have learned more about the nature of racial discrimination and the means by which it might, one day, be eliminated.

The character of dialogue varies. Drawing upon my personal recollections, I recall an occasion when an Arab State was represented by a lawyer for whom the use of law to prevent racial discrimination was a completely novel consideration. An Arabic-speaking Committee member, himself a diplomat, understood the State representative's difficulties and, speaking in Arabic, took him through the main points like a tutor; the State representative was very appreciative. This was a constructive experience. By contrast, on one occasion the representative of a reporting State acted like a trial lawyer engaged to defend a client. He argued very vigorously that his State's laws were sufficient and brushed aside the arguments of some Committee members about desirable improvements. The exchanges continued, and came to a halt only because when the committee business has gone well past the time allocated for the session the interpreters simply depart. On this occasion there was an inadequate dialogue and little by way of conclusion.

The issue that gives rise to proceedings in a court is usually identified before the parties appear before the tribunal. A report presented to a treaty body, however, may be designed to advertise the State's successes and it is for committee members to identify what they regard as the main issues.

Court proceedings within States are paid for either by the State or by the users. In the case of the ICERD, the premises and administration of Committee sessions was to be provided by the UN. Article 8(6) of the Convention provided that the travel and subsistence expenses of members when attending the Committee's twice-yearly meetings was a charge upon States parties; they would have to refund the UN. A significant number of States parties failed to pay. They were freeloaders, seeking to ride at the expense of others. Consequently, one of CERD's two meetings scheduled for 1986 had to be cancelled. In 1987 it could meet for four weeks, in 1988 for two, in 1989 for four, in 1990 for three, in 1991 for six, in 1992 for two, and in 1993 for six weeks.

Among the States parties, a minority held to the principle that the user should pay, but eventually there was an agreement that the charges should fall upon the UN's budget (a principle that has applied to later treaty bodies). The agreement required that States parties formally accept the amendment to Article 8(6) agreed at the fourteenth meeting of States parties. A list of States that have accepted the amendment is included each year in CERD's annual report. The report for 2015 lists forty-six States. The failure of other States to meet this simple requirement indicates how low a priority many States would give to any proposal that depended upon treaty change. CERD owes its existence to the tolerance showed to freeloaders.

CERD 1986–2000

My election to membership of CERD[4] was towards the end of the Cold War between East and West. For example, it brought me into a bitter controversy over a new policy in Bulgaria designed to achieve by force the assimilation of that country's ethnic Turkish minority.[5] With the change in the international political climate by the end of the decade, however, many of the old restraints upon CERD fell away. Helped by the restoration of the previous periodicity of committee meetings, steps could be taken to improve the Committee's effectiveness.

It was agreed that, instead of reporting the views expressed by individual members, the Committee would agree a collective statement about the results of its examination of a State report. Nevertheless, some members – and not only serving diplomats – at times continued to behave as representatives of their States rather than as members of a legal team. As there was a general expectation that decisions should

---

4 It was the outcome of circumstances described in Michael Banton, *International Action Against Racial Discrimination* (Oxford: Oxford University Press, 1996), p. 139.

5 *Ibid.*, pp. 134–7.

be taken by agreement, the opposition of a single member might suffice to defeat a proposal. Then, gradually, it became possible to decide more matters by taking a vote.

New procedures were introduced regarding the appointment of country rapporteurs, the agreeing of Concluding Observations, and action in connection with States whose reports were seriously overdue.[6] Then, a little later after the fall of the Berlin Wall in 1989, there were major changes in the tone and content of periodic reports from States in the East European group.

At the beginning of the 1990s, proceedings in CERD often concentrated on the implementation of obligations under Articles 3 and 4. Much attention was paid to the perspective of State institutions and relatively little to the State's obligation to act against discriminatory behaviour by individuals.[7] The changed atmosphere meant that more attention could be paid to the implementation of Article 5 on the civil, political, economic, social and cultural rights of individuals and to the monitoring of discrimination within member States.

To discharge their obligation under Article 4 to 'declare an offence punishable by law', States had to extend their criminal codes. In the UK the first proposals for anti-discrimination laws also envisaged criminal proceedings, but then in 1964 those most concerned 'were impressed by North American evidence that anti-discrimination laws were more likely to be effectively enforced by administrative machinery than by proceedings in the criminal courts'.[8] It took time for the significance of this evidence to be appreciated elsewhere. In 1991, when the UN Human Rights Centre prepared draft model anti-discrimination legislation, it relied on criminal law to provide all forms of protection. CERD found these proposals quite inadequate.

The Committee's ability to respond to new circumstances was exemplified in 1993 when, in December of that year, and in consultation with the Government of the Federal Republic of Yugoslavia (Serbia and Montenegro), the Committee sent a good offices mission of three CERD members to visit the State party. Among other things, the mission proposed a number of specific steps, particularly in the fields of education and health care, with a view to normalising the situation in Kosovo.[9]

6 *Ibid.*, pp. 47–156.

7 Michael Banton, 'Colour as a ground of discrimination', in N. Ghanea and A. Xanthaki (eds), *Minorities, Peoples and Self-Determination Essays in Honour of Patrick Thornberry* (Leiden Martinus Nijhoff, 2004), p. 239.

8 Anthony Lester and Geoffrey Bindman, *Race and Law* (Harmondsworth: Penguin, 1972), p. 111.

9 UN Doc. A/49/18, paras. 21–5.

Early warning and urgent action

A very significant initiative succeeded in 1994, when, at its forty-fifth session, the Committee considered the Secretary General's report *An Agenda for Peace*. It used the occasion to agree innovatory procedures for 'early warning and urgent action' of a kind that that would have been inconceivable at the start of the decade. In stark contrast with the opinions expressed in the Committee's first years, CERD accepted the view that innovation sprang from the nature of its mandate.[10]

To illustrate the range and significance of matters considered in the course of a single three-week meeting, it may be noted that CERD established early warning and urgent action procedures as a regular and principal agenda item. In addition to its continuing examination of periodic reports from States, at that session CERD also gave consideration to the situations in Israel and Papua New Guinea, adopted decisions on the human rights situations in Rwanda, in Burundi, and on racist acts of terrorism (mentioning the attack on a Jewish organisation in Buenos Aires, and the attack in London). These decisions offered a basis for political action in other parts of the UN. CERD also agreed that a mission to Croatia be undertaken by one member of the Committee.

Among other innovations, it may be noted that in 2000 CERD held a thematic discussion on discrimination against the Roma, and used that discussion as the basis for General Recommendation (GR) 27 (2000) on the subject.[11] This Recommendation has been followed by others, including the lengthy GR 35 (2013) on combating racist hate speech.[12]

Communication between CERD and the States parties has been improved. In 1998 an afternoon meeting between the Committee and State party delegates was held, but, strangely, such occasions are not mentioned in CERD's annual reports. From 1996 onwards, some States have sent comments on Concluding Observations concerning their dialogue with the Committee; these have been published in CERD's annual reports. In this period the character of State reports, and of CERD's annual report, underwent changes that made them more fit for their purposes. The preparation by States of 'common core' documents has reduced duplication and saved much Committee time.

---

10 Banton, *International Action Against Racial Discrimination*, pp. 161–5.

11 CERD, 'General Recommendation 27 on Discrimination against Roma', UN Doc. A/55/18, Annex V at 154 (2000).

12 CERD, 'General Recommendation 35 on Combating racist hate speech', UN Doc. CERD/C/GC/35 (2013).

Relations with NGOs have been put on an institutional basis.[13] Dialogue is much richer when, as in the case of the UK, the United States, and some West European States, a reporting State can supply statistical information that bears on the incidence of racial discrimination, and when NGOs have been able to supply perspectives of their own. When NGOs are active, and send representatives to Geneva, the examination of State reports is more rigorous.

Those who drew up the Convention looked for action on two fronts: law enforcement and education. They looked to education as something that was delivered in schools and colleges. Experience in Europe and North America over the last half century suggests that wider social changes, especially those in the mass media, including television, newsprint and cinema, foreign travel, together with contact with persons from other world regions and changes resulting from changes from one generation to the next, have been very influential in achieving the objectives of ICERD's Article 7. These are fields in which CERD members have little expertise.

There have also been increases in some forms of social and economic inequality. Differential behaviour on grounds of race is sometimes inseparable from differential behaviour on grounds of socio-economic status. This complicates action on both the political and the legal tracks.

Political action 1971–2001

In the UN General Assembly, on a proposal from the USSR, 1971 was designated as the International Year to Combat Racism and Racial Discrimination. Then 'the ten-year period beginning on 10 December 1973' was designated 'the Decade for Action to Combat Racism and Racial Discrimination'. No explanation was offered about any advantage to be gained by adding 'racism' to the definition of racial discrimination in ICERD.

In 1993 the Commission on Human Rights appointed a special rapporteur on contemporary forms of racism, racial discrimination and xenophobia and related intolerance. His, and the three subsequent appointments to the position, have all been males and from among States in the African group. The special rapporteur has visited particular States and has issued reports on his findings. His work complements, but overlaps, that of CERD.

Each of the decades has concluded with a World Conference to Combat Racism and Racial Discrimination. The first two, held in

13 Michael Banton, 'States and civil society in the campaign against racial discrimination', Nationalism and Ethnic Politics, 18:4 (2012), 385–405.

Geneva in 1978 and 1983, were diverted by the politics of the Middle East. A senior UN official at the time described the first conference as a disaster and the second as a non-event. These conferences were diplomatic assemblies. The third, in Durban in 2001, was a more popular event. It showed that politicians had not learned the lessons of the previous failures and it descended into negative campaigning. Some delegations were withdrawn, so a valuable opportunity to publicise and strengthen action along the legal track was squandered.[14] Worse than the previous conferences, it was a calamity.

The Conference Declaration affirmed that universal adherence to and full implementation of the ICERD was of paramount importance, and continued in paragraph 79: 'We firmly believe that the obstacles to overcoming racial discrimination and achieving racial equality mainly lie in the lack of political will, weak legislation and lack of implementation strategies and concrete action by States', but the possibilities of pressure upon States were not discussed. Malaysia voted for the Conference Declaration but has not ratified the Convention and would need to amend its constitution to conform with its provisions.[15]

Some action was subsequently taken in the case of Fiji, made a party to ICERD at a time when it was a colony of the United Kingdom. As an independent state, it restricted the rights of persons of immigrant ethnic origin. Because of its failure to hold democratic elections, in 2009 Fiji was suspended from participation in the Pacific Islands Forum and from the Commonwealth of Nations. Actions by the World Bank, the International Monetary Fund and other financial institutions inflicted greater damage. Fiji took steps towards its redemption. A commission headed by a veteran Kenyan lawyer, Yash Ghai, drew up a new constitution. Then, in 2013, Fiji's military ruler rejected the draft constitution.

Article 14

CERD's duty to consider complaints against States that have made the Article 14 declaration came into effect in 1984. By the end of 2014 it had registered fifty-four complaints concerning twelve States parties. Of them, one had been discontinued and eighteen declared inadmissible. CERD had adopted final decisions on the merits of thirty complaints and found violations of the Convention in thirteen of them. Complaints pending consideration numbered five. Like the judgments of the International Court of Justice, the decisions are advisory opinions.

---

14 Banton, *The International Politics of Race*, pp. 142–69.
15 Banton, 'States and civil society', 393–4.

When it considers individual complaints, a treaty body has to act like a court. The increase in the number of such complaints means that the States parties will need to elect more persons having the appropriate qualifications and experience. More attention will have to be paid to the strictly legal components of the Convention's provisions.

Discussion of CERD's work under Article 14 has to start from the definition of racial discrimination in Article 1, paragraph 1:

> In this Convention, the term 'racial discrimination' shall mean any distinction, exclusion, restriction or reference based on race, colour, descent, or national or ethnic origin which has the purpose or effect of nullifying or impairing the recognition, enjoyment or exercise, on an equal footing, of human rights and fundamental freedoms in the political, economic, social, cultural or any other field of public life.

CERD drew the attention of States parties to certain features of this definition in its GR 14 (1993).[16] More concisely, it may be said that the definition identifies five grounds of behaviour, or causes of action, whether conscious or not; it states that if an act is based on any of them, whether purposely or not, and may have a given effect in public life, then it is unlawful.

How is a court to decide if an action is based on race? The word 'race' entered West European languages from the fifteenth century onwards. In ordinary language it was used in a metaphorical sense to identify a set of persons sharing a common ancestry. Then, from the end of the eighteenth century, there was an attempt to give the word a technical or scientific meaning. By the end of the nineteenth century, that attempt had failed. It was not a suitable word for differentiating people of African, Asian or European origin, or blacks, browns, whites and yellows. But, as Darwin regretted in 1871, 'from long habit the term "race" will perhaps always be employed' [in this popular sense].[17] In the twenty-first century, a court may have to consider whether an act was based on a popular idea of 'race'. In such circumstances sophisticated discussions of the meaning given to the word can be laid aside.

The word 'colour' is more straightforward. Differences of complexion are observable. An example has been given of a case before an Industrial Tribunal in Bristol in which an employer asked a Jobcentre if a particular job seeker was coloured. The Tribunal found that this was evidence of direct racial discrimination. The differentiation of direct and indirect discrimination corresponds to ICERD's differentiation of purpose and effect.

---

16 CERD, 'General Recommendation 14 on Definition of racial discrimination', UN Doc. A/48/18 at 114 (1993).

17 See further Michael Banton, What We Now Know About Race and Ethnicity (New York and Oxford: Berghahn Books, 2015).

The official classification of persons by colour for administrative purposes in the Dominican Republic, and its relation to proceedings in CERD, has been discussed elsewhere.[18] With the growth in the numbers of persons of multiple ancestry, colour as a ground of discrimination may be used more frequently in the future, so it may be regretted that the European Union Racial Equality Directive 2000/43/EC fails to specify this as a prohibited ground.

The character of descent as a ground of action is discussed in this volume by the editors.

National or ethnic origin can be assigned administratively. In its GR 8 (1990) CERD stated that, after having considered reports from States parties about the ways in which individuals were identified as being members of racial or ethnic groups, it 'is of the opinion that such identification shall, if no justification exists to the contrary, be based on self-identification by the individual concerned'.[19]

How is the ground of an action established? In 1997, speaking to the periodic report of Burundi, Ambassador Nsanze maintained that his country's independence had been broken by struggles for power that had resulted in the creation of artificial ethnic groups. He denied that people had been massacred on account of their ethnicity; the motivations had been political. He implied that whether or not an act was discriminatory depended upon intention.

In a separate article,[20] it has been noted that the definition of racial discrimination in ICERD was modelled on the International Labour Organization's Discrimination (Employment and Occupation) Convention 111 of 1958; this lists 'political opinion' as a prohibited ground of action, as does Article 2(1) of the International Covenant on Civil and Political Rights. In the ILO Convention the intention may have been to restrain any action by an employer to discriminate against an employee on the grounds of that person's membership of a political party or support for a political movement.

It may also be noted that on one occasion a representative of Israel objected to a request of CERD for information on the territories occupied by Israel on the grounds that the conflict there was neither racial nor religious but national and political. That is a

18 Banton, 'Colour as a ground of discrimination', pp. 237–47.

19 CERD, 'General Recommendation 8 on Membership of racial or ethnic groups based on self-identification', UN Doc. A/45/18 at 79 (1991).

20 Michael Banton, 'Political motives as grounds of racial discrimination', in F. Coomans, F. Grünfeld, I. Westendorp and J. Willems (eds), Rendering Justice to the Vulnerable: Liber Amicorum in Honour of Theo van Boven (The Hague: Kluwer, 2000), pp. 61–68.

characterisation of a situation; it does not claim to describe the cause of a particular action.

The definition in ICERD focuses on particular actions. It does not depend upon motivation or the subjective causes of actions. When deciding cases of direct and indirect discrimination, courts in the United Kingdom have adopted the 'but for' test, in which they ask whether the alleged victim would have been treated less favourably *but for* his or her membership of a class of protected persons. The court makes an objective determination of the grounds of action.

When CERD's jurisprudence is more substantial it may be possible to comment on its character. For example, since the case of *Tyrer* v. *UK* (1978) the European Court of Human Rights' (ECtHR) adoption of an evolutionary interpretation of expected standards of conduct has attracted comment.[21] ICERD has proven a living instrument in the sense that it has been used to consider matters that were not in contemplation in 1965 (like discrimination against the Roma), but there has been no new interpretation of the standards to be expected. CERD has shown that the standards envisaged in 1965 can be applied to new categories of persons.

The United Kingdom has under review the possibility of making a declaration under Article 14, and has issued comments in its State reports which illustrate opposition to making the declaration.[22] It comments:

> The Government remains to be convinced of the added practical value to people in the United Kingdom of rights of individual petition. The United Kingdom has strong and effective laws under which individuals may seek remedies in the courts or in tribunals if they feel that their rights have been breached. By contrast, the treaty monitoring committees are not courts, and they cannot award damages or produce a legal ruling on the meaning of the law.[23]

The treaty body system

Successive UN High Commissioners for Human Rights have, from 1994, attempted to harmonise the operation of the treaty bodies. In 2006, the then High Commissioner commissioned a report from one of the few experts with a grasp of the whole system, Mr Philip Alston.

21 *Tyrer* v. *United Kingdom* (1978), 58 ILR 339, 353.

22 CERD, 'State Report: United Kingdom (2011)', CERD/C/GBR/18–21, paras. 358–62.

23 *Ibid.*, para. 359.

In her Concept Paper she launched a proposal to replace the existing treaty bodies with a single unified treaty body.[24]

The Concept Paper reviewed the achievements of the treaty bodies in providing authoritative guidance on the meaning of international human rights standards, stimulating the creation of constituencies at the national level, with dialogue and opportunity for public scrutiny of government policies. Individual complaints procedures had often resulted in individual relief for victims. Various parts of civil society, regional bodies and UN agencies had benefited from the treaty monitoring process.

The system nevertheless faced serious challenges, some of them linked to its successes. Many States accepted the human rights treaty system only on a formal level and did not, in public, play any very active part. If they were to do so, and presented all the reports they have undertaken to submit, the treaty bodies would be unable to cope with the burden of work. In particular:

> [T]reaty bodies, composed of part-time, unremunerated experts nominated by States parties from among their nationals and elected by States parties for fixed renewable terms, have been uneven in terms of expertise and independence, as well as geographical distribution, representation of principal legal systems and gender balance. Competing demands have also meant that some treaty body members have been unable to devote the time required to the work of their Committees and some have been unable to attend sessions. As there is no limitation on the number of terms members may serve, several members have served for long and unbroken periods.[25]

The proposed unified standing treaty body might well have had to operate by dividing into chambers operating along functional, treaty, thematic or regional lines. Limiting the length of time that experts can serve on treaty bodies might be a means to increase the degree to which the committees are representative of the general population, but it would have disadvantages. My experience is that it takes time for a committee member to understand how the system operates, and how amendments of various kinds can be introduced. Institutional memory can also be important.

Little progress has been recorded along the lines the High Commissioner proposed. Instead, her successors have convened regular meetings of the chairpersons of treaty bodies and pressed for the harmonisation of their working methods. A successful innovation in one treaty body may be recommended to others. One example is the adoption of follow-up procedures that improve the dialogue with

---

24 United Nations Secretariat, 'Concept paper on the High Commissioner's proposal for a unified standing treaty body' (2006), HRI/MC/2006/2.

25 Ibid., para. 22.

States. Significant improvements may be achieved by such simple measures as insisting on time limits for speeches by State party delegates, committee chairpersons and members.[26]

The complexity of the treaty body reporting system may explain why the work of the committees has attracted very little academic comment. Like other institutions, CERD can benefit from constructive criticism. Yet there are few people outside the OHCHR who are able to provide such criticism. There are also few people other than diplomats who would be able to offer informed comment on the interdepartmental relations within governments that may affect the policies adopted by States parties.

Conclusion

The treaty body system is a creation of States, made possible by the commitment of individual politicians and officials who at times may press other States to observe standards their own States cannot always satisfy. It is testimony to the better side of human nature, financed on the cheap.

CERD has no life of its own. It has to be given life, first by the States parties, such as by the character of the persons they elect to membership of CERD, and by the attention they pay to CERD's reports, with respect both to the implementation of their own obligations and as a means of extending the rule of law in the wider world.

Second, CERD and other treaty bodies depend upon the United Nations, for the provision of the requisite services, the work of the secretariat, and, through the High Commissioner for Human Rights, for action on any opportunity for rationalising the human rights treaty system as a whole.

Third, the treaty body system depends ultimately upon public understanding of human rights and upon support for politicians willing to run risks in opposing nationalist attacks upon international norms. The contributions of NGOs to the work of CERD (playing a role that would have been inconceivable to many delegates in the General Assembly in 1965) testify to increasing public support. Sometimes the UN cannot act without the support of regional bodies. As this chapter is written, in early 2016, the news of ethnic conflicts in Burundi sadly recalls the history of Tutsi–Hutu tensions since the 1870s, and the international failure to prevent or halt the genocidal mass slaughter of

---

26 For examples of the scope for improvement, see Michael Banton, 'Decision-taking in the Committee on the Elimination of Racial Discrimination', in P. Alston and J. Crawford (eds), The Future of UN Human Rights Treaty Monitoring (Cambridge: Cambridge University Press, 2000), pp. 55–78.

Tutsi in Rwanda during 1994. Effective international action (including action in the International Criminal Court) often needs the support of regional bodies and heads of state. Africa's record is disappointing, and that of the Association of Southeast Asian Nations even more so.

Fourth, there are some problems that politicians (and voters) regard as 'too difficult', such as, for example, the way that in some regions the supply of labour is increasing so much more rapidly than the demand for labour. So it is unsurprising if governments regard excess population growth as 'too difficult' a problem. In 1945, international action against racial discrimination would have been considered 'too difficult'. Not now!

Chapter 2

Knowing and doing with numbers: disaggregated data in the work of the Committee on the Elimination of Racial Discrimination

Joshua Clark

The Committee on the Elimination of Racial Discrimination (CERD/ the Committee) has asked that States provide it with population statistics broken down by race, ethnicity or nationality for most of its history, but never with as much priority as in the last fifteen years. This chapter analyses CERD's evolving approach to using these disaggregated data to monitor and promote implementation of the International Convention on the Elimination of All Forms of Racial Discrimination (ICERD/ the Convention). When I speak of 'disaggregated data', I refer to socio-demographic, economic and administrative statistics created from information that is coded by individuals' racial, ethnic or national identity or origin.[1] States gather such data through a variety of tools, including censuses, surveys, birth or conscription registries, and social-service records. Using documents spanning the Committee's history, secondary literature and ethnographic material from observation and interviews at CERD sessions, I track the debates that have shaped the Committee's policies and practices on disaggregated data over its first forty-five years.[2]

The increasing interest at CERD in using statistics to track States' obligations is not unusual in the treaty body system, but it has a distinct historical trajectory from the recent rise of 'indicators' elsewhere in human rights governance.[3] One significant feature of this history is

1 I use the term *disaggregated data* rather than *demographic data* because it better encompasses the range of data with which CERD has engaged under the rubric of 'information on the demographic composition of the population'. This category is distinct from another set of statistics of interest to the Committee – those on complaints, prosecutions and sentences related to acts of discrimination – which I do not discuss here.

2 The author carried out ethnographic research at CERD's August sessions in 2010, 2013 and 2015.

3 See Sally Engle Merry, 'Measuring the world: Indicators, human rights, and global governance', *Current Anthropology*, 52:s3 (2011), s83–s95 ['s' = supplement]; and

the fact that many reporting States have long resisted gathering data on the subject matter of interest to CERD. Unlike other demographic variables relevant to human rights treaty monitoring – sex and age, for example – racial, ethnic, and national identities or origins are often left out of official (State) statistics.[4] Throughout CERD's existence, the United Nations Statistics Division (UNSD) has deemed this topic optional for population censuses, and declined to adopt precise guidelines for those States that choose to record it.[5] This places CERD in the unique position of having to justify why and how States should produce even the basic data it seeks, often in the face of strident opposition.[6]

CERD has regularly requested disaggregated data on groups protected under the Convention since it issued a general recommendation on the matter in 1973; however, its policies have tended to be broad and conducive to discrepant applications. Former CERD chair Michael Banton describes the Committee's position as being that States 'usually need to' collect and monitor demographic data in some form, adding that these views 'have not been challenged and therefore have a place in the developing international law on the prevention of racial discrimination'.[7] This description accurately summarises CERD general recommendations and reporting guidelines, but it also reflects those policy statements' ambiguity concerning some consequential questions. If

AnnJanette Rosga and Margaret Satterthwaite, 'The trust in indicators: Measuring human rights', *Berkeley Journal of International Law*, 27 (2009), 253–315.

4 For a global survey of the 2000 round of censuses, see Ann Morning, 'Ethnic classification in global perspective', *Population Research and Policy Review*, 27 (2008), 239–72.

5 See United Nations Statistics Division, *Principles and Recommendations for the 1970 Population Censuses*, Statistical Papers, Series M, No. 44 (New York: United Nations, 1967), paras. 175, 245–6; and United Nations Statistics Division, *Principles and Recommendations for Population and Housing Censuses* (Revision 2), Statistical Papers, Series M, No. 67 (New York: United Nations, 2008), paras. 2.160–2.162. Morning has criticised the UNSD's reticence regarding ethno-racial enumeration guidelines. See Morning, 'Ethnic classification'.

6 I prefer the term *produce* over *collect*, recognising that, as Alain Desrosières reminds us, 'contrary to what the etymology of the unfortunate term "data" suggests, very few "data" are actually "given"'. Alain Desrosières, 'How real are statistics? Four possible attitudes', *Social Research*, 68 (2001), 347. Rather, data – and perhaps especially ethno-racially disaggregated data – are products of numerous choices, and sometimes heated debates, concerning methods of elicitation, validation and collation. See for example the study of Costa Rica's 2011 census in Joshua Clark, *The Global Fight against Racial Discrimination: Counting, Representation, and Responsibility in Costa Rica and at the United Nations* (PhD dissertation, University of California, Irvine, 2016).

7 Michael Banton, 'Ethnic monitoring in international law: The work of CERD', in Andrea Krizsán (ed.), *Ethnic Monitoring and Data Protection: The European Context* (Budapest: Central European University Press, 2001), p. 81.

States must *usually* provide demographic data, what circumstances justify exceptions? What is the substantive scope and level of detail of the data CERD requires? How do these particular data relate to States' obligations under the Convention? This chapter focuses on how CERD has answered these questions in practice – through its deliberations over State reports and its Concluding Observations. I show that the Committee's practices have varied across time and States, in relation to both the data States report and their arguments for not reporting. Tracking these variations offers a clearer understanding of this international expert body's evolving vision for the role of ethno-racially disaggregated data in eliminating racial discrimination in all its forms.

One particularly salient variation I highlight is between two distinct types of data that CERD has elicited since its 1973 general recommendation. A first type consists of figures on the size and distribution of ethno-racial sub-populations; a second is comprised of statistics representing the living conditions of protected groups, especially in comparison to the rest of the population. Though CERD initially anticipated receiving only the former of these, one of the fruits of its under-specified information requests was that some States began reporting the latter as well. This in turn altered CERD reporting expectations, and both types of data have since become vehicles for pursuing provisions of the Convention that previously eluded assessment. But the distinction between the two is significant because each type points towards different rights issues and ways of knowing racial discrimination. CERD's work has most fully reflected the Convention's broad agenda for combating discrimination in both purpose and effect where it has insisted that States report both types of data in as much detail as possible.

A second point of variation is in CERD's acceptance of limits and exceptions to its demands that States provide one or both types of data. Overall, CERD has become less tolerant of State resistance to data-reporting requirements, and fittingly so given the expanding uses of data for assessment just mentioned. But CERD's deliberations over the reasons particular States might not use ethno-racial statistical categories show that it is not driven by an unmitigated 'will to know'. Rather, CERD deploys its data-reporting requirements critically and differentially, taking into account wider concerns about what its efforts to know *do*. Specifically, CERD members weigh questions about how ethno-racial data disaggregation is likely to impact different countries' domestic social dynamics and policy processes. In doing so, they accept that quantification and measurement projects always produce more than knowledge, and that their own involvement constitutes them as social actors who must consider both dimensions of *knowing* and *doing* with numbers.[8] Here we see illustrated a larger, often-overlooked tension with which CERD constantly grapples – that between efforts to rigorously assess and to effectively promote implementation of the Convention. CERD practice tends to favour a pragmatic, nuanced approach in which the kinds of knowledge the Committee requires depend on the particular circumstances of each State party in question.

I find here a lesson for social scientists interested in generating research that strengthens the work of the treaty bodies. That lesson is that there is greater need for rich empirical accounts of what measurement does in diverse social and policy settings than there is for the development of further standardised indices and measurement tools. If treaty bodies like CERD prefer flexibility and the discretion to pursue 'what works' for each State's implementation process, then critical, in-depth studies of the situated effects of quantitative-knowledge production could contribute a great deal to their strategies.

Data requests in CERD's first decade

CERD began requesting that States parties provide data on population groups in the first years of its work. This practice was hardly inevitable though; initially, some Committee members considered States' abstention from ethno-racial identification to be good anti-discrimination practice. In 1973, for example, CERD members commended Brazil for *not* possessing statistical data on the country's racial composition, saying that this reflected the Government's 'enlightened policy' on racial distinctions and integration.[9] It is helpful to recall that in CERD's first

8 These insights are central to anthropological and sociological scholarship on quantification and measurement. See for example Wendy Nelson Espeland and Mitchell Stevens, 'A sociology of quantification', *European Journal of Sociology*, 49 (2008), 401–36; Martha Lampland, 'False numbers as formalizing practices', *Social Studies of Science*, 40 (2010), 377–404; Jane I. Guyer *et al.*, Special section: 'Number as inventive frontier', *Anthropological Theory*, 10 (2010), 36–197; and Kregg Hetherington, 'Waiting for the surveyor: Development promises and the temporality of infrastructure', *Journal of Latin American and Caribbean Anthropology*, 19 (2014), 195–211.

9 CERD, 'Summary record of the 130th meeting'. Hereafter all CERD summary records will be cited as 'SR.[meeting number]', e.g. SR.130. The 1970 Brazilian census to which the CERD member's comments refer was actually the only one of the country's last eight decennial censuses that did not classify respondents by race/colour. CERD's apparent naivety about the role of racial/colour difference in social stratification in Brazil is surprising given contemporaneous domestic policy debates, social movements, and more than a decade of scholarship – beginning with path-breaking works sponsored by UNESCO – deconstructing the myth of Brazilian 'racial democracy'. See Jan Hoffman French, '*Mestizaje* and law making in indigenous identity formation in northeastern Brazil', *American Anthropologist*,

years of examining State reports, members were still deciding what kinds of information they needed, and feedback they should transmit, to fulfil their mandate. The issue was a pressing one from the start, as an astonishing number of States sent reports to CERD claiming that racial discrimination simply did not exist in their countries.[10] Dubious as these claims may have been, CERD often accepted them, leaving unclear how a biannual reporting cycle should thus proceed. Where States had 'no difficulties' related to racial discrimination, could the Committee ask them to report about their 'successful experiences', which could then serve as examples for other governments?[11] If CERD doubted a State's claims, what further information could it request to better understand the country's ethno-racial context?

One answer to the latter quandary came in General Recommendation 4, which CERD adopted in 1973. The recommendation states that CERD,

> *Bearing in mind* the need for the reports sent by States parties to the Committee to be as informative as possible,
>
> *Invites* States parties to endeavor to include in their reports under article 9 relevant information on the demographic composition of the population referred to in the provisions of article 1 of the Convention.[12]

It is occasionally argued at CERD that reading General Recommendation 4 as a request for *statistical* information is a misinterpretation, but there is no evidence that this or anything else about the statement caused controversy at the time of adoption.[13] During the following year, CERD solicited comments from States parties and received just seven responses, none of them expressing opposition.[14] When one State, Madagascar, responded by sending CERD demographic figures on the general population, CERD even explained that

---

106 (2004), 663–74; Michael George Hanchard, *Orpheus and Power: The Movimento Negro of Rio de Janeiro and São Paulo, Brazil, 1945–1988* (Princeton: Princeton University Press, 1994); and George Reid Andrews, 'Brazilian racial democracy, 1900–90', *Journal of Contemporary History*, 31 (1996), 483–507.

10 See Michael Banton, *International Action against Racial Discrimination* (Oxford: Oxford University Press, 1996), pp. 106–7.

11 SR.45. See also CERD, 'General Recommendation 2 on States parties' obligations' (1972), which affirms that States must submit reports irrespective of whether they acknowledge that racial discrimination exists in their countries.

12 CERD, 'General Recommendation 4 on Information on the demographic composition of the population', UN Doc. A/9018 at 106 (1973).

13 Indeed, the recommendation was adopted unanimously and without formal debate. See SR.161. This unanimity is surprising given that it came just a few months after Committee members had praised Brazil for abstaining from collecting ethno-racial data.

14 See Report of the CERD, General Assembly Official Records, UN Doc. A/9618 (1974), pp. 98–9.

such figures should be broken down in terms of the protected classes covered by the Convention. Its interest, CERD stated, was in 'statistical data and other particulars on the various ethnic groups' in each country.[15] Subsequent state responses to General Recommendation 4 regularly made reference to censuses, suggesting that there was little doubt that 'information on the demographic composition of the population' meant numbers.[16]

States' acceptance of General Recommendation 4 showed that most were prepared to allow the reporting procedure to go beyond what some CERD members previously understood as a very limited mandate: to 'detect an incompatibility between the domestic laws of a country and a specific provision of the Convention'.[17] The Convention itself defines its scope more broadly than this, and CERD requests for data on the ethno-racial breakdown of populations underscored that States parties must eliminate racial discrimination not only in law, but also in fact. For CERD to be able to ask the right questions, and assess the actual status and treatment of protected groups, it needed to know which groups existed and how many individuals belonged to each. This was the function initially envisaged for disaggregated data in the reporting procedure.[18]

Still, CERD continued to accept the absence of disaggregated data from State reports throughout the 1970s. Many States did not collect data on racial, ethnic or national origin, and CERD was not sure that telling States to change their data-gathering practices was within its competence. CERD took up this question in 1976, during its review of Kuwait's State report. The ensuing debate offers a unique view into CERD's thinking at the time, as this report was discussed without a State representative present.

Mr Valencia-Rodríguez began the discussion of the Kuwaiti report with praise that seems out of place in light of General Recommendation 4. He announced that he 'readily appreciated that in States such as Kuwait or Brazil where no racial discrimination existed, the census authorities, when preparing statistical data, were "not allowed to base the distribution of the population on ethnic origin", since to make such a breakdown could in itself be considered as a form of discrimination'.

15 *Ibid.*, p. 38.

16 See for example CERD dialogues with Yugoslavia in SR.422, the Philippines in SR.321, Austria in SR.273, and Mexico in SR.303.

17 SR.29.

18 Thomas Buergenthal, 'Implementing the UN racial convention', *Texas International Law Journal*, 12 (1977), 191–2. As Mr Ingles stated as early as 1970, 'Since racial discrimination could exist only in countries where the population was not homogeneous, the Committee should know whether there were racial minorities in a given State in order to be aware of the possibility of discrimination'. See SR.34.

Mr Pahr disagreed, arguing that every State party must comply equally with CERD's general recommendations. When Mr Sayegh countered that Kuwait could not be expected to provide census statistics on ethnic origin if it did not collect them, Mr Ingles questioned whether the omission 'was legally mandatory or ... simply the result of a policy decision'. He proceeded to say that a State's failure to collect information on the distribution of population groups could undermine its ability to ensure these groups' protection, and thus might 'run counter to the Convention's aims'. If the decision not to collect data in this way was not prescribed by law, but rather left to census authorities' discretion, Kuwait might be asked to reconsider it.[19]

Ultimately, CERD would not pursue this proposal, or at least not in this first period of its work. Though no decision was taken formally, dissenting voices on CERD prevailed. Mr Aboul-Nasr expressed disappointment that Kuwait had not abided by General Recommendation 4, but pointed out that the Convention itself did not require that States parties provide demographic information. Mr Sayegh, a Kuwaiti national and diplomat, went further. He argued that States could only be asked for information already at their disposal, and that '[t]he Committee would be exceeding its rights if it requested the Government of Kuwait to change its census policy'.[20] Unchallenged, Mr Sayegh would repeat this position during the 1978 examination of Brazil's report, saying that CERD 'had no alternative but to respect' that country's choice not to record race or ethnic origin in censuses.[21] CERD concluded its first decade thus – with requests for statistical breakdowns of countries' population groups, but not the boldness to compel them.

The 1980s and 1990s

CERD began the 1980s consolidating and codifying reporting-procedure practices it had developed the decade before. These included its requests that States report demographic breakdowns of their populations. During its twenty-first session in 1980, CERD adopted 'General Guidelines regarding the form and contents of reports by States parties'. This document elaborated upon the vague instructions on State reporting CERD issued in a January 1970 communication,[22]

19 See SR.280.

20 *Ibid.* See also Report of the CERD, General Assembly Official Records, UN Doc. A/31/18 (1976), para. 98.

21 See SR.395, para. 41. Again, the fact that Brazil's most recent census at the time had no such variable was an aberration. Race/colour categories were reinstated on its subsequent census two years later.

22 See CERD Communication, UN Doc. CERD/C/R.12 (28 January 1970).

and added relevant text from CERD's five general recommendations adopted since then. Accordingly, the General Guidelines reaffirmed that 'Information should also be provided in [the first] part [of States' reports] in connexion [*sic*] with General Recommendation IV ... on the demographic composition of the population'.[23]

During this period, CERD also began responding to States parties' objections to coding data by race, ethnicity or nationality. In its 1983 report to the UN General Assembly, CERD discussed an exchange with an unnamed reporting State that opposed 'group[ing] the population according to ethnic origin' on grounds that this 'would go against the principles of equality laid down in the Convention'. Though this position was anomalous – 'for the most part, States parties were providing such information in their reports' – CERD considered it important to respond. Members acknowledged that not all States collect 'statistics on the ethnic composition of their populations', and accepted that where doing so is 'considered improper' or where 'there were genuinely no ethnic differences', States 'could not be expected to respond in the same way as multi-ethnic States'. Nonetheless, CERD was 'of the opinion that information on the demographic composition was of relevance to many articles of the Convention and that the Committee could not effectively deal with the problem of racial discrimination without having such information'. Thus, members made the compromise that 'such information need not be precise demographic statistics but at least percentages of the total population'.[24]

This formulation sought to accommodate both CERD's general information needs and States' perceived differences of national circumstance. States employed numerous arguments against coding demographic data by race, ethnicity or nationality. These included not only claims that their populations were homogenous, but also objections based on principles of liberal citizenship, socialism and Islam,[25] as well as pragmatic objections about the need to foster unified national identities in postcolonial settings.[26] Then-Committee member Karl Partsch recalls that CERD often lacked consensus about how to deal with such objections, but generally reinforced 'the practical importance of receiving [demographic] information'.[27] What is clear in the language

23 See Report of the CERD, General Assembly Official Records, UN Doc. A/35/18 (1980), Annex IV, para. 7.

24 Report of the CERD, General Assembly Official Records, UN Doc. A/38/18 (1983), paras. 512–13.

25 Algeria in fact cited both of the latter sources in 1984. See Report of the CERD, General Assembly Official Records, UN Doc. A/39/18 (1984), para. 97.

26 Banton, *International Action against Racial Discrimination*, Ch. 11.

27 Karl Josef Partsch, 'The Committee on the Elimination of Racial Discrimination', in Philip Alston (ed.), *The United Nations and Human Rights: A Critical Appraisal* (Oxford: Oxford University Press, 1992), p. 351.

quoted above is that CERD's rationale continued to be that this information provided basic knowledge of ethno-racial diversity in a country, allowing the Committee to know where, and with respect to which groups, discrimination could potentially crop up.

That rationale began to be displaced in the late 1980s and early 1990s by one that drew on a broader conception of discrimination. By that time, several States had reported unemployment, education and income figures on minoritised groups that made clear that such groups experienced widespread socio-economic disadvantage. Most States parties argued before CERD that these conditions were caused by something other than racial discrimination, and for several years CERD accepted their arguments.[28] But by the early 1990s, those arguments faced obsolescence as key CERD members reiterated that neither causation nor lack of discriminatory intent limited the scope of their work. The Convention's definition of discrimination included anything less than the de facto equal enjoyment of all human rights across groups; thus, the ethno-racial distribution of social and economic rights so clear in State-reported statistics was indeed the Committee's concern.

As statistics registering inequality helped return CERD's attention to the Convention's broad scope, they also sharpened the focus of CERD's requests for disaggregated data moving forward. In a 1990 dialogue with Finland, for example, CERD members stated that they needed 'comparative data on rates of school enrolment, access to health care, the rate of unemployment, infant mortality, life expectancy, [etc.]'. These were necessary 'to be able to gain a clearer idea of the situation of the Samis and the Romanies in relation of the remainder of the Finnish population'.[29] This request diverges from earlier ones, which sought data that characterised a country's diversity as background knowledge for tracking down discriminatory acts. It focuses instead on socio-economic conditions, and suggests that groups' *relative outcomes* themselves imply discrimination *in effect*.[30]

28 See for example the CERD's 1985 dialogue with Mexico in SR.706 and SR.707. For an excellent discussion and typology of States' forms of denying the existence of racial discrimination in Latin America, see Ariel Dulitzky, 'A region in denial: Racial discrimination and racism in Latin America', in Anani Dzidzienyo and Suzanne Oboler (eds), *Neither Enemies nor Friends: Latinos, Blacks, Afro-Latinos* (New York: Palgrave Macmillan, 2005).

29 Report of the CERD, General Assembly Official Records, UN Doc. A/45/18 (1990), para. 91.

30 Here we see an instance in which meaning lies not in numbers' absolute terms, but in the relations articulated between them. See Gary Urton, *The Social Life of Numbers: A Quechua Ontology of Numbers and Philosophy of Arithmetic* (Austin: University of Texas Press, 1997). That is, it is when read against the context of all Finns' life expectancy rates that those particular to the Sami people become knowledge pertinent to discrimination.

This approach to disaggregated data is evident in CERD's 1992 Concluding Observations on Costa Rica,[31] and spelled out in those on Greece:

> In order to determine whether the social differentiation of Muslims, Pomaks, Gypsies, Armenians and others … had the effect of impairing the human rights and fundamental freedoms of members of those groups, the Committee called upon the Government of Greece to include in its next periodic report information on the economic, social and cultural circumstances of those groups.[32]

At around this time, CERD also took up the question of *how* individuals should be identified by race, ethnicity or nationality. This matter was a tricky one for at least two reasons. First, the Convention defines discrimination in a way that intentionally avoids reifying race or ethnicity.[33] It discusses these terms only as grounds upon which discrimination occurs (without affirming their 'true' character), thereby providing little guidance about the bases on which individuals *ought to be* identified. Second, any debate about how to identify individuals again raises questions about CERD's competence – namely, whether it may say anything at all to States about their methods for collecting official data.

These issues notwithstanding, CERD members turned their support for the criterion of self-identification – and worries that other criteria could endanger certain groups' rights claims – into a general recommendation on the matter.[34] From the outset, CERD limited the scope of what would become General Recommendation 8 to the issue of how individuals are formally identified, declining to attempt 'a general definition of ethnic groups'.[35] Members agreed that they should advocate self-identification – or, 'basing identification on an individual's expressed desire' – but took great care to ensure that their wording was neither too strong nor weak. They considered, for example, if self-identification should be called a 'rule' or 'an inherent right', and whether too categorical a statement might dissuade States from producing disaggregated data at all.[36] Notably, no member mentioned the possibility of a universal 'objective' criterion of racial, ethnic or national identity, leaving no suggestion that the Committee

31 See Report of the CERD, General Assembly Official Records, UN Doc. A/47/18 (1992), para. 112.
32 *Ibid.*, para. 91.
33 See Banton, *International Action against Racial Discrimination*, Ch. 4.
34 See SR.867 and CERD, 'General Recommendation 8 on Membership of racial or ethnic groups based on self-identification', UN Doc. A/45/18 at 79 (1991).
35 *Ibid.*
36 See SR.883.

believed such a thing existed. Members ultimately agreed upon the following text:

> *Having considered* reports from States parties concerning information about the ways in which individuals are identified as being members of a particular racial or ethnic group or groups,
>
> [the Committee i]s *of the opinion* that such identification shall, if no justification exists to the contrary, be based upon self-identification by the individual concerned.[37]

As CERD focused on comparative disaggregated data as means of knowing discrimination 'in effect', some States' opposition to producing them grew. This was the case for several African countries, whose leaders worried that producing statistics tied to ethnicity could destabilise already fragmented populations. Any socio-economic disparities revealed by these data would reinforce citizens' belief that resources were distributed through ethnic favouritism and patronage networks. Further, some States argued that opposition political factions could deploy such data to stoke interethnic competition and conflict.[38]

In some cases this type of objection resembled States admitting that if citizens could see the extent of their country's inequality in concrete figures, they would likely revolt. Though CERD's job was not to protect governments from dissatisfied constituents, growing ethnic conflicts in Yugoslavia, Burundi and Rwanda made threats to peace and public security loom large in members' minds.[39] When CERD updated its reporting guidelines in 1993, CERD member Mr Banton advocated flexibility on the issue of ethno-racial data coding. Noting that 'some States parties refrained from collecting information on the ethnic origin of their populations in their periodic censuses', Banton suggested that, 'Those States could be reminded that, if it was not possible for them to provide the data through censuses, it was permissible for them to inform CERD of their demographic situation in another way'.[40] The text proposed and adopted for the revised guidelines thus read:

> Many States consider that, when conducting a census, they should not draw attention to factors like race lest this reinforce divisions they wish to overcome. If progress in eliminating discrimination based on race, colour, descent, national and ethnic origin is to be monitored, some indication is needed of the number of persons who could be treated less favourably on the basis of these characteristics. States which do not collect information on these characteristics in their censuses, are therefore requested to provide information on mother tongues as indicative of ethnic differences,

37 SR.884.
38 Banton, *International Action against Racial Discrimination*, pp. 250–1, 268–9.
39 *Ibid.*, pp. 187–9, 255–61.
40 SR.984.

> together with any information about race, colour, descent, national and ethnic origins derived from social surveys. In the absence of quantitative information, a qualitative description of the ethnic characteristics of the population should be supplied.[41]

This 1993 formulation reads as something of a retreat from CERD's increasing turn towards using disaggregated data to spotlight socio-economic disparity as a breach of the Convention. First, it repeats an earlier era's rationale for requesting such data, specifically that 'some indication is needed of the number of persons who could be treated less favourably on the basis of these characteristics'. Again, this is a purpose apart from that of disaggregating educational, health, income and other data to compare figures on different groups. Though it does not prevent States from providing such figures, nor stop the Committee from identifying discriminatory effects in them, it fails to codify either practice. Indeed, it suggests that having socio-economic statistics broken down by racial, ethnic, or national identity or origin need not be the point. Relatedly, the guideline's allowances do not support the tracking of inequality through time. If 'a qualitative description of the ethnic characteristics of the population' is acceptable, it is unclear how CERD could assess progress in reducing relative disadvantage – concepts that appear logically and discursively dependent upon the 'strong language' of comparative statistics.[42]

But if the revised guideline seems to grant considerable deference to States, there is little evidence that it constrained CERD in practice. To the contrary, CERD's Concluding Observations for the rest of the decade frequently pressed for not only breakdowns of the demographic composition of their populations, but also information and indicators on the distinct social and economic circumstances of different ethno-racial groups.[43] Banton has since stated that the 1993 guideline 'was drafted so as to take account of the sensitivity in black African countries of the recording of ethnic origin in the national census'.[44] If it served a more general purpose, it may have been to present a policy that was formally consistent and universal, but also broad enough to grant CERD discretion about the specifics of what to demand from which States. CERD could continue to push the issue of discrimination 'in effect' through calls for robust disaggregated statistics from

41 CERD, 'General guidelines regarding the form and contents of reports by States parties' (Revision 3), UN Doc. CERD/C/70/Rev.3 (1993), para. 8.

42 See Talal Asad, 'Ethnographic representation, statistics and modern power', *Social Research*, 61 (1994), 55–88.

43 Banton reproduces an extensive list of Concluding Observations on ethno-racial data spanning the years 1994 to 2000 in 'Ethnic monitoring in international law', pp. 68–78.

44 *Ibid.*, p. 79.

less 'sensitive' States. But where it judged doing so would risk alienating a State party from the reporting procedure, it could settle for simpler descriptions of the population's diversity – at least for the time being.

Data disaggregation in the twenty-first century

In the decade of the 2000s, the production of statistical data disaggregated by race, ethnicity or nationality approached becoming a full-fledged human-rights imperative. Language urging the practice was included in the Programme of Action adopted at the 2001 World Conference against Racism, Racial Discrimination, Xenophobia and Related Intolerance in Durban, South Africa.[45] In 2006, when the human rights treaty body system established 'harmonized guidelines' on treaty reporting, they too instructed States to generate disaggregated information and indicators on the various 'demographic and ethnic' segments of the population.[46] For its part, CERD received disaggregated data in more state reports than ever before, and showed increasing impatience with States that continued to refuse to collect them.

This mounting consensus notwithstanding, CERD did not rigidify its stance on ethno-racially disaggregated data in its updated 2007 reporting guidelines. Those guidelines retain the 1993 language so ambiguous about which types of ethno-racial data are mandatory for which States.[47] In practice, however, the countries CERD exempted from pressure for disaggregated data were few and far between. During the five years following the revised guidelines, 80 per cent of CERD's Concluding Observations included at least one recommendation concerning disaggregated statistics.[48] In the vast majority of cases, these recommendations called on States to change their data-collection practices – to improve current methodologies or to gather data the State might not presently – above and beyond simply providing data

45 This provision owes a great deal to the lobbying efforts of civil-society leaders, in particular an emerging transnational network of Afro-descendants from Latin America. See Corinne Lennox and Carlos Minott, 'Inclusion of Afro-descendents in ethnic data collection: Towards visibility', *International Journal on Minority and Group Rights*, 18 (2011), 257–75.

46 See Inter-Committee Technical Working Group, 'Harmonized guidelines on reporting under the international human rights treaties', HRI/MC/2006/3 (10 May 2006).

47 See CERD, 'Guidelines for the CERD-specific document to be submitted by States parties', UN Doc. CERD/C/2007/1 (2007), para. 11.

48 Over the years 2008–12, the Committee examined ninety-eight State reports, and in seventy-eight cases its Concluding Observations urged the State to provide, improve or collect ethno-racial statistical data. Where States received no such recommendation, it was usually because they had already reported enough to satisfy the Committee.

the State already possessed.[49] African States were no more likely to be exempted from these requests, despite the role their objections played in tempering official reporting requirements.

By the 2010s, CERD also more readily confronted States regarding such objections. In August 2010, for example, Mr Lahiri firmly rejected the French claim that collecting ethno-racial data undermined the equality of French citizenship. Such data, he said, were a means of identifying de facto discrimination, and 'refusing to measure its extent did not make that discrimination any less real'.[50] Mr Cali Tzay echoed this point in CERD's 2011 dialogue with Spain, arguing that ignoring race/ethnicity in official statistics did not help discrimination go away, but rather masked it.[51] In its Concluding Observations, CERD acknowledged these States' avowedly principled objections to producing disaggregated data only to overrule them. Particularly noteworthy is CERD's assertion that ethno-racial statistical production is not contrary to the French constitutional guarantee of all citizens' equality without distinction, assuming it is based on individuals' 'anonymous and purely voluntary self-identification'.[52] Even in the case of Rwanda – a country torn apart by genocide less than two decades earlier – CERD in 2011 applauded the removal of ethnic classifiers from national identity cards, while still promoting such identification for socio-economic data, where they could illustrate the relative standing of different groups.[53] In these and other exchanges, CERD's adamancy about monitoring ethno-racially disaggregated data reinforced economic and social rights' place on the implementation agenda.

CERD's calls for disaggregated data in the 2000s also served as a vehicle for foregrounding the Convention's requirement that States enact 'special and concrete measures' wherever fundamental rights are enjoyed unequally across groups. CERD members advocated using disaggregated data to determine whether socio-economic conditions obliged such measures, and, once in place, whether the measures were in fact ameliorating disparities. This argument reiterated the crucial

49 CERD members in this period advised States on what they should collect, how to collect it, and social conditions they should address in order to prevent under-reporting of minority identities. See, for example, CERD, 'Concluding Observations: Colombia', UN Doc. CERD/C/COL/CO/14 (2009); the CERD's 2011 dialogue with Paraguay (SR.2095, paras. 62, 75–6); and CERD, 'Concluding Observations: Paraguay', UN Doc. CERD/C/PRY/CO/1–3 (2011).

50 See SR.2026, para. 47.

51 See SR.2065, para. 46.

52 See CERD, 'Concluding Observations: France', UN Doc. CERD/C/FRA/CO/17–19 (2010), para. 12; on Spain, see CERD, 'Concluding Observations: Spain', UN Doc. CERD/C/ESP/CO/18–20 (2011), para. 8.

53 See CERD, 'Concluding Observations: Rwanda', UN Doc. CERD/C/RWA/CO/13–17 (2011), paras. 6, 10.

point that, under ICERD, discriminatory outcomes compel remedial policies, programmes or other State actions even without proof of discriminatory acts. Having made these connections in dialogues with individual State delegations, in 2009, CERD codified them in a general recommendation. The recommendation recalls that ICERD aims to secure 'substantive or *de facto* equality in the enjoyment and exercise of human rights', a principle that provides the general normative grounds for States to enact preferential policies or programmes for minoritised groups.[54] But whether such 'special measures' can or must be adopted in a particular context was an empirical question:

> Appraisals of the need for special measures should be carried out on the basis of accurate data, disaggregated by race, colour, descent and ethnic or national origin and incorporating a gender perspective, on the socio-economic and cultural status and conditions of the various groups in the population and their participation in the social and economic development of the country.[55]

The position enunciated in this recommendation has largely replaced the earlier rationale for requesting disaggregated data simply to know how many people are susceptible to discriminatory acts. By 2013, CERD's appeals for demographic and socio-economic statistics were so ubiquitous that members sometimes qualified them by assuring State delegations that they raised the issue in every dialogue. But this wholesale insistence that States code data by race, ethnicity or nationality has sparked a backlash on the Committee. Some members worry that CERD's sweeping demands uncritically emphasise means at the expense of ends. This recent challenge to disaggregated data's place in CERD's work came out in a debate among CERD members in August 2013.

The debate in question began during the examination of Burkina Faso, in which various CERD members suggested that the State include ethnic identity in official statistics. This, they said, would allow it to identify and address patterns of inter-group inequality before they lead to conflict. Mr Lindgren however objected to this position, noting that many countries' group-based animosities – such as those between herders and farmers – are not experienced by their protagonists as 'ethnic'. In such cases, collecting and disaggregating socio-economic data in ethnic terms fosters and legitimises lines of division that entrench hostility and fragment society. Mr. Thornberry responded by acknowledging validity in both positions, saying that while states need

54 CERD, 'General Recommendation 32 on The meaning and scope of special measures in the ICERD', UN Doc. CERD/C/GC/32 (2009), paras. 6–8.

55 *Ibid.*, para. 17.

to possess information on sub-populations to direct policy, there are sometimes 'legitimate concerns about data collection focusing identities around limited categories'. In the end though, he concluded, 'most countries manage the dilemma without fragmentation', and in his view, 'more friction is possible due to a lack of adequate policies than any administrative data effort'. During the subsequent review of Belarus, Mr Lindgren countered that 'recent experiences in Europe, Asia, and Africa' attest that the distinctions disaggregation reinforces 'can easily be used to foster resentment, unrealistic claims, refusal to integrate, separation, and war'.[56]

This debate is significant because it finds CERD members grappling with the fact that ethno-racial quantification is not only a means of knowing but also a social intervention. Here CERD is indeed less worried about how disaggregated data help it assess local conditions than how a State's statistical production might impact those conditions. Both Mr Lindgren and Mr Thornberry echo various scholarly critiques of institutional systems for classifying people, including that they amplify the socially perceived importance of certain types of difference, authorise a reduced set of identities and solidify otherwise permeable boundaries between them.[57] On the other hand, a State that does not generate ethno-racial data may be ill-equipped to ameliorate inequalities distributed along already socially salient lines, and could even be accused of complicity in those inequalities for having rendered them 'statistically invisible'.[58] Faced with this dilemma, in most cases CERD continues to press States to produce disaggregated statistics, and praises those that already do so. But lest we doubt that CERD members take the dilemma seriously, following the debate just described, CERD abstained from such recommendations in its Concluding Observations on both Burkina Faso and Belarus.[59]

---

56 Quotations in this paragraph are taken from the author's ethnographic field notes and a print copy of Mr Lindgren's comments on the State report of Belarus.

57 See for example Ian Hacking, 'Making up people', in T. C. Heller, M. Sosna and D. E. Wellbery (eds), *Reconstructing Individualism* (Stanford: Stanford University Press, 1986); Benedict Anderson, *Imagined Communities* (London: Verso, revised edn, 1991); Pierre Bourdieu, 'Rethinking the state: Genesis and structure of the bureaucratic field' (Loic J. D. Wacquant and Samar Farage, trans.), *Sociological Theory*, 12 (1994), 1–18; Jane Collier, Bill Maurer and Liliana Suárez-Navaz, 'Sanctioned identities: Legal constructions of modern personhood', *Identities*, 2 (1995), 1–27; and David I. Kertzer and Dominique Arel (eds), *Census and Identity: The Politics of Race, Ethnicity, and Language in National Censuses* (Cambridge: Cambridge University Press, 2002).

58 See Clark, *The Global Fight against Racial Discrimination*, Ch. 2; and Lennox and Minott, 'Inclusion of Afro-descendents in ethnic data collection'.

59 See CERD, 'Concluding Observations: Burkina Faso', UN Doc. CERD/C/BFA/CO/12–19 (2013); and CERD, 'Concluding Observations: Belarus', UN Doc. CERD/C/BLR/CO/18–19 (2013), respectively.

My interviews with CERD members offer further evidence that Mr Lindgren is not the only one apprehensive about CERD pressing for ethno-racial data from every reporting State. After one CERD member told a State delegation that the Committee needed to support various claims with indicators, I asked this member how the Committee evaluates the credibility of such indicators. The CERD member pointed out that my question assumed that CERD requests data simply to judge compliance, but this is not necessarily the case. There are many sources of information available, the member continued, and CERD can usually assess States' shortcomings under the Convention without official (State) ethno-racial statistics. What makes it worthwhile to push States to produce their own indicators is if doing so sparks a wider state process – the establishment of targets, plans for achieving those targets, and subsequent measurement of success. That is, quantification is valuable inasmuch as it mobilises State action. Another CERD member similarly described data disaggregation as necessary only in relation to specific, instrumental goals. For example, to request ethno-racial data is justified where a State denies that discrimination – or ethno-racial heterogeneity itself – exists in its country, as was long the case for most Latin American States.[60] Here the data are useful because they destabilise such presumptions, and thereby push States parties into a more in-depth engagement with the Convention and the Committee. But whether data disaggregation is a productive means of advancing a State's implementation process depends on the circumstances of the particular State. Where it is not, the numbers alone are not very useful to CERD.

Together, these commentaries exhibit a pragmatic orientation to the reporting procedure in which CERD members gauge the value of information less on basis of what it *reveals* than what it *does*. More than in the past, CERD considers the potential societal and policy by-products of quantification when debating whether to advocate ethno-racial statistical production. Disaggregated data are deemed valuable not because they disclose a more 'objective' truth, but if, and insofar as, they serve as a channel or 'infrastructure' for State action.[61] For most CERD members, the burden is still upon those States – or CERD colleagues – who argue that data disaggregation does more harm than good for a particular country's realisation of non-discrimination and equality. Some however insist on posing the question on a case-by-case – or State-by-State – basis, arguing that ethno-racial statistical

60 See Dulitzky, 'A region in denial'.

61 For recent anthropological treatments of these two types of socio-political investment in quantitative measurement, see respectively, Merry, 'Measuring the world' and Hetherington, 'Waiting for the surveyor'.

production often brings only wasted political energy, and potentially much worse. These represent the contending positions at CERD on the eve of the fiftieth anniversary of the International Convention on the Elimination of All Forms of Racial Discrimination.

Conclusions

The current state of CERD's debate over disaggregating data by race, ethnicity and/or nationality in some ways echoes those of the past. As Banton says, CERD has always wanted some type of information on the ethno-racial characteristics of countries whose governments report to it. The questions have concerned the types of information to be included, who decides the limits, and upon what basis. In its early years, CERD restricted itself to requesting data that States already possessed, uncertain that CERD's mandate allowed it to speak to States' statistical practices. As States increasingly submitted data, CERD found in them new ways of ascertaining knowledge of discrimination, which in turn strengthened its argument that other States did indeed need to generate disaggregated statistics. These data have helped CERD move beyond impasses with States that claim their countries are ethno-racially homogenous, opened new vistas on minoritised groups' social and economic rights, and provided a concrete form of knowledge for judging whether States must enact special measures benefiting those groups. With these advances in the reporting procedure, CERD increasingly made the case for State production of disaggregated data, while maintaining policies that allowed for exceptions.

Today CERD is cautious about pressing for ethno-racial statistics only where it judges that the production thereof may create new social divisions, or be treated by a State as an end in itself rather than a means. CERD's awareness of such dynamics demonstrates its increased attention to wider socio-legal contexts and pragmatics of combating racial discrimination through the reporting procedure. That which best allows CERD to know or assess may not always be the best strategic step for moving a country towards better fulfilling the Convention's aims. CERD then has maintained some ambiguity in its position on State reporting of disaggregated data – a position that it negotiates in relation to the particular dilemmas and objections encountered in dialogue with specific States parties. If this amounts to standards not fully standardised, the result is to preserve a space of flexibility and discretion for CERD members to seek advances in treaty implementation effectively and appropriately for all and each State.

Nonetheless, we can see that overall CERD's demands for States to produce, analyse and take action based on ethno-racial statistics have expanded as the stakes of doing so have increased. What CERD requests today is not only background information on how many people could be exposed to discrimination, but statistics showing which self-identified groups benefit most and least from the country's policies and resources. Such data are suggestive of forms of indirect or de facto discrimination that are otherwise difficult to pinpoint – whether for CERD, States parties, or the affected populations themselves. In countries in which it is an open secret that socio-economic inequalities track lines of ethno-racial difference, these data can be powerful levers for pushing the issue onto policy agendas, particularly with reference to ICERD's provision that targeted measures to benefit minoritised groups be used whenever 'circumstances so warrant'. It is not clear whether CERD or groups protected under ICERD can effectively mobilise that provision where States continue not to produce disaggregated data. Thus, exceptions to the general policy favouring such data production should be made with the awareness that State refusal to disaggregate makes it less likely that protected groups will see important parts of ICERD's robust framework for combating discrimination applied to them.

Chapter 3

Racial discrimination and gender justice

Nozipho January-Bardill

Introduction

The commemoration of the fiftieth anniversary of the United Nations International Convention on the Elimination of all Forms of Racial Discrimination (ICERD/the Convention) in November 2015 occurred during an important year when the UN also celebrated the twentieth year of the adoption by UN member States of the Beijing Declaration and Platform for Action (PFA) during the fourth UN World Conference on Women in China in 1995.[1] Of additional interest is the fact that 2015 also marked the year when the global community reached consensus on the 2030 Agenda for Sustainable Development goals for the post-2015 era and agreed that gender equality has to be a lived reality for all women and girls irrespective of their race, nationality, ethnicity, social class, age, disability and other identities.[2]

At the Women's Conference in Beijing member States of the United Nations agreed on a blueprint for the achievement of gender equality and accepted that gender, like race, is a social and not a biological construct. They also understood that both men and women are gendered beings whose experience of life is historically, politically and culturally constructed and socially determined, in particular through the ideologies of patriarchy (sexism) and racism; and that there are important conceptual differences between women's rights and gender power relations. Feminists across the globe had for decades before Beijing argued that women need not be seen in isolation but within a system of gender relationships that privilege men and subordinate women. But it was in Beijing, at this last conference on women, that the community of nations provided the context for a comprehensive analysis by the UN

1 United Nations, 'Report of the Fourth World Conference on Women', Beijing 4–15 September 1995, UN Doc. A/Conf.177/20/ Rev.1 (1996).

2 UNWomen, *Progress of the World's Women 2015–2016: Transforming Economies, Realising Rights* (New York: UNWomen, 2015), p. 10.

of the dynamics of gender discrimination, and how it leads to the violation of women's rights and gender justice. The UN for the first time acknowledged that women's rights are human rights.

The UN World Conference Against Racism, Racial Discrimination, Xenophobia and related Intolerance (WCAR), held in Durban, South Africa in 2001,[3] six years after Beijing and seven years after the demise of apartheid in South Africa, created a similar opportunity for the family of nations to engage in a global dialogue on past as well as contemporary forms of racism and racial discrimination, xenophobia and related intolerance. The final conference declaration and programme of action reaffirmed that all forms of racism, racial discrimination, xenophobia and related intolerance constitute a negation of the purpose and principles of the Charter of the United Nations.[4] The declaration also reaffirmed that 'states have the duty to protect and promote the human rights and fundamental freedoms of all victims and that they should apply a gender perspective, recognising the multiple forms of discrimination which women face, and that the enjoyment of their civil, political, economic, social and cultural rights is essential for the development of societies throughout the world'.[5]

Four preparatory regional conferences that included strong civil society participation prior to the WCAR had spent a considerable amount of time examining and analysing the intersectionality of race, ethnicity and gender. The United Nations Division for the Advancement of Women (DAW) in collaboration with the Office of the High Commissioner for Human Rights (OHCHR) and the United Nations Development Fund for Women (UNIFEM) organised an Expert Group Meeting on Gender and Racial Discrimination to deepen understanding on the issue, and support the Secretary General's report to the Commission on the Status of Women at its forty-fifth session as well as the WCAR.[6]

This effort by women in the UN system and women from across the world resulted in both conferences positively refining and accepting the notion that there is a clear relationship between race, ethnicity and gender, and that these social and ideological constructs intersect

3 Durban, South Africa, was chosen to host the Conference since a new non-racial democracy had replaced years of colonialism and institutionalised racism under apartheid.

4 United Nations, 'Declaration and Programme of Action: World Conference Against Racism, Racial Discrimination, Xenophobia and Related Intolerance', UN Doc. A/CONF.189/12 (2002), p. 7.

5 *Ibid.*, p. 11.

6 United Nations, 'Gender and Racial Discrimination', Report of the Expert Group Meeting, Zagreb, Croatia (21–24 November 2000).

and co-exist in ways that affect the life experience of racial groups differently.[7]

Discussions on the use of race and gender relations as tools for analysing both historic and contemporary forms of racial and gender discrimination have remained central to the implementation of the outcomes of these two world conferences. Gender relations in this context are understood as the social, economic, political and legal roles of women and men within society. Issues of gender equality, women's empowerment and racial justice are very complex in most societies and cultures across the globe. Manifestations of structural or institutional racism against women and men of African descent, national and ethnic minorities, indigenous peoples, migrants, refugees and asylum seekers remain a grave concern for defenders of human rights, gender justice and racial equality.

This chapter offers a description and a critical and personal perspective on the normative rights frameworks that have served as international legal instruments to set norms and standards to help governments address race and gender discrimination, as well as their effects on the lives of people who reside in their jurisdictions. It will also identify some key aspects of the United Nations treaty system and, in particular, the work of the Committee on the Elimination of Racial Discrimination (CERD/the Committee) that have served to both help and hinder the achievement of a fairer social system for those who are the main victims and survivors of racial and gender injustice.

ICERD and CEDAW

On 21 December 1965 at the UN General Assembly 106 States adopted the oldest of the UN's human rights binding legal instruments directed at the elimination of racism and racial discrimination, ICERD.[8] UN member States had witnessed and were appalled by the ravages of anti-Semitism in Europe and, in particular, by the 1961 Sharpeville massacre of unarmed and peaceful black South African demonstrators and human rights activists.[9] The international community had in solidarity concurred with UN member States that apartheid was a crime

7 Celina Romany and Katherine Culliton, 'The UN World Conference against Racism: A race–ethnic and gender perspective', *Human Rights Brief*, 9:2 (2002), 14–17 and 29.

8 GA Res. 20/2106, 'International convention on the elimination of all forms of racial discrimination', UN Doc. A/RES/20/2106 (21 December 1965).

9 Rudiger Wolfrum, 'The elimination of racial discrimination: Achievements and challenges', in The United Nations Educational, Scientific and Cultural Organization, *United to Combat Racism: Selected Articles and Standard-Setting Instruments* (Paris: UNESCO, 2001), pp. 23–55.

against humanity that gravely disturbs international peace and security; and the global anti-apartheid movement had made it their mission to end one of the most repressive forms of racism and racial oppression in the history of the world.

One hundred and seventy-seven states have ratified and are currently parties to ICERD. The 1963 Declaration by the UN General Assembly that preceded the adoption of the Convention had targeted racism as an ideology.[10] It asserted that any doctrine of racial differentiation or superiority was scientifically false, morally condemnable, socially unjust and dangerous. Thus, there was no justification for racism in theory or practice. It also set out the moral path for the future by affirming that:

> Discrimination between human beings on the grounds of race, colour or ethnic origin is an offense to human dignity and shall be condemned as a denial of the principles of the charter of the United Nations [and] as a violation of the human rights and fundamental freedoms proclaimed in the Universal Declaration of Human Rights.[11]

Article 1 of ICERD defines racial discrimination widely as 'any distinction, exclusion, restriction or preference based on race, colour, descent, or national or ethnic origin which has the purpose or effect of nullifying or impairing the recognition, enjoyment or exercise, on an equal footing, of human rights and fundamental freedoms in the political, economic, social, cultural and other fields of public life'.[12] Although it was specifically intended to apply to the treatment of the black population under apartheid in South Africa, it was not confined to this notorious institutionalised racism and discrimination. Instead it covers all acts of racially motivated discrimination in any country, whether based on race, colour, descent, or national or ethnic origin, whether intentional or unintentional, and has the purpose or effect of nullifying or impairing a person's dignity.

The Declaration on the Elimination of All Forms of Discrimination against Women was adopted by the General Assembly in 1967 soon after ICERD, and a year after the General Assembly adopted the International Covenant on Civil and Political Rights. This was followed by the adoption of the Convention on the Elimination of All Forms of Discrimination against Women (CEDAW) in 1979,[13] four years after the first World Conference on Women in Mexico in 1975,

10 GA Res. 18/1904, 'United Nations declaration on the elimination of all forms of racial discrimination', UN Doc. A/RES/18/1904 (20 November 1963).

11 *Ibid.*, Article 1.

12 GA Res. 20/2106, Article 1, para. 1.

13 GA Res. 34/180, 'Convention on the elimination of all forms of discrimination against women', UN Doc. A/RES/34/180 (18 December 1979).

and during the UN Decade for the Advancement of Women (1976–85). Three world conferences on women were subsequently held in 1980, 1985 and 1995. Similar to ICERD, CEDAW defines discrimination against women as:

> any distinction, exclusion or restriction made on the basis of sex and which has the effect or purpose of impairing or nullifying the recognition, enjoyment and exercise by women, irrespective of their marital status, on a basis of equality of men and women, of human rights and fundamental freedoms in the political, economic, social, cultural, civil or any other field.[14]

Article 2 of CEDAW requests States parties to 'condemn discrimination against women in all its forms, agree to pursue, by all appropriate means and without delay, a policy eliminating discrimination against women, and, to this end, undertake to embody the principle of equality of men and women in their national constitutions or other appropriate legislation'.[15]

At the Beijing Conference in 1995 participants from 189 countries (including 70,000 attendants and 30,000 NGO activists), unanimously agreed on the most visionary, comprehensive progressive blueprint to date, for advancing women's rights and the social, economic and political empowerment of women. Importantly the Conference Declaration also asserted that women's rights are human rights. This milestone platform for action drew significant attention to the fact that socio-economic circumstances as well as race, ethnicity, disability and age create specific obstacles for women and girls. The PFA provided the framework for the acceptance of the fact that multiple and co-existing forms of discrimination that violate women's human rights continue to limit their social, political and economic advancement and cause untold violence, deprivation and poverty. It strongly advanced the need for positive actions to be taken by States parties to the convention to reverse the negative impact of sex and gender discrimination.

States that agree to be bound by ICERD and CEDAW not only have a duty to refrain from acts of discrimination, they are also required to condemn all acts of discrimination against racialised groups and women in all its forms. Article 3 of ICERD urges States 'to condemn racial segregation and apartheid and prevent, prohibit and eradicate all practices of this nature in territories under their jurisdiction'.[16] Article 4 condemns all forms of propaganda based on theories of racial superiority including promoting racial hatred and acts of violence or incitement to such acts. Such acts shall be punishable by law.

14 *Ibid.*, Article 1.
15 *Ibid.*, Article 2.
16 *Ibid.*, Article 3.

The two conventions accord all women and racialised groups or individuals equal enjoyment of their human rights and fundamental freedoms. Women and racial groups are guaranteed equality before the law and the enjoyment of a range of civil, economic, social and cultural rights. They commit States to change national laws and policies that directly and indirectly discriminate against such groups. Both conventions rightfully state that it is not sufficient to refute or deny discriminatory intent behind a particular policy or action. States obligations go much further and beyond that. They are required to ensure that private and public persons do not engage in or promote policies that are discriminatory in effect. In addition, it is imperative that they take positive steps and design effective remedies to eliminate all forms of racial and gender discrimination from all aspects of public and private life, such as in housing, employment, access to justice, education and migration.[17]

Treaty bodies/committees of ICERD and CEDAW

CERD and CEDAW are autonomous bodies central to the implementation of the two conventions. The committees are known formally as treaty bodies and members are nominated by their governments and elected by member States of the UN in New York through a voting system. They comprise men and women from diverse geographies, nationalities, cultures and disciplines who are experienced 'experts' in the field of human rights and related disciplines and acknowledged to be of high moral standing and impartiality.[18] They serve in their personal capacity and governments are not permitted to instruct or influence the members' participation in the committee.

High level delegations from the States parties present periodic written and verbal reports to the committees in Geneva, Switzerland, under the auspices of the OHCHR. These periodic reports mostly describe what legislative, judicial and administrative measures States parties to the conventions have developed and implemented to give effect to key normative provisions of ICERD and CEDAW. They form the basis for robust discussions, in the spirit of open and constructive dialogue, between the committee members and the complying States.

The country reporting process also includes contributions by other UN agencies, UN mandate holders and independent experts such as

17 Sapana Pradhan-Malla, 'Racism and gender', in United Nations, *Dimensions of Racism* (New York and Geneva: United Nations, 2005), pp. 179–91.

18 Centre for Human Rights, *The Committee on the Elimination of Racial Discrimination*, Fact Sheet 12 (Geneva: UN Centre for Human Rights, 1991), pp. 4–5.

the Special Rapporteurs on Racism and Minority Rights, national human rights institutions, ombudspersons and other international human rights bodies. Shadow reports by non-governmental organisations and anti-racist and gender equality activists in civil society complement and sometimes contradict the formal reports submitted by States parties to the OHCHR and the secretariats of each of the treaty bodies. The committees actively advocate for the participation of such civil society groups. In addition, CERD's open dialogues are widely accessible to the public through the internet. Webcasting has provided many civil society and other interested organisations and individuals the opportunity to listen to the Committee's formal deliberations with States parties.

Article 14 of ICERD also provides CERD with the competence to receive and examine allegations and complaints by individuals and groups provided their governments have made the declaration under Article 14 of the Convention.[19] CERD's early warning and urgent action procedure,[20] adopted in 2004, has enabled the Committee to act and prevent very critical problems from escalating into conflicts. Indigenous peoples, for example from Latin America, Canada and the United States, have utilised this procedure to protect their rights in the wake of massive exploration by the extractive industries on some of their lands and cultural heritage sites. CERD'S Concluding Observations in its reports also encourage States to implement the 2001 Durban Programme of Action designed to guide States in combating all forms of racism, racial discrimination, xenophobia and related intolerances. This is frequently reputed to be one of the best programmes of action, despite the fact that it emerged from what was in many ways a controversial UN World Conference.[21]

In addition, CERD consistently advocates for the universal ratification of ICERD, as well as the withdrawal by states parties of reservations on some articles in the Convention. CERD furthermore regularly requests that States parties, that have not done so, make the declaration pursuant to Article 14 of the Convention that permits the Committee to hear and process individual complaints. It consistently recommends to States parties that they establish national human rights institutions that monitor, investigate and manage alleged cases of racial discrimination to assist the implementation of ICERD; communicate strategies

---

19 Some State parties to the Convention have chosen not to be bound by some of the individual articles.

20 CERD, 'Guidelines for the Early Warning and Urgent Action Procedure', UN Doc. A/62/18 (2007).

21 With some states withdrawing from the Conference prior to the adoption of the Declaration and Programme of Action.

to combat racism; raise awareness of racial discrimination; promote training and sensitisation of public servants and ensure appropriate follow-up to CERD observations and recommendations.

The adoption by CERD of General Recommendation 25

In March 2000, CERD took a momentous step by adopting General Recommendation (GR) 25 on the gender related dimensions of racial discrimination.[22] This was in line with its practice of organising occasional and broader 'thematic discussions' during some of its sessions. During this fifty-sixth session of the examination of country reports, CERD acknowledged and accepted the fact that racial discrimination does not always affect women and men equally or in the same way. 'Some forms of racial discrimination have a unique and specific impact on women only.'[23] This breakthrough was a familiar position to some members of the Committee, though less so for others. In particular, it represented a significant gain for the black women on the Committee. More especially it was a gain for all women of African descent, women from national and ethnic minority groups, Roma women, indigenous and migrant women, women who are non-citizens, and women seeking refugee status and political asylum.

The fact that GR 25 was adopted on the eve of the 2001 WCAR was significant. In its contribution to the conference, CERD was able to request States parties to the Convention to integrate gender in their analysis of racial discrimination and pay special attention to gender and the violations of the human rights of vulnerable women. The activism of the NGO forum and civil society participants in and before the Durban Conference during preparatory meetings accelerated the acceptance of 'intersectionality' as a concept. Anti-racist groups and feminists also placed xenophobia and the plight of indigenous peoples and people of African descent on the world stage in the fight for racial justice.

In more recent years and in the face of increased Islamophobia and other forms of religious intolerance, conservatism and extremism, the Committee has engaged States parties on the intersection of race, religion and gender. These social trends are reported to have slowed down progress towards gender equality. They have been instrumental in restricting the sexual and reproductive health and rights of women and girls, have increased violence against them, and negatively affected their autonomy. For these reasons, CERD has been diligent in

---

22 CERD, 'General Recommendation 25 on Gender-related dimensions of racial discrimination', UN Doc. A/55/18, Annex V at 152 (2000).

23 *Ibid.*, para. 3.

acknowledging the value of the Durban Declaration and Platform for Action and the effectiveness of an intersectional, multi-disciplinary, collective and inclusive approach to combating racial discrimination, xenophobia and related intolerance.[24]

GR 25 was not only strengthened by the Durban Conference. The visibility of black and minority women was also enhanced within the States they lived. States parties to ICERD had to include them specifically in their official analysis of racial diversity and race relations in their jurisdictions, as well as in the strategies to combat racial inequality and injustice. The rights of all these women became the subject of much discussion between CERD and States parties to the Convention including recommendations in a number of Concluding Observations that governments provide it with detailed gendered analyses of the situation of minority and other racially vulnerable women in their countries.

In addition, CERD made a decision to recommend to all States parties that they include information in their periodic reports on all efforts to implement the Durban Platform for Action. Reporting requirements included, amongst others, disaggregated data showing how and the extent to which the civil, political, social and cultural lives of women were negatively affected by direct and indirect forms of racial discrimination, and detailed descriptions of the legal, administrative and judicial measures introduced to prevent, combat and punish such acts of discrimination, as well as an assessment of their effectiveness.

Similarly, non-governmental organisations, academic institutions, think tanks, social movements and other data-gathering institutions were encouraged to use gender as a cross-cutting variable in their analysis of racial discrimination and related intolerances. Such encouragement was promoted both directly, through formal and informal interactions of the Committee with such groups, and indirectly through the dissemination of information to them by the States parties. Moreover, CERD itself had to learn the art of looking at the world through gender lenses in its examination of the reports by States parties to the Convention. The 'intersectionality' of race and gender rapidly became part of the discourse in Committee discussions and dialogues with States parties. Female victims and survivors of racial discrimination could utilise ICERD to protect and promote their fundamental right to civic, social, political and economic justice, as well as to express the fact that they have particular needs, expectations, views and priorities.

24 UN Secretary General, 'Review and appraisal of the implementation of the Beijing Declaration and Platform for Action and the outcomes of the 23rd special session of the General Assembly', UN Doc. E/CN.6/2015/3 (20 March 2015), p. 110.

By adopting GR 25 and a range of other general recommendations, including the most recent on racial hate speech and racial violence,[25] CERD has enhanced the normative standards for the protection of the rights of vulnerable racial and national minorities such as the Roma in Europe, people who have been the victims of descent-based discrimination, people of African descent, indigenous peoples and non-citizens. These measures have served to stretch the utility of ICERD as a legal international instrument, thereby addressing some of the shortcomings of the 1965 Convention. CERD has made it possible for all these groups, and the women who identify themselves as belonging to them, to legitimise the claim that they experience race and gender discrimination simultaneously in their private and public lives. These claims might deliver them little or no transformative changes in societal political, cultural and economic relations, but can at least deliver them recourse from the institutions of the State that ostensibly protect their rights as human beings under international human rights laws.

The utilisation of GR 25 continues to provoke a degree of controversy within CERD with the change of membership of the Committee, as was the case recently when CERD addressed the impact of political uprisings that have led to violent conflicts in Africa, the Middle East, Eastern Europe and other parts of the world. With less than full support from some colleagues,[26] it was the women on CERD who invoked Security Council Resolution 1325[27] and recommended that States parties involved in armed conflict observe the impact of war on racial and ethnic minorities, racially vulnerable women and girls in particular, and take measures to ensure that they are included in conflict resolution, humanitarian and peace building efforts. The female members of CERD further urged such conflicting parties to take special measures to protect women and girls from gender-based violence, in particular rape and other forms of violent sexual abuse.

Similarly, and at its November 2015 sitting, the women on CERD invited all members to align themselves with the '16 days of activism against violence against women'[28] campaign coordinated by UNWomen, the UN entity mandated to convene action to promote, protect and advocate for the rights of women, and coordinate efforts

25 CERD, 'General Recommendation 35 on Combating racist hate speech', UN Doc. CERD/C/GC/35 (2013).

26 Some of whom felt that, as this was a Security Council Resolution, it essentially fell outside the mandate of the Committee.

27 UN Security Council Resolution 1325 (2000), 'Women, Peace and Security', UN Doc. S/RES/1325 (31 October 2000).

28 10 November–16 December marks the sixteen days of activism against gender-based violence, a campaign initiated by the Centre for Global Leadership, Rutgers University in 1991.

to achieve gender parity throughout the UN system. Such an act of solidarity with the Secretary General and UNWomen, would help, it was argued, to demonstrate the value of united and collective action by the UN system.

Achievements and challenges

Like all conventions and treaty bodies, CERD and CEDAW are creations of their Conventions and the UN General Assembly. The Conventions define the scope of their work and diplomacy, and consensual decision-making are their modus operandi. The diversity and independence of the Committee members is valuable and offers each member the opportunity to interpret the Convention from their own vantage points. The downside of this independence is the lack of an explicit and common vision concerning the purpose of the Committee and the type of society that it aspires to see and contribute to in the examination of States party reports.

Individual Committee members approach the examination of country reports from their own personal and political stance as well as their own racial, gender, regional and nationality perspectives. Some have been essentially liberal and legalistic in their interventions while others have been more radical in their approach, focusing on the broader structural, socio-economic and cultural factors that underpin race and gender power relations in society. Whilst CERD's reports and recommendations have undoubtedly assisted many States parties in strengthening and improving their legal human rights obligations and institutional machinery, its emphasis on consensus has sometimes led to compromises and lost opportunities to demand more from States parties to ICERD, particularly in terms of proactively addressing the underlying causes of continuing race and gender inequalities in society. This has been a difficult challenge but also a significant lesson on how to agree to disagree.

Many States parties to CERD and CEDAW have enacted constitutional provisions on non-discrimination and equality based on race, gender and ethnicity. Some have criminalised discrimination and have initiated special measures to address the negative impacts of discrimination.

A number of States parties to ICERD, however, have also presented challenges to the work of CERD. Some have denied the existence of racism and racial discrimination in their jurisdictions primarily because, unlike in South Africa, racial discrimination was not formally institutionalised through legal statutes. The caste system, for example, has been a source of much contention in CERD discussions and engagements with States where caste distinction is accepted as a way of life. Such States have argued that this category falls outside the scope of the definition of racial discrimination in the Convention. More recently, there has been a tendency in other States, and particularly those from the European Union and other Western countries, to adopt a generic approach to difference and avoid any effort to disaggregate the composition of racially or ethnically diverse societies to address racism and racial discrimination. The rhetoric of 'I do not see colour' and 'there is no such thing as race' are part of a range of expressions being used to promote contemporary notions of race and colour blindness. Such States ignore the reality that visible physical differences are still loaded with social significance that assign group membership, rank, social and economic status, to individuals.[29] Racial profiling, for example, remains one of the most widely used forms of racial discrimination in the world. These race-neutral approaches are of grave concern to all members of CERD and particularly those on the Committee who have first-hand experience of the insidious nature of racial and gender stereotyping and discrimination. It also has the effect of diminishing the real experience of 'people of colour' and others with distinct and visible and linguistic differences.

Many reports presented by civil society organisations show that some civil servants and police in law enforcement agencies, judges and magistrates in judicial systems, teachers and social workers in social institutions, tellers and bankers in financial institutions and immigration officers at points of entry into countries and employers in the private sector are all to a larger or lesser degree influenced by physical and other differences that can lead to racial and gender discriminatory behaviour in intent or effect. The absence of complaints to law enforcement agencies and judicial institutions about such infringements does not necessarily imply the absence of institutionalised racism and discrimination. Guillaumin aptly argues that 'race exists and does not exist; although an imaginary formation and an ideological construct it is real, a brutal and tangible reality'. She goes further and states that both racism and sexism are operative and function to exploit and sometimes to kill, and should therefore not be eradicated from our critical vocabulary.[30]

These conflicting approaches to difference have not been helpful. Neither has the tendency to depoliticise the issue of racial and gender discrimination. To deny the presence of segregation does not guarantee its absence in some States parties. The divorce of law from politics has been one of the most frustrating aspects to some CERD members.

---

29 Michael Banton, *Race Relations* (London: Tavistock Publications, 1967).

30 Colette Guillaumin, *Racism, Sexism, Power and Ideology* (London: Routledge, 1995), p. 19.

Racism and sexism have much to do with ideologies, bias, and access to opportunity, and the unequal distribution of resources. Changing outcomes and systems of social relations seems to be the ultimate object of being a custodian of international human rights law generally and CERD in particular.

Race, gender and power

Human rights laws and conventions, including ICERD and CEDAW, can undoubtedly serve to legitimise the claims that victims of discrimination make against perpetrators. They also remain important symbols of democracy and freedom and offer victims some protection from powerful State and social institutions. Courts and judicial systems in the States that are bound by ICERD offer recourse, albeit to varying degrees, to complaints from individuals and groups that are victims of racial discrimination and marginalisation. However, such laws and conventions do not always change racial or gender power relations that are systemic and fuelled by ideologies of racial and gender superiority and inferiority. Legal individual rights do not by themselves solve fundamental social and political inequalities and injustices that are structural in essence and require more fundamental transformative changes in the status quo.

The CERD and CEDAW Committees can and have effectively used their influence to strengthen national legislation that prohibit certain policies, practices and behaviours that discriminate against the rights of people that these conventions are meant to protect. However, they cannot address racism and sexism effectively without making any reference to power relations and the political and structural aspects of race and gender discrimination. Patriarchy, for example, continues in most countries to contribute to the sexism that women of all colours, nationalities, ethnicities and social classes experience. According to the UN Secretary General, 'violence against women and girls persists at alarmingly high levels in many forms, in public and private spaces'. His report notes the limited presence of women in decision-making and the setbacks caused by their under-representation at the highest levels of political leadership.[31] This is an indication of who has power in society and the workplace, how such power is exercised and how it is shared. Many who benefit or not from the status quo are typically active in maintaining it.

31 UN Secretary General, 'Review and appraisal of the implementation of the Beijing Declaration and Platform for Action and the outcomes of the 23rd special session of the General Assembly', p. 6.

Though the Committees have effected important changes in States parties that have acceded to the provisions of the Conventions, understating the systemic practice of racial and gender discrimination in some of their deliberations has compromised their influence and effectiveness in recommending broader transformative goals to states. First, the work of having to assess the activities of sovereign states in a multilateral context such as the United Nations results in a degree of self-censorship. Second, the different backgrounds, expertise and ideological viewpoints of the Committee members are invaluable and complementary, but the need to compromise and achieve consensus can sometimes be limiting. Thirdly, the UN has compartmentalised and fragmented specific categories of discrimination rather than adopt a more holistic approach. This fragmentation and separation of issues has been the cause of a degree of divisiveness and wasteful utilisation of resources by the many institutions of the UN system. 'Intersectionality' is not a central tenet of international human rights law and some of the language of the Conventions, such as the use of 'discrimination' has led to a watering down of complex concepts that hinder rather than help the analysis of society and its insidious social relations.

Lastly, the lack of available resources to oversee the implementation of the Conventions has also been an important constraint, especially in the current international economic climate. As long as member States are responsible for selecting members of the Committees, and the structure, resources and activities of the Committees remain subject to the rules of the General Assembly of the United Nations, including the practice of consensus politics and voluntary contributions, it is unlikely that the work of the Committees will be able to lead to fundamental changes in the underlying structures of those societies with legacies of racism, sexism and other forms of intolerance. The UN itself has struggled to attain the race and gender parity in its own institutions that its member States have advocated for.

Addressing racism and sexism: the South African experience

The removal of racism and sexism from the statute books of the South African legal system has had many positive effects. The 1996 Constitution of the Republic of South Africa is reputed to be one of the best and most comprehensive in the world and the institutions that monitor its implementation have been relatively successful given the deep-seated challenges of the legacies of the *apartheid* state. However, given the history of colonialism and apartheid, it is not surprising that many of the structural dimensions of racism and sexism in the society still remain and will likely take generations to eliminate.

In this regard, Susan Bazilli, in an edited publication entitled *Putting Women on the Agenda*, offers an interesting feminist analysis of the intersection of race and gender in the South African struggle for freedom and democracy and says the following:

> We have often used the term 'rights' and 'human rights' to characterize what we have been fighting for. From the 1948 Universal Declaration of Human Rights, the attainment of fundamental human rights has come to symbolize the essence of our struggle, most eloquently framed in the Freedom Charter.[32] But what do we mean by women's rights? When rights intersect with 'law' the real issue is 'power'. Who has the power to demand and who has the power to cede these rights? How do we attain our rights in the face of structural and systemic inequality? And in South Africa, the legacy of the legislated and instituted inequality of apartheid is legion. The history of 'rights' has developed from the liberal notion of equality under the law in an individual capacity, and not from the structural inequalities of race, class and gender. But the extension of 'rights' is associated with the foundations of democracy and freedom: the protection of the weak against the strong, the individual against the state. To couch a claim in terms of rights is a major step towards recognition of a social wrong. Such a right gives legitimacy to a claim. Where we must be vigilant is to recognize that if the gender power relations remain the same, legal individual rights do not solve problems but rather transpose the problem into one that is defined as having a legal solution.[33]

Murray and O'Reagan go further and argue that the claims in the Charter will not end the subordination of women, and to think so would be to accept the 'myth of rights' that changing the laws does change society.[34] The contributions in Bazilli's book were presented at a conference organised by the South African Lawyers for Human Rights in Johannesburg in November 1990, a few months after the release of Nelson Mandela from his twenty-seven years of incarceration. This was at a time when many anti-apartheid activists were grappling with the challenges of breaching the deep divisions between black and white people in South Africa, as well as divisions that were entrenched within the country's robust patriarchal structure.

The argument she presents effectively highlights the difference between individual rights under the law and structural inequalities sustained by unequal power relations underpinned by notions of race,

---

32 The Freedom Charter was adopted in 1955 by the African National Congress and its partners in the South African Congress Alliance, as the blueprint for equality in a future free and democratic South Africa.

33 Susan Bazilli, 'Introduction', in Susan Bazili (ed.), *Putting Women on the Agenda* (Johannesburg: Ravan Press, 1992), pp. 1–26, at p. 13.

34 Christine Murray and Catherine O'Regan, 'Putting women into the Constitution', in Bazilli, *Putting Women on the Agenda*, pp. 33–55, at p. 45.

class, gender and other social, biological and cultural differences. Many South African women of all races understood very clearly the dynamics of double discrimination and the intersection between race, gender, ethnicity and class; and that, while black and white women were in the same boat steered by the apartheid patriarchal state, they were sitting on separate decks and were experiencing the ride very differently.

Many conversations and debates that had in fact begun in the 1950s had intensified in the late 1980s and early 1990s on the eve of the first free and fair elections in South Africa. Gender activists had experienced and witnessed the institutionalised oppression of black people and black women. They had witnessed and experienced how the apartheid regime, through its racist and sexist ideologies and State apparatus, including its unjust laws and courts, had violated the human rights of its majority black population and women in ways that led to the structural inequalities and poverty that remain the legacies of apartheid.

As the anti-apartheid movement in South Africa and the world increased its call for an end to legalised racism, women's voices were prominent in the robust discussions that took place in shaping the agenda for a future based on non-racialism and a shared universal sisterhood in the new South Africa.[35] Discussions on the 'intersectionality' of race, gender and class not only tested the notions of double and triple oppression, but also interrogated the assumption that black, coloured[36] and Indian women experienced sexism in the same way as white women. Black women made strong assertions that being a woman is not distinct from being either black or working class or heterosexual. The 'difference' debate, as it was called then, had a distinctly 'disruptive' effect.[37] Women made it very clear that a hierarchical approach that prioritised racism over sexism would not be entertained. Neither would the two forms of oppression and discrimination be treated in parallel and mutually exclusive ways. On the contrary, the apartheid State had used 'intersectionality' and interconnectedness with such skill and efficiency that it achieved one of most severe forms of racial and gender oppression in the world. Injustice and human rights violations affected the weakest and most vulnerable black South African children, women and men, including documented and undocumented

---

35 In 1992, for example, the Women's National Coalition was formed to take such issues and debates forward. This represented a broad front of seventy political and civil society organisations linking women across racial and ideological positions.

36 The expression 'coloured' was and still is used in South Africa to refer to people of 'mixed' descent.

37 Cheryl De la Rey, 'South African feminism, race, and racism', *Agenda*, 32 (1997), 6–10.

migrants and workers from neighbouring states, in ways that will take generations to turn around.

As the new Constitution was being shaped, the message that women had to be central to the process gained significant momentum, particularly in the crafting of the Constitution's Bill of Rights for the achievement of a non-racist and non-sexist society. In the period since 1994 this has been reflected in the increasing representation of black people and women at senior levels in government, and to a noticeable but more limited extent in the private sector. Currently women comprise 41 per cent of both the Cabinet and the National Assembly, which compares very favourably to many other countries in the world. Black Africans also now occupy over 70 per cent of the senior management positions in the public sector. Such advances have been promoted by a range of legislative interventions, including affirmative action, designed to reverse the legacy of discrimination and inequality, including the Employment Equity Act, the Labour Relations Act, the Promotion of Equality and the Prevention of Unfair Discrimination Act, and the Broad Based Black Economic Empowerment Act.

A strong human rights framework has also been put in place, through the Constitution, an independent judiciary, vibrant civil society organisations and the operation of constitutionally mandated bodies such as the Human Rights Commission, the Gender Commission and the Public Protector. At the same time, however, the persistence of depressingly high rates of unemployment, poverty and inequality, almost exclusively amongst the black population, and the very high levels of violence and abuse against women and girls, highlights the fact that progress in terms of legally entrenched rights has not as yet translated into more fundamental forms of socio-economic equality and race and gender justice.

Conclusion

As a long-serving member of CERD there is little doubt that personal experiences and perspectives[38] have significantly informed my approach to the examination and analysis of State party reports. It was difficult to take a purely legal approach to human rights for the achievement of a greater purpose – that of transforming power relations in diverse societies in order to achieve the UN principles of equality, justice, non-discrimination, peace and security and the rule of law.

38 As a race and gender trainer and anti-apartheid activist in exile in the United Kingdom during the 1980s and early 1990s, as a human rights advocate and practitioner in South Africa in the period since 1993, and as the Chief of Staff for UNWomen in New York during 2014–15.

There is much evidence that the law sometimes does not extend agency to those responsible for racial and gender disadvantage, deprivation and poverty. There are visible limits to what regulation can reach because impunity and lack of accountability by the very custodians of the law is rampant. The least that can be expected are clear policies and their focused implementation. Justice Albie Sachs, an anti-apartheid activist and a member of the Constitutional Court in the post-apartheid dispensation, highlighted quite profoundly that 'no one gives us rights. We win them in struggle. They exist in our hearts before they exist on paper. Our debates are about power rather than rights. We speak about human rights only in terms of how they are violated and not in terms of how they can affirm and legitimize a new society'.[39]

The UN system, without any doubt, served an important role in exposing, shaming and exercising rigid sanctions against the apartheid State. It used its convening powers very effectively to galvanise global resistance against the South African Government for violating the human rights of its black citizens, men and women, and for dehumanising its people. Although they received support from many other quarters, it was however South Africans themselves who struggled and died for racial and gender equality and justice, and are still, almost twenty-two years later, in the process of developing a 'new' society. That struggle goes on in a world where the gap between the rich and poor is increasing and fuelling racism and sexism in many countries. Many gains have been made by the United Nations and those in civil society who have made it a mission to resist these age old and resilient systems of oppression. It has been a privilege to have been a part of the South African struggle and to have made a modest contribution in the struggle for racial equality and gender justice at a local and global level.

39 Albie Sachs, *Protecting Human Rights in a New South Africa* (Cape Town: Oxford University Press, 1990), p. vii.

Part II

Groups and general recommendations

Chapter 4

CERD's contribution to the development of the rights of indigenous peoples under international law

*Jérémie Gilbert**

Introduction

The rights of indigenous peoples under international human rights law have greatly evolved in the last two decades, notably with the adoption of the United Nations Declaration on the Rights of Indigenous Peoples (UNDRIP) in 2007 which came to light after more than twenty years of negotiations.[1] In terms of international legal standards, there are two main approaches to the rights of indigenous peoples, one stemming from the specialised body of law dedicated to the rights of indigenous peoples, which includes the UNDRIP but also the ILO Convention no. 169, and the more general approach based on universal human rights standards applied to indigenous peoples.[2] While certainly the first specialised approach is important, and has been the centre of attention, the second – using the general standards of human rights to make them adequate to the specific needs of indigenous peoples – has been equally effective. An important aspect of this latter approach relates to the fundamental fact that across the globe most, if not all, indigenous peoples are facing serious historically embedded forms of

* The author would like to thank Fergus Mackay for comments on an earlier draft of this chapter.

1 See: Claire Charters (ed.), *Making the Declaration Work: The United Nations Declaration on the Rights of Indigenous Peoples* (Copenhagen: International Work Group for Indigenous Affairs (IWGIA), 2009); Stephen Allen and Alexandra Xanthaki (eds), *Reflections on the UN Declaration on the Rights of Indigenous Peoples* (Oxford: Hart Publishing, 2011); Jérémie Gilbert, 'Indigenous rights in the making: The United Nations Declaration on the Rights of Indigenous Peoples', *International Journal on Minority and Group Rights*, 14:2/3 (2007), 207–30.

2 See James Anaya, *Indigenous Peoples in International Law* (Oxford: Oxford University Press, 2004) and Patrick Thornberry, *Indigenous Peoples and Human Rights* (Manchester: Manchester University Press, 2002).

discrimination and racism.[3] This has been highlighted by the consistent work of the Committee on the Elimination of Racial Discrimination (CERD/the Committee) which has systematically focused its attention on the rights of indigenous peoples, making it clear that discrimination against indigenous peoples is racial discrimination. Based on its mandate to eliminate racial discrimination, CERD has greatly contributed to the development of the specific body of indigenous peoples' human rights and to the interpretation of general human rights law to make it adequate and relevant to indigenous peoples.[4] CERD was notably the first human rights treaty monitoring body to adopt a general recommendation specifically on indigenous peoples, General Recommendation 23 on rights of indigenous peoples.[5] More widely, throughout its work CERD has been adopting detailed and responsive Concluding Observations and recommendations to States parties regarding the rights of indigenous peoples, including under its follow-up, and early warning and urgent action, procedures.

The present chapter examines CERD's contribution to the development of indigenous peoples' rights. It reviews and analyses the role of the Committee regarding the overall development of indigenous peoples' rights under international human rights law. In examining the role of the Committee, this chapter explores how it has given depth to the International Convention on the Elimination of all Forms of Racial Discrimination (ICERD/the Convention) to ensure it can cover several key issues faced by indigenous peoples, making it one of the most relevant human rights treaties for indigenous peoples globally. To undertake this review, the first section focuses on CERD's effort to invite States to adopt effective measures to combat structural forms of racial discrimination. The second section examines how CERD has developed a strong approach to protect indigenous peoples' rights to lands and territories. The third section explores how CERD has played an important role to ensure indigenous peoples' access to and control over their natural resources. Finally, the fourth section examines how CERD has been able to use the early warning and urgent action procedures to address some of the pressing issues faced by indigenous peoples.

---

3 See Suhas Chakma and Marianne Jensen (eds), *Racism against Indigenous Peoples* (Copenhagen: IWGIA No. 105, 2001).

4 For an in-depth analysis, see Fergus Mackay, 'Indigenous peoples' rights and the UN Committee on the Elimination of Racial Discrimination', in Solomon Dersso (ed.), *Perspectives on the Rights of Minorities and Indigenous Peoples in Africa* (Pretoria: Pretoria University Law Press, 2010), pp. 155–202.

5 CERD, 'General Recommendation 23 on Rights of indigenous peoples', UN Doc. A/52/18, Annex V at 122 (1997).

Fighting structural discrimination

ICERD does not mention 'indigeneity' or 'autochthony' as one of the grounds for discrimination. Nonetheless, very early on, CERD adopted a proactive approach to ensure that indigenous peoples are protected under the Convention. ICERD designates 'racial or ethnic groups or individuals requiring … protection' (Article 1(4)), and 'racial groups or individuals belonging to them' (Article 2(2)). In GR 23 on indigenous peoples, CERD highlighted that 'discrimination against indigenous peoples falls under the scope of ICERD and that all appropriate means must be taken to combat and eliminate such discrimination'.[6] The subsequent General Recommendation 24 (1999) on information on the demographic composition of the population affirmed that according to the definition in Article 1(1), ICERD 'relates to all persons who belong to different races, national or ethnic groups or to indigenous peoples'.[7] In terms of the development of international law, the specific inclusion of indigenous peoples within the racial or ethnic groups requiring protection under ICERD contributes to the development of international law in several important ways. It notably addresses the 'raging' debate relating to the definition of indigenous peoples in highlighting how indigenous peoples face extreme forms of discrimination due to the fact that they are indigenous.

Regarding the debate on definition, it is important to bear in mind that whenever indigenous peoples' rights are mentioned, the reaction of some governments is denial. Thus for many States, the first reaction to CERD raising issues of discrimination against indigenous peoples is denial that there are any indigenous peoples within their territories. This includes many States across Africa and Asia that have rejected the 'concept' of indigenous peoples as not being applicable outside the situation of white settler colonisation.[8] While this debate did not take place only within the remit of ICERD, CERD played an important role in addressing such claims in systematically inviting States to recognise indigenous peoples. Importantly, while the debate on the definition of indigenous peoples had been dominating international policies for decades, CERD very promptly highlighted

6 CERD, GR 23, para. 1

7 CERD, 'General Recommendation 24 on Information on the demographic composition of the population', UN Doc. A/54/18, Annex V at 103 (1999), para. 1.

8 See Report of the African Commission's Working Group of Experts on Indigenous Populations/Communities, submitted in accordance with 'Resolution on the Rights of Indigenous Populations/Communities in Africa', adopted by the African Commission on Human and Peoples' Rights at its twenty-eighth ordinary session, DOC/OS(XXXIV)/345 (2003); Benedict Kingsbury, 'Indigenous peoples in international law: A constructivist approach to the Asian controversy', *American Journal of International Law*, 92 (1998), 414–57.

the importance of self-identification.[9] Rejecting the adoption of any specific definition of indigenous peoples, CERD has systematically put the emphasis on the importance of self-identification for the peoples concerned. Several of its Concluding Observations have invited States to ensure that self-identification by indigenous peoples should be a central factor of their identification as indigenous peoples.[10] This has included situations where States are refusing to recognise indigenous peoples, for example, recent Concluding Observations regarding Japan's lack of recognition of the Ryukyu/Okinawa as indigenous peoples,[11] or the Democratic Republic of Congo's 'reluctance to acknowledge the existence of indigenous peoples in its territory'.[12] An important aspect of this focus on self-identification relates to the fact that, in the view of the Committee, it is essential that indigenous peoples themselves use a terminology that respects their cultural identity, as seen in CERD's Concluding Observations regarding the situation in Laos, noting the reluctance of the Government to recognise indigenous peoples:

> The Committee recommends to the State party that it recognize the rights of persons belonging to minorities and indigenous peoples as set out in international law, regardless of the name given to such groups in domestic law. It invites the State party to take into consideration the way in which the groups concerned perceive and define themselves. The Committee recalls that the principle of non-discrimination requires that the specific characteristics of ethnic, cultural and religious groups be taken into consideration.[13]

There has been a consistent approach by the Committee towards the issue of definition, putting forward the fact that self-identification is essential no matter what terminology is used at national level.[14]

The other extremely important factor regarding the inclusion of indigenous peoples as a 'category' of specific rights-holders under ICERD relates to the need to tackle the structural discrimination faced by indigenous peoples; as such, CERD has often referred to the

---

9 CERD, 'General Recommendation 8 on Membership of racial or ethnic groups based on self-identification', UN Doc. A/45/18 at 79 (1991).

10 For a review and analysis, see Mackay, 'Indigenous peoples' rights', pp. 155–202.

11 CERD, 'Concluding Observations: Japan', UN Doc. CERD/C/JPN/CO/7–9 (2014), para. 21.

12 CERD, 'Concluding Observations: Democratic Republic of Congo', UN Doc. CERD/C/COD/CO/15 (2007), para. 14.

13 CERD, 'Concluding Observations: Lao Peoples' Democratic Republic', UN Doc. CERD/C/LAO/CO/15 (2005), para. 17.

14 See also prolonged debates between the Committee and the government of India on the use of the term 'Scheduled Tribes' – CERD, 'Concluding Observations: India', UN Doc. CERD/C/IND/CO/19 (2007), para. 10.

systemic discrimination faced by indigenous peoples.[15] Most, if not all, of CERD's Concluding Observations call on States to fight structural discrimination faced by indigenous peoples, highlighting the fact that in most societies indigenous peoples are facing embedded forms of discrimination. All the Concluding Observations adopted by CERD concerning countries where indigenous peoples live invite States to specifically address the discrimination faced by indigenous peoples. This underlines how, in most societies, indigenous peoples are facing systematic and often historically embedded forms of discrimination. It is worth noting that CERD's approach towards the structural discrimination faced by indigenous peoples is innovative under international law insofar as it interprets and extends non-discrimination norms from an almost exclusively individual context to encompass collective rights and non-discrimination against collectives, rather than just their members. This is an important element, as indigenous peoples have consistently been pushing the human rights legal framework to embrace a more collective approach to their rights. While ICERD does make mention of groups, its intent and focus was initially on protection of individuals on account of the membership of the specified groups rather than the groups themselves.[16] CERD's more recent approach has firmly carved out non-discrimination norms as applying to the group, especially indigenous peoples, rather than only the individual members of the group.

CERD has consistently invited States to put in place special measures to fight such structural discrimination faced by indigenous peoples as a group. In many of its Concluding Observations, CERD has underlined the need for States to put in place serious and efficient measures to combat structural forms of discrimination faced by indigenous peoples. As indicated by the Committee, there are two main obligations on States to address discrimination. The first is the general obligation to secure human rights on a non-discriminatory basis to persons and groups subject to their jurisdiction. The second relates to the need to adopt temporary special measures designed to secure to disadvantaged groups the full and equal enjoyment of human rights and fundamental freedoms. The two approaches are complementary but should not be confused. CERD has clarified that indigenous peoples' rights, which are permanent rights, should not be confused with

15 See CERD, 'Concluding Observations: Brazil', UN Doc. CERD/C/64/CO/2 (2005), para. 12; CERD, 'Concluding Observations: Colombia', UN Doc. CERD/C/304/Add.1 (1996), para. 10.

16 For example, CERD, GR 24, reads that: 'according to the definition given in article 1, paragraph 1, of the International Convention on the Elimination of All Forms of Racial Discrimination, the Convention relates to all *persons who belong to* different races, national or ethnic groups or to indigenous peoples' [emphasis added].

temporary 'special measures'. On this issue CERD has clearly indicated that 'special measures' are necessary to tackle embedded forms of discrimination faced by indigenous peoples, and that such special measures should not be treated as 'privileges'. Many governments, especially in Africa and Asia, often put forward the fact that integrating special rights for indigenous peoples within their internal legal framework would amount to constituting a 'privilege' for indigenous peoples. This 'privilege argument' is based on the notion that designing specific rights for indigenous peoples would create a category of rights-holders who would have privilege over other citizens of the State. As made clear by CERD, to treat in an equal manner persons or groups whose situations are objectively different will constitute discrimination in effect, just as much as will the unequal treatment of persons whose situations are objectively the same. As noted in its General Recommendation 14 on the definition of racial discrimination: 'differentiation of treatment will not constitute discrimination if the criteria for such differentiation, judged against the objectives and purposes of ICERD, are legitimate.'[17] The important aspect is not to confuse special measures with specific rights pertaining to indigenous peoples. As noted by CERD in General Recommendation 32 on special measures:

> States parties should carefully observe distinctions between special measures and permanent human rights in their law and practice. The distinction between special measures and permanent rights implies that those entitled to permanent rights may also enjoy the benefits of special measures.[18]

This clear statement from CERD undoubtedly helps address the so-called 'privilege' argument which is so often put forward by States to avoid ensuring proper legal protection for indigenous peoples under their national legislation.

Another important contribution regarding CERD's focus on the structural discrimination faced by indigenous peoples relates to discrimination faced by indigenous women. On many occasions, CERD has explicitly acknowledged the 'multiple forms' of discrimination that indigenous women face due to being indigenous and being women. For example, in a recent Concluding Observation regarding the situation in Paraguay, it stated: 'the situation of indigenous women is of particular concern to the Committee, as they are subject to multiple, intersectional forms of discrimination because of their ethnic origin,

17 CERD, 'General Recommendation 14 on Definition of racial discrimination', UN Doc. A/48/18 at 114 (1994), para. 2.

18 CERD, 'General Recommendation 32 on The meaning and scope of special measures in the ICERD', CERD/C/GC/32 (2009), para. 15.

gender, occupational status and poverty.'[19] Throughout its reporting mechanism, CERD has been systematically addressing the discrimination faced by indigenous women, in the process constructing one of the most effective platforms for addressing multiple forms of discrimination. In the words of MacKay:

> one could argue, for instance, that indigenous women may be better served bringing many of their complaints to the CERD Committee rather than to the Committee on the Elimination of Discrimination against Women. This is because ICERD offers the potential to address a wide range of concerns that are often raised by indigenous women, whereas the latter, although improving in recent years, remains reluctant to address questions of ethnicity and sometimes adopts recommendations that run counter to the stated wishes of indigenous women.[20]

Overall, the systematic focus on structural discrimination faced by indigenous peoples has supported the development of a strong human rights-based approach to fighting the embedded forms of discriminations faced by indigenous peoples across the globe. An important contribution of CERD has been to highlight that when it comes to fighting discrimination, indigenous peoples should be regarded as specifically vulnerable as in most societies they are still facing structural and historically embedded forms of discrimination. As such CERD has been consistently inviting States to develop special measures of protection, as well as effective guarantees for the permanent rights for indigenous peoples, to ensure the elimination of such discrimination.

Land rights as racial discrimination

Access, ownership and control over their lands and territories constitute an essential element for indigenous peoples who have made it clear that land rights are integral to their survival. Legally, land rights usually fall within the categories of land laws, land tenure agreements or planning regulations, but are rarely associated with human rights law. In terms of international human rights, apart from the specialised ILO Convention no. 169, no treaty or declaration refers specifically to a human right to land.[21] This lack of a proper legal framework relating to land rights for indigenous peoples has been addressed by CERD, which has developed a very strong jurisprudence regarding land rights.

19 CERD, 'Concluding Observations: Paraguay', UN Doc. CERD/C/PRY/CO/1–3 (2011).

20 Mackay, 'Indigenous peoples' rights', p. 202.

21 Jérémie Gilbert, 'Land rights as human rights: The case for a specific right to land', *SUR Journal on Human Rights*, 18 (2014), 114–35.

In its Article 5, ICERD expressly requires State parties to guarantee the right of everyone without distinction as to race, colour, or national or ethnic origin, the enjoyment of civil rights, including 'the right to own property alone as well as in association with others' and 'the right to inherit'. It is under this specific mention of property rights that CERD has developed a comprehensive approach to land rights for indigenous peoples. Based on Article 5, CERD has highlighted that States need to:

> recognise and protect the rights of indigenous peoples to own, develop, control and use their communal lands, territories and resources and where they have been deprived of their lands and territories traditionally owned or otherwise inhabited or used without their free and informed consent, to take steps to return these lands and territories.[22]

Based on this approach, CERD has developed a systematic jurisprudence inviting States to develop adequate protection for the rights of indigenous peoples to own, use and control their traditional lands, territories and resources. In the view of the Committee, the non-recognition of land rights for indigenous peoples constitutes in itself racial discrimination. Thus, by expressly requiring States parties to guarantee the right of everyone to own property without distinction as to race, colour, or national or ethnic origin, CERD significantly opens the door to indigenous peoples' collective approach to property in lands, something which was missing under international human rights with property rights seen more through the lens of individual title.[23]

Another important contribution by CERD regarding land rights relates to the obligation for States to recognise indigenous peoples' own land tenure systems. On many occasions, CERD has highlighted that indigenous peoples' land rights derive from their own customary laws and forms of land tenure, and that as such they exist as valid and enforceable rights notwithstanding the absence of formal recognition by the government. For example, in the case of Canada, CERD has expressed concerns about 'the difficulties which may be encountered by Aboriginal peoples before the courts in establishing Aboriginal title over land'. It recommended that Canada 'examine ways and means to facilitate the establishment of proof of Aboriginal title over land in procedures before the courts'.[24] The non-recognition of such systems of land tenure constitutes racial discrimination. Hence governments need to recognise customary land tenure systems as a source of

22 CERD, GR 23, para. 5.
23 See Jérémie Gilbert, *Indigenous Peoples' Land Rights under International Law: From Victims to Actors* (Leiden, Boston and Tokyo: Brill, 2nd edn, 2016).
24 CERD, 'Concluding Observations: Canada', UN Doc. A/57/18 (2002), para. 330.

rights, highlighting that those customary rights must also be effectively protected under the national legal system. The role and place of customary land tenure systems undoubtedly constitutes an important contribution of CERD, which has since then been extensively used as an important reference by the other human rights institutions, including in the jurisprudence of the Inter-American and African systems.[25]

Another important contribution of CERD regarding land rights relates to its approach to the right to remedies and restitution. Restitution and reparation for loss of lands and territories constitute a very complex and controversial issue.[26] In its GR 23, CERD addressed the issue:

> where they have been deprived of their lands and territories traditionally owned or otherwise inhabited or used without their free and informed consent, to take steps to return those lands and territories. Only when this is for factual reasons not possible, the right to restitution should be substituted by the right to just, fair, and prompt compensation.[27]

Hence, restitution of lands should be the main form of remedy and only when it is not factually possible would other forms of redress, such as compensation, apply. This approach is based on the fact that other forms of compensation, such as providing monetary compensation, would not acknowledge that land ownership is not merely a source of individual economic security but the core of indigenous cultures. It is worth noting that CERD's approach towards restitution follows the approach adopted in Article 28 of the UNDRIP, namely that restitution should be the main principle, and that 'lands, territories and resources equal in quality, size and legal status' should be the preferred form of compensation, with monetary compensation or 'other appropriate redress' being the less preferable mode of compensation.

Overall, it is certain that CERD has played an important role in highlighting how essential land rights are for indigenous peoples, and in emphasising the fact that the non-recognition of land rights derived from customary tenure and law does in itself constitute racial discrimination. Knowing that there is no main human rights treaty specifically including land rights, CERD's approach linking discrimination,

---

25 See Inter-American Court of Human Rights: *Sawhoyamaxa Indigenous Community* v. *Paraguay*, 29 March 2006, para. 248; the *Mayagna (Sumo) Awas Tingni Community* case, 31 August 2001, Series C No. 79, paras. 148–51; African Commission on Human and Peoples' Rights, *Centre for Minority Rights Development (Kenya) and Minority Rights Group International on behalf of Endorois Welfare Council* v. *Kenya*, Communication 276/2003 (2010).

26 See Federico Lenzerini (ed.), *Reparations for Indigenous Peoples: International and Comparative Perspectives* (Oxford: Oxford University Press, 2008).

27 CERD, GR 23, para. 5.

property rights and land rights has undoubtedly proven to be extremely important to make human rights law relevant to indigenous peoples.

Exploitation of natural resources and the private sector

Access and control of the natural resources that are within the territory of indigenous peoples is another essential element of indigenous peoples' rights. On that issue, CERD has contributed to the protection of such access to natural resources by notably focusing on the right to participate in decision-making relating to the use of the natural resources. In its GR 23, CERD has put the emphasis on the fact that 'no decisions directly relating to their rights and interests are taken without their informed consent'. In light of its GR 23, CERD urges States parties to establish practical mechanisms for implementing the right to consultation in a manner that respects the free, prior and informed consent of the affected peoples and communities and to ensure that consultations are carried out systematically and in good faith. CERD has frequently addressed the right of indigenous peoples to participate and consent to decisions concerning the exploitation of natural resources located in their territories, highlighting that the 'right to prior consultation and consent is frequently violated in conjunction with megaprojects relating to infrastructure and natural resource exploitation, such as mining, oil exploration or monoculture'.[28] For example, in its 2013 report on the situation in Belize, CERD called on the Government to 'stop granting leases and oil concessions without obtaining the prior, free and informed consent of Maya people'.[29] CERD has put a lot of emphasis on the need to obtain consent, and that mere consultations would not be enough. This focus by CERD, very early on – what would be phrased as the right to free, prior and informed consent (FPIC) within the UNDRIP – supported the development of the very important notion that indigenous peoples do have a right to consent to decisions affecting the use of their natural resources. The application of FPIC in the context of the exploitation of natural resources has been an important feature of CERD's approach to indigenous peoples' rights.

An important, and ground-breaking, aspect of this focus on FPIC relates to its application to the private sector, and notably multinational corporations involved in the exploitation of natural resources. Over the last few years, the agenda on business and human rights has gained

28 CERD, 'Concluding Observations: Colombia', UN Doc. CERD/C/COL/CO/14 (2009), para. 20.

29 CERD, 'Concluding Observations: Belize', UN Doc. CERD/C/BLZ/CO/1 (2012), para. 10

prominence, notably with the adoption of the UN Guiding Principles on Business and Human Rights in 2011.[30] However, well before the business and human rights agenda rose to prominence within UN circles, CERD had already engaged with the issue of corporations and their responsibilities under human rights law. On many occasions the Committee has highlighted that States have a strong obligation to ensure that corporations do not violate indigenous peoples' rights. For example, in its 2008 Concluding Observations regarding the situation in Russia, CERD stated that:

> The grant of licences to private companies for activities such as logging, extraction of subsoil resources and the construction of pipelines or hydroelectric dams leads to privatization and ecological depletion of territories traditionally inhabited by indigenous peoples.[31]

In itself, the focus on the need for States to control the way licences are granted to corporations is not ground-breaking, as it mainly highlights States' obligations to respect indigenous peoples' land rights and right to FPIC. However, the approach of CERD towards extraterritorial obligations of the governments towards multinational corporations is ground-breaking. In many situations, the corporations operating on indigenous lands are multinational corporations often based in rich countries. In these situations, CERD has highlighted that governments have an obligation to regulate the actions of private corporations, even when operating abroad, when these violate indigenous peoples' rights. For example, in its Concluding Observations on Canada in 2007, CERD noted 'reports of adverse effects of economic activities connected with the exploitation of natural resources in countries outside Canada by transnational corporations registered in Canada on the right to land, health, living environment and the way of life of indigenous peoples living in these regions (article 2(1)(d), article 4(a) and article 5(e)'.[32] On this issue CERD recommended that the Government should 'take appropriate legislative or administrative measures to prevent acts of trans-national corporations registered in Canada which negatively impact on the enjoyment of rights of indigenous peoples in territories outside Canada. In particular, CERD recommends to the state party that it explore ways to hold trans-national corporations registered in Canada accountable'.[33] CERD has made similar comments

30 Office of the High Commissioner for Human Rights, 'Guiding Principles on Business and Human Rights: Implementing the United Nations "Protect, Respect and Remedy" Framework' (New York and Geneva: United Nations, 2011).

31 CERD, 'Concluding Observations: Russian Federation', UN Doc. A/63/18 (2008), para. 374.

32 CERD, 'Concluding Observations: Canada', UN Doc. CERD/C/CAN/CO/18 (2007), para. 17.

33 *Ibid.*

in its Concluding Observations regarding Norway, the United States and the United Kingdom.[34] CERD has also used its early warning and urgent action mechanism to raise the issue of uranium extraction by a registered French company operating in Niger, highlighting the obligation of the French Government to monitor the action of the company.[35] On the issue of extraterritoriality, it is worth noting that despite the fact that the UN Guiding Principles on Business and Human Rights seem to be quite precarious as regards the issue of extraterritoriality,[36] CERD has clearly indicated that it does apply when it comes to violations of indigenous peoples' rights over their natural resources.

Another relevant contribution of CERD when it comes to the exploitation of natural resources relates to the mention of a right of indigenous peoples to benefit from such exploitation. As noted by the Committee, as part of their right to own, develop, control and use their communal lands and resources, indigenous peoples have a 'right to exclusive benefit of renewable natural resources situated on their lands'.[37] For example, in the case of Ecuador it noted that 'the equitable sharing of benefits to be derived' from the exploitation of natural resources should be ensured.[38] CERD has recommended changes when a State does not provide for such equitable sharing of benefits for the exploitation of natural resources. It has recently welcomed the fact that Bolivia has established a process to ensure profit-sharing when natural resources are extracted from the territories of indigenous peoples.[39] Likewise, it has invited Peru to: 'guarantee that indigenous peoples affected by natural resource activities in their territories receive compensation for damage or loss suffered and participate in the benefits arising out of such activities',[40] highlighting that benefit sharing should not be regarded as compensation, but as independent

34 CERD, 'Concluding Observations: Norway', UN Doc. A/66/18 (2012), para. 17; CERD, 'Concluding Observations: United Kingdom', UN Doc. A/66/18 (2012), para. 59 (29); CERD, 'Concluding Observations: United States', UN Doc. A/63/18 (2008), paras. 500–1.

35 CERD, 'Letter to the French Government', 28 September 2009.

36 The Guidelines note: 'At present States are not generally required under international human rights law to regulate the extraterritorial activities of businesses domiciled in their territory and/or jurisdiction. Nor are they generally prohibited from doing so, provided there is a recognized jurisdictional basis.' OHCHR, 'Guiding Principles on Business and Human Rights', p. 3.

37 CERD, 'Concluding Observations: Bolivia', UN Doc. CERD/C/63/CO/2 (2003), para. 9

38 CERD, 'Concluding Observations: Ecuador', UN Doc. CERD/C/62/CO/2 (2003), para. 16.

39 CERD, 'Concluding Observations: Bolivia', UN Doc. CERD/C/BOL/CO/17–20 (2011), para. 7.

40 CERD, 'Concluding Observations: Peru', UN Doc. CERD/C/PER/CO/18–21 (2014), para. 15.

entitlement for indigenous peoples whenever natural resources found on their lands and territories are exploited.

Overall, CERD has played an important role in highlighting that indigenous peoples have a right to control the exploitation of the natural resources that are found on their territories. This is an important contribution of CERD knowing that international norms regarding the control of natural resources are highly complex and contested under international law.[41] As such CERD has highlighted that under human rights law, this includes a right for indigenous peoples to consent to, but also to benefit from, the exploitation of these resources.

Early warning and urgent action

Human rights treaty monitoring bodies are known for their lack of 'teeth' to enforce their decisions and recommendations.[42] CERD has been working hard to ensure that its observations and decisions have an impact and are followed by States. It has for example established a 'follow-up' procedure and a 'follow-up coordinator'. But probably one of the most relevant procedural developments for indigenous peoples came with the establishment of an Early Warning and Urgent Action (EW/UA) procedure in 1993. Early warnings are preventive measures aiming at preventing existing situations escalating into conflicts, whereas urgent action procedures are aimed at responding to problems requiring immediate attention. These mechanisms have been extremely useful for indigenous peoples. Based on such mechanisms, CERD has adopted several decisions directly concerning the rights of indigenous peoples.[43] One of the indicators for early warning procedures relates to '[e]ncroachment on the traditional lands of indigenous peoples or forced removal of these peoples from their lands, in particular for the purpose of exploitation of natural resources'.[44]

This mechanism has proven particularly efficient in addressing situations where draft legislation negatively affecting indigenous peoples' rights was to be adopted. This was the case regarding the adoption of an amendment to the legislation governing aboriginal land

41 See Jérémie Gilbert, 'The right to freely dispose of natural resources: Utopia or forgotten right?', *Netherlands Quarterly of Human Rights*, 31:2 (2013), 314–41.

42 For a very interesting article tackling this issue, see Pammela Saunders, 'The integrated enforcement of human rights', *New York University Journal of International Law and Politics*, 45 (2012), 97.

43 This notably includes the Philippines, Suriname, New Zealand, Australia, Mexico, Papua New Guinea and the United States. For a review of these situations see Mackay, 'Indigenous peoples' rights'.

44 CERD, 'Guidelines for the use of the early warning and urgent action procedure', advanced unedited version [copy available with author], August 2007.

rights in Australia,[45] the proposal to adopt a revised Mining Act in Suriname,[46] and the adoption of the Foreshore and Seabed Act 2004 in New Zealand.[47] In all these situations, this procedure has allowed CERD to quickly intervene to highlight how these new proposed legislations might negatively impact the right of indigenous peoples.[48] Likewise, this EW/UA mechanism has allowed CERD to intervene urgently when specific governmental measures were going to affect indigenous peoples. This has included Australia's decision in relation to the Northern Territory Emergency Response, or regarding the cutting of legal aid, the United States' decision to build a wall on its border with Mexico, or a ski resort on indigenous territories. This mechanism was also extremely useful when in 2013 the Government of Cameroon started the process of drafting a new forest law and concerns were raised regarding the lack of integration and consultation of indigenous communities in this process. Overall, the EW/UA mechanism has allowed indigenous peoples to quickly raise issues with CERD, and in turn this has allowed CERD to quickly react to actions that might threaten indigenous peoples' rights, becoming a very efficient and rapid way to address human rights violations outside the rigid time period fixed by the reporting mechanism.

Conclusion

Undeniably, CERD has played a prominent role in the development of indigenous peoples' rights under human rights law. While the rights of indigenous peoples are now well established and have received considerable attention from other human rights bodies, CERD was a pioneer in adopting a specific general recommendation on the rights of indigenous peoples, and by systematically focusing its attention on the rights of indigenous peoples. The significance of CERD's contribution is not only about having been at the forefront of this movement, but also relates to the content of its approach.

45 CERD, 'Decision 1(54): Australia', UN Doc. A/53/18 (1998), and CERD, 'Decision 2(54): Australia', UN Doc. A/54/18 (1999). See further Sarah Pritchard, 'Stirrings: Early warning/urgent action decision concerning Australia from the UN Committee on the Elimination of Racial Discrimination', *Indigenous Law Bulletin*, 4:15 (1999), 17.

46 CERD, 'Decision 1(67): Suriname', CERD/C/DEC/SUR/2 (2005); and CERD, 'Decision 1(69): Suriname', CERD/C/DEC/SUR/3 (2006).

47 CERD, 'Decision 1(66): New Zealand', CERD/C/DEC/NZL/1 (2005).

48 See the letter for urgent action sent to the Government of Papua New Guinea in 2011, which directly resulted in the withdrawal of amendments to the Environmental Protection Act that would have limited indigenous peoples' access to judicial remedies.

CERD has very early on established important principles regarding indigenous peoples' rights under human rights law, such as their fundamental rights to land and resources and their right to consent to any decisions affecting them. As highlighted earlier, its approach to the obligations of States to ensure that private actors, including corporations, do not violate indigenous peoples' rights is also an important contribution. As concluded by Mackay: 'CERD now routinely addresses indigenous peoples' rights and does so with a degree of detail that far surpasses the other UN treaty bodies responsible for monitoring the implementation of human rights instruments.'[49]

The list of contributions that CERD has made to the development of indigenous peoples' rights would probably be too long to list here, but it is worth highlighting that such contributions have been generated by CERD's extremely proactive and open approach to the direct participation of indigenous peoples themselves. When it comes to human rights law, and more specifically UN-led human rights mechanisms, indigenous peoples have often found a wall in front of them. For not being State actors, for being marginalised in their own country, and for not being able to have direct access to international institutions, indigenous peoples have often been left out in the cold, not having access to law making and monitoring processes. While the situation has recently been addressed notably with the establishment of the UN Permanent Forum on Indigenous Issues, giving indigenous peoples direct access to UN circles, it is important to recognise that very early on CERD has been much more willing to receive information directly from indigenous peoples themselves, opening the doors of what is otherwise generally a very closed diplomatic circle. One of the strengths of CERD has been its willingness to engage with civil society actors, and notably with indigenous peoples' organisations. CERD has been effective at gathering additional information from indigenous peoples and their representative organisations. It is also worth noting that in 2014 CERD nominated an indigenous person as its president. Francisco Cali Tzay is the first indigenous expert to hold such a position in the UN system. Hence, overall, there is no doubt that CERD has played a very important role in ensuring the protection of indigenous peoples under human rights law. Apart from the ILO Convention 169, there is no universal binding international human rights specialised treaty regarding indigenous peoples' rights. However it could be argue that de facto, ICERD has played such a role, notably thanks to CERD's effort to systematically focus its attention on the plight of indigenous peoples across the globe.

49 Mackay, 'Indigenous peoples' rights', p. 202.

Chapter 5

CERD and discrimination against Roma

*Claude Cahn**

Introduction

Recently while browsing at a used book store, I came upon a 1982 volume called *Extraordinary Groups: The Sociology of Unconventional Life-Styles*, by a certain William M. Kephart of the University of Pennsylvania. This included chapters on the 'Old Order Amish', the Oneida Community, the Father Divine Movement, the 'Shakers', the Mormons and the Hutterites.

The book, however, opens with a chapter called 'The Gypsies'. This began as follows: 'The Gypsies are an incredible people; in fact, the more one studies them, the more incredible they become!'[1] Kephart then proceeds to summarise key features of conservative Romani culture, interspersed with comments such as 'Gypsies have made a remarkable adaptation to their environment'; 'Through it all, the Gypsies have survived. Gypsies always survive'; 'Like so many aspects of Gypsy life, their origins are draped in mystery'.[2] Under the heading 'Adaptability: The Gypsy Trademark', Kephart asserts: 'It is doubtful whether the Roma spend much time thinking about the causes of discrimination. Being realists, they expect it. And being Gypsies, they learn to live with it.'[3] It is a worthy thought experiment to substitute the word 'Gypsies' with 'Jews' or 'African Americans' in these passages. It is more-or-less unimaginable that such superficial generalisations would be acceptable in mainstream discourse.

Why does the current chapter begin with passages from a marginal pop/academic publication from 1982? To make the following

* The views in this article are those of the author and do not necessarily reflect the views of the United Nations.

1 William M. Kephart, *Extraordinary Groups: The Sociology of Unconventional Life-Styles* (New York: St. Martin's Press, 1982, 2nd edn), p. 5.

2 *Ibid.*, pp. 5–7.

3 *Ibid.*, pp. 43–4.

observation: first of all, today, it is probably no longer conceivable that Roma or 'Gypsies' would make an appearance in a serious publication otherwise devoted to religious communities, as if the two might be elided under the general grouping of 'unconventional lifestyles'. Second, and crucially, the general confusion surrounding Roma – lifestyle choice? 'Unconventional group'? Collectivity of deviant behaviour? – has steadily given way to an understanding that the heterodox set of groups broadly identifying as Romani or Gypsy or Traveller are in fact to be understood as ethnic groups, one with a history of persecution and powerful contemporary discrimination, particularly, although not only, in Europe. The Committee on the Elimination of Racial Discrimination (CERD/the Committee) has played a central role in the developments which have brought about this fundamentally changed understanding. Unfortunately, these changes have been driven due to CERD's growing awareness of and concern with the very palpable wave of anti-Romani sentiment and action in Europe following the major political changes with the collapse of Communism in 1989. Equally unfortunately, despite CERD's best efforts, a fundamental change in the human rights situation of Roma, particularly in Europe, remains elusive.

Roma in Europe and around the globe

The Romani and related ethnic groups are a diverse set of peoples and communities living in Europe, the Americas and parts of Africa, related to similar groups in the Middle East and Central Asia, called 'Lom' and 'Dom'. Roma are believed to be descended from groups of people who left India approximately 1,000 years ago and arrived in Europe in successive waves beginning in or around the fourteenth century. A lack of written community records makes Romani history an extremely difficult field, intensely reliant among other things on sources such as the historical imprint left on the various Romani dialects.[4] The history of Roma in Europe is not a happy one. Soon after their arrival in Europe Roma were excluded in Western Europe, and periodically subjected to raw persecution.[5] In the Ottoman Empire, Roma occupied a low status, even when members of the privileged Muslim community.[6] Roma were enslaved in the Romanian

4 See especially Yaron Matras, *Romani: A Linguistic Introduction* (Cambridge: Cambridge University Press, 2002).

5 See Sir Angus Fraser, *The Gypsies* (Oxford: Blackwell, 1992).

6 See Elena Marushiakova and Vesselin Popov, *The Gypsies in the Ottoman Empire* (Hatfield: University of Hertfordshire Press, 2001). Roma in Europe tend to be Christian or Muslim, although in some cases religious practice involves particular

principalities.[7] From the beginning of the modern State, significant efforts were periodically undertaken – with mixed success – to assimilate Roma forcibly.[8] Roma were targeted for genocide during the Second World War.[9] The period since 1989 has seen a renewal of active anti-Romani antipathy throughout the European continent. Tens of thousands of Roma were ethnically cleansed from Kosovo in the period 1999–present.[10] Outbreaks of anti-Romani racism have plagued every European society without exception.

CERD's engagement with discrimination against Roma

Before 1992

Rooker divides examination of CERD's engagement with Roma into the period before 1992 and the period after it, noting a shift in the internal modus operandi of CERD around 1992.[11] She writes that, as a rule, Communist States denied that racial discrimination existed under Communism, but observes that a different reality at times emerged from reporting by States: 'one member of CERD agreed with the Czechoslovak statement that "the problem is to solve the contradiction between the historical backwardness of Gipsies on the one hand, and the level achieved by the rest of society and the need of its social development on the other hand"'.[12] Some States – notably Bulgaria – told CERD in the 1980s that there was no Romani community in the country.[13]

With direct reference to Bulgaria's contentions before CERD – and in particular in light of systematic campaigns in Bulgaria during the 1970s and 1980s against Muslims (including Roma), Turks and

---

Romani forms. There are major Romani evangelical movements, one a centre of Romani empowerment movements, as well as a major source of written Romani.

7 See Achim Viorel, *The Roma in Romanian History* (Budapest: Central European University Press, 2004), pp. 27–132.

8 See David Crowe and John Kolsti (eds), *The Gypsies of Eastern Europe* (Armonk: M. E. Sharp Inc., 1991).

9 See, *inter alia*, Michael Zimmermann, *Verfolgt, Vertrieben, Vernichtet: Die Nationalsozialistiche Vernichtungspolitik gegen Sinti und Roma* (Essen: Klartext, 1989); Donald Kenrick and Grattan Puxon, *Gypsies under the Swastika* (Hertfordshire: University of Hertfordshire Press, 1995).

10 See Claude Cahn, 'Birth of a nation: Kosovo and the persecution of pariah minorities', *German Law Journal*, 8:1 (2007), 81–94.

11 Marcia Rooker, *The International Supervision of the Protection of Romany People in Europe* (Nijmegen: Nijmegen University Press, 2002), p. 104.

12 *Ibid.*, p. 105.

13 *Ibid.*, p. 109.

Pomaks – Rooker quotes Banton, then a member of CERD, to the effect that 'up until 1988, CERD was in no position to act against any but a pariah state'.[14] Rooker concludes:

> [U]ntil the end of the Cold War, members of CERD asked few critical questions and hardly reacted to discriminatory statements [by members of government delegations] with respect to Romany people. Some states submitted information on remedies for racial discrimination against Romany people, but it was totally up to States whether they chose to submit such information. ... The quality of the reports and of the dialogues with state representatives definitely changed in the 1990s.[15]

The 1990s

The extent to which racism returned as a dynamic force to the European continent was among factors which propelled CERD to much more engaged action than previously. Generally, the civil wars of the former Yugoslavia, the steady advance of the Front National in France, as well as the inclusion in the Austrian Government in 1999 of the Freedom Party of Austria (FPO), an openly racist party, heightened the view that ethnic hatred was among – if not at the heart of – core human rights issues in Europe after the collapse of Communism. More specifically as concerns Roma, the Eastern European post-Communist transition featured violent pogroms in Romania, Bulgaria and other States; neo-Nazi skinhead movements targeted Roma for attack in the Czech Republic, Slovakia, Hungary, Serbia, Croatia, Poland, Russia and Bulgaria; and near-constant reports of abuse by police officers in all of the countries of the region. In Western Europe, the early 1990s featured mobilised efforts by States such as Belgium, Italy, Austria and Germany to expel Eastern European Roma. Following the withdrawal of Serbian forces from Kosovo in June 1999, Roma and the related groups Ashkalis and Egyptians were ethnically cleansed from the province.

By the second half of the decade, CERD began serious engagement with States on issues related to discrimination against Roma. This was particularly the case with countries where CERD received credible information from civil society as to violations of the International Convention on the Elimination of all Forms of Racial Discrimination (ICERD/the Convention) – the treaty monitored by CERD. Insofar as information coming to the attention of the Committee drew heavily, during this period, from the European Roma Rights Centre (ERRC),

14 *Ibid.*

15 *Ibid.*, pp. 109–10.

CERD's efforts were very engaged with respect to countries with a strong ERRC research presence, such as the Czech Republic, Greece, Hungary, Slovakia, Romania, Bulgaria and Italy, as well as with countries where Roma were already at the centre of concerns relating to racial discrimination, such as Spain. In this period, CERD focused heavily on several key thematic areas – matters such as racially motivated violence by racist skinheads or police, and the failure of the justice system to rectify these harms, as well as racial segregation in schooling and housing. CERD also expressed concern at particular issues in given country contexts, such as the impact of the 1993 Czech citizenship law in rendering thousands of Roma de facto stateless. This focus was strongly a result of the kind of information brought to the attention of CERD during this period.

Thus, for example, in its March 1998 review of the Czech Republic, CERD expressed:

> concern ... at the persistence of racial hatred and acts of violence, particularly by skinheads and others, towards persons belonging to minority groups, especially Roma and people of African or Asian origin ... Concern is expressed at information indicating that the number of charges and convictions, including those of skinheads, is low relative to the number of abuses reported. It is also noted with concern that perpetrators of racial crime are often lightly punished and that, in a number of cases, prosecutors have been reluctant to identify a racial motive. Moreover, in the light of evidence of unnecessarily long proceedings and slow investigations of acts of racial crime, concern is raised about judicial effectiveness in this respect.[16]

Additionally:

> In light of reports indicating discrimination against Roma in areas such as housing, transport and employment, it is noted with concern that the State party does not have civil or administrative law provisions expressly outlawing discrimination in employment, education, housing and health care and that there exists no administrative regulation explicitly prohibiting racial discrimination by public institutions and agencies. The denial of access to public places such as restaurants, pubs, discotheques and similar establishments by persons belonging to some ethnic minorities, especially Roma, is also noted with concern.[17]

However, CERD during this period appears keen to agree with the Czech Government that it has no express policy of discriminating against Roma. CERD during this period begins a preoccupation

16 CERD, 'Concluding Observations: Czech Republic', UN Doc. CERD/C/304/Add.47 (1998), paras. 8–9.

17 *Ibid.*, para. 12.

with the segregation of Roma in education which continues to the present day:

> The marginalization of the Roma community in the field of education is noted with concern. Evidence that a disproportionately large number of Roma children are placed in special schools, leading to de facto racial segregation, and that they also have a considerably lower level of participation in secondary and higher education, raises doubts about whether article 5 of the Convention is being fully implemented.[18]

Also, as noted above, CERD raised concerns with respect to the 1993 Czech citizenship law, adopted in the context of the break-up of Czechoslovakia:

> It is noted that the 1993 law on the acquisition of Czech citizenship (Law No. 40/1990) has resulted in widespread criticism from a number of international institutions and non-governmental organizations for its discriminatory effects, especially vis-à-vis Roma. While it is noted that the State party has taken steps to mitigate the negative consequences of the law, it is stressed that the act of rendering people stateless entails the deprivation of fundamental rights linked to citizenship, as well as exposing them to the risk of expulsion. Concern is expressed that there remain groups of the population for whom the question of citizenship has not yet been addressed in a satisfactory manner ... many of whom are of Roma origin.[19]

General Recommendation 27 on Discrimination against Roma

On 16 August 2000, drawing together CERD's work in this area up to that point, as well as recognising the commonalities of issues faced by Roma in many countries – and in particular throughout the European continent – CERD issued General Recommendation (GR) 27 on Discrimination against Roma.[20] GR 27 provides a comprehensive overview of CERD's approaches to Roma up to that time, and in many ways, they have not changed drastically since. It is organised into six sub-sections, reflecting CERD's thematic preoccupations at end of the 1990s: (1) Measures of a General Nature; (2) Measures for Protections Against Racial Violence; (3) Measures in the Field of Education; (4) Measures to Improve Living Conditions; (5) Measures in the Field of the Media; and (6) Measures Concerning Participation in Public Life.

---

18 *Ibid.*, para. 13.
19 *Ibid.*, para. 14.
20 CERD, 'General Recommendation 27 on Discrimination against Roma', UN Doc. A/55/18, Annex V at 154 (2000).

As concerns measures of a general nature, GR 27 starts by extending basic provisions of ICERD to explicitly cover the situation of Roma. Thus, paragraph 1 calls on States parties: 'To review and enact or amend legislation, as appropriate, in order to eliminate all forms of racial discrimination against Roma as against other persons or groups, in accordance with the Convention.'[21] Particular issues soon emerge however; GR 27 importantly recognises the 'deportation and extermination' harms suffered by Roma during the Second World War,[22] although as a result of internal community disputes over the name(s) of these events, it avoids using terms such as 'Holocaust'. Similarly, reflecting growing concerns within the diverse Romani and related communities, CERD urges respect for 'the wishes of Roma as to the designation they want to be given and the group to which they want to belong'.[23]

Some issues, however, remain muted. Thus, although GR 27 recognises that Romani women 'are often victims of double discrimination'[24] and urges States parties to take into account Romani women when planning policies and programmes, GR 27 makes no mention of coercive sterilisation, a matter with which CERD was to become preoccupied during the 2000s, particularly in relation to the Czech Republic, Slovakia and Hungary. GR 27 is similarly muted as to concerns around the expulsion of Roma from Western Europe, preferring the abstract formulation that States should 'take all necessary measures in order to avoid any form of discrimination against immigrants or asylum-seekers of Roma origin'.[25]

The section of GR 27 on protection against 'racial violence' covers important ground by highlighting the need for protection against both acts by racist vigilantes such as skinheads, as well as against such acts by police. CERD in this sense was ahead of the European Court of Human Rights, which first found any State in violation of the European Convention's discrimination provisions in a case concerning Roma only in 2004.[26] GR 27 further calls on States 'to encourage

21 *Ibid.*, para. 1.
22 *Ibid.*, para. 10.
23 *Ibid.*, para. 3.
24 *Ibid.*, para. 6.
25 *Ibid.*, para. 5.
26 *Nachova and Others* v. *Bulgaria* (Application nos. 43577/98 and 43579/98), Judgment (Grand Chamber) of 6 July 2005. On the development of the jurisprudence of the European Court of Human Rights in cases concerning Roma, as well as on the very troubled nature of the Court's work on racial discrimination until the mid-2000s, see Claude Cahn, 'Roma and racial discrimination: The jurisprudence of the European Court of Human Rights', in Didier Bigo, Sergio Carrera and Elspeth Guild (eds), *Foreigners, Refugees and Minorities? Rethinking People in the Context of Border Controls and Visas* (Farnham: Ashgate, 2013), pp. 55–73.

appropriate arrangements for communication and dialogue between the police and Roma communities and associations, with a view to preventing conflicts based on racial prejudice and combating acts of racially motivated violence against members of these communities',[27] as well as 'to encourage recruitment of members of Roma communities into the police and other law enforcement agencies'.[28] GR 27 further urges 'action in post-conflict areas … to prevent violence against and forced displacement of members of the Roma communities'.[29]

As concerns education, GR 27 includes some interesting moments, worthy of comment. In the first place, its stops short of condemning segregation in education absolutely, calling on States only 'to prevent and avoid *as much as possible* the segregation of Roma students'[30] [emphasis added]. It is unclear what motivated this approach, which is both at odds with Article 3 of ICERD, as well as with later approaches by CERD itself. The rest of the same paragraph of GR 27 urges 'keeping open the possibility for bilingual or mother tongue tuition'.[31] At this juncture, CERD appeared unclear as to whether it might possibly favour education for Roma in Romani, potentially even in separate environments. This issue became more settled during the 2000s, with a number of key rulings by the European Court of Human Rights in education cases – including the rejection by the Court's Grand Chamber of separation justified by language tuition[32] – as well as the increasingly clear calls coming from within the Roma movement on ending segregation in education.

Also evident in the education section of GR 27 is the increasing need to manage tensions between issues relating to Roma on the one hand, and matters related to Travellers on the other.[33] Thus GR 27

27 CERD, GR 27, para. 14.
28 *Ibid.*, para. 15.
29 *Ibid.*, para. 16.
30 *Ibid.*, para. 18.
31 *Ibid.*
32 *Oršuš and Others* v. *Croatia* (Application no. 15766/03), Judgment (Grand Chamber) of 16 March 2010.
33 The Council of Europe, Europe's premier human rights institution, treats Roma and Travellers within one policy cluster. The lead document of its human rights approach in this area is the 2011 report of the Council of Europe Human Rights Commissioner on the 'Human Rights of Roma and Travellers in Europe'. This provides, *inter alia*: 'The various Traveller minorities of Europe are primarily distinguished by their travelling lifestyle, although many members of this minority are nowadays semi-sedentary or completely sedentary … It is not always clear who should be included and who should be excluded from these categories. The minorities labelled "Roma", "Gypsies" and "Travellers" in fact comprise a multitude of ethnicities and distinct linguistic communities, heterogeneous groups that are viewed as a unit primarily by outsiders. This report uses the term "Roma and Travellers". This umbrella grouping is not intended to deny the self-identification of any person or group and is used solely for the purposes of not

includes a recommendation, based in particular on the experience of States parties with developed Traveller outreach policies such as the United Kingdom, '[T]o take the necessary measures to ensure a process of basic education for Roma children of travelling communities, including by admitting them temporarily to local schools, by temporary classes in their places of encampment, or by using new technologies for distance education'.[34]

GR 27 similarly nods to Traveller issues when it urges States parties 'to take the necessary measures, as appropriate, for offering Roma nomadic groups or Travellers camping places for their caravans, with all necessary facilities'.[35] This recommendation is something of a digression from the rest of section 4 on improving living conditions, the rest of which is focussed predominantly if not exclusively on measures to bring Roma into situations equivalent to majority communities. GR 27 momentarily departs to some extent from ICERD when it treats the motivation for efforts to improve Roma access to health care as grounded not in the need to combat discrimination, but rather in 'their disadvantaged situation due to extreme poverty and low level of education, as well as to cultural differences'.[36]

The fact that GR 27 focuses on media in section 5, while only arriving at representation of Roma in public life in section 6, is itself noteworthy. The media section, in addition to provisions closely harmonised with ICERD on eliminating ideas of racial or ethnic superiority,[37] wanders far into territory in (at least implicit) tension with the Article 19 right to freedom of expression of the International Covenant on Civil and Political Rights (ICCPR) when it encourages 'methods of self-monitoring by the media, through a code of conduct for media organizations, in order to avoid racial, discriminatory or biased language'.[38]

The focus on improving the representation of Roma in public life was to grow stronger during the 2000s. It included efforts such as the now-failed (or at least much-diminished) Council of Europe endeavour, the European Roma and Travellers Forum.[39] GR 27 was adopted at a time when there was some attention to the possibility of Roma parties as a mode for securing Roma inclusion, and this is visible in

---

repeatedly using long chains of group and subgroup names.' Council of Europe Human Rights Commissioner, 'Human Rights of Roma and Travellers in Europe' (Strasbourg: Council of Europe, 2011), pp. 31–2.

34 CERD, GR 27, para. 21.
35 *Ibid.*, para. 32.
36 *Ibid.*, para. 34.
37 *Ibid.*, para. 36.
38 *Ibid.*, para. 40.
39 European Roma and Travellers Forum, www.ertf.org.

the text.[40] Nevertheless, GR 27 covers broadly the need to strengthen Roma representation and inclusion, noting the extreme paucity of involvement of Roma in public life throughout Europe; at the time of the adoption of GR 27, the number of Roma in elected positions anywhere in Europe was in the tens, with literally only two or three Roma in elected positions anywhere in Western Europe including a councillor in the Vienna local government, as well as – sporadically – Roma MEPs from Spain.

Finally, GR 27 concludes with a recommendation that the World Conference against Racism, Racial Discrimination, Xenophobia and Related Intolerance (WCAR), held in Durban in September 2001, 'give due consideration to the above recommendations, taking into account the place of the Roma communities among those most disadvantaged and most subject to discrimination in the contemporary world'.[41]

2000s and beyond

In the fifteen years since the adoption of GR 27, CERD has not fundamentally changed any of the basic aspects of its approach towards Roma. There is little question, however, that CERD's work has been enriched both by its own deepening expertise in the factual matters of Roma exclusion in various particular countries, as well as by the broadening range of civil society actors intervening, as well as by the growth of State policies and expertise in this area. Thus, Concluding Observations vis-à-vis States have become more detailed and concrete, as well as in some cases more bold in the expression of discontent with States' actions. Furthermore, new issues have emerged in the review of States. In addition, the Committee has found States in violation of ICERD within the complaints procedure set out under Article 14. Finally, CERD has expanded the geographic range of its concerns beyond Europe.

In thematic terms, the 2000s brought issues to CERD that it had not previously examined. Major new areas included the coercive sterilisation of Romani women – a matter of increasing urgency throughout the 2000s in relation to the Czech Republic, Hungary and Slovakia. Thus, for example, in its 2013 Concluding Observations following review of Slovakia, CERD stated:

---

40 CERD, GR 27, para. 42. It reads: 'To develop modalities and structures of consultation with Roma political parties, associations and representatives, both at central and local levels, when considering issues and adopting decisions on matters of concern to Roma communities.'

41 *Ibid.*, para. 49.

> While noting three judgments of the European Court of Human Rights against Slovakia on forced sterilization of Roma women, the Committee draws the attention to the lack of effective investigation by the State party regarding this practice throughout the country and the lack of compensation to the victims (arts. 2, 5 and 6). The Committee recommends that the State party implement fully recent decisions of the European Court of Human Rights and ensure full reparation and compensation for all victims of these practices. The Committee urges the State party to thoroughly investigate all incidents of forced sterilization of Roma women and prosecute those responsible. Bearing in mind its general recommendation No. 25 (2000) on gender-related dimensions of racial discrimination, the Committee encourages the State party to adopt appropriate measures, including the implementation of the 2012 Decree related to the cases of illegal sterilization of women and the organization of special training for all medical staff on how to obtain informed consent before carrying out sterilization, on sensitization of medical staff on respecting diversity of members of the Roma community.[42]

Another area raised for the first time during the 2000s was the right to vote for thousands of Travellers in France, a matter to which CERD returned repeatedly throughout the decade. Thus, for example, during regular review of France's compliance with ICERD in 2010, CERD stated that it 'remains very concerned at the difficulties faced by travellers, particularly regarding their freedom of movement, exercise of the right to vote and access to education and decent housing. In this respect, the Committee notes with concern that, despite the recommendations formulated in its previous Concluding Observations, the State party has still not provided travellers with the necessary number of encampment areas'.[43]

Slovakia is a particularly extreme case, and it is worth examining CERD's 2013 Concluding Observations on Slovakia to see how far it has come in terms of the depth, breadth and detail of concerns and recommendations raised. The section on 'Stigmatization of and discrimination against minorities, in particular Roma' runs to multiple pages, not including the section on coercive sterilisation noted above. These address, among other things, 'the continued stigmatization of, and discrimination against Roma and their ongoing precarious socio-economic situation', including their absence from police and local government; the 'continued de facto segregation in the education system'; 'Limited measures have been undertaken towards promoting Roma's right to adequate housing and ending spatial segregation';

42 CERD, 'Concluding Observations: Slovakia', UN Doc. CERD/C/ SVK/CO/9–10 (2013), para. 13.

43 CERD, 'Concluding Observations: France', UN Doc. CERD/C/FRA/CO/17–19 (2010), para. 16.

'lack of basic facilities such as sanitation, electricity, drinking water, sewage system and waste disposal'; 'Walls and barriers ... in some areas including Prešov, Michalovce, Partizánske or Trebišov, to segregate Roma from the rest of the population'; 'forced evictions and demolitions of Roma settlements are taking place without alternatives for Roma'; 'persistent negative perception of the majority population towards the minorities, particularly Roma'; as well as 'limited effectiveness of the State party's reaction to some of the decisions of local bodies in denying Roma access to housing and in other cases financing the construction of walls to separate Roma settlements from the rest of the population'.[44] CERD does not hesitate to go into the details of issues in particular localities, requesting that the Government 'include in its next periodic report any measures taken to address the situation of Roma in Plavecky Stvrtok', having been alerted to forced eviction issues in that community.[45]

During the 2000s, CERD also for the first time raised concerns about the treatment of Roma outside Europe. Thus, for example, in its 2004 review of Brazil, the Committee expressed 'allegations concerning discrimination faced by Gypsies with regard to birth registration and access to schools for their children'.[46]

A significant development in the 2000s is the adjudication by CERD of cases brought by Roma under the ICERD Article 14 individual complaints procedure. Although a number of cases were submitted in the 1990s, CERD only began examining these cases from the year 2000. CERD's first finding of a violation came on 8 August 2000, in the case of *Anna Koptova* v. *Slovakia*.[47] Ms Koptova alleged that the adoption of a ban on the entry of Roma into two towns in eastern Slovakia violated her rights under ICERD. CERD agreed, finding a violation of Article 5(d)(i) of ICERD.[48] CERD again found Slovakia in violation of ICERD provisions in March 2005, in the case of *L.R. et al.* v. *Slovakia*.[49] The case concerned the actions of the municipality of Dobsina, which agreed to cancel a social housing project that would have benefited Roma in the town. The cancellation followed a petition campaign against Roma receiving such housing,

---

44 CERD, 'Concluding Observations: Slovakia' (2013), paras. 10–12, 14 and 16.
45 *Ibid.*, para. 12.
46 CERD, 'Concluding Observations: Brazil', UN Doc. CERD/C/64/CO/2 (2004), para. 17.
47 *Anna Koptova* v. *Slovakia* (2000), CERD Communication No. 13/1998, UN Doc. CERD/C/57/D/13/1998.
48 *Ibid.*, para. 10.1.
49 *L.R. et al. v. Slovakia* (2005), CERD Communication No. 31/2003, UN Doc. CERD/C/66/D/31/2003.

mounted by local non-Roma, and ultimately garnering some 2,700 signatures locally.

CERD did not find Slovakia in violation of ICERD in August 2001 in the case of *Miroslav Lacko*, in which the Committee held that Slovakia's failure at that time to provide a remedy to a Romani man refused service in a restaurant did not violate the treaty. CERD considered in the case that the fact that the perpetrator had been sentenced to pay a fine of 5,000 Slovak Crowns for the crime of incitement to ethnic hatred was sufficient to avoid a violation of ICERD.[50] CERD did however find Serbia and Montenegro in violation of the Convention in 2006, in a similar case concerning a ban on access to public services, *inter alia* as a result of 'the State party's failure to investigate and adjudicate the case effectively'.[51]

CERD did not find Germany in violation of the Convention in a 2008 case concerning a publication by a police union, involving derogatory and demeaning statements against Roma. CERD grounded its decision *inter alia* in its view that the publication at issue was not a State organ, as well as the fact that the publication 'has carried consequences for its author, as disciplinary measures were taken against him'.[52] In 2011, CERD deemed inadmissible a complaint against the Russian Federation concerning leaflets appealing to expel Roma from the town of Pskov, on grounds that the petitioners lacked standing to file the complaint.[53]

Finally, Roma and Traveller matters now feature regularly as requests for information from CERD within one year of review, in accordance with Article 9, paragraph 1, of the Convention and rule 65 of its amended rules of procedure.[54] Discrimination against Roma also features to a certain extent among issues raised under the early warning and urgent action procedures. Although CERD's website indicates that it has not to date taken any decisions under the early warning and urgent action procedure in this regard, it has sent letters to the governments of the Czech Republic, Italy, Slovakia and the United Kingdom in cases concerning Roma.[55]

---

50 *Miroslav Lacko* v. *Slovakia* (2001), CERD Communication No. 11/1998, UN Doc. CERD/C/59/D /11/1998.

51 *Dragan Durmic* v. *Serbia and Montenegro* (2006), CERD Communication No. 29/ 2003, UN Doc. CERD/C/68/D/29/2003.

52 *Zentralrat Deutscher Sinti und Roma et al.* v. *Germany* (2008), CERD Communication No. 38/2006, UN Doc. CERD/C/72/D/38/2006.

53 *A.S.* v. *Russian Federation* (2011), CERD Communication No. 45/2009, UN Doc. CERD/C/79/D/45/2009.

54 See for example CERD, 'Concluding Observations: Slovakia' (2009) and CERD, 'Concluding Observations: France' (2013).

55 See further CERD, 'Early-Warning Measures and Urgent Procedures', available at: www.ohchr.org/EN/HRBodies/CERD/Pages/EarlyWarningProcedure.aspx.

Conclusion

The work of CERD has been very important in moving forward the understanding that anti-Romani sentiment is racism and anti-Romani action is racial discrimination in the sense of ICERD. It has also been instrumental in moving forward – in concert with other international actors such as the Council of Europe, the European Union, and the Organisation for Security and Cooperation in Europe (OSCE) – policy and action by governments and States to strengthen Roma inclusion. In the two-and-a-half decades since the fall of the Berlin Wall, CERD can be proud of its record in supporting broadly civic movements aiming to end Romani racism and finally to tackle the severe forms of exclusion resulting from anti-Gyspyism.

There are good examples of States acting on CERD's recommendations. A recent review of Moldova's implementation of the 2011 CERD Concluding Observations[56] indicated relatively strong compliance, including on the Roma recommendations, which were by far the most far-reaching within the given review. That said, there are still many examples of governments ignoring CERD's recommendations concerning Roma. One particularly glaring recent example has been the French Government's flouting of CERD's recommendations concerning stopping the forced eviction of Roma. CERD has repeatedly engaged in this area, most recently in its June 2015 Concluding Observations concerning France, in which it expressed concern at 'repeated breaches' of the right of Roma to housing, 'many of which take the form of forced evacuations of Roma from their camps without, in many cases, any alternative type of lodging being offered'.[57] Utterly disregarding this recommendation, as well as the efforts of a range of French civic organisations and the French Ombudsperson Jacques Toubon as well as international organisations, French authorities in late August 2015 dismantled the shantytown known as 'Samaritain' in the town of La Courneuve – a municipality in Ile-de-France (greater Paris) – and forcibly evicted the circa 150–300 Roma living there, primarily persons from Romania. The settlement was reportedly the oldest existing Roma migrant slum in France, having been in place since 2008. There are plenty of other examples of States parties disregarding CERD's recommendations in relation to the Roma.

It will thus take further work by many actors to render CERD's work on the human rights of Roma effective. This can only be done by

56 CERD, 'Concluding Observations: Moldova', UN Doc. CERD/C/MDA/CO/8–9 (2011).

57 CERD, 'Concluding Observations: France', UN Doc. CERD/C/FRA/CO/20–21 (2015), para. 9.

concerted efforts by States, civil society actors and others to strengthen attention to and action on the concerns raised by authoritative human rights bodies, CERD among them. It will also require serious attention to the continuing role played by anti-Romani sentiment – anti-Gypsyism – in shaping the societies in which we live.

Chapter 6

CERD and caste-based discrimination

Annapurna Waughray and David Keane

Introduction

On 19 January 2016, BBC News ran a story from India with the headline 'Rohith Vemula: The student who died for Dalit rights'.[1] The story concerned a twenty-six-year-old PhD student who killed himself inside the campus of Hyderabad Central University. It explained that Mr Vemula 'was a member of the Ambedkar Students' Association, which fights for the rights of Dalit (formerly known as untouchable) students on the campus' and that '[t]hough he did not blame anyone for his death, the contents of the [suicide] letter show that he was upset over the discrimination shown to Dalits like him'.[2]

Four months previously, on 22 September 2015, BBC News had reported a UK story headlined 'Woman awarded £184k in "first caste discrimination" case', concerning an Indian woman recruited from India to be a domestic servant for a family in the UK: 'Permila Tirkey, 39, was discriminated against because of her "low caste", her lawyers said, describing it as the first successful case of its kind.'[3]

---

1 Dalit is a political term of self-identification meaning 'crushed' or 'broken'. Since the 1970s it has been used in India and internationally by many those at the bottom of the caste hierarchy, formerly known as 'untouchables'. The Indian constitutional, legal and administrative term for Dalits is 'Scheduled Castes'. In this chapter, the term Scheduled Caste is used in these contexts. Otherwise, the term Dalit is used, albeit that it is not adopted by all people of so-called untouchable origin.

2 Omer Farooq, 'Rohith Vemula: The student who died for Dalit rights', *BBC News*, 19 January 2016, available at: www.bbc.co.uk/news/world-asia-india-35349790

3 'Woman awarded £184k in "first caste discrimination" case', *BBC News*, 22 September 2015, available at: www.bbc.co.uk/news/uk-34330986. A further £83,700 was awarded in damages for indirect religious discrimination and unlawful harassment on the ground of race, specifically ethnic origins which in this case was deemed capable of capturing caste; see Tamar Burton, 'Remedy in Tirkey v Chandhok', *Cloisters – Discrimination and Equality*, 10 December 2015, available at: www.cloisters.com/latest/remedy-in-tirkey-v-chandhok. The claimant in

These news stories, one from India and one from the UK, provide a snapshot of manifestations of caste-based discrimination as a contemporary, global phenomenon. In both cases the ground of discrimination referred to was *caste*, a form of social organisation based on inherited status, traditionally associated with South Asia. This chapter explains and assesses the role of the Committee on the Elimination of Racial Discrimination (CERD/the Committee) in the conceptualisation of discrimination on grounds of caste as a form of descent-based racial discrimination under the International Convention on the Elimination of All Forms of Racial Discrimination (ICERD/the Convention) and hence a violation of international human rights treaty law.

For over 2,000 years, oppression and discrimination based on caste has affected many millions of people in South Asia, and latterly the diaspora,[4] yet the term caste is not present in any international human rights instrument, and there is no specialised international instrument prohibiting caste-based discrimination. Historically and today, the primary victims of caste discrimination in the Indian sub-continent are the Dalits, formerly known as 'untouchables', officially referred to as Scheduled Castes in Indian constitutional, administrative and legal terminology.[5] Caste discrimination is estimated to affect some 260 million people worldwide, the majority in South Asia. India's Dalits number around 167 million people, many of whom are subject to extreme socio-economic deprivation and exclusion and violations of their civil, political, economic and social rights as well as systemic caste-based violence.[6] The Constitution of

---

this case was an Adivasi, a term which refers to members of India's indigenous tribes, known as Scheduled Tribes in Indian constitutional, legal and administrative terminology. In sociological terms the distinction between castes and tribes 'is to some extent arbitrary and reified by law'; tribal groups 'have a different history of non-integration, but also suffer inequality, marginalisation, and social separation'; Meena Dhanda, Annapurna Waughray, David Keane and David Mosse, 'Caste in Britain: Socio-legal Review'; Equality and Human Rights Commission (EHRC) Research Report 91 (Manchester: EHRC, 2014). The EHRC 'Caste in Britain' research team included the present authors.

4 Susan Bayly, *Caste, Society and Politics in Modern India from the Eighteenth Century to the Modern Age* (Cambridge: Cambridge University Press, 1998), pp. 13, 28; Oliver Mendelsohn and Marika Vicziany, *The Untouchables: Subordination, Poverty and the State in Modern India* (Cambridge: Cambridge University Press, 1998), pp. 25–6.

5 The term Scheduled Castes refers to those formerly 'untouchable' castes listed in a Schedule to the Indian Constitution. The Schedule lists those castes entitled to the benefit of affirmative action policies and the protection of criminal legislation outlawing caste discrimination and caste hate crimes; see Annapurna Waughray, 'India and the paradox of caste discrimination', *European Yearbook of Minority Issues*, 8 (2010), 413–52.

6 International Dalit Solidarity Network (IDSN), 'Caste Discrimination', available at: http://idsn.org/caste-discrimination/ See also Waughray, 'India', 416–17.

India 1950, drafted following India's independence from the British in 1947, prohibits discrimination on grounds of caste and abolishes and criminalises its most egregious manifestation, the practice of 'untouchability'.[7] Subsequently, criminal legislation outlawing caste discrimination and caste hate crimes ('atrocities') was enacted, and constitution-based affirmative action policies ('reservations') were introduced; yet, in the post-independence period, widespread discrimination based on caste persisted, alongside an increase in anti-Dalit violence. Dalit non-governmental organisations (NGOs) in India adopted a variety of strategies to publicise and challenge caste-based discrimination and violence, but the response of successive Indian governments was to downplay the severity of the problem while insisting that India had sufficient domestic measures in place to tackle it, albeit that this would take time.[8]

Outside India, caste was an unfamiliar and largely unrecognised ground of discrimination. From the early 1980s, frustration with the slow pace of change led Dalit activists in India and the diaspora to turn to international NGOs as well as the UN human rights treaty bodies and charter mechanisms in the search of an international response to their grievances.[9] The challenge faced by Dalit activists was the apparent lack of an international frame or category within which to locate caste. Of the UN bodies and mechanisms with which Dalit activists sought to engage, the most important have been the UN Sub-Commission for the Promotion and Protection of Human Rights, and CERD. Of these, CERD has played a crucial role in the international recognition of caste discrimination as a human rights issue and as an international human rights treaty violation.

The legal source of CERD's engagement with caste is the category of descent in Article 1 of the Convention. In 1996, in its Concluding Observations on India's 9th–14th State report, CERD stated that the term descent in Article 1 did not solely refer to race, and affirmed for

---

7 Constitution of India 1950, Articles 15 and 17. Untouchability is not defined in the Indian Constitution. On the practice of untouchability see Navsarjan Trust and Robert F. Kennedy Center for Justice & Human Rights, 'Understanding Untouchability: A Comprehensive Study of Practices and Conditions in 1589 Villages' (2010), pp. 3–4.

8 Mendelsohn and Vizciany, *The Untouchables*, pp. 118–28, at pp. 147–8; Hugo Gorringe, 'Dalit politics: Untouchability, identity and assertion', in Atul Kohli and Prerna Singh (eds), *Routledge Handbook of Indian Politics* (Routledge: London, 2012), pp. 119–28; India: tenth to fourteenth reports to CERD; UN Doc. CERD/C/299/Add.3, 29 April 1996.

9 Clifford Bob, '"Dalit Rights are Human Rights": Caste discrimination, international activism and the construction of a new human rights issue', *Human Rights Quarterly*, 29:1 (2007), 167–93.

the first time that the situation of the Scheduled Castes in India fell within the scope of the Convention, under the rubric of descent.[10] In 2001, Dalit activists failed to secure the inclusion of caste as a form of racial discrimination in the outcome document of the UN World Conference Against Racism, Racial Discrimination, Xenophobia and other Related Forms of Intolerance (WCAR), but their presence at the WCAR served to raise international awareness of caste discrimination. In 2002, CERD issued General Recommendation 29 on Article 1(1) of the Convention (Descent) (GR 29) which confirms that the term descent in Article 1 does not solely refer to race but has a meaning and application which complement the other prohibited grounds of discrimination in Article 1; reaffirms that discrimination based on descent includes discrimination against members of communities based on forms of social stratification such as caste and analogous systems of inherited status which nullify or impair their equal enjoyment of human rights; and condemns descent-based discrimination, such as discrimination on the basis of caste and analogous systems of inherited status, as a violation of the Convention.[11]

The inclusion of caste in 'descent' is rejected by India which does not accept that discrimination against the Scheduled Castes falls within the scope of ICERD. However, other states questioned by CERD on the existence of caste discrimination in their territories (for example Nepal, Pakistan, Bangladesh, the UK) have accepted or at least not challenged CERD's use of descent to cover caste.

ICERD is a Convention of a general nature in that, aside from the case of apartheid, it makes no reference to specific forms of racial discrimination, nor does it identify specific groups as victims of racial discrimination. Interpretation of ICERD follows the 'living instrument' approach which facilitates the application of the Convention to new and emerging forms and understandings of racial discrimination. The living instrument principle applies to the Convention's structures and processes as well as its substantive content, resulting in innovative developments in procedure, for example the introduction of thematic debates on proposed general recommendations.[12]

Since the early 2000s there have been calls from some Dalit activists and human rights actors for a caste-specific treaty.[13] This seems less

---

10 UN Doc. A/51/18 (1996), para. 352.

11 CERD, 'General Recommendation 29 (2002) on Discrimination based on descent', UN Doc. A/57/18 at 11.

12 Patrick Thornberry, 'Confronting racial discrimination: A CERD perspective', *Human Rights Law Review*, 5:2 (2005), 266.

13 See for example Barbara Crosette, 'Putting Caste on Notice', *The Nation*, 9 November 2009 in which the former UN High Commissioner for Human Rights, Navi Pillay, suggests that a caste specific treaty may be required.

likely to emerge than a treaty on descent-based discrimination: India is unlikely to support a caste-specific instrument which it might construe as targeting India alone, while descent is a wider legal category than caste, with a wider geographical and social reach. It is possible that a recent UN OHCHR study on work and descent-based discrimination may lead to a Declaration on this issue, which in turn may lead to a treaty; however, neither the Indigenous Peoples' Declaration nor the Minorities Declaration have yet been converted into legally binding treaties. In the absence of a caste or descent-specific treaty, ICERD remains the pre-eminent human rights treaty for addressing caste discrimination.

GR 29 affirms that caste is a facet of descent. It was preceded by a thematic discussion on descent-based discrimination within CERD, in the course of which CERD member Pillai suggested that unless the Committee could find some common denominator identifying all discriminatory social practices as caste discrimination, it should employ the term 'caste' only with reference to countries where, in their own terms, castes existed.[14] This would confine the use of the term caste to its paradigmatic meaning, namely the form of social organisation associated with South Asia and its diaspora. The remit of this chapter being caste-based discrimination rather than its parent category, descent-based discrimination, the term caste is used here in its paradigmatic sense, as a specific form of descent-based discrimination primarily associated with South Asia and its diaspora.

The focus of ICERD is racial discrimination. During CERD's thematic discussion of descent-based discrimination, the issue of 'cultural intrusion' was raised. Former CERD member Thornberry explains that the thrust of GR 29 'is not against the caste or any other cultural system as such' but against discrimination on the basis of descent; nevertheless 'the Recommendation goes some way in the direction of a severe critique of that particular form of social and religious organisation'.[15] NGOs and civil society organisations have played a key role in CERD's engagement with caste discrimination, as non-State sources of information about a form of discrimination falling within the purview of the Convention. CERD, writes Thornberry, could not ignore the experience of Dalits and other victims of caste discrimination, notwithstanding the value CERD places on cultural diversity:

---

14 CERD/C/SR.1531, 16 August 2002, para. 8.

15 Patrick Thornberry, 'The Convention on the Elimination of Racial Discrimination, indigenous peoples, and caste/descent-based discrimination', in Joshua Castellino and Niamh Walsh (eds), *International Law and Indigenous Peoples* (Leiden: Martinus Nijhoff, 2005), p. 42.

> The massive contestation of caste systems by Dalits and others and the overwhelming evidence of oppression suffered by those made subject to it could hardly escape the attention of CERD in the light of its duty to be faithful to the norms of the convention. While the Committee demonstrates a high level of respect for cultures, there are always limits, there are always practices which are open to a human rights critique, even if the human rights brought to bear on the practice may themselves possess a degree of openness to cultural context.[16]

This chapter examines the emergence of the issue of caste-based discrimination as a violation of ICERD, beginning in the 1990s with the application of 'descent' in Article 1(1) to caste groups in the context of India's 1996 State report, and the development of the issue from there. It charts the evolution and adoption of General Recommendation 29 on Article 1(1) (Descent), in which the scope and meaning of descent is elaborated in detail, with a definition of descent-based discrimination as including caste and analogous systems of inherited status. In addition to examining the meaning of caste and the nature of rights violations that occur, the chapter engages with State opposition to CERD's interpretation, in particular from India, which rejects the categorisation of caste as a form of descent-based discrimination and therefore a form of racial discrimination. While CERD considers the treaty to be a living instrument, and interprets it so as to bring newly recognised marginalised groups under its protection, States parties may not accept these interpretations, leading to disagreement and even conflict with the Committee and beyond. The issue of caste challenges the interpretive approach to the treaty which CERD has adopted from the outset.

Understanding caste

According to the *International Encyclopedia of the Social Sciences*,

> [t]he term caste refers, paradigmatically, to a social institution in India and elsewhere in South Asia in which endogamous descent groups, known as castes or subcastes, are hierarchically ranked. It has also been used to describe hereditary forms of social stratification in non–South Asian contexts, such as Japan, the American South, and elsewhere. The validity of usage outside of South Asian contexts, however, ultimately turns on how we are to understand the paradigmatic Indian case – a matter of considerable and ongoing debate.[17]

---

16 *Ibid.*, p. 43.

17 Nate Roberts, 'Caste, anthropology of', in W. Darity (ed.), *International Encyclopedia of the Social Sciences*, 2nd edn (Detroit: Macmillan, 2007), pp. 461–63. See also Dhanda *et al.*, 'Caste in Britain', pp. 3–6.

Sociologically, caste may typically be summed up as

> a 'closed system' of stratification where social groups, often divided on the basis of their occupation, strictly follow the code of behaviour prescribed by tradition regarding marriage and kinship alliance. Caste groups are unequal, ranked on a scale of hierarchy based on their ritual status, from pure to impure. Their 'status' or position in the system determines with whom they can interact and with whom they cannot. The idea and practice of untouchability is an integral part of the caste system.[18]

Anthropologist Gerald Berreman explained caste as being, in empirical terms, about fundamental social, economic and political inequalities, stating that it entails

> [i]nstitutionalised inequality; guaranteed differential access to the valued things in life ... [t]he human meaning of caste for those who live it is power and vulnerability, privilege and oppression, honor and denigration, plenty and want, reward and deprivation, security and anxiety.[19]

These written definitions cannot easily convey the reality of caste oppression. Numerous studies exist by national and international organisations, activists, practitioners and scholars, as well as official datasets on caste hate crimes, personal testimonies, literature and poetry, which attest to the social, economic and psychological effects of caste discrimination on those at the bottom of the social hierarchy, and of the inequality and denial of rights and dignity which the reality of caste entails.

As is well-known, the term caste comes from the Portuguese *casta* meaning race or breed. In South Asia and its diaspora the term is used for two concepts, *varna* and *jati*. *Varna*, a concept in ancient Sanskrit religious texts, refers to the textual division of Hindu society into four hierarchical and mutually exclusive categories or *varnas* related to occupation or social function and involving the notion of 'innate characteristics':[20] Brahmins (priests), Kshatriyas (warriors and rulers), Vaisyas (traders and artisans) and Shudras (labourers and servants). Outside the *varna* framework is a fifth category – the Dalits, formerly known as 'Untouchables'. Caste is also used to refer to *jati*. *Jatis* are the thousands of local or regional endogamous birth groups, linked to hereditary occupation and hierarchically ranked within a geographical locality. Unlike *varna*, the concept of *jati* is not exclusive to Hinduism

18 Surinder Jodhka, *Oxford India Short Introductions: Caste* (New Delhi: Oxford University Press India, 2012), pp. xi, 1.

19 Gerald Berreman, *Caste and other Inequities* (Meerut: Folklore Institute, 1979), p. 159.

20 Wendy Doniger, *The Hindus: An Alternative History* (Oxford: Oxford University Press, 2010), p. 211.

but is found across religious communities. While there are only four *varnas* the number of *jatis* has always varied as existing groups merge and new groups emerge.

Despite the textual link with the ancient Hindu *varna* classification system, caste is neither solely 'religious' nor is it religion-specific; the concept of caste and the existence of Dalit castes are found among adherents of Hinduism as well as Islam, Sikhism and Christianity notwithstanding the doctrinal absence or rejection of caste in these religions. Caste membership is hereditary, i.e. acquired by birth, involuntary and generally considered permanent.[21] It is generally accepted that caste as an institution is maintained and reproduced by endogamy (whereby marriage must be within the same caste).[22] The origins of caste are disputed but, notwithstanding the role of colonialism in the 'construction' of caste as a pan-Indian concept, academic consensus is that its roots in the Indian sub-continent long pre-date British rule, as the link suggested by recent scholarship between agrarian slavery and the emergence of untouchability and Dalit status illustrates.[23] In contrast to earlier scholarly representations of caste as a 'consensual, functional and harmonious system'[24] it is now widely acknowledged that throughout history both the concept of caste itself and the discrimination, exploitation and inequality it engenders have been challenged by those on the 'receiving end' of caste oppression.[25] In the twentieth century the preeminent campaigner for the eradication of caste was Dr B. R. Ambedkar (1891–1956), a Dalit and a British-educated lawyer, one of India's greatest political leaders and legal scholars, chair of the Drafting Committee of India's Constitution, and responsible for the inclusion in the Indian Constitution of provisions on rights and non-discrimination, and on social, economic and political equality for Dalits and non-Dalits alike.[26]

---

21 For exceptions to this rule see Annapurna Waughray, *Capturing Caste in Law: The Legal Regulation of Caste-based Discrimination* (Routledge, 2018, forthcoming), Ch. 1.

22 See Dhanda *et al.*, 'Caste in Britain', p. iii.

23 Mendelshohn and Vizciany, *The Untouchables*, pp. 17–18. See also Rupa Viswanath, *The Pariah Problem: Caste, Religion, and the Social in Modern India* (New York: Columbia University Press, 2014).

24 Gorringe, 'Dalit politics', pp. 119, 128, 120.

25 *Ibid.*; Mendelshohn and Vizciany, *The Untouchables*, pp. 21–5.

26 On Ambedkar see Christophe Jaffrelot, *Dr Ambedkar and Untouchability: Analysing and Fighting Caste* (New Delhi: Permanent Black, 2005); Eleanor Zelliot, 'The leadership of Babasaheb Ambedkar' and 'Gandhi and Ambedkar: A study in leadership', in *From Untouchable to Dalit: Essays on the Ambedkar Movement* (New Delhi: Manohar, 1998). See also Valerian Rodrigues (ed.), *The Essential Writings of B.R. Ambedkar* (New Delhi: Oxford University Press, 2002).

There is no definition of caste or untouchability in the Constitution of India or in Indian legislation. In 1993 in the leading case of *Indra Sawhney* v. *Union of India* the Indian Supreme Court defined caste as a socially homogenous class and also an occupational grouping, membership of which is involuntary and hereditary.[27] GR 29 does not contain a definition of descent, but lists some of the factors on the basis of which the existence of descent-based discrimination, including discrimination on the basis of caste and analogous systems of inherited status, may be recognised:

> [I]nability or restricted ability to alter inherited status; socially enforced restrictions on marriage outside the community; private and public segregation, including in housing and education, access to public spaces, places of worship and public sources of food and water; limitation of freedom to renounce inherited occupations or degrading or hazardous work; subjection to debt bondage; subjection to dehumanizing discourses referring to pollution or untouchability; and generalized lack of respect for their human dignity and equality.

Caste as a social institution has shown a remarkable capacity over the centuries to modify and adapt to changing economic, political and social contexts. In recent years it has been argued that India's transition to modern capitalism has hastened the decline of the 'caste system' as traditionally understood, leading some scholars and commentators to claim that caste is 'dead'; conversely, others argue that the traditional, hierarchical caste system has simply given way to a new form of caste as 'difference' rather than hierarchy.[28] In this understanding of caste, caste groups are seen as identity-based groups and caste as a form of cultural or 'community' identity to be celebrated with pride, rather than as an ascribed, inherited status involving privilege for some and inequality and discrimination for others. In the case of the Dalits this concept of caste as cultural identity may take the form of 'Dalit pride' yet, as Hugo Gorringe observes, there is a paradox in attacking discrimination based on caste but not caste itself.[29] Ambedkar famously advocated the annihilation of caste, not just an end to caste discrimination.[30] Balmurli Natrajan argues that the conceptualisation of caste as simply a form of cultural difference or cultural identity (what he terms the 'culturalisation' of caste) is deeply dangerous, and warns that representing caste as 'natural' or 'pre-existing' cultural identity

27 A.I.R.1993 SC 477, para. 82.

28 Balmurli Natrajan, *The Culturalisation of Caste in India: Identity and Inequality in a Multicultural Age* (Abingdon: Routledge, 2012), pp. 1–28.

29 Gorringe, 'Dalit politics', p. 123.

30 Bhimrao Ramji Ambedkar, 'The annihilation of caste', in Rodrigues, *The Essential Writings of B. R. Ambedkar*, pp. 263–305.

masks the reality of caste, namely 'socioculturally constructed relations of ascribed status and antagonism (inequality, domination and exploitation)'.[31]

ICERD and caste discrimination as an emerging issue: 1965–2001

ICERD was drafted as a response to anti-Semitism, colonialism and apartheid. Its specific purpose was to address racial discrimination. A suggestion that the Convention should address both racial and religious discrimination was rejected at the early stages of drafting.[32] Article 1(1) of ICERD defines racial discrimination as

> any distinction, exclusion, restriction or preference based on race, colour, descent, or national or ethnic origin which has the purpose or effect of nullifying or impairing the recognition, enjoyment or exercise, on an equal footing, of human rights and fundamental freedoms in the political, economic, social, cultural or any other field of public life.

As Patrick Thornberry has pointed out, the umbrella term of the Convention is 'racial discrimination', not 'race'.[33] The prohibited grounds of racial discrimination in Article 1(1) are race, colour, descent, or national or ethnic origin. There is no mention of caste or caste groups. Descent is the ground under which discrimination based on caste has been addressed by CERD since 1996; but descent was not included in the original draft of the Convention, which listed four grounds: race, colour, national or ethnic origin. Descent was introduced into Article 1 by an amendment initially proposed by India to resolve disagreements over the meaning of national origin; India's suggestion was to replace 'national origin' with 'descent' and 'place of origin'. This amendment was replaced by a second amendment proposed jointly by India and eight other states which retained the original four grounds (including national origin) and added 'descent' (but not 'place of origin'). The joint amendment proposing the addition of descent was adopted unanimously with minimal debate and no discussion as to the meaning of the term.[34]

Since 1996 India has repeatedly rejected CERD's position that caste-based discrimination falls within the scope of Article 1 of ICERD under descent. It has been suggested elsewhere that descent was proposed by India to meet two concerns: first, the legacy of colonialism whereby Indians had suffered racial discrimination in their own land;

31 Natrajan, *The Culturalisation of Caste in India*, p. 5.
32 David Keane, *Caste-based Discrimination in International Human Rights Law* (Surrey: Ashgate/Routledge, 2007), pp. 168–71.
33 Thornberry, 'Confronting racial discrimination', p. 250.
34 Keane, *Caste-based Discrimination in International Human Rights Law*, pp. 227–8.

and second, racial discrimination against Indians in South Africa,[35] moreover, that India, at least, had caste in mind during the debates on Article 1(4) and Article 2(2) on special measures, when the Indian representatives in the UN General Assembly Third Committee explicitly identified the Scheduled Castes as groups to which the special measures provisions would apply. The discrepancy between India's contribution to the drafting of the special measures provisions, and its subsequent position that caste is not covered by the Convention, was pointed out by former CERD member Van Boven in 1996.[36]

During the drafting of the Convention many countries insisted that there was no racial discrimination in their country. Ratification was a political act intended to signal a State's opposition to apartheid and colonialism and its support for the anti-apartheid movement and decolonisation.[37] The majority of ratifying States did not appear to consider ICERD to be relevant to their internal domestic situation.[38]

India ratified ICERD in 1969. India's position, similar to many other States, was that there was no racial discrimination in India,[39] and this has remained its position. Almost thirty years after ratifying the Convention, in its 1996 report, India asserted: 'Categorical distinctions of race or national or ethnic origin have ceased to exist and race itself as an issue does not impinge on the consciousness or outlook of Indian citizens in their social relations', moreover 'race as a ground for discrimination has never been invoked before the courts of law of India so far'.[40] At the time ICERD was drafted, India saw itself and its people as both victims and principal opponents of racial discrimination, not as perpetrators. With regard to its tribal populations, India did not – and still does not – consider that ICERD applies to them as indigenous peoples, a category covered by the Convention;[41] its view is that from the moment of independence and the departure of the colonisers, all Indians are to be regarded as indigenous.[42]

---

35 See Waughray, *Capturing Caste in Law*, Chapter 4. See also UN Doc. CERD/C/SR.1796, 2 March 2007, para. 7.

36 UN Doc. CERD/C/SR.1162, 13 August 1996, para. 15.

37 Michael Banton, *International Action Against Racial Discrimination* (Oxford: Oxford University Press, 1996), pp. 99, 305. See also India: tenth to fourteenth report. UN Doc. CERD/C/299/Add.3, 29 April 1996, para. 13.

38 Thornberry, 'Confronting racial discrimination', p. 241.

39 See for example CERD/C/R.3/add.3/Rev.1, 30 March 1970, para. 19; UN Doc. A/9018 (1973) para. 238.

40 CERD/C/299/Add.3, 29 April 1996, paras. 5, 10.

41 See Fergus Mackay, 'Indigenous peoples' rights and the UN Committee on the Elimination of Racial Discrimination', in Solomon Dersso (ed.), *Perspectives on the Rights of Minorities and Indigenous Peoples in Africa* (Pretoria: Pretoria University Law Press, 2010), pp. 155–202.

42 UN Doc. CERD/C/SR. 1797, 26 March 2007, para. 15.

Between 1969 and 1982, India submitted seven reports to CERD. In each report, India provided detailed information on its affirmative action (i.e. special) measures for the Scheduled Castes. During this period CERD continued to ask for information on the situation of the Scheduled Castes and Tribes; but neither CERD nor India made it clear whether they considered the Scheduled Castes to fall within the purview of Article 1(1) of the Convention. Successive post-independence governments in India failed to treat the problem of discrimination against the Dalits as anything more than a 'marginal issue'; caste was seen as antithetical to modern India and there was an assumption that caste and hence the problems of the Dalits would disappear as India modernised.[43] In the immediate post-war years the Congress Party sought and secured Dalit political support in return for promises of change, which did not materialise,[44] while for the Left, class not caste was the key political and social enemy. Meanwhile, Dalits continued to suffer egregious discrimination; for them, freedom from colonial rule did not mean freedom from caste oppression.

Hugo Gorringe explains how, starting in the 1970s and through the 1980s, the slow pace of change led to the rise of 'new Dalit movements' in India which confronted the failure of successive governments and co-opted Dalit politicians to bring about meaningful change for Dalits.[45] There was little international awareness outside of South Asia of caste as a ground of discrimination. By the early 1980s Dalit activists in India and the diaspora, frustrated by the limited success of domestic measures to combat caste discrimination, had turned towards the United Nations in an attempt to 'internationalise' their situation as a human rights issue.[46] In the course of the next decade Dalit activists sought to raise international awareness and to secure international recognition of caste-based discrimination by lobbying and appearing before a wide variety of international human rights bodies including the UN Commission on Human Rights, the UN Working Group on Indigenous Peoples, the UN Working Group on Minorities, the Committee on the Rights of the Child, and at the UN World Conference on Human Rights in Vienna.[47]

The 1990s was a decade of huge economic and social change in India, prompted in part by the economic liberalisation programme

43 Mendelsohn and Vizciany, *The Untouchables*, pp. 44, 118.
44 Gorringe, 'Dalit politics', p. 122; Mendelsohn and Vizciany, *The Untouchables*, p. 118.
45 Gorringe, 'Dalit politics', p. 122.
46 Bob, 'Dalit Rights are Human Rights', p. 175.
47 *Ibid.*, p. 177; Corinne Lennox, 'Norm-entrepreneurship on caste-based discrimination', in David Mosse and Luisa Steur (eds), *Caste Out of Development? The Cultural Politics of Identity and Economy in India and Beyond* (Routledge, 2015).

introduced in 1991 by the then Finance Minister Manmohan Singh (later Prime Minster of India 2004–14). This decade also witnessed what activists have termed the 'internationalisation' of caste, meaning both the efforts of Dalit activists to bring the problem of caste discrimination and caste-based violence to the attention of international actors – politicians, international organisations, civil society, NGOs and the wider public – and an increase in global awareness and visibility of the discrimination and violence associated with caste.

CERD Concluding Observations, India, 1996

In 1996, in its 10th–14th report, India asserted categorically for the first time its view that ICERD did not apply to the Scheduled Castes and Scheduled Tribes, stating: 'the policies of the Indian Government relating to Scheduled Castes and Scheduled Tribes do not come under the purview of Article 1 of the Convention'.[48] According to India,

> [T]he term 'caste' denotes a 'social' and 'class' distinction and is not based on race, [having] its origins in the functional division of Indian society during ancient times.[49]

India's report noted that Article 1 of ICERD includes in the definition of racial discrimination the term descent. India argued that although both castes and tribes were systems based on descent since people are normally born into a particular caste or tribe, it was however 'obvious' that the use of the term descent in the Convention 'clearly referred to race'.[50] Therefore, 'as conveyed to the Committee during the presentation of India's last periodic report', India's policies relating to Scheduled Castes and Scheduled Tribes did not come under the purview of Article 1 of the Convention.[51]

During the presentation of its report in 1996 before CERD, India reiterated that caste denoted a social or class distinction, and was originally occupation-oriented; it was not a racial issue.[52] While

> the notion of 'race' was not entirely foreign to that of 'caste'; according to experts on such questions, racial differences were secondary compared to cultural ones (economic and occupational status, language and dynastic or

48 CERD/C/299/Add.3, 29 April 1996, para. 6.
49 CERD/C/299/Add.3, 29 April 1996, para. 7.
50 CERD/C/299/Add.3, 29 April 1996, para. 7.
51 CERD/C/299/Add.3, 29 April 1996, para. 7. The reference was to the view expressed orally by the Indian representative in 1987 at CERD's examination of India's 8th–9th Report that Article 1 of ICERD did not apply to the Scheduled Castes and Scheduled Tribes; see CERD/C/SR.796, 30 November 1987, para. 26; CERD/C/SR.797, 30 November 1987, paras. 60–1.
52 CERD/C/ SR 1162, 13 August 1996, paras. 35, 36.

national loyalties), and the principle of race had never really been a determinant for caste.[53]

Constitutionally (in India) the concept of race was distinct from caste.[54] Given that (in India's view) descent referred solely to race, and caste was not a racial issue, the Indian Government's policies on caste discrimination therefore did not fall under descent or indeed under the Convention at all. CERD did not accept the argument that descent referred solely to race, or that because caste and race were distinguished from each other in the Indian Constitution therefore descent in Article 1 could not capture caste. During its consideration of India's report, CERD member Wolfrum stated that India's interpretation of the term 'descent' was not acceptable. If 'descent was the equivalent of "race", it would not have been necessary to include both concepts in the Convention. The State party's position on the question could not fail to be of concern to the Committee'.[55] CERD member Chigovera argued that the fact that castes (and tribes) were based on descent brought them strictly within the Convention under the terms of Article 1.[56] CERD member De Gouttes took a similar position, arguing that although the problem was complex, it was unacceptable to say that the serious discrimination against certain castes, especially the untouchables, was not within the Committee's competence.[57] Indeed, in its previous report India had provided information on the development and protection of Scheduled Castes and had therefore clearly recognised that the Convention was applicable to the (caste) situation in India. Yet the 10th–14th periodic report stated that information on matters dealt with in Article 1 of the Convention would be provided only as 'a matter of courtesy'. In its Concluding Observations CERD reiterated that descent in Article 1 did not solely refer to race, and affirmed that the situation of the Scheduled Castes and Tribes in India fell within the scope of the Convention. It emphasised its great concern that in discussion its report, there was no inclination on the side of India to reconsider its position.[58] This was the first time that CERD had explicitly identified caste discrimination as coming within the purview of the Convention, and by extension as an international human rights violation. Its observations were widely welcomed by Dalit activists and their supporters. The Committee's concern with caste and caste-related discrimination had been kindled by information provided by

53 CERD/C/SR.1163, 20 November 1996, para. 3.
54 CERD/C/SR.1162, 13 August 1996, para. 35.
55 CERD/C/SR.1161, 1 November 1996, para. 20.
56 CERD/C/SR.1162, 13 August 1996, para. 22.
57 De Gouttes; CERD/C/SR.1161, 1 November 1996, para. 32.
58 UN Doc. CERD/A/51/18 (1996) para. 352.

non-State sources including shadow reports from human rights NGOs, urging CERD to raise the issue of caste discrimination with India.[59] According to Corinne Lennox,

> [t]his [was] reportedly the first time any NGO had submitted a shadow report on caste-based discrimination to a UN treaty body. It was an auspicious move for subsequent norm entrepreneurship on caste because it pushed CERD into taking a juridical position on whether caste fell within the remit of the committee.[60]

The discussions with India during the presentation of its report did not result in India changing its position. The Indian Government considered that CERD was guilty of a misinterpretation of the term descent. India rejected the accusation of racial discrimination which CERD's Concluding Observations implied; in its report India had stressed the key role it had played in the fight against apartheid since Indian independence, and its role as a founding member of the Non-Aligned Movement which was associated with the elimination of racial discrimination, exploitation and inequality.[61] Nevertheless, 'the dialogue positioned CERD as an early ally of advocates on caste and ICERD as a relevant international standard'.[62]

Corinne Lennox describes 1998 as the start of the 'second wave' of post-war Dalit activism. It saw the foundation of the NGO National Commission on Dalit Human Rights (NCDHR) in India, and the First World Dalit Convention in Kuala Lumpur organised primarily by Dalit NGOs from the United States, United Kingdom and Canada.[63] In 1999 the NGO Human Rights Watch published a highly influential report, *Broken People: Caste Violence Against India's "Untouchables"*. In the same year the NCDHR published a 'Black Paper' documenting violence against Dalits in India. In 2000, following intensive lobbying by Dalit organisations and their supporters, the former UN Sub-Commission for the Promotion and Protection of Human Rights adopted Resolution 2000/4 condemning discrimination based on work and descent as a violation of international human rights law, although the resolution contained no definition of this form of discrimination. This led to the development of a parallel advocacy track challenging caste discrimination via the concept of discrimination based on work and descent, a new international legal category which includes but is wider than caste discrimination.

59 CERD/C/SR.1161, 1 November 1996, paras. 11, 22; CERD/C/SR.1162, 13 August 1996, para 23.
60 Lennox, 'Norm-entrepreneurship on caste-based discrimination'.
61 CERD/C/299/Add.3, 29 April 1996, para. 13 [India 1996 report]
62 Lennox, 'Norm-entrepreneurship on caste-based discrimination'.
63 *Ibid.*

The 'work and descent' terminology was adopted to encompass caste and similar systems of inherited status without focusing on any one state. Three expert reports in 2001, 2003 and 2004, commissioned by the UN Sub-Commission, identified work and descent-based discrimination, including discrimination based on caste, as a worldwide problem. In 2004 two UN Special Rapporteurs on Discrimination Based on Work and Descent were appointed by the Sub-Commission, producing two further reports in 2005 and 2006 and, in 2009, a set of Draft Principles and Guidelines for the effective elimination of work and descent discrimination. Caste discrimination has also been repeatedly condemned by many of the UN special procedures, in particular successive UN Special Rapporteurs on contemporary forms of racism. 2000 also saw the establishment of a transnational advocacy network, International Dalit Solidarity Network (IDSN), based in Copenhagen, Denmark. IDSN has played an important role in further 'internationalising' caste discrimination by engaging with UN bodies, including CERD, and other international and regional actors such as the European Union (EU), although the transnational advocacy model is not without pitfalls.[64] In the same year, a UK-based Dalit non-governmental organisation, Voice of Dalit International, organised an International Conference on Dalit Human Rights in London which called for caste to be added to UK discrimination law, demanding that 'laws which address discrimination based on racism should take cognisance of casteism and place it on a par with racism'.[65] At the end of the millennium Dalit activists turned their attention to the WCAR held in Durban in 2001, where they sought through intensive lobbying both before and at the conference to secure the inclusion of caste in the conference's Final Declaration and Programme of Action. This was unsuccessful due to the opposition of the Indian Government, but their lobbying succeeded in greatly raising international awareness of the problem of caste discrimination.[66]

The 'lines in the sand' for the range of actors on caste in international human rights law are apparent from 2001, and have not

64 *Ibid.*; Bob, 'Dalit Rights are Human Rights'; J. Lerche, 'Transnational advocacy networks and affirmative action for Dalits in India', *Development and Change*, 39:2 (2008), 239–261; David Mosse and Lisa Steur, 'Dalit rights and the development agenda: The promise, progress, and pitfalls of NGO networking and international advocacy'. Dalit communities in India and diaspora: agency and activism, research and representation. Conference paper. University of Lisboa. July 2012.

65 Satpal Muman, 'Caste in Britain', in *Dalits in the New Millennium: Report of the Proceedings of the International Conference on Dalit Human Rights*, 16–17 September 2000 (London: Voice of Dalit International, 2000), p. x.

66 See Bob, 'Dalit Rights are Human Rights'; Lennox, 'Norm-entrepreneurship on caste-based discrimination'.

shifted substantially since. From the perspective of the UN, caste comes under the purview of the international human rights *system*, its agencies and mechanisms, a position apparent through various references to or representations on caste in UN bodies from the 1980s onwards at, if not an informal, at least an un-formalised level. Distinct from this, 1996 marked the formal recognition by the UN of caste in international human rights *law*, situating caste within the definition of racial discrimination in Article 1(1) ICERD, under descent. That the term 'descent' would be the legal home for caste is reflected and continued in the parallel Charter-based mechanisms that date from 2000, under the nebulous 'work and descent' category. Hence the international legal understanding of caste generated a wider international legal category of descent that had not been elaborated in any form in the UN system prior to 1996. It clearly includes caste as practised in India and elsewhere, but is a wider concept whose parameters are not yet fully delineated.

The year 1996 also marks the formal opposition of India to the recognition of caste in international human rights law under Article 1(1) ICERD. India is not necessarily opposed to the inclusion of caste in the international human rights *system*. It may be inclined to contest the raising of caste in international bodies, but this is not necessarily formal or legal. By contrast, it is clearly formally opposed to the inclusion of caste in international human rights law via ICERD. The question is whether its objection is based on an international legal recognition of caste per se, which did not happen expressly in any international forum prior to 1996; or an international legal recognition of caste *as a form of racial discrimination*. The experience in Durban, involving an international document on racism and not on human rights more generally, suggests that it is the latter. This is affirmed when it is considered that India reports to other UN treaty bodies on caste, for example extensively discussing caste in a 2005 report to the Committee on the Elimination of Discrimination Against Women.[67] Hence formal or legal Indian opposition is to the international legal understanding of caste as a form of racial discrimination, and not to the 'internationalisation' of caste per se, although it may oppose or contest this in other ways. This distinction has not been clearly enunciated by India, but its State practice suggests that there is no evidence that it is opposed to caste-based discrimination in international human rights law; just to the inclusion of caste in the international prohibition on racial discrimination.

---

67 CEDAW, 'State Report: India', UN Doc. CEDAW/C/IND/2–3 (2005). For example, among the many references there is a paragraph entitled 'Caste-based discrimination, including violence, suffered by women of [the] dalit community' (para. 20).

From 2001, these positions would be consolidated. CERD would evolve its work on 'descent', which includes caste; India would continue its formal opposition to the international legal recognition of caste as a form of racial discrimination; and NGOs would seek the further 'internationalisation' of caste across the UN system. Caste would emerge as a cross-cutting theme in the UN human rights bodies, treaty-based and Charter-based, although clarifying its relationship with descent and related terms such as work and descent, engaging with or overcoming State opposition, and understanding its application in an international context in particular outside South Asia – in contradistinction to descent – would not find easy resolution.

2001–15

General Recommendation 29 (2002) on Descent

In August 2002 CERD issued General Recommendation 29 on Article 1(1) of the Convention (Descent) (GR 29).[68] Former CERD member Thornberry writes:

> The General Recommendation followed the debacle (for Dalits and others) at the Durban World Conference when the caste issue was talked out by vigorous diplomacy by India. The Committee had independent reasons to go ahead and explore the issue: to understand better a key term in the Convention; to understand better the contemporary scope of such discrimination; and, to respond to the victims who impressed the Committee so greatly. There are issues here: the target of the General Recommendation is not or should not be the caste system itself, but discrimination – although the distinction is a thin one. In the author's view, powerful victim perspectives greatly influenced the Committee.[69]

GR 29 was preceded by an informal discussion on the concept of descent with NGOs and States parties (including India), followed by a thematic debate within the Committee – only the second time this had happened. The style, format and the drafting process of the general recommendation were modelled on General Recommendation 27 on discrimination against Roma which was preceded by the first thematic discussion within the Committee.[70] In November 2001 the Committee had proposed holding a thematic debate on descent in the next session, preceded by a preliminary exchange of views. Although the term was included in Article 1, the Committee had never studied it in any depth and it had received little attention to date. A thematic debate on

68 UN Doc. A/57/18, 111–17.
69 Thornberry, 'Confronting racial discrimination', at p. 264.
70 Keane, *Caste-based Discrimination in International Human Rights Law*, p. 219.

descent, it was suggested, would also enable CERD to collaborate with the UN Sub-Commission which was working on discrimination based on work and descent. Due to the complex nature of 'descent', it was felt that the Committee should study the concept carefully in order to clarify the basic notion as well its scope.[71]

On the use of thematic debates, Thornberry explains that these are not a departure from the Convention's formal structures and processes but a manifestation of members' desire to develop their expertise in a particular direction. The thematic debate on descent was not a political response to the absence of caste in the WCAR Final Declaration, rather 'an exercise by the Committee *proprio motu*, strictly tied to the Convention'.[72] Nonetheless, it represented an important milestone for Dalit activists and their supporters. The debate on descent and descent-based discrimination took place in August 2002 in two stages; first, a session with NGOs, experts from the UN Sub-Commission on the Promotion and Protection of Human Rights, and governments; and second, a thematic discussion within CERD.[73] As with the discussion which preceded GR 27 on Roma, it was essential, writes Thornberry, that affected communities themselves be involved so that the voices of victims and their representatives could be heard.[74] The twenty-plus representatives of Dalit NGOs gave detailed accounts of the 'harsh reality' of caste-based discrimination.[75] They urged the Committee to name caste-based discrimination as a primary form of descent-based discrimination, whilst also stressing that descent-based discrimination should not be equated solely with the Dalit issue in India nor be polarised in a manner that overlooks caste discrimination against communities in other parts of the world.[76] The Indian Government reiterated that its Constitution abolished untouchability and recognised the situation of the Dalits and the need to address it. Members of the UN Sub-Commission for the Promotion and Protection of Human Rights felt that caste-based discrimination came under the competence of CERD and was captured by descent. The Sub-Commission was conducting its own further studies on descent and caste discrimination. It was felt that the problem of caste should not be seen in relation to a

71 UN Doc. CERD/C/SR/1493, 12 November 2002, paras. 38–44.

72 Patrick Thornberry, 'Race, descent and caste under ICERD', in Kenji Nakano, Mario Jorge Yutzis and Ryo Onoyama (eds), *Peoples for Human Rights*, Vol. 9, 'Descent-based Discrimination' (Tokyo: International Movement Against all Forms of Discrimination and Racism, 2004), pp. 119–37, at p. 126.

73 *Ibid.*, pp. 125–6.

74 *Ibid.*, p. 126.

75 UN Doc. CERD/C/SR.1531, 16 August 2002, para. 11.

76 Thematic debate, unofficial contemporaneous notes; S. Prasad, Dalit Human Rights Watch, 8 August 2002; copy on file with author.

particular country; the debate should also include countries other than those in the Indian subcontinent.

In its thematic discussion, CERD members agreed that the scope and meaning of the Convention must be seen as inclusive not exclusive.[77] The term descent implied one generation inheriting from another specific characteristics that were positively or negatively evaluated by society.[78] On the specific issue of caste, CERD member Thornberry explained that caste systems represented hierarchy, not equality; segregation, not integration; bondage, not freedom; and value determined at birth without regard for morality, achievement, intelligence or character. The existence of caste discrimination was a matter of fact. He agreed with CERD member Pillai that the scope of descent was wide, and that caste was one of its facets.[79] A final definition of descent-based discrimination was not necessary; the term was clear, and encompassed caste and other analogous systems of social stratification based on birth.[80] The focus of the GR should be on the need to encourage governments to report on the existence of castes, and to take action in a constructive spirit to eliminate such discrimination, paying particular attention to the double discrimination suffered by Dalit women.[81]

These views were reflected in the General Recommendation. Drafted by a working group comprising CERD members Sicilianos, Pillai and de Gouttes, coordinated by CERD member Thornberry,[82] GR 29 does not offer a definition of descent-based discrimination. The tone is 'hortatory rather than critical', encouraging states to adopt measures appropriate to their circumstances.[83] The Preamble confirms the Committee's view that the term descent in Article 1 does not solely refer to race and has a meaning and application which complement the other prohibited grounds of discrimination in Article 1. It 'strongly reaffirms' that 'discrimination based on descent includes discrimination against members of communities based on forms of social stratification such as caste and analogous systems of inherited status which nullify or impair their equal enjoyment of human rights'. The Preamble concludes by strongly condemning descent-based discrimination, such as discrimination on the basis of caste and analogous systems of inherited status, as a violation of the Convention. The Recommendation does not provide a full definition of descent-based

77 CERD/C/SR.1531, 16 August 2002, para. 7.
78 *Ibid.*, para. 18.
79 *Ibid.*, para. 13.
80 *Ibid.*, para. 12.
81 *Ibid.*, paras. 14, 25.
82 *Ibid.*, para. 54.
83 Thornberry, 'Race, descent and caste under ICERD', p. 128.

discrimination; rather, paragraph 1 on general measures to be taken by States parties explains that

> descent-based communities are those who suffer from discrimination, especially on the basis of caste and analogous systems of inherited status, and whose existence may be recognized on the basis of various factors including some or all of the following: inability or restricted ability to alter inherited status; socially enforced restrictions on marriage outside the community; private and public segregation, including in housing and education, access to public spaces, places of worship and public sources of food and water; limitation of freedom to renounce inherited occupations or degrading or hazardous work; subjection to debt bondage; subjection to dehumanizing lack of respect for their human dignity and equality.

The emphasis is on 'discrimination against individuals locked into a system from which they aspire to escape and which they find degrading, a system which involves "a total lack of social mobility, for the status of the individual was determined by birth or social origin and could never change regardless of personal merit"'.[84]

In paragraph 1, States are asked *inter alia* to take steps to identify communities suffering from descent-based discrimination, to review or enact legislation prohibiting descent-based discrimination, to adopt special measures in favour of descent-based communities in order to ensure their enjoyment of human rights and fundamental freedoms, and to audit and provide disaggregated information on the de facto economic and social situation of descent-based communities, including a gender perspective. This is followed by operative paragraphs on multiple (intersectional) discrimination against women, segregation, hate speech, administration of justice, civil and political rights, economic and social rights, and right to education. The sequence of the operative paragraphs and the style of the Recommendation follows the format of the Convention, and General Recommendation 27 on the Roma. The operative paragraphs drew on the NGO submissions in the thematic discussion, which reflected a wide geographical and cultural range.[85] The emphasis on the provision of information on the de facto economic and social situation of groups covered by the Recommendation is particularly relevant to States which have already enacted legislation prohibiting descent-based discrimination and/or adopted special measures in favour of groups suffering from such discrimination. The Recommendation was not intended to be exhaustive; it was expected that the Recommendation would apply differently, and

84 CERD member de Gouttes, UN Doc. CERD/C/SR.1531, 16 August 2002, para. 40, cited in Thornberry, 'The Convention on the Elimination of Racial Discrimination', p. 41.

85 Thornberry, 'Race, descent and caste under ICERD', p. 127.

different strategies would be followed, in different societies according to their own problems.[86]

On the use of ICERD to address caste discrimination, former CERD member Thornberry explains,

> [I]f the various 'grounds' of discrimination in Article 1 do not immediately translate themselves into recognisable varieties of community vulnerable to discrimination, the practice of the Committee has served to put a human face to the targets of discriminatory practices.[87]

He argues that caste or analogous forms of social stratification 'are appropriately brought within the frame of Article 1' because they have 'a "race-like" quality on a par with the other descriptors in Article 1 ... even if the surest of the specific descriptors [in Article 1] remains that of "descent"'.[88] On the choice of descent for capturing caste, Thornberry explains that descent is a term 'which suggests a wide span of possibilities'.[89] Descent

> has the most open character, since all human beings have a 'descent'. However much it may shade into other concepts, it is an appropriate term to act as a normative safety net for clear cases of group-based discrimination based on inherited characteristics which are not easily caught by other, narrower descriptors.[90]

In this respect, he writes,

> [T]he thrust of the Convention towards the elimination of 'all forms' of racial discrimination suggests that an expansive reading of its scope is not unreasonable. There are overlaps among the Article 1 descriptors, and the *travaux* suggest that not every descriptor was clearly understood as marking out a sharply defined conceptual space or class of victim. [Former CERD member] Diaconu accounts for the Article 1 *travaux* by suggesting that 'the definition was composed by adding as many concepts as possible, in order to avoid any lacunae'.[91]

Through the 'living instrument' principle, human rights protection can be extended to groups who are not directly referred to in existing instruments:

> We need not exaggerate the normative quality of the step taken by CERD. The recommendation stems from [the Convention] which is general in nature, and is thus only a partial substitute for a free-standing instrument

86 *Ibid.*, p. 128.
87 Thornberry, 'Confronting racial discrimination', pp. 257–8.
88 Thornberry, 'Race, descent and caste under ICERD', p. 122.
89 Thornberry, 'The Convention on the Elimination of Racial Discrimination', p. 37.
90 Thornberry, 'Race, descent and caste under ICERD', p. 123.
91 Thornberry, 'Confronting racial discrimination', p. 258.

> on caste, such as a UN General Assembly Declaration or a dedicated international convention. Nevertheless, it illustrates the possibilities inherent in elaborating existing instruments on human rights to benefit particular communities, even in the absence of direct reference to the community in question ... CERD has also elaborated ... recommendations on minorities and indigenous peoples which are also not referred to in the body of the Convention.[92]

The perspectives of victims 'greatly' impressed the Committee, in Thornberry's view, and played a key role in the development of GR 29;[93] the Preamble refers specifically to CERD's receipt of oral and written information from individuals and NGOs which provided the Committee with further evidence of the extent and persistence of descent-based discrimination around the world. The Committee considered the issue of cultural intrusion during the thematic debate; some Committee members, explains Thornberry, were more troubled about this than others, but ultimately the Committee could not accept a 'cultural' defence of caste 'when there is massive disaffection and dissent, and group "membership" is heavily contested'.[94] While the target of GR 29 is discrimination on the basis of descent (including caste discrimination), rather than caste or any other particular cultural or social system, the distinction, as Thornberry readily acknowledges, is 'a thin one'.[95] His observation speaks to the paradox, mentioned previously, of attacking caste discrimination but not the concept of caste itself.

Beyond General Recommendation 29

In its 2006 report India reiterated its position that caste cannot be equated with race, nor is it covered under descent under Article 1 of the Convention.[96] It repeated this position in 2007 when presenting its report, insisting that it 'had no doubt that the ordinary meaning of the term "racial discrimination" did not include caste', and that caste discrimination was an issue outside the purview of racial discrimination under Article 1(1).[97] Consequently 'India was not in a position to accept reporting obligations [on caste] under the Convention'.[98] In

92 Thornberry, 'Race, descent and caste under ICERD', pp. 119–20.
93 Thornberry, 'Confronting racial discrimination', p. 264.
94 UN Doc. CERD/C/SR.1531, 16 August 2002, paras. 12, 30–1; Thornberry, 'The Convention on the Elimination of Racial Discrimination', pp. 42–43; Thornberry, 'Confronting racial discrimination', p. 264.
95 Thornberry, 'Confronting racial discrimination', at p. 264.
96 UN Doc. CERD/C/IND/19, 19 March 2006, para. 16.
97 UN Doc. CERD/C/SR.1796, 2 March 2007, paras. 3, 7.
98 *Ibid.*, para. 3.

its 2007 Concluding Observations CERD noted India's view that discrimination based on caste falls outside the scope of Article 1 of the Convention, but reaffirmed its position, as expressed in GR 29, that such discrimination is fully covered by Article 1 of the Convention.[99] India has not reported to CERD since 2006. At its Universal Periodic Review examination in 2011, India accepted no recommendations relating to caste discrimination, which may suggest a widening of its opposition within international human rights law, in line with comments above. Effectively, the 1996 and 2007 oral dialogues between India and CERD have resulted in a stalemate on the issue of caste discrimination, highlighting the limitations of the treaty body system and the constructive dialogue principle. On the other hand, the dialogue and Concluding Observations mechanisms render government positions more transparent, which is extremely useful for NGOs and civil society organisations campaigning for change.

India has not been the sole focus of CERD's attention on caste. Within South Asia CERD has examined the issue of continuing de facto caste discrimination in Nepal,[100] Pakistan,[101] Bangladesh[102] and Sri Lanka,[103] despite constitutional provisions in Nepal, Pakistan and Sri Lanka prohibiting discrimination based on caste and, in the case of Nepal, a constitutional provision and legislation outlawing untouchability. None of these states has objected to CERD's deployment of descent to address caste-based discrimination; Sri Lanka, in 1986, asserted that the caste system in its country was 'a racial phenomenon' found among Tamils and Sinhalese despite the lack of racial distinction between the two communities.[104]

CERD has also engaged with the UK on caste. Caste was barely acknowledged in the UK public domain as a ground of discrimination until the early 2000s, when UK Dalits, spurred by the 'internationalisation' of caste, began to draw attention to the existence of caste discrimination within UK South Asian communities, calling for casteism to be treated on a par with racism within domestic law.[105] The UK's 2003 State report to CERD was silent on caste. Unlike India, the UK did not contest CERD's application of descent to caste; instead, during presentation of its report it dismissed calls to introduce legislation

99 CERD/C/IND/CO/19, 5 May 2007, para. 8.
100 See CERD/C/64/CO/5, paras. 12, 14, 15.
101 CERD/C/PAK/CO/20, paras. 11,12.
102 CERD/C/304/Add.118, paras. 8, 11.
103 UN Doc. A/42/18 (1987) para. 293.
104 *Ibid.*
105 See Muman, 'Caste in Britain'. See also Annapurna Waughray, 'Caste discrimination: A twenty-first century challenge for UK discrimination law?', *Modern Law Review*, 72:2 (2009), 182–219.

on caste-based discrimination on the grounds that there was no obvious need for such legislation. In its 2003 Concluding Observations, CERD referred to GR 29 and recommended that the UK include a prohibition of descent-based discrimination, such as discrimination based on caste, in domestic legislation.[106]

In 2010, new equality legislation was enacted in the UK. The Equality Act 2010 prohibits discrimination on nine grounds including race, defined as 'including' colour, nationality, and ethnic or national origins. The legislation did not include a prohibition of caste or descent-based discrimination; instead, a ministerial power to make caste 'an aspect of race' at some point in the future was inserted.[107] The term caste was used instead of descent because of fears that descent might open the door to social or class-based claims.[108] In its 2010 report to CERD, the UK explained that it had declined to include an immediate prohibition of caste discrimination in the new Equality Act 2010 because it had 'seen no firm evidence on whether caste-based discrimination in the fields covered by the Convention exists to any significant extent in the UK'.[109] CERD responded in its 2010 Concluding Observations by recalling GR 29, referring to information received from NGOs as well as government-commissioned research, and recommending the addition of caste to the legislation.[110]

In 2013 the power to add caste to the Equality Act 2010 was converted into a statutory duty to do so; but, as at the time of writing, caste has still not been added to the legislation. The UK reported again to CERD in 2015. The delay in adding caste to the Equality Act 2010, it explained, was because the Government was 'considering the implications' of a 2014 Employment Appeal Tribunal decision which

> opened the possibility that there was an existing legal remedy for claims of caste-associated discrimination under current domestic legislation, namely through the 'ethnic origins' element of section 9 [race] of the Equality Act 2010.[111]

That decision – in *Chandhok* v. *Tirkey* – established that in certain circumstances ethnic origins could be construed so as to provide for caste

106 CERD/ C/63/CO/11, 10 December 2003, para. 25.

107 Equality Act 2010 c 15; section 9(5)(a). See Annapurna Waughray, 'Capturing caste in law: Caste discrimination and the Equality Act 2010', *Human Rights Law Review*, 14:2 (2014), 359–79.

108 See Waughray, *Capturing Caste in Law*.

109 CERD/C/GBR/18–20, 13 August 2010, para. 42.

110 [CERD 2011 COs to UK] 14 September 2011, para. 30. See also H. Metcalfe and H. Rolfe, 'Caste discrimination and harassment in Great Britain' (London: Government Equalities Office, 2010).

111 CERD/C/GBR/21–23, 16 July 2015, paras. 8–11.

to be part of race.[112] As this volume was being prepared, the UK was due to present its 21st–23rd State report (2015) at the ninetieth session of CERD in August 2016. Also while this volume was being prepared, an NGO shadow report was being compiled by the Runnymede Trust (an independent race equality think-tank). The draft refers to NGO criticism of the Government for failing to add caste to the Equality Act 2010 as an aspect of race, as required by parliament, arguing that the legislation as currently drafted does not adequately protect victims of caste discrimination and that the Government's assertion that the law now provides for a legal remedy for caste discrimination is 'misleading and incorrect'.[113]

The emergence of caste discrimination as a domestic issue within the UK since the early 2000s has increased the visibility of ICERD among British activists, NGOs, parliamentarians, lawyers and the judiciary. At the same time, successive UK governments have resisted CERD's recommendations in 2003 and 2010 to enact caste discrimination legislation, not because they object to the application of ICERD to caste issues per se, but because they disagree with CERD as to the necessity or desirability of legislation. The UK, while abiding by its reporting obligations under ICERD, has clearly not felt obliged to comply with recommendations with which it disagrees.

Looking ahead

Caste discrimination is not a problem of the past but a contemporary human rights violation occurring every day across South Asia and the diaspora, albeit one which remains insufficiently recognised. CERD's deployment of descent in 1996 to address caste discrimination in India helped propel caste discrimination into wider public view. This interpretation of descent – affirmed by CERD in 2002 in GR 29 – has been vigorously resisted by India, which argues that descent was never intended to cover caste and should not, decades after the Convention was drafted, be deployed in this way. By contrast, CERD member Thornberry considered that

> the intention of the drafters was less important than the text they had drafted. As a basis of discrimination, the term 'descent' signified forms of inherited status. Under the Convention some – though not all – instances of descent-based discrimination might equally be addressed under the criteria

112 *Chandhok and Anor* v. *Tirkey* [2014] UKEAT/0190/14/KN; *Tirkey* v. *Chandhok and Anor* [2015] ET/3400174/2013; Annapurna Waughray, 'Is caste discrimination in the UK prohibited by the Equality Act 2010?', *International Labor Rights Case Law*, 2 (2016), 70–6.

113 See www.odysseustrust.org/CERD/CERD.pdf.

> of race or colour, and ethnic or national origin. The term 'descent' indeed added something to the Convention and, like the other human attributes mentioned in article 1, it was non-negotiable. The question of communities of inherited status was analogous to other terms in the Convention in that the group concerned might be treated as though it were a separate race or ethnicity. By the same token, the Committee had also shown great concern for the status of minorities and indigenous peoples.[114]

CERD's examination of caste-based discrimination under the rubric of descent, while unchallenged by states such as Nepal, Pakistan and the UK, has resulted in a stalemate with India which categorically rejects the application of ICERD to the issue of caste. CERD's experience with India on caste illustrates the limits of the constructive dialogue approach, and raises the question of what CERD can achieve on caste with India if India refuses to engage with CERD on the issue. After all, India undertook decades ago many of the steps recommended in GR 29 as regards legislation and special measures. Perhaps there is also a danger that India's outright opposition to CERD on the question of caste could affect India's view of CERD's credibility and legitimacy on other issues. In 2003, CERD member January-Bardill argued that CERD should be consistent in its approach by referring to caste and descent-based discrimination in other countries where it occurs, aside from India.[115] The Committee has followed this advice and has examined the problem of descent-based discrimination in a range of countries outside South Asia, for example Japan, Yemen and Mauritania. Nevertheless, India continues to provide the paradigmatic example of caste discrimination, which is the most recognised form of descent-based discrimination, and in 2006, CERD member January-Bardill asked India why it regarded the Convention as a threat rather than an opportunity to challenge the caste system. She asked whether the Government could not use ICERD as a tool to assist in the fraternity project aimed at building substantive citizenship. She also challenged the Government's assertion that there was no discrimination in India. While discrimination was not embedded in the law, social practice had discriminatory effects, and she urged the Government to consider this in order to facilitate a more constructive dialogue with the Committee in future.[116] As noted, India has not reported to CERD since 2006; it remains to be seen how India approaches the issue of caste in its next report.

The potential to engage the full range of CERD mechanisms in relation to caste-based discrimination has yet to be explored. The

114 CERD/C/SR.1531, para. 11.
115 CERD/C/SR.1607, 30 October 2003, para. 60.
116 CERD/C/SR.1796, 2 March 2007, paras. 48–50.

early warning and urgent action measures and procedures could apply to situations involving caste discrimination, if it became necessary to address serious violations in an urgent manner in accordance with the indicators set out in CERD's 2007 guidelines.[117] It is possible to foresee the use of these procedures in relation to atrocities or other severe manifestations of casteism. Individual or group communications alleging violations of ICERD on the basis of caste could be taken before the Committee, however none of the States parties discussed in this chapter have made the requisite declaration under Article 14, including India, Nepal and the UK. It is possible a communication involving caste discrimination in the diaspora could emanate from Australia or South Africa, who have made the requisite Article 14 declaration, but clearly CERD has a wider task in convincing the majority of its State parties to recognise its communications procedure.

More immediately, collaboration with the full range of human rights bodies on caste-based discrimination will continue to evolve its understanding at the international level. This is already in evidence, where treaty bodies such as CEDAW or the Committee on the Rights of the Child (CRC) are providing Concluding Observations on caste where relevant to States parties. Yet the emergence of caste in international human rights law is still at a relatively early stage; for example India has not reported to the Human Rights Committee since 1997.[118] Although that reporting cycle did raise caste-based discrimination,[119] it would appear essential that the Human Rights Committee would view the next State report from India as an opportunity to engage with its contestation of international standards, in particular GR 29, in consultation with CERD. The heightened role of NGOs in the monitoring process across the UN bodies has been significantly highlighted in relation to caste, and these groups will continue to drive the evolution of standards by producing shadow reports, testimonies and information, as well as their implementation. The Dalit NGO groupings among others provide a template for effective interaction between UN bodies and civil society and, in relation to CERD, illustrate the Committee's willingness to listen closely to victims of discrimination.

117 CERD, 'Guidelines for the Early Warning and Urgent Action Procedures', UN Doc. A/62/18, Annexes, Chapter III (2007), para. 12.

118 Human Rights Committee, 'Concluding Observations: India', UN Doc. CCPR/C/79/Add.81 (1997).

119 *Ibid.*, para. 15. The Human Rights Committee noted 'with concern that despite measures taken by the government, members of the Scheduled Castes ... continue to endure severe social discrimination and to suffer disproportionately from many violations of their rights under the Covenant ... It regrets that the de facto perpetuation of the caste system entrenches social differences and contributes to these violations'.

It is now twenty years since CERD formalised and legalised caste-based discrimination as a form of racial discrimination, affirming binding international obligations on States parties for its elimination. Since that time, caste-based discrimination has become part of the lexicon of international human rights law, with treaty bodies and Charter bodies evolving standards or applying their provisions to the issue. It is undeniable, and uncontested, that caste has a place within the international human rights system. The difficulty lies in the fact that the primary source or node for caste-based discrimination in international human rights law, as a form of racial discrimination under Article 1(1) of ICERD, is contested by the State most associated with caste, India. It should also be noted that some States, such as Japan, contest the application by CERD of the wider term descent-based discrimination to groups on their territories. However generally, in treaty body and Charter body mechanisms, caste discrimination is raised without formal or legal objection. Furthermore, recent work by the UN OHCHR may lead to a Declaration on descent-based discrimination, including discrimination on the basis of caste and analogous systems of inherited status.

The CERD–India stalemate is likely to recede in importance as it becomes dwarfed by a wider international understanding of caste and descent. Eventually, India may become convinced that the language of racial discrimination in the twenty-first century is to be understood differently than it was fifty years ago. CERD's contemporary remit, involving a range of groups of inherited status analogous to other terms in the Convention, should clearly include Dalits and other caste groups. The question is not principally one of civil and political rights; or economic, social and cultural rights; or gender; or children, although it will engage all of these aspects; it is the historic and continued subordination of a group on the basis of an unalterable status upon birth. Hence caste-based discrimination is primarily the domain of CERD, and principled interpretive stances will not alter this. CERD has been a pioneer in raising caste at the international level, and will continue to evolve these standards. It will continue its work on behalf of the victims of caste-based discrimination in fulfilment of its mandate, until, eventually, all States parties come on board.

Chapter 7

General Recommendation 34: *a contribution to the visibility and inclusion of Afro-descendants in Latin America*

Pastor Murillo and Esther Ojulari

Introduction

In a context of *mestizo*[1] national identities and the 'myth of racial democracy',[2] the issue of racial discrimination was largely denied in many Latin American countries for much of the twentieth century. Reflecting this, Afro-descendants were an 'invisible group' within international law, with no specific norms or mechanisms responding to their particular rights claims until the twenty-first century. However, long before this, the Committee on the Elimination of Racial Discrimination (CERD/the Committee), the monitoring mechanism of the International Convention on the Elimination of All Forms of Racial Discrimination (ICERD/ the Convention), began to draw attention to racial discrimination against Afro-descendants through its Concluding Observations and recommendations to Latin American States, challenging dominant discourses on the inexistence of racial discrimination. In

1 The Spanish term *mestizo* refers to people of mixed race/ethnicity. In the Latin American context it has historically been used to refer particularly to the 'mixing' of white European and Indigenous people but is sometimes extended to include Afro-descendant people as well. *Mestizo* national identities and ideologies of *mestizaje* were promoted in many countries following independence as part of the construction of the new nations.

2 The idea that Latin American societies were racial democracies free of racial inequality and racism relied heavily on the notion of *mestizaje* and was largely influenced by the ideas of Brazilian writer Gilberto Freyre in the 1930s. However this idea has since been argued to be a 'myth' or a romanticisation of race relations and experiences in the region. See further Edward Telles, *Race in Another America: The Significance of Skin Color in Brazil* (Princeton: Princeton University Press, 2004) and Henry Gates Jr., *Black in Latin America* (New York and London: New York University Press, 2011).

2011 it strengthened this component of its work with the adoption of General Recommendation 34 on racial discrimination against people of African descent (GR 34).[3]

As we celebrate the fiftieth anniversary of ICERD, this chapter traces the role that ICERD and CERD have played in contributing to the emerging visibility of Afro-descendants in Latin America. It begins with a brief overview of historical racial discourses in the region and the emergence of a framework for Afro-descendant rights at the international level. With reference to several country examples it then demonstrates how CERD has used Concluding Observations and recommendations to draw attention to Afro-descendants in Latin America. Finally it discusses the more recent adoption of GR 34. While still too early to analyse its impact, GR 34 has opened the door for greater possibilities within the emerging normative framework on the human rights of Afro-descendants.

Background and context

Afro-descendants[4] make up around 30 per cent of the population of Latin America and the Caribbean.[5] While their population sizes vary from country to country there are Afro-descendant communities in every country in the region. For example, Afro-descendant people represent over 50 per cent of the population of Brazil, 10.5 per cent in Colombia and 8.82 per cent in Panama, whilst in Honduras, Nicaragua and Guatemala they represent 0.9 per cent, 0.45 per cent and 0.04 per cent, respectively.[6] It is important to note that due to issues around census data, including capacity needs in data collection processes and self-identification, population figures

---

3 CERD, 'General Recommendation 34 on Racial discrimination against people of African descent', UN Doc. CERD/C/GC/34 (2011).

4 This chapter uses both the terms 'people of African descent' and 'Afro-descendant'. The term 'Afro-descendants' is used to refer to descendants of the enslaved Africans that were taken to the Americas during the transatlantic slave trade. The term 'people of African descent' is used in relation to UN norms and documentation of which all people of African descent around the world (including Afro-descendants from the Americas but also Africans or African descent migrants in other parts of the world) are subjects.

5 Inter-American Commission on Human Rights (IACHR), 'The Situation of People of African Descent in the Americas', OEA/Ser.L/V/II, Doc. 62 (Washington, DC: Organization of American States, 2011).

6 UNDP, 'Visibilidad Estadística: Datos Sobre Población Afrodescendiente En Censos Y Encuestas de Hogares de América Latina' (Panamá: United Nations Development Programme, 2012).

on Afro-descendants are often considered to underestimate true population sizes.[7]

Despite recent economic growth, reductions in poverty, and even reductions in income inequality in many countries in the region, Afro-descendant people (along with indigenous peoples) continue to be over-represented among the poorest communities and in some countries the gaps are widening.[8] Available socio-economic indicators demonstrate disparities that Afro-descendants face in all areas of their lives from access to health, education and employment, to adequate housing, access to justice and political participation.

In Uruguay, for example, the National Institute of Statistics (INE) reported in 2011 that 28.1 per cent of Afro-descendants lived below the poverty line, more than twice the national average of 13.7 per cent.[9] In Ecuador the 2006 Life Conditions Survey demonstrated that illiteracy among Afro-Ecuadorians over fifteen years of age was 12.6 per cent and as high as 23.3 per cent in rural areas compared to a national average of 9.1 per cent. Further, it showed that enrolment of Afro-Ecuadorians in higher education was only 8.15 per cent, just under half of the national average of 17.9 per cent.[10] In Colombia in 2009 the Government reported that the infant mortality rate for Afro-Colombians was 48.1 per thousand and as high as 77.5 per thousand in the Chocó, the region with the largest Afro-descendant population, compared to the national average of 26.9 per thousand.[11]

Racial discrimination, whether direct or indirect (including structural discrimination and institutional racism), is at the root of many of these inequalities.[12] Therefore efforts to realise the human rights of Afro-descendants must include measures to directly address and

7 See Corinne Lennox and Carlos Minott, 'Inclusion of Afro-descendants in ethnic data collection: Towards visibility', *International Journal on Minority and Group Rights*, 18 (2011), 257–75.

8 IACHR, 'The Situation of People of African Descent in the Americas'; see also Kevin Leighton, 'The scandal of inequality in Latin America and the Caribbean' (Christian Aid, 2012).

9 Daniel Martínez Cué, Walter Menéndez and Sandra Cesilini, 'Situación Socioeconómica de La Población Afrodescendiente Del Uruguay' (Panamá: United Nations Development Programme, 2013), p. 40.

10 Jhon Antón Sánchez, 'Implementación de Los Pactos Y Los Convenios Internacionales Relacionados Con Los Derechos Civiles, Culturales, Económicos, Políticos Y Sociales de La Población Afrodescendiente de Colombia, Ecuador, Perú Y Venezuela' (Panamá: United Nations Development Programme, 2010), p. 133.

11 Comisión Intersectorial para el Avance de la Población Afrocolombiana (Panamá: United Nations Development Programme, 2009).

12 Margarita Sánchez and Maurice Bryan, 'Macro study: Afro-descendants, discrimination and economic exclusion in Latin America' (London: Minority Rights Group International, 2003).

eliminate racism and discrimination in all its forms. Despite this, for a long time the issues of racism and racial discrimination were largely denied or ignored in many countries, with a lack of legislation and policy to recognise the particular situations of Afro-descendants.

The invisibility of racism and racial discrimination must be understood in historical context. Following independence and during processes of nation building, many new governments promoted *mestizo* national identities which, while seemingly celebrating the countries' rich racial mixing, also served to assimilate and subjugate both indigenous and Afro-descendant peoples, cultures and languages.[13] The histories, cultures and contributions that Afro-descendants had made to the development of their nations were rendered 'invisible' in the national stories.[14] By the mid-twentieth century, influenced largely by the ideals of Brazilian writer Gilberto Freyre in his book *The Masters and the Slaves*,[15] many countries adopted images of 'racial democracy', claiming that in contrast to the Jim Crow segregation laws of the Southern states of the United States, Latin American countries were characterised by racial mixing and harmony, where racism and racial inequality simply did not exist.[16]

The racial democracy discourse served to deny the existence of racism, concealing racist structural practices, attributing disparities to class inequalities, and further creating obstacles to both the development of Afro-descendant identities and their claims for racial justice.[17]

---

13 See among others Nina S. De Friedemann and Jaime Arocha, 'Colombia', in Pedro Pérez Sarduy and Jean Stubbs (eds), *No Longer Invisible: Afro-Latin Americans Today* (London: Minority Rights Group International, 1995), pp. 47–76; P. Wade, *Race and Ethnicity in Latin America* (London and Chicago: Pluto Press, 1997); George Reid Andrews, *Afro-Latin America, 1800–2000* (Oxford: Oxford University Press, 2004); Telles, *Race in Another America*; and M'Baré N'gome, 'Inclusión, interculturalidad y etnoeducación en el Perú y en América latina', in Centro de Desarrollo Étnico, *Desde Adentro: Etnoeducación E Interculturalidad En El Perú Y América Latina* (Lima: Centro de Desarrollo Étnico – CEDET, 2011), pp. 315–24.

14 See further Sarduy and Stubbs, *No Longer Invisible*.

15 Gilberto Freyre, *The Masters and the Slaves* (New York: Knopf, 1946), first published in 1933 as *Casa Grande & Senzala*.

16 See Telles, *Race in Another America*, and Gates Jr., *Black in Latin America*.

17 See Carlos Hasenbalg, 'Racial inequalities in Brazil and throughout Latin America: Timid responses to disguised racism', in Elizabeth Jelin and Eric Hersheberg (eds), *Constructing Democracy: Human Rights, Citizenship, and Society in Latin America* (Boulder: Westview Press, 1996), pp. 161–76; Helen Safa, 'Race and national identity in the Americas', *Latin American Perspectives*, 25:3 (1998), 3–12; Jesus Maria Herrera Salas, 'Ethnicity and revolution: The political economic of racism in Venezuela', *Latin America Perspectives*, 32(2) (2005), 72–91; Rachel Reichmann, *Race in Contemporary Brazil: From Indifference to Inequality* (Philadelphia: Pennsylvania State University Press, 1999); Judith Morrison, 'Social movements in Latin America: The power of regional and national networks', in

A large body of academic research has since demonstrated that this idea of racial democracy is a 'myth', pointing to the very real existence of racial inequalities and racial discrimination.[18]

Towards the end of the 1980s and beginning of the 1990s many countries in Latin America underwent multicultural citizenship reforms, adopting new constitutions which recognised for the first time the multicultural and pluri-cultural nature of their societies.[19] Largely influenced by ILO Convention 169 on the Rights of Indigenous and Tribal Peoples (1989), the constitutions enshrined provisions for non-discrimination, respect for cultural diversity, and collective rights around justice, land, education, languages, culture, and political participation for indigenous peoples and in some cases Afro-descendants.[20]

However, as Hooker demonstrates, of the fifteen States that underwent multicultural citizenship reforms only six included provisions for Afro-descendants, and in most cases these rights were much more limited in scope than those provided for indigenous peoples.[21] Further, those Afro-descendant communities that have been successful in gaining visibility and rights recognition are those whose situations resemble more closely those of indigenous 'autochthonous' peoples and possess distinct cultures, languages and traditions, and have been able to frame their struggles within the existing indigenous rights framework.[22]

For example, some Afro-descendant *Garífuna* communities in Central America, *Quilombola* communities in Brazil, and rural Afro-descendant communities in Colombia have made claims around land, cultural identity and language rights.[23] In the context of the myth of

---

Kwame Dixon and John Burdick (eds), *Comparative Perspectives on Afro-Latin America* (Gainesville: University Press of Florida, 2012), pp. 243–63.

18 See for example Robert J. Cottrol, 'The long, lingering shadow: Law, liberalism, and cultures of hierarchy and identity in the Americas', *Tulane Law Review*, 76 (2001), 11–80; Juliet Hooker, 'Indigenous inclusion, black exclusion: Race, ethnicity and multicultural citizenship in Latin America', *Journal of Latin American Studies*, 37:2 (2005), 285–310; Elisabeth Cunin (ed.), *Mestizaje, Diferencia Y Nación: Lo 'negro' En América Central Y El Caribe* (Mexico: Instituto Nacional de Antropología e Historia, 2010); and Edward Telles, *Pigmentocracies: Ethnicity, Race, and Color in Latin America* (Chapel Hill: University of North Carolina Press, 2014).

19 See for example the Constitutions of Colombia (1991) and Ecuador (1998, reformed in 2008).

20 See Rachel Sieder, *Multiculturalism in Latin America: Indigenous Rights, Diversity and Democracy* (Basingstoke: Palgrave Macmillan, 2002).

21 Hooker, 'Indigenous inclusion, black exclusion'. Brazil, Colombia, Ecuador, Guatemala, Honduras and Nicaragua extend (some) collective rights to their Afro-descendant populations.

22 *Ibid.*

23 Eva Thorne, 'Land rights and Garifuna identity', *North American Congress on Latin America*, 38:2 (2004), 21–5; Mark Anderson, 'When Afro becomes (like)

racial democracy, it was much harder to secure concrete steps and commitments to address racism and racial discrimination, thus further perpetuating the exclusion and invisibility of Afro-descendants and their particular human rights issues.

It can be argued to a certain extent that the invisibility at the domestic and regional level of Afro-descendants and of the particular racial discrimination they face, reflected a similar invisibility within the international human rights system. While there has long been a wide framework on indigenous rights it was not until the beginning of the twenty-first century that a specific set of rights responding to the situations and needs of people of African descent began to emerge.

An emerging international framework for Afro-descendants

Afro-descendants may be considered as a relatively new group in terms of human rights protections. Since the foundation of the United Nations Human Rights system an increasing number of group-specific rights instruments and mechanisms have emerged. These include for example the Convention relating to the Status of Refugees (1951), ILO Convention 107 on Indigenous and Tribal Populations (1957), the Convention on the Elimination of all Forms of Discrimination against Women (1979), ILO Convention 169 on Indigenous and Tribal Peoples Convention (1989), the UN Convention on the Rights of the Child (1989), International Convention on the Protection of the Rights of All Migrant Workers and Members of their Families (1990) and the Declaration on the Rights of Persons Belonging to National or Ethnic, Religious and Linguistic Minorities (1992), as well as other mechanisms such as Special Rapporteurs, Working Groups and Permanent Forums.

Many of these instruments and mechanisms may be relevant for Afro-descendants, particularly taking into account the compound and intersecting forms of discrimination that women, children and migrants of African descent, for example, may face. Indeed people of African descent who are more recent migrants, particularly in Europe and North America, may have certain rights as migrant workers or as refugees. However, those Afro-descendants whose ancestors were trafficked to the Americas during the transatlantic slave trade, particularly in Latin America, occupied a rather ambiguous space somewhere between the indigenous rights and minority rights frameworks. As mentioned above, while rural traditional communities may be considered as indigenous or 'tribal peoples' under ILO Convention 169,

indigenous: Garifuna and Afro-indigenous politics in Honduras', *Journal of Latin America and Caribbean Anthropology*, 12:2 (2007), 384–413.

many Afro-descendant communities who live in urban contexts, or who do not maintain traditional languages and cultural practices, may not meet such criteria. Further, in the context of *mestizaje*, the term minorities has rarely been employed in Latin America.

Thus, until the end of the twentieth century, there was a glaring gap for specific protections recognising the particular histories and experiences of Afro-descendants. However, this changed during the process of the Third World Conference on Racism (WCAR) held in Durban in 2001. The Durban Conference is seen as the main catalyst to the emergence of a framework focusing on the rights of Afro-descendants, contributing to both their greater visibility and protection.[24]

During the regional preparatory Conference for Durban, held in Santiago de Chile in 2000, Afro-descendant civil society organisations from all over the region raised issues and made demands of their governments concerning the rights of their communities. This was to some extent the first opportunity for many such organisations to be able explicitly to address issues of racism and racial discrimination with their governments.[25] The outcome document of the conference, the Santiago Declaration, made a series of demands around the economic, social, cultural, civil and political rights of Afro-descendants which were taken to Durban the following year.

The final outcome document of the Durban Conference, the Durban Declaration and Programme of Action (DDPA), contained several paragraphs recognising the specific situations and histories of people of African descent and calling upon states to take specific steps to realise their rights.[26] The Conference also led to the creation of the UN Working Group of Experts on People of African Descent (WGPAD), mandated to investigate the problems of racial discrimination facing people of African descent around the world, and make thematic and country specific recommendations to States.[27]

During the Durban Review Conference, held in 2009, CERD proposed the adoption of an international decade on people of African

24 See Michael J. Turner, 'The road to Durban – and back', *NACLA Report on the Americas*, 35:6 (2002), 31–5; Mala Htun, 'From racial democracy to affirmative action: Changing state policy on race in Brazil', *Latin American Research Review*, 39:1 (2004), 60–89; Corinne Lennox, 'Reviewing Durban: Examining the outputs and review of the 2001 World Conference against Racism', *Netherlands Quarterly of Human Rights*, 27:2 (2009), 209–13.

25 Lennox, 'Reviewing Durban'.

26 These include paragraphs 13–14; 32–35; and 103 of the Declaration, and paragraphs 4–14 of the Programme of Action.

27 Originally mandated through Commission on Human Rights (CHR) Resolution (Res) 2002/68, and later renewed through CHR Res 2003/30, Human Rights Council (HRC) Res 9/14, HRC Res 18/28 and HRC Res 27/25.

descent. This initiative, led by the Colombian expert member of the Committee, was later presented by the State of Colombia to the General Assembly, leading first to the proclamation of 2011 as the International Year for People of African Descent (GA Res 64/69), and later to the International Decade, 2015–24 (GA Res 68/237).

The international year aimed to raise awareness of the situations of people of African descent and to increase their participation in all economic, social and political life, with a theme of 'recognition, justice and development'. It is in the context of the International Year for People of African Descent that CERD drafted and adopted its General Recommendation 34 on racial discrimination against people of African descent, which will be discussed in detail below.

In December 2013 the UN General Assembly proclaimed the International Decade for People of African Descent with the continued theme of 'People of African descent: recognition, justice and development'.[28] The programme of activities for the Decade, adopted in November 2014, calls upon States to strengthen national, regional, and international action and cooperation for the rights of people of African descent, to promote a greater knowledge of and respect for their cultures and contributions to development, and to strengthen legislation and policy.[29]

Despite the fact that these important processes began during the Durban and Santiago Conferences, Afro-descendants had nevertheless been on the radar of CERD for a much longer period.

CERD observations and recommendations concerning Afro-descendants

CERD is without doubt the most notable mechanism in terms of the recognition of Afro-descendants within the international sphere. For a number of decades CERD has issued observations and recommendations to States parties, during the consideration of periodic reports, which have resulted in greater visibility of Afro-descendants, and of the challenges facing both States and the international community.

CERD has been performing the task of catalysing current and potential tensions by periodically promoting a kind of *intercultural dialogue* within the States that it examines. This dialogue, concerning States' level of compliance with ICERD, has especially focussed on the situations of their ethnic/racial groups, including Afro-descendants.

For example, during its thirty-fourth session in 1987 CERD asked the State of Brazil to clarify whether it viewed Afro-Brazilians as a

28 UN Doc. A/RES/68/237.
29 UN Doc. A/RES/69/16.

'separate ethnic group', thus drawing early attention to the issue of the identification of Afro-descendant communities in the region.[30] In its Concluding Observations to Brazil in the forty-ninth session in 1996, it requested the state to provide indicators on the social difficulties encountered by Afro-Brazilians and raised issues of state violence and land rights.[31]

In the case of Peru, a country where the Afro-descendant population was particularly invisible at the national level,[32] CERD has increasingly encouraged the State to pay greater attention to the situation of this population in its reporting. In Concluding Observations to the forty-sixth session in 1995, CERD requested information on measures taken to address the discrimination, poverty and social prejudice affecting the 'black minority of Peru'.[33] In the session in 1999 it raised particular issues of concern including socio-economic underdevelopment, racial discrimination in employment and access to education, requesting the State to include more information in its next report.[34]

More recently, CERD's eighty-seventh session in August 2015 included the examination of two countries in Latin America where the issue of Afro-descendants has been at the centre of recent public debate. In Colombia, where Afro-descendants are one of the principle victims of the internal armed conflict, on 3 August 2015, just as CERD's examination began, news was received of the assassination of Afro-Colombian community leader and human rights defender Genaro García. Responsibility for this assassination would later be recognised by the FARC guerrilla group, creating tensions for the ongoing negotiations with the Government at the peace negotiation table in Havana, Cuba.

The issue of violence against Afro-descendant leaders in Colombia has been a concern of CERD for some time. In Concluding Observations from its seventy-fifth session in 2009 CERD expressed concern over threats and killings of Afro-descendant and indigenous leaders and recommended the State to strengthen protection mechanisms.[35] During the eighty-seventh session it reiterated its alarm at the situation of violence against community leaders, with specific mention

30 UN Doc. A/42/18, para. 556.
31 CERD, 'Concluding Observations: Brazil', UN Doc. CERD/C/304/Add.11 (1996), paras. 19–20.
32 See further N'gome, 'Inclusión, interculturalidad y etnoeducación en el Perú y en América latina'.
33 CERD, 'Concluding Observations: Peru', UN Doc. A/50/18 (1995), para. 183.
34 CERD, 'Concluding Observations: Peru', UN Doc. CERD/C/304/Add.69 (1999), paras. 12, 20, 23.
35 CERD, 'Concluding Observations: Colombia', UN Doc. CERD/C/COL/CO/14 (2009), para. 15.

of the assassination of Genaro García and again recommending strengthening mechanisms for protection.[36]

In Costa Rica during May and June 2015 there was great turmoil due to the revival of a polemic debate around the obligatory use in schools of the children's book *Cocorí*, in which the main character, an Afro-descendant boy, is associated with a chimpanzee. Responding to this current situation, CERD expressed concern at the use of such texts in schools and recommended that the State take measures within the education system to ensure that all texts with racist connotations are removed from obligatory reading lists.[37]

CERD's concern over Afro-descendants and people of African descent goes beyond the region of Latin America. In the last year, ICERD has been challenged by a series of incidents occurring in the United States as well as hate speech against migrants from African, Asia and the Middle East, particularly in Europe. For example, there have been growing racial tensions in the Netherlands following complaints from members of the African descent community about the Christmas tradition 'Black Pete', which depicts a stereotyped African character as Santa Claus's helper, and is seen as a reference to slavery. In 2013 around 3,600 racist incidents against people of African descent were reported, and more than two million people took to social media, many expressing insults against people of African descent. CERD also closely follows the growth of the practice of racial profiling and hate speech against Afro-descendants, including migrants, stressing the importance of implementing its General Recommendation 35 on combating racist hate speech. In addition there is growing attention to the issue of racism within football of which Afro-descendants are the principle victims.

Fundamental to the monitoring of ICERD is the participation of civil society actors who draw important attention to issues of concern in their countries. Afro-descendant organisations are increasingly expressing themselves through shadow reports and attending the informal civil society dialogue sessions with CERD prior to the examination of State party reports. For example, during the eighty-seventh session, Afro-descendant organisations from Colombia, such as PCN[38] and

36 CERD, 'Concluding Observations: Colombia', UN Doc. CERD/C/COL/CO/15–16 (2015), paras. 27–8.

37 CERD, 'Concluding Observations: Costa Rica', UN Doc. CERD/C/CRI/CO/19–22 (2015), para. 15.

38 See Proceso de Comunidades Negras (PCN), La Conferencia Nacional de Organizaciones Afrocolombianas (CNOA), Movimiento Nacional Cimarrón (MNC), Asociación Casa Cultural El Chontaduro and International Institute on Race, Equality and Human Rights, 'Informe alternativo para el Examen de

ACONC[39] among others, and from Costa Rica such as ADMNC,[40] presented reports highlighting the issues mentioned above.

CERD now addresses the issue of Afro-descendants systematically when examining States parties. The principle areas of interest and concern include: *the demand for statistical information; the criminalisation of racism; the adoption of affirmative action measures; and most recently, the adoption of measures to combat structural discrimination.*

The demand for statistical information about the Afro-descendant population is perhaps the issue which has been most emphasised by CERD. The requirement of disaggregated statistical information on ethnic/racial groups is provided in the guidelines for reporting to CERD, and CERD in turn systematically makes observations and recommendations concerning this issue. For example in the recommendations issued during the penultimate examination of Venezuela, CERD states that it:

> notes with concern that the State party does not have disaggregated statistical data on the Afro-descendants. The Committee recalls that such information is necessary for evaluating the implementation of the Convention and for monitoring policies that affect minorities. The Committee recommends that the State party include in its next periodic report disaggregated statistical data on Afro-descendants, which would make it possible to evaluate their situation more accurately.[41]

Colombia de los 15° y 16° informes periódicos (UN Doc. CERD/C/COL/15–16) sobre su cumplimiento con la Convención Internacional sobre la Eliminación de todas las Formas de Discriminación Racial: Colombia: el flagrante incumplimiento y sistemática violación de ICERD' (2015), available at: http://tbinternet.ohchr.org/Treaties/CERD/Shared%20Documents/COL/INT_CERD_NGO_COL_21183_S.pdf.

39 Association of Community Councils in the North of Cauca (ACONC), Franciscan Family of Colombia, Franciscans International, 'Alternative Report for the Review of Colombia 15th and 16th periodic reports (UN Doc. CERD/C/COL/15–16) on its compliance with the International Convention on the Elimination of All Forms of Racial Discrimination: Structural Discrimination in Colombia: Differential Impact of Mining on the Rights of Afro-descendant people' (2015), available at: http://tbinternet.ohchr.org/_layouts/treatybodyexternal/Download.aspx?symbolno=INT%2fCERD%2fNGO%2fCOL%2f21105&Lang=en.

40 Asociación para el Desarrollo de las Mujeres Negras Costarricenses (ADMNC), Red Nacional de Juventud Afrocostarricense, 'Informe alternativo sobre la implementación de la convención internacional sobre la eliminación de todas las formas de discriminación racial en Costa Rica: Informe alternativo al informe del estado consolidado de los periodos 19, 20, 21 and 22' (2015), available at: http://tbinternet.ohchr.org/Treaties/CERD/Shared%20Documents/CRI/INT_CERD_NGO_CRI_21035_S.pdf.

41 CERD, 'Concluding Observations: Venezuela', UN Doc. CERD/C/VEN/CO/18 (2007), para. 14.

The issue of statistical data is also one in which we can observe the greatest responsiveness from States, in particular in Latin America. Indeed, in response to the repeated recommendations by CERD as well as demands from civil society, a growing number of countries are now incorporating the variable black/Afro-descendant in their national population censuses, and in other instruments for statistical information.[42]

The administration of criminal justice is another area in which CERD has often made requests of States parties. Under Article 4 of ICERD, and reiterated in General Recommendation 31 on the prevention of racial discrimination in the administration and functioning of the criminal justice system, States parties are obliged to prosecute all racist acts referred to in the provision, through criminal law. In particular this includes the spreading of ideas based on racial superiority or hate, incitement to racial hatred, violence or incitement to racial violence, racist propaganda and activities by racist organisations. Further, it encourages States parties to include racial motivation as a general aggravating circumstance in offences in their criminal law.

This is another of the areas in which the majority of States, including many in Latin America, have demonstrated commitment to CERD, although there are still challenges in terms of effective implementation. The concerns of the Committee refer to the need for legislation that is in harmony with the provisions of Article 4 of ICERD and the recommendations of CERD.

In Concluding Observations to Bolivia in 2003, CERD:

> notes with concern the lack of legislative provisions punishing the dissemination of ideas based on racial superiority or hatred, as well as acts of violence or incitement to violence and the organizations promoting racial discrimination, as required under article 4 of the Convention. In this regard, the Committee reiterates its previous recommendation urging the State party to fulfil its obligation to make all forms of racial discrimination, as specified in article 4 of the Convention, punishable by law.[43]

In 2010, Boliva adopted Law No. 45: The Law against racism and all forms of discrimination. This law aims to establish mechanisms and

42 UNDP, 'Visibilidad Estadística', p. 11. In the 2000s Brazil, Colombia, Costa Rica, Ecuador, El Salvador, Guatemala, Honduras and Nicaragua all included questions in their census which would allow people to identify as being of African descent. In the census round starting in 2010, Argentina, Panama, Uruguay and Venezuela included similar questions. Further, Bolivia, Brazil, Colombia, Ecuador, Guatemala, Honduras, Nicaragua, Peru and Uruguay have included questions on racial/ethnic identity in national household surveys.

43 CERD, 'Concluding Observations: Bolivia', UN Doc. CERD/C/63/CO/2 (2003), para. 12.

procedures for the prevention, sanction and elimination of racist acts and all forms of discrimination, including a national committee, and to strengthen public policy for protection and prevention of crimes of racism and all forms of discrimination.

In 2014 the State of Mexico strengthened its criminal law against racism and racial discrimination by introducing amendments to the Federal Law against Discrimination, adopted in 2003. In line with concerns and recommendations expressed by CERD in 2012[44] the law now includes racial discrimination within its definition of discrimination. The amendments also sanction new forms of racism and racial discrimination, including those that manifest in the area of sports. Likewise, in 2011 Colombia adopted Law 1482 which penalises racism and racial discrimination, and Venezuela adopted the Organic Law against racial discrimination.

All of these advances can be seen as the result of a number of influences and processes including the tireless campaigning, organising and advocacy of Afro-descendant civil society in their respective countries and internationally, the growing visibility of Afro-descendants and of the issue of racism and racial discrimination, and the ever strengthening normative framework and mechanisms at the international and regional levels, including ICERD. In 2011, ICERD strengthened its focus on Afro-descendants further still.

CERD General Recommendation 34: foundations for an International Declaration on the Rights of People of African Descent

CERD General Recommendation 34 (GR 34) on racism and racial discrimination against people of African descent represents a significant advance along the road towards *recognition, justice and development* for Afro-descendants. It situates the rights of Afro-descendants in the sphere of international human rights law, and paves the way towards their full recognition as subjects of international law, understood in its wider sense. GR 34 recognises that, as for indigenous peoples, collective rights are attributable to Afro-descendants and that ILO Convention 169 on Indigenous and Tribal Peoples is applicable to them.

It also recognises that the racial discrimination that affects Afro-descendants is structural in character (para. 5) and that therefore it should be combated through special measures or affirmative action (para. 7). Finally GR 34 understands the intersectional nature of discrimination and makes clear the need to adopt specific

44 CERD, 'Concluding Observations: Mexico', UN Doc. CERD/C/MEX/CO/16–17 (2012), para. 11.

measures in favour of the most vulnerable groups within the Afro-descendant population including women (paras. 22–4) and children (paras. 25–6).

In line with CERD practice, the adoption of GR 34 was preceded by a thematic debate which included the participation of delegates from the States parties to ICERD, specialised agencies, bodies and human rights mechanisms of the UN, national human rights institutions, intergovernmental and non-governmental organisations, academic institutions and other relevant organisations and interested individuals.

GR 34 provides for the following collective rights that should be recognised for Afro-descendants:

a) The right to property and to the use, conservation and protection of lands traditionally occupied by them and to natural resources in cases where their ways of life and culture are linked to their utilization of lands and resources;
b) The right to their cultural identity, to keep, maintain and foster their mode of life and forms of organization, culture, languages and religious expressions;
c) The right to the protection of their traditional knowledge and their cultural and artistic heritage;
d) The right to prior consultation with respect to decisions which may affect their rights, in accordance with international standards. (Para. 4)

Further, GR 34 recognises that Afro-descendants are victims of structural racism and discrimination as a consequence of slavery, and it provides indicators for identifying the existence of racism within states. These indicators include:

> their grouping, together with indigenous peoples, among the poorest of the poor; their low rate of participation and representation in political and institutional decision-making processes; additional difficulties they face in access to and completion and quality of education, which results in the transmission of poverty from generation to generation; inequality in access to the labour market; limited social recognition and valuation of their ethnic and cultural diversity; and a disproportionate presence in prison populations. (Para. 6)

The recognition of the structural character of discrimination against Afro-descendants is now a constant element within the Concluding Observations of CERD, and in dialogue with the delegations of the States parties, especially those from Latin America. In order to combat structural discrimination CERD recommends the adoption of special measures or affirmative action as provided for in ICERD (Articles 1.4

and 2.2), CERD General Recommendation 32 on the meaning and scope of special measures, and GR 34 (para. 7).

With these and other legally relevant contributions, GR 34 has opened the door to the possibility of an International Declaration on the Rights of Afro-descendants. The Committee proposed this in a 2012 Declaration entitled *Contributions for the Plan of Action for the Decade on People of African Descent*, presented to the WGPAD during its eleventh session.[45] This proposal for a Declaration on the Rights of People of African descent was included in the Draft Programme of Action on the Decade[46] and was later welcomed by the UNGA in its Resolution 69/16 of 2014 on the Programme of Activities for the Decade.[47]

CERD maintains an active relationship with other specialised bodies and agencies of the United Nations. The Declaration on contributions to the decade mentioned above, aimed to increase the effectiveness of ICERD, calling for both a Declaration and a World Summit on people of African descent among other action points. An expert member of CERD regularly attends the sessions with the WGPAD, through which it is able to promote these and other initiatives, which are also transmitted to the General Assembly. All of the Concluding Observations to States parties now contain a standard paragraph on the Decade, in which CERD asks States to adopt a national action plan for Afro-descendants and requests periodic information on the progress in the implementation of the Decade.

Conclusions

The historic invisibility of the rights of people of African descent in the international human rights normative framework has been directly proportional to the space that issues relevant to Afro-descendants have occupied in the interior of their countries in Latin America. However, ICERD has been at the centre of the legal framework which is increasingly invoked in the journey towards recognition, justice and development of Afro-descendants. From its earliest Concluding Observations and Recommendations pushing States parties to begin to examine and report on the situations of their Afro-descendant populations, to the adoption of GR 34 to strengthen the meaning and scope of the ICERD, and advocacy by individual CERD members for the International Decade and a Declaration on people of African descent,

45 See UN Doc. A/HRC/21/60, para. 29
46 UN Doc. A/HRC/21/60/Add.2, para. 28(f).
47 UN Doc. A/RES/69/16, para. 29(h).

CERD has been fundamental to the growing visibility and inclusion of this population at both international and domestic levels.

It is now up to the Afro-descendant social movement to continue the journey mapped out by CERD and the Durban process. Afro-descendants must help integrate their aspirations into the expanding international legal framework, just as has happened with other social collectives that have achieved a certain level of recognition, such as women and indigenous peoples. The possibility of the adoption of an International Declaration on the Rights of People of African Descent depends on this. CERD General Recommendation 34 represents a good starting point in this perspective, as it covers many of the relevant rights for Afro-descendants.

Part III
Conflict and resolution

Chapter 8

Genocide and the ICERD

William Schabas

Although there is no reference to genocide in the International Convention on the Elimination of All Forms of Racial Discrimination (ICERD/the Convention), the Committee on the Elimination of All Forms of Racial Discrimination (CERD/the Committee) has shown a special interest in the subject. Ironically, CERD examined the periodic report of Rwanda in March 1994, only a few weeks before the outbreak of the worst episode of genocide since the adoption of the Convention on the Prevention and Punishment of the Crime of Genocide in 1948. On 17 March 1994, CERD adopted Concluding Observations that addressed problems of impunity with respect to ethnic violence in the country, requesting that Rwanda provide further information by the end of June 1994.[1] Alas, there was no such follow-up. By the end of June 1994, hundreds of thousands of Tutsi had perished. In mid-August 1994, CERD adopted a Decision '[e]xpressing its deep concern and grave alarm over the tragic loss of life of genocidal dimensions in Rwanda'.[2]

Reporting to the Secretary General of the United Nations, CERD explained that in reviewing Rwanda's periodic report, it had taken note of the findings of a Commission composed of non-governmental organisations published in early 1993 that had warned of genocide. 'Subsequent events have proved the accuracy of that report's diagnosis of the threats to peace in Rwanda', said the Committee. It added that the Commission's recommendations were 'well judged, but they received too little support from the international community – with

1 CERD, 'Concluding Observations: Rwanda', UN Doc. A/49/18 (1994), paras. 61–71.

2 CERD, Decision 1 (45), 'The human rights situation in Rwanda', UN Doc. A/49/18 (1994), Annex III.

results that have been only too tragic'. CERD said that procedures for early warning and urgent action 'desperately need improvement'.[3]

Declaration on the Prevention of Genocide

CERD returned to the subject in 2005. Following a thematic dialogue on the subject of genocide with NGOs and other relevant actors within the United Nations and other international organisations, including the Special Adviser on Genocide, on 11 March 2005 CERD adopted a Declaration on the Prevention of Genocide.[4] The document was directly inspired by proposals in the Secretary General's presentation at the Stockholm International Forum in January 2004.[5] The Preamble to the Declaration noted that 'genocide is often facilitated and supported by discriminatory laws and practices or lack of effective enforcement of the principle of equality of persons'. It said that 'the international community had failed to prevent the genocides in Rwanda and Srebrenica because of lack of will'. The Declaration placed strong emphasis on the use of force to prevent genocide, and the responsibility of developed countries to contribute to peace operations in order to facilitate rapid deployment. At the same time as it adopted the Declaration, CERD considered the specific case of Darfur. Summary records of the Committee suggest it was divided about the legal description of the atrocities.[6] Its decision on Darfur, adopted only weeks after presentation of the report of the United Nations Commission of Inquiry commissioned by the Security Council,[7] spoke of 'war crimes, crimes against humanity and the risk of genocide'.[8]

Following the Declaration, CERD prepared a list of indicators relevant to the prevention of genocide, although it entitled them 'indicators of patterns of systematic and massive racial discrimination'. These include: lack of a legislative framework and institutions to prevent racial discrimination; systematic official denial of the existence of particular distinct groups; systematic exclusion – in law or in fact – of

3 Letter of transmittal, Report of the Committee on the Elimination of Racial Discrimination, Forty-ninth Session, UN Doc. A/49/18 (1994), p. vii.

4 CERD, 'Declaration on the Prevention of Genocide', UN Doc. CERD/C/66/1 (1995); also UN Doc. A/60/18 (2005), para. 459. For the debates, see: UN Doc. CERD/C/SR.1700/Add.1 (2005); UN Doc. CERD/C/SR.1701 (2005).

5 UN Doc. CERD/C/SR.1700/Add.1, para. 1.

6 E.g. UN Doc. CERD/C/SR.1701, paras. 18–40; UN Doc. CERD/C/SR.1714 (2005), paras. 31–46.

7 Report of the International Commission of Inquiry on Violations of International Humanitarian Law and Human Rights Law in Darfur, UN Doc. S/2005/60 (2005).

8 CERD, Decision 2 (66), Situation in Darfur, UN Doc. CERD/C/DEC/SDN/1 (2005).

groups from positions of power, employment in State institutions and key professions; compulsory identification against the will of members of particular groups, including the use of identity cards indicating ethnicity; grossly biased versions of historical events in school textbooks and other educational materials as well as celebration of historical events that exacerbate tensions between groups and peoples. Many of the factors feature in all discussions about racial discrimination. To an extent, one or more of them is present in most countries. CERD cautioned that 'as these indicators may be present in States not moving towards violence or genocide, the assessment of their significance for the purpose of predicting genocide or violence against identifiable racial, ethnic or religious groups should be supplemented' by consideration of other indicators, including a prior history of genocide or violence against a group, a policy or practice of impunity, and the 'existence of proactive communities abroad fostering extremism and/or providing arms'.[9]

However, since that flurry of activity, CERD has not devoted much attention to issues that concern genocide specifically. In 2007, it adopted new Guidelines for the Early Warning and Urgent Action Procedure in which it takes note of the earlier work of the Committee on genocide prevention.[10] It also refers to the Declaration and Decision on Follow-up in a General Recommendation on the Durban Review Conference.[11] In 2013, CERD issued General Recommendation (GR) 35 entitled 'Combating racist hate speech'. It mentions genocide in four places, but generally as part of an enumeration including terms like 'human rights' and 'crimes against humanity'.[12] In one paragraph, the Recommendation states: 'Discourses which in one context are innocuous or neutral may take on a dangerous significance in another: in its indicators on genocide the Committee emphasized the relevance of locality in appraising the meaning and potential effects of racist hate speech.'[13]

Exceptionally, in August 2014 CERD invoked its early warning and urgent action procedures as well as its Declaration on Genocide, issuing a Decision with respect to activities of 'Islamic State' in Iraq that

---

9 CERD, 'Decision on Follow-up to the Declaration on the Prevention of Genocide: Indicators of Patterns of Systematic and Massive Racial Discrimination', UN Doc. CERD/C/67/1 (2005); UN Doc. A/60/18, para. 20.

10 CERD, 'Guidelines for the Early Warning and Urgent Action Procedure', UN Doc. A/62/18 (2007), Annex III, para. 10.

11 CERD, 'General Recommendation 33 on Follow-up to the Durban Review Conference', UN Doc. CERD/C/GC/33 (2009), Preamble para. 7.

12 CERD, 'General Recommendation 35 on Combating racist hate speech', UN Doc. CERD/C/GC/35 (2013)', paras. 3, 6, 14.

13 *Ibid.*, para. 15.

included the following paragraph: 'Deeply concerned by the mass killings, the ethnic cleansing, the massive forced displacement of populations, the violence against women and children and the other crimes against humanity, which constitute blatant violations of the ICERD and increase the risk of genocide…'[14]

Obviously, the promise of much greater attention to genocide by CERD, that seemed to emerge in 2005, has not been borne out. One explanation may be that responsibility for genocide-related issues within the UN system as a whole has been taken up by the Special Adviser to the Secretary General on the Prevention of Genocide.

Defining genocide and racial discrimination

The relationship between racial discrimination, which is at the heart of CERD's mandate, and genocide, defined in the 1948 Convention on the Prevention and Punishment of the Crime of Genocide as the intentional destruction of a national, ethnical, racial or religious group, may seem so obvious as to deserve no further comment or examination. Yet the debate continues, in case law, at the political level, and in the academy, about whether the objective in preventing genocide is to protect racial groups and their cognates from what Theo van Boven has described as the 'ultimate and most evil corollary of racial and religious discrimination'.[15]

Before proceeding, a comment on terminology is required. Article 2 of the 1948 Genocide Convention refers to 'national, ethnical, racial or religious' groups. It is remarkably similar to the definition of 'racial discrimination' in Article 1(1) of ICERD: 'based on race, colour, descent, or national or ethnic origin'. The Genocide Convention includes 'religious' groups whereas the term is not used in ICERD. Probably the drafters of the Genocide Convention understood the notion of 'religious group' to overlap with the other three categories. It also seems likely that religious groups were not included in ICERD because at the time a separate convention on religious discrimination was contemplated. For the purposes of this chapter, it is assumed that the meaning of the term 'racial' in Article 2 of the Genocide Convention and Article 1(1) of ICERD is very similar if not entirely identical.

The word 'genocide', as conceived by Raphael Lemkin in 1944, was clearly directed at 'racial groups' as this term is later understood

14 CERD, Decision 1 (85), 'Prevention of Racial Discrimination, Including Early Warning and Urgent Action Procedures', 2313th meeting (2014).

15 Theo van Boven, 'Racial and religious discrimination', in Rüdiger Wolfrum (ed.), *The Max Planck Encyclopedia of Public International Law*, Vol. VIII (Oxford: Oxford University Press, 2012), pp. 608–17, at p. 609.

in the 1948 Genocide Convention and the 1965 Convention on Racial Discrimination. Lemkin saw his proposal as an attempt to reinforce the legal regime of protection of national minorities that had emerged in the treaties and declarations adopted following the First World War.[16] The chapter in his book *Axis Rule in Occupied Europe* where the term 'genocide' made its debut referred to 'political' genocide and 'economic' genocide, but by that Lemkin meant the attempted destruction of a racial (or national, ethnic or religious) group by means of destroying the political and economic institutions of the group.[17]

In 1946, largely due to the personal campaign of Raphael Lemkin, the UN General Assembly adopted a resolution recognising genocide as a crime in international law.[18] Lemkin's initial draft,[19] presented to the Assembly by Cuba, Panama and India, referred to 'national, racial, ethnical or religious groups'.[20] There was a substantial debate in the Sixth Committee of the General Assembly but without any suggestion that the enumeration of groups be amended. A subcommittee was assigned to finalise the drafting of the resolution. Then there was a mysterious change, whereby the final text of the Resolution referred to 'racial, religious, political and other groups' and to a crime 'committed on religious, racial, political or any other grounds'. Nothing in the official records of the Sixth Committee or the General Assembly sheds any light on the origin of this change, the reasons for it, or the identity of the government or governments who were responsible. A biographer of Lemkin suggests it was 'an intervention "by the British delegation at a very late hour of a tiresome genocide meeting in Lake Success"' although the origin of the reference is unclear.[21]

Two years later, the reference to 'political' was removed in the Convention whose preparation was mandated by the 1946 General Assembly Resolution. The debates are part of the public record although they have been somewhat misrepresented in some of the academic accounts. The Soviet Union opposed the inclusion of political groups, as all of the writers point out, but it was hardly alone in

16 *Prosecutor* v. *Krstić* (IT-98–33-T), Judgment, 2 August 2001, paras. 554–60.
17 Raphael Lemkin, *Axis Rule in Occupied Europe* (New York: Carnegie Endowment for World Peace, 1944), pp. 79–97.
18 The Crime of Genocide, GA res. 96(I).
19 Donna-Lee Frieze (ed.), *Totally Unofficial: The Autobiography of Raphael Lemkin* (New Haven and London: Yale University Press, 2013), pp. 118–32.
20 Draft resolution relating to the crime of genocide, proposed by the delegations of Cuba, India and Panama, UN Doc. A/BUR/50.
21 John Cooper, *Raphael Lemkin and the Struggle for the Genocide Convention* (Basingstoke: Palgrave Macmillan, 2008), p. 86.

taking this position. Lemkin himself as well as Jewish organisations interested in the text of the Convention also favoured the omission of political groups. Moreover, archival materials suggest that the United States, which initially took a public position supporting inclusion of political groups in the Convention, was itself more than agreeable to dropping the term.[22]

Criticism of the definition

One of the earliest academic writers on the Genocide Convention, Pieter Drost, discussed what he called the 'Deficient Definition in Article II'. He said that '[b]y leaving political and other groups beyond the purported protection the authors of the Convention also left a wide and dangerous loophole for any government to escape the human duties under the Convention by putting genocide into practice under the cover of executive measures against political or other groups for reasons of security, public order or any other reason of state'.[23] Drost said that 'in order to achieve its purpose such convention must extend its protection to all groups of human beings'. He linked his approach to the central non-discrimination clause in the Universal Declaration of Human Rights: 'When including all human groups a genocide convention would in effect provide international criminal protection of human rights and freedoms without distinction of any kind such as mentioned in Article 2 of the Universal Declaration.'[24] Drost considered that genocide was 'a violation of fundamental freedoms of human beings collectively considered'.[25]

A similar view was taken up by Benjamin Whitaker, the special rapporteur designated by the United Nations Sub-Commission on the Prevention of Discrimination and the Protection of Minorities. Whitaker pointed to a 'considerable number of commentators' who had criticised the Convention for 'its omission to protect political, economic, sexual or social groups, despite the inclusion in the examples of genocide cited in resolution 96/1 of the destruction of "racial,

22 Letter, 14 July 1948, Acting Legal Adviser to James Rosenberg, National Archives, United States of America, 501.BD-Genocide, 1945–9; Memorandum of Conversation, 16 July 1948, Between John Maktos and Raphael Lemkin, National Archives, United States of America, 501.BD-Genocide, 1945–9; Minutes of the Ninth Meeting of the United States Delegation, Paris, Hotel d'Iéna, 30 September 1948, in *Foreign Relations of the United States, 1948*, Vol. I (Washington: United States Government Printing Office, 1975), pp. 295–7 at p. 296.

23 Pieter N. Drost, *Genocide, United Nations Legislation on International Criminal Law* (Leiden: A. W. Sythoff, 1959), p. 123.

24 *Ibid.*

25 *Ibid.*, p. 124.

religious, political and other groups"'.[26] Whitaker focused on the exclusion of political groups, which he seemed to blame on the Soviet Union, reprising the arguments that were made on both sides of the debate.[27] Whitaker wrote that '[o]ne possible solution to the problem of killings of political and other groups which would be considered in the absence of consensus, would be to include this provision in an additional optional protocol'.[28]

The argument for enlargement of the definition of genocide continues to get a limited amount of traction among academic commentators. In a recent and quite exhaustive study of the issue of 'groups' protected by the Genocide Convention, David L. Nersessian has set out a case for recognising 'a crime of political genocide', noting that '[t]he reprehensible underlying violence involved in political genocide is identical to that of genocide against enumerated groups'.[29] Nersessian makes a persuasive plea for the international criminalisation of 'political genocide'. However, that the intentional physical destruction of political groups should be punishable as an international crime is not really very controversial. It already is punishable, under one or more headings of crimes against humanity. In other words, the real argument should be not whether the extermination of political groups is a crime, subject to the jurisdiction of international tribunals like the International Criminal Court, but whether it should migrate from the category of crimes against humanity to that of genocide.

Another scholar, Larry May, has suggested modifying the Convention definition of genocide as part of 'some proposed changes in international law'. He would change the wording of Article 2 of the 1948 Convention as follows: '"genocide" means any of the following acts committed with intent to destroy, in whole or in part, *a group, such as* a national, ethnical, racial or religious group, as such'. The modification is italicised. According to Professor May, 'such a change will allow for other groups that are very much like the four originally listed types of groups also to be the object of genocidal harms that can be redressed in international law'. He proposes a further amendment in order to direct the interpretation of the words 'such as', adding the words 'a group that is relatively stable and significant for the identity of its members'.[30]

---

26 Revised and Updated Report on the Question of the Prevention and Punishment of the Crime of Genocide, UN Doc. E/CN.4/Sub.2/1985/6 (1985), para. 34.

27 *Ibid.*, paras. 35–6.

28 *Ibid.*, para. 37.

29 David L. Nersessian, *Genocide and Political Groups* (Oxford: Oxford University Press, 2010), p. 182.

30 Larry May, *Genocide: A Normative Account* (New York: Cambridge University Press, 2010), p. 57.

Resistance to amendment

However, despite these repeated appeals for a revision of the definition of genocide from what we might call the Lemkinian perspective – one that, by the way, coincides with Article 1(1) of ICERD – there has been little interest at the governmental level. Shortly after Whitaker's report was issued, international criminal law entered its most dynamic phase, one characterised both by the creation of new institutions, like the International Criminal Tribunal for the former Yugoslavia and the International Criminal Court, and the elaboration of new international norms, standards and crimes. In particular the definitions of international crimes derived from the post-Second World War period went through a virtual revolution, with war crimes being enlarged to encompass non-international armed conflict and crimes against humanity being extended to acts perpetrated in peacetime. The seminal moment was the October 1995 judgment of the Appeals Chamber of the International Criminal Tribunal for the former Yugoslavia known as the *Tadić Jurisdictional Decision*.[31] Three years later, this dramatic exercise in judicial law-making was confirmed in Articles 7 and 8 of the Rome Statute of the International Criminal Court.

Seemingly, momentum to modify the definitions of war crimes and crimes against humanity had been building for many years, just as it had for genocide. But to the surprise – and dismay – of many, the attitude taken by international lawmakers to genocide did not benefit from the same spirit of change and innovation. The proposals of Drost, Whitaker and others were not followed. This was not for want of opportunity. Drafting of the Rome Statute provided the perfect occasion to revise and reform the outdated texts they had inherited from the 1940s. As has been mentioned, they embraced this with enthusiasm when it came to war crimes and crimes against humanity. With respect to genocide, however, as M. Cherif Bassiouni has explained, the delegates missed an 'historic opportunity' to expand the scope of the Convention.[32] There were some rather isolated attempts to amend the definition of genocide in order to include political or economic and social groups.[33] A footnote to the final draft of the Preparatory Committee declares: 'The Preparatory Committee took note of the suggestion to examine the possibility of addressing "social

31 *Prosecutor* v. *Tadić* (IT-94–1-AR72), Decision on the Defence Motion for Interlocutory Appeal on Jurisdiction, 2 October 1995.

32 M. Cherif Bassiouni, *The Legislative History of the International Criminal Court: Introduction, Analysis and Integrated Text*, Vol. I (Ardsley: Transnational, 2005), p. 92, fn. 208.

33 Preparatory Committee 1996 Report, Vol. I, pp. 17–18, para. 60; Preparatory Committee 1996 Report, Vol. II, p. 57.

and political" groups in the context of crimes against humanity.'[34] At the Rome Conference, in 1998, Cuba argued for inclusion of social and political groups. Ireland answered, stating 'we could improve upon the definition if we were drafting a new genocide convention', but explained that this was not the case, and that it was better to stick with the existing definition.[35] The Bureau of the Conference proposed that the definition be taken literally from the 1948 Convention[36] and there was virtually no objection.[37] Herman von Hebel and Daryl Robinson have observed that '[a]t the Rome Conference, the definition of the crime of genocide was not discussed in substance'.[38] No proposals at the Conference were ever submitted concerning any substantive changes to the definition.

This reluctance to change or expand the definition of genocide is also manifested in judicial interpretation over the past two decades. With relatively rare exceptions, judges of the International Criminal Tribunals for the former Yugoslavia and Rwanda, the International Criminal Court and the International Court of Justice have maintained a relatively strict construction of the crime of genocide. Occasional manifestations of creativity have focused on the material elements of the crime rather than on the protected groups. The great exception is the *Akayesu* judgment of a Trial Chamber of the International Criminal Tribunal for Rwanda. Because it was the first judgment of an international criminal tribunal on the interpretation of the definition of genocide drawn from the 1948 Convention, it has probably received an inordinate amount of attention from commentators. Considered from a contemporary perspective, nearly two decades after the decision was

34 Preparatory Committee 1996 Report, Vol. I, p. 11, fn. 2. See also: Decisions Taken by the Preparatory Committee at its Session Held from 11 to 21 February 1997, UN Doc. A/AC.249/1997/L.5, p. 3, fn. 2; Zutphen Report, p. 17, fn. 11.

35 Author's personal notes of debate, Committee of the Whole, 17 June 1998.

36 Discussion Paper, Bureau, UN Doc. A/CONF.183/C.1/L.53 (1998), p. 1; also UN Doc. A/CONF.183/C.1/L.59 (1998), p. 2.

37 UN Doc. A/CONF.183/C.1/SR.3 (1998), paras. 2, 18, 20 (Germany), 22 (Syria), 24 (United Arab Emirates), 26 (Bahrain), 28 (Jordan), 29 (Lebanon), 30 (Belgium), 31 (Saudi Arabia), 33 (Tunisia), 35 (Czech Republic), 38 (Morocco), 40 (Malta), 41 (Algeria), 44 (India), 49 (Brazil), 54 (Denmark), 57 (Lesotho), 59 (Greece), 64 (Malawi), 67 (Sudan), 72 (China), 76 (Republic of Korea), 80 (Poland), 84 (Trinidad and Tobago), 85 (Iraq), 107 (Thailand), 111 (Norway), 113 (Côte d'Ivoire), 116 (South Africa), 119 (Egypt), 122 (Pakistan), 123 (Mexico), 127 (Libya), 132 (Colombia), 135 (Iran), 137 (United States of America), 141 (Djibouti), 143 (Indonesia), 145 (Spain), 150 (Romania), 151 (Senegal), 153 (Sri Lanka), 157 (Venezuela), 161 (Italy), 166 (Ireland), 172 (Turkey), 174.

38 Herman von Hebel and Darryl Robinson, 'Crimes within the jurisdiction of the Court', in Roy S. Lee (ed.), *The International Criminal Court: The Making of the Rome Statute, Issues, Negotiations, Results* (The Hague, London and Boston: Kluwer Law International, 1999), pp. 79–126, at p. 89.

issued, and in light of an enormous volume of case law, the teachings of the *Akayesu* Trial Chamber cannot really be said to have stood the test of time.

With respect to the groups protected by the criminalisation of genocide, the Trial Chamber in *Akayesu* held that the drafters of the 1948 Convention had meant to encompass all 'stable' and 'permanent' groups.[39] It was a somewhat extravagant reading of the *travaux*, based on isolated comments by a few delegations and, moreover, it appeared to contradict a finding elsewhere in the judgment that the Tutsi were an ethnic group for the purposes of charges of crimes against humanity.[40] According to Guénaël Mettraux, '[a]lthough the meritorious agenda behind such a position is obvious, this proposition would appear to be, unfortunately, unsupported in law and at the time of its exposition in fact constitute purely judicial law-making'.[41] The novel interpretation was repeated in two subsequent decisions of the same Trial Chamber, although in a rather more guarded fashion: 'It appears from a reading of the *travaux préparatoires* of the Genocide Convention that certain groups, such as political and economic groups have been excluded from the protected groups, because they are considered to be "mobile groups" which one joins through individual, political commitment. That would seem to suggest *a contrario* that the Convention was presumably intended to cover relatively stable and permanent groups.'[42]

The 'stable and permanent' theory put forward by Trial Chamber I of the International Criminal Tribunal for Rwanda was not subsequently followed in any other decisions of the Tribunal itself[43] or those of its companion, the International Criminal Tribunal for the former Yugoslavia. Indeed, it had been effectively forgotten until the Darfur Commission of Inquiry revived the matter in its January 2005 report. According to the Commission, the 'interpretative expansion' effected by the Trial Chamber in Akayesu was 'in line with the object and scope of the rules on genocide (to protect from deliberate annihilation essentially stable and permanent human groups, which can be differentiated on one of the grounds contemplated by the Convention

39 *Prosecutor* v. *Akayesu* (ICTR-96-4-T), Judgment, 2 September 1998, para. 515.
40 *Ibid.*, para. 652.
41 Guénaël Mettraux, *International Crimes and the Ad Hoc Tribunals* (Oxford: Oxford University Press, 2005), p. 230.
42 *Prosecutor* v. *Rutaganda* (ICTR-96–3-T), Judgment and Sentence, 6 December 1999, para. 57; *Prosecutor* v. *Musema* (ICTR-96–13-T), Judgment and Sentence, 27 January 2000, para. 162 (reference omitted).
43 George William Mugwanya, *The Crime of Genocide in International Law: Appraising the Contribution of the UN Tribunal for Rwanda* (London: Cameron May, 2007), p. 67.

and the corresponding customary rules)'. The Commission suggested that the theory had been generally accepted by both Tribunals, adding that 'perhaps more importantly, this broad interpretation has not been challenged by States'. Therefore, '[i]t may ... be safely held that that interpretation and expansion has become part and parcel of international customary law'.[44] But this analysis is clearly a misreading of the authorities.

By way of explanation

The purpose of this discussion has not been to examine in detail the notion of 'groups' within the definition of genocide. Its more modest ambition is a search for some common thread linking the 1948 Genocide Convention with the 1965 Convention on the Elimination of All Forms of Racial Discrimination. The protected categories largely overlap. But whereas the scope of Article 1(1) of ICERD seems well-accepted, the same cannot necessarily be said of Article 2 of the Genocide Convention. The debate actually began with the 1946 General Assembly Resolution, even before the 1948 Convention, although virtually nothing is known about the discussions at the time in order to usefully inform our contemporary understanding. What emerges from the sources, however, is that the frequent complaints about the scope of Article 2 of the Genocide Convention have, by and large, not led to concrete changes in the law. There is some evidence in national legislation for larger definitions of genocide. However, the thorough review of these definitions in the appendix to David Nersessian's study[45] tends to confirm that the addition of categories to the list in Article 2 is very much the exception, and this therefore confirms the rule.

The Rome Conference should not be viewed a 'missed opportunity'. The drafters of the Rome Statute filled the gaps that had been left by the international legal framework of the 1940s that formed the starting point for their work. However, they just chose to fulfil this task by expanding the definitions of war crimes and crimes against humanity rather than that of genocide. The result is a seamless package of measures dealing with impunity for atrocity crimes. Unhappiness with the decision to leave the definition of genocide untouched cannot really be justified as a legal shortcoming. It merely manifests an obsession with semantics, with the demagogic magic of the 'g-word' rather than the legal reality. Early critics, like Drost and Whitaker, were concerned

---

44 Report of the International Commission of Inquiry on Violations of International Humanitarian Law and Human Rights Law in Darfur, UN Doc. S/2005/60 (2005), para. 501.

45 Nersessian, *Genocide and Political Groups*, pp. 267–72.

about legal loopholes left by the 1948 codification. With the adoption of the Rome Statute, that is no longer a serious objection. More modern critics, like Nersessian and May, do not have the same excuse.

The complaint that it is irrational, or unacceptable, to limit the scope of genocide to national, ethnical, racial and religious groups is one that might also be levelled at ICERD. Just as Drost pointed to Article 2 of the Universal Declaration of Human Rights as a rationale for enlarging the scope of Article 2 of the Genocide Convention, one might similarly point to Article 1(1) of ICERD. Of the enumeration in Article 2 of the Universal Declaration, the Convention addresses discrimination directed against only a few categories: race and colour, and perhaps language, religion and national origin. It ignores other terms in the list: sex, political or other opinion, social origin, property, birth or other status, as well as unenumerated categories such as disability, age and sexual orientation. This 'omission' has been only partially rectified with the UN treaty system, through the Convention on the Elimination of All Forms of Discrimination Against Women[46] and the Convention on the Rights of Persons with Disabilities.[47] In other words, critics of the limited scope of the definition of genocide in the 1948 Convention should, logically, favour an 'International Convention for the Elimination of All Forms of Discrimination'. Why should racial discrimination be entitled to any special treatment?

Why indeed. In fact, there is a compelling case to be made that the limited scope of both treaties, the 1948 Genocide Convention and the 1965 Convention on Racial Discrimination, is to be understood as a logical and appropriate choice by international lawmakers. It should not be viewed as the result of irrational oversight and Machiavellian compromise. There is much wisdom in this common thread that links both treaties, namely the focus on racial groups, described as 'national, ethnic, racial and religious groups', and on racial discrimination, explained as 'race, colour, descent, or national or ethnic origin'.

It should be unnecessary to demonstrate the link between the fresh memories of the Nazi holocaust and the codification of the crime of genocide by the United Nations General Assembly in 1946 and 1948. Lemkin himself was a survivor, having fled Poland following the German invasion. Weeks before the final judgment in the Nuremberg trial, he learned that his entire family had perished at the hands of the Nazis.[48] As for the Convention on Racial Discrimination, reference is often made to reports of anti-Semitism that prompted the General Assembly to initiate work on a declaration and, subsequently, the

46 (1981) 1249 UNTS 13.
47 (2008) 2515 UNTS 3.
48 Cooper, *Raphael Lemkin*, pp. 72–73.

Convention itself.[49] However, the General Assembly had been expressing concern about racial discrimination from its earliest sessions.[50] Racial discrimination has also featured in the work of subsidiary bodies, notably the Sub-Commission on the Prevention of Discrimination and the Protection of Minorities, and agencies, in particular UNESCO.

Built on the ashes of the most destructive war in history, the United Nations focused its attention on racial discrimination out of a common understanding that ideas of racial superiority and related practices were in some way responsible for the devastation and misery that humanity had inflicted upon itself. The Holocaust was only the most immediate manifestation of this. The root of the problem was more visceral and it could not be blamed on the Nazis alone. Its manifestations included the scourge of slavery and the slave trade, by then abolished but of recent and enduring memory, and colonialism, very much a reality as the United Nations addressed the corrupted mandate system it had been bequeathed by the League of Nations. Understood from this perspective, a focus on racial discrimination rather than on some broader and ultimately amorphous notions of inequality is entirely justifiable, as is a focus on national, ethnical, racial and religious groups, despite the very important issues confronting attacks on political groups.

If genocide is conceived of more broadly, as a crime contemplating the protection of groups in general, then it loses its proximate relationship with racial discrimination. To the extent that it retains its more narrow focus, the two concepts and the two Conventions are joined at the hip. This is even more justifiable today than it was some decades ago given the larger scope recognised for crimes against humanity in modern international criminal law. The criticism that the Genocide Convention leaves a big loophole or an impunity gap cannot now be sustained, even if this might once have been the case. The complementary nature of the Genocide Convention and ICERD should not be understated. To the extent that ICERD is close to 'the soul of the United Nations', the Genocide Convention cannot be very far away.

49 Preparation of a Draft Declaration and a Draft Convention on the Elimination of All Forms of Racial Discrimination, GA Res. 1780(XVII).

50 Persecution and discrimination, GA Res. 103(1).

Chapter 9

CERD, the State, mining corporations and indigenous peoples' rights: the experience of the Subanon in the Philippines

*Cathal Doyle**

Introduction

In 1997, the Philippines Congress passed the Indigenous Peoples' Rights Act (IPRA), a law which effectively incorporated the then draft UN Declaration on the Rights of Indigenous Peoples into the national legislative framework, providing for the recognition of indigenous peoples' ancestral domain and self-determination rights.[1] This led to the establishment of the National Commission on Indigenous Peoples (NCIP) mandated to implement the IPRA law. That same year, the UN Committee on the Elimination of Racial Discrimination (CERD/the Committee) issued its General Recommendation (GR) 23 on rights of indigenous peoples – a document which would become a key touchstone for State recognition of indigenous peoples' rights.[2] In

* The author assisted the Subanon in the preparation of their submission to CERD in 2007 and in their subsequent engagements with CERD. He also assisted the network of indigenous peoples' organisations in the Philippines with the preparation of their indigenous peoples CERD shadow report in 2008–9. He wishes to thank the Subanon leaders as well as Geoff Nettleton and Zherwinah Mosqueda for the insights they provided into the Subanon peoples' situation over the course of this engagement with CERD.

1 Indigenous Peoples Rights Act of 1997 (Republic Act No. 8371), An Act to Recognize, Protect and Promote the Rights of Indigenous Cultural Communities/Indigenous Peoples, Creating a National Commission on Indigenous Peoples, Establishing Implementing Mechanisms, Appropriating Funds Therefor, and for other Purposes.

2 CERD, 'General Recommendation 23 on Rights of indigenous peoples', UN Doc. A/52/18, Annex V at 122 (1997). For an account of the background to CERD's drafting of GR 23, see Cathal Doyle, *Indigenous Peoples, Title to Territory, Rights and Resources: The Transformative Role of Free Prior and Informed Consent* (London: Routledge, 2015), pp. 166–7.

1997, the Philippines Government also submitted a State party report to CERD, which was to be its last for over twelve years, prompting the Committee to commend its effort in drafting the IPRA, but also to express its concerns in relation to the negative impacts development projects were having on the country's indigenous peoples.[3]

The year 1997 was also the year that the Subanon community, located at the foot of Mt Canatuan, on the Zamboanga Peninsula of Mindanao, obtained their Certification of Ancestral Domain Claim (CADC) from the Philippines' Department of the Environment and Natural Resources (DENR) and commenced their engagement with the new procedures for strengthened rights recognition under the IPRA. This convergence of events offered the promise of a future based on respect for their inherent rights to the Philippines' indigenous peoples such as the Subanon of Mt Canatuan. At the time the Subanon were involved in a struggle to protect their territories from the encroachment of a junior Canadian mining company, TVI Resources Development Philippines, Inc. (TVIRD). Of particular concern to the Subanon was the company's intent to develop an open pit gold mine, thereby destroying the peak of their sacred mountain, Mt Canatuan. As a component of their long-running struggle the Subanon turned to CERD for assistance in 2007. This chapter seeks to provide an overview of the Subanon experience and the role which their engagement with CERD has played in their quest for meaningful implementation of their rights, and the rights of other Philippine indigenous peoples, which are recognised under the law but not yet realised in practice.

Subanon context

To understand the position of the Subanon, and the events that unfolded at Mt Canatuan, it is first necessary to briefly address the Subanon beliefs and their experience in the years leading up to TVIRD's entry into their lands. The Subanon of Mt Canatuan form part of the greater Subanen people of the Zamboanga Peninsula whose total population is estimated to be approximately 330,000 people. The Zamboanga Peninsula also happens to be one of the priority mining areas targeted under the Government's mining policy. The Subanon are among the indigenous peoples in Mindanao, collectively referred to as Lumads, whose ancestors resisted conversion to both Islam and Christianity, retreating from the coastal regions in order to do so. The community living at the foot of Mt Canatuan take their name from the mountain which they hold to be the sacred and to be intimately connected

3 CERD, 'Concluding Observations: Philippines', UN Doc. CERD/C/304/Add.34 (1997), para. 17.

with their history and well-being. According to Subanon oral history, recounted by their Timuoy (chieftains determined by Subanon customary law), their ancestor Apu Manlang made a peace pact with the supreme-being to protect Mt Canatuan in return for guaranteeing their safety and protection from disease.[4] This is commemorated by the Subanon in a thanksgiving ritual known as the Buklog held every seven years. The mountain constituted a source of medicinal plants for the Subanon and its peak was considered out of bounds for occupation or any types of construction or interference.

This practice of attributing particular significance to specific mountains is not unique to the Subanon of Mt Canatuan. Mt Pinukis in the territories of the Subanan[5] of Midsalip, in the neighbouring province of Zamboanga del Sur, is another mountain held sacred by the local Subanen. The mountain range of which it forms a part is rich in iron ore, and like Mt Canatuan has also been targeted for mining. In that case, in 1997 Rio Tinto recognised the sacredness of the mountain to the Midsalip Subanan communities and abandoned its plans to mine the area given the absence of Subanan consent.[6] As outlined below, TVIRD adopted a very different approach in relation to Mt Canatuan.

The steps taken by the Subanon of Mt Canatuan to protect their mountain prior to, and following, TVIRD's entry into Mt Canatuan reflect the extent to which they repeatedly sought in good faith to engage with the national mechanisms aimed at protecting their rights, and the consistent pattern of failure on the part of State institutions to fulfil their duties. Over the course of the decade preceding TVIRD's arrival, the Subanon had faced waves of encroachments by outsiders into Mt Canatuan. Prior to the arrival of large-scale gold mining on their lands, the Subanon had successfully prevented logging from impacting on the peak of Mt Canatuan.[7] The Subanon of Mt

---

4 Raymundo D. Rovillos and Victoria Tauli-Corpuz, 'Development power and identity politics in the Philippines', in Suzana Sawyer and Edmund Terence Gome (eds), *The Politics of Resource Extraction: Indigenous Peoples, Multinational Corporations and the State* (London: Palgrave Macmillan, 2012), pp. 129–52, at p. 141; Penelope Sanz, 'The politics of consent: The state, multinational capital and the Subanon of Canatuan', in Augusto B. Gatmaytan (ed.), *Negotiating Autonomy Case Studies on Philippines Indigenous Peoples' Land Rights* (Quezon City and Cogenhagen: IWGIA, LRC-KsK/FOE-Phils, 2007), pp. 109–35, at pp. 112–13.

5 The spelling of Subanen varies by community. For the Mt Canatuan community it is Subanon while in Midsalip it is Subanen.The spelling used when referring to the entire people is Subanen.

6 Cathal Doyle, Clive Wicks and Frank Nally, 'Mining in the Philippines: Concerns and conflicts' (London: Society of St Colomban, 2007), p. 3, available at: www.eccr.org.uk/dcs/MininginthePhilippines-ConcernsandConflicts.pdf.

7 Subanon of Mt Canatuan, 'Submission to the CERD regarding Discrimination against the Subanon of Mt Canatuan, Siocon, Zamboanga del Norte, Philippines,

Canatuan, together with their leader Timuoy Jose Anoy, then resisted an influx of small-scale miners and eventually managed to regulate small-scale mining activities in a way that avoided any operations threatening the mountain peak.[8]

A component of the Subanon strategy to protect their mountain was to engage with successive national legislative processes, each of which afforded increasing recognition to their inherent rights over their territories. Under a 1982 Presidential Decree, which encouraged local forest management, the Subanon had applied for a Community Forestry Stewardship Agreement (CFSA), which they obtained in 1992. Upon the issuance of the DENR Administrative Order no. 2 in 1993, the Subanon applied to have this forestry agreement converted into a new legal instrument, the CADC, which was awarded to them in 1997.[9] Then again, immediately following the adoption of the IPRA, and in an effort to further strengthen their rights and control over their ancestral domain, they immediately applied to have the CADC converted into a Certification of Ancestral Domain Title (CADT). They were, as a result, among the first communities in the country to be awarded a CADT in 2003, with the president attending the award ceremony together with the local Subanon Timuoy, Jose Anoy.

Despite this consistent engagement with a progressive rights-affirming legal regime, the Subanon nevertheless found themselves in a situation whereby their rights recognised under the law were subverted in practice in the context of a mining concession and operations of TVIRD. In 1994 the company signed an 'Exploration Agreement with Option to Purchase' covering Mt Canatuan with a Philippine mining company, the original claim of the Philippine company having been obtained under dubious circumstances.[10] In 1996, the DENR approved TVIRD's Mineral Production Sharing Agreement (MPSA) despite Subanon opposition and without their prior consent as required by the 1995 Mining Act, Section 16 of which states that '[n]o ancestral lands shall be opened for mining operations without the prior consent of the indigenous cultural communities'. In the years that followed, further permissions continued to be granted to the company and were associated with a series of rights violations in the context of violence and threats, on occasion leading to killings. Mining activities proceeded in

---

in the context of large-scale gold mining on their ancestral domain', CERD Seventy-first Session, 30th July – 17th August (2007), para. 52.

8 *Ibid.* See also J. R. Jacobe-Asperin, 'Community perspectives on the business responsibility to respect human rights in countries affected or threatened by conflict' (Institute for Human Rights and Business, Collaborative Learning Projects, 2010), p. 11.

9 Subanon of Mt Canatuan, 'Submission to CERD' (2007), para. 19.

10 Doyle *et al.*, 'Mining in the Philippines', p. 4.

the absence of the consent of the Subanon people despite the adoption of the IPRA with its strengthened free, prior and informed consent (FPIC) requirement and its self-determination based rights recognition framework.

The Subanon took their complaint to the UN Working Group on Indigenous Populations in 2002, prompting an investigation by the Commission on Human Rights in the Philippines (CHRP). The investigation held that the problems at Mt Canatuan stemmed from the

> approval of the MPSA by the DENR on October 23 1996 covering an area of 508.34 hectares within the ancestral land of the Subanon … The violation committed by TVI and its personnel to include the company guards and the Special Civilian Armed Auxiliary (SCAA) who are assisting the company guards; The failure of the TVI to obtain free prior consent from the indigenous peoples as the law requires.[11]

However, despite the Commission's recommendation that revocation of the MPSA was required to rectify the wrongs and address the problems,[12] the NCIP, the Government agency responsible for upholding indigenous peoples' rights, instead facilitated the creation of a 'Siocon Council of Elders', which proceeded to give the necessary 'consent' to TVIRD, thereby circumventing the long-standing opposition of the local Subanon leaders and community to the project.

In 2004, having attempted to engage all available State based judicial and non-judicial mechanisms – which included a request for an injunction filed by Timuoy Jose Anoy – to no avail, the Subanon were faced with the commencement of TVIRD's mining operations without having obtained their legitimate consent.[13]

Dual rights assertion strategy

From 2004 onwards the Subanon adopted an alternative strategy based on two mutually reinforcing rights assertion approaches. The first approach was to invoke their own customary legal system. This resulted in the issuance of two rulings, one against the State in 2004

11 Commission on Human Rights in the Philippines, 'Resolution in the Matter of Investigation conducted on the Subanon Case at Tabayo, Siocon, Zambonga del Norte', Case No IX 2002–1770 (2002).

12 Subanon of Mt Canatuan, 'Submission to CERD' (2007).

13 The case was also subject to a Congressional Hearing in the Philippines in 2006 at which many of the Subanon concerns were raised, but despite the Committee's recommendations no action was forthcoming from the responsible Government agencies. See Congress of the Philippines, 'Plight of Indigenous People in Zambo Province Looked Into', National Cultural Communities, 13(86), 16 January 2006.

and the other against the company in 2007 for violations of Subanon customary law.

In 2003, the *Gukom sog Pito Kobogolalan sog Pito ko Dolungan* (referred to as *Gukom of the Seven Rivers*), the highest Subanon judicial authority in the area which consists of the Timuoy of Mt Canatuan and the Timuoy of the surrounding Subanon territories, informed the NCIP of its concern over the manipulation of indigenous structures and processes in the granting of 'consent' to TVIRD. The NCIP formally recognised the authority of the *Gukom* to settle the dispute according to their customary law, stating that 'any judgment arrived at by the *Gukom* may be referred to the NCIP for enforcement'.[14] In 2004, the Subanon of Mt Canatuan convened the *Gukom of the Seven Rivers* which ruled that the consent obtained by TVIRD was void as the body which had provided it, the Siocon Council of Elders, was 'illegitimate, illegal and an affront to the customs, traditions, and practices of the Subanon'.[15] The *Gukom* also noted the sacred nature of Mt Canatuan and demanded that the traditional leader, Timuoy Jose Anoy, be recognised and the community's FPIC sought. The *Gukom* ruling, which was submitted to the NCIP, imposed penalties on the agency and instructed it to immediately nullify any agreements authorising mining to proceed. No response or action on the ruling was forthcoming from the NCIP, thereby enabling TVIRD to proceed with its mining operations.

The *Gukom* was again convened in Mt Canatuan in September 2007 and condemned the destruction of the sacred Mt Canatuan and performed a traditional ritual associated with the mountain.[16] That December it held a second traditional judicial hearing, following a complaint filed by Timuoy Jose Anoy against TVIRD. The hearing addressed issues arising from the company's non-consensual presence and its mining operations in the area. The *Gukom* ruling imposed fines on TVIRD for disrespecting Subanon customary protocols and laws, including for the destruction of their sacred mountain and for 'violation (blasphemy/ mockery) against customary laws', and required it to conduct a cleansing ritual in atonement for desecrating Mt Canatuan.[17]

14 Subanon of Mt Canatuan, 'Submission to CERD' (2007), para. 29.

15 Gukom of the Seven Rivers Assembly Resolution No. 01–2004, *Tupo Nog Pito Kobogolalan Pogokbit Nog Gulal Sog Pito Kodolungan* 'Resolution on the Decision Pertaining to the Composition and Legitimacy of the Siocon Council of Elders and the Official Position on the Issue of Leadership and Representation of the Canatuan Subanön Community', 3rd Assembly of the Gukoms (2004), para. 4.

16 The ritual is called *Glongosan sog Dongos nog Konotuan*.

17 Gukom of the Seven Rivers, 'Verdict upon complaint by Timuay Jose Anoy against TVIRD for its failure to respect customary laws within the territory of Timuay Jose Anoy', Gukom of the Seven Rivers (2007), pp. 3–6.

The second approach was to focus on international fora in which to seek remedies for their grievances. In 2005 the Subanon again presented their issues at the UN Working Group on Indigenous Peoples (WGIP) in Geneva and also went to Canada, the home country of TVIRD, to raise their issues. A Standing Committee of the Canadian Parliament on Foreign Affairs and International Trade investigated their case and stated that it was 'deeply concerned about the possible impact of the activities of TVI Pacific Inc. [TVIRD], a Canadian mining company, on the indigenous rights and the human rights of people in the area'.[18] While in Canada the Subanon considered submitting a complaint to the Canadian OECD National Contact Point (NCP). They ultimately decided against doing so as they felt that the NCP lacked the capacity and, based on its track record at the time, also the will to address the issues that were of core concern to them. Having examined the range of available international mechanisms they decided to make a detailed submission to CERD. The decision to do so was based on CERD's in-depth understanding of indigenous issues and its consistent focus on them since the issuance of its 1997 General Recommendation, as well as its repeated invocation of its innovative early warning urgent action procedure in relation to similar cases of indigenous peoples elsewhere.[19]

The submission was made prior to the Committee's seventy-first session, in August 2007 and included the ruling of the *Gukom*, outlining the Subanon's issues, alleged rights violations and associated requests for assistance. Among other things, the Subanon alleged that the Government had granted the concession and associated permissions authorising the mining activities of TVIRD in their sacred mountain despite their repeated objections and contrary to the requirement for their FPIC in both the 1995 Mining Act and the 1997 IPRA. They emphasised that the Siocon Council of Elders, from which the NCIP and the company had obtained consent, had no standing under their customary laws and had been found to be illegitimate by their judicial authority, the *Gukom of the Seven Rivers*. The submission also

18 Cathal Doyle, 'Indigenous peoples and the Millennium Development Goals: "Sacrificial lambs" or equal beneficiaries?', *The International Journal of Human Rights*, 13:1 (2009), 44–71, at 60, citing *Fourteenth Report of the Standing Committee of the Canadian Parliament on Foreign Affairs and International Trade*.

19 See Cathal Doyle and Andrew Whitmore, *Indigenous Peoples and the Extractive Industries: Towards Rights Respecting Engagements* (Manila and London: Tebtebba, Middlesex University, PIPLinks, 2014), pp. 61–73, and Doyle, *Indigenous Peoples, Title to Territory, Rights and Resources*, for an overview of CERD's engagement with indigenous issues in the context of the extractive industry. An empirical analysis of CERD's early warning urgent action procedures indicates that in excess of 30 per cent of the Committee's work is focused on indigenous peoples' issues.

alleged that serious human rights violations were suffered as a result of TVIRD's non-consensual mining operations and the associated presence of armed paramilitary groups in their territories and included affidavits of community members in this regard. Finally, the Subanon pointed to the failure of the FPIC guidelines of the NCIP to adhere to the spirit and letter of the IPRA and the fact that this was impacting on indigenous peoples' rights throughout the country.

Two Subanon Timuoy, Timuoy Boy and Timuoy Nanding, both members of the *Gukom of the Seven Rivers*, attended the session in Geneva providing further written and oral input to CERD's Early Warning Urgent Action Committee. Following the session, CERD issued a letter to the Philippine Government expressing its concern at the situation and requesting information into the alleged violation of the rights of the Subanon of Mt Canatuan. The Government replied on 24 January 2008, denying the allegations but failing to address the specific issues raised by the Subanon. The Subanon and support organisations responded to the Government reply both in writing and in person at the seventy-second session of CERD in March 2008. Meanwhile, in response to the CERD communication the NCIP finally overturned the certification of ancestral domain title to the Subanon, in an award ceremony to Timuoy Jose Anoy, and ensured its registration at the Register of Deeds, some five years after it had been initially officially awarded to the Subanon. This recognition by the NCIP was important in a context where the company was attempting to undermine the Timuoy's legitimacy. However, it also reflected the incoherence in the NCIP's approach as it continued to support the Siocon Council of Elders.

The Committee again communicated to the Government expressing its on-going preoccupation in relation to the situation of the Subanon of Mt Canatuan and requested 'further clarification and additional information' in relation to the issues already raised in August 2007. The Government replied in June 2008 and took the highly unorthodox step of attaching a letter from the company. For the second time the Government's response failed to address the specific issues raised by the Committee. Meanwhile, the letter submitted by TVIRD included a strong attack on the legitimacy of Timuoy Jose Anoy, questioning his lineage as a Subanon Timuoy. TVIRD also repeated its rejection of the fact that Mt Canatuan was sacred to the Subanon on the grounds that it had found no archaeological evidence to support their claim.[20] This

20 TVI Resource Development (Phils.) Inc., TVIRD letter submitted by Government of the Philippines to CERD (2008, on file with author); see also TVIRD, 'There is NO Sacred Mountain', Social and Environmental Review, available at: www.tvird.com.ph/stakeholders/nosacredmountain.html.

was despite repeated Subanon assertions of its sacredness, including in their submissions to CERD, and their explanation that constructions were prohibited on the mountain precisely because of its scared nature.

Once again a detailed written and oral response was provided by the Subanon at the seventy-third session of the Committee in August 2008. Philippine Government representatives also attended the seventy-third session and provided an oral briefing to the Committee in a closed-door session. In light of the 'contradictory information' received from the Government and the Subanon, the Committee requested that the Government provide 'a written note of the points made during the [Government] briefing, in addition to any further information which the State party may wish to provide'.[21] No written response was provided by the Government.

In response to information submitted by the Subanon, and supported by other indigenous peoples,[22] that the issues at Mt Canatuan were reflective of similar problems elsewhere in the Philippines, CERD invited the Government to present a long overdue periodic report at its August 2009 session. The State party periodic report submitted for review at that session failed to address the situation of the Subanon. However, in the public dialogue with CERD, the CHRP acknowledged that there had been a failure to obtain Subanon consent and that there had been violations of the Subanon rights as a result.[23] Following the session, CERD reiterated its concern in relation to the absence of prior consent for the mining operations and regarding 'the status of actions taken to address the violations of the Subanon people's rights and destruction of their sacred mountain'.[24] It urged the Government 'to consult with all concerned parties in order to address the issues over Mt. Canatuan in a manner that respects customary laws and practices of the Subanon people' and welcomed 'information from the State party in relation to further developments.'[25] A response was requested from the Government by August 2010 as part of CERD's follow-up procedure. No response was forthcoming.

---

21 CERD, 'Early Warning Urgent Action letter to the Government of the Philippines' (2008), available at: www.ohchr.org/EN/HRBodies/CERD/Pages/EarlyWarningProcedure.aspx.

22 A supporting statement was submitted to CERD by a broad range of indigenous peoples and organisations in the Philippines.

23 Minutes of CERD seventy-fifth session on file with author; see also CERD, 'Summary record of the 1957th meeting', UN Doc. CERD/C/SR.1957 (19 March 2010), paras. 20–3.

24 CERD, 'Concluding Observations: Philippines', UN Doc. CERD/C/PHL/CO/20 (2009), para. 25.

25 *Ibid.*

The Subanon submitted further information at the seventy-seventh session of CERD in August 2010. In response CERD again issued a communication to the Government noting that, according to information received, mining operations had caused irreparable destruction to the Subanon's sacred site and that the Government had not yet implemented its recommendation in relation to consultation with the Subanon in order to resolve the issues.[26] It again requested that the Government provide it with information in relation to steps taken to implement its recommendation, in accordance with its follow-up procedure by January 2011. In 2012, at its eighty-first session, following further updates from the Subanon, CERD again communicated with the Government, noting that the requested responses in relation to its Concluding Observation of September 2009, and its letter of the 27 August 2010, had not been received.[27] It again reiterated its recommendation that the Government of the Philippines 'consult with all concerned parties in order to address the issues regarding Mount Canatuan in a manner that respects customary laws and practices of the Subanon people'.[28] Importantly, in addition it also requested that the State provide information on 'concrete measures taken to ensure that the sacred character of Mount Canatuan is respected; and, appropriate consultation conducted with the Subanon people and culturally appropriate reparation provided to them'.[29]

Current situation at Mt Canatuan

As of September 2015 the Government has not responded to CERD's request for updated information or taken the necessary measures to implement the recommendation in relation to reparations. The NCIP, and other government agencies involved, such as the Mines and Geosciences Bureau of the DENR, have yet to acknowledge their wrong-doing at Mt Canatuan and to conduct the appropriate consultations with the Subanon of Mt Canatuan in order to ensure that culturally appropriate reparations are realised. Alarmingly, rather than address these serious issues, the Government established a worrying precedent by presenting TVIRD's mining activities at Mt Canatuan as

26 CERD, 'Early Warning Urgent Action letter to the Government of the Philippines' (2010), available at www.ohchr.org/EN/HRBodies/CERD/Pages/EarlyWarningProcedure.aspx.

27 CERD, 'Early Warning Urgent Action letter to the Government of the Philippines' (2012), available at www.ohchr.org/EN/HRBodies/CERD/Pages/EarlyWarningProcedure.aspx.

28 *Ibid.*

29 *Ibid.*

an example of good practice within the framework of the Extractive Industry Transparency Initiative (EITI).[30]

In 2011, after fifteen years of sustained resistance to the mining project, the Subanon decided that further resistance was unlikely to bring substantive changes and that their priority was to resolve the serious divisions which the project had caused in their community. On this basis, while still maintaining their complaint at CERD against the Government and seeking reparations, they decided to enter into negotiations with TVIRD. For its part, TVIRD, which had done its utmost to discredit the traditional leadership while destroying the Subanon sacred mountain, and added insult to injury by denying its sacred nature, finally recognised the Mt Canatuan traditional leadership and their governance structures. On 17 May 2011, TVIRD performed the mandatory cleansing ritual called *Bintungan nog gasip bu doladjat* 'in atonement for desecrating the sacred Mt. Canatuan', and agreed to negotiations regarding penalties for harms caused.[31] Following this shift in its approach to the community and their authorities, TVIRD was invited to participate in hearings whenever the traditional local advisory council (the *Pigbogolan*, headed by Timuoy Jose Anoy) was addressing community grievances in relation to the company's actions.[32] The company would then investigate the issues and report back to the *Pigbogolan*, with recourse to external quasi-legal or legal process available if either part was not satisfied with the resolution of the issues. The case, when viewed in light of its historical context and unaddressed remedial issues, therefore offers valuable lessons in terms of the potential role of customary law in operational-level grievance mechanisms.[33]

The negative publicity which the CERD complaint generated undoubtedly contributed to TVIRD's decision to alter its approach toward the Subanon customary institutions. The decision was also in keeping with the company's objectives of expanding its presence into other Subanen territories in the Zamboanga Peninsula, something

---

30 Extactive Industries Transparency Initiative, 'Philippines Extractive Industries Transparency Report', Vol. 1 (2014), pp. 145–6, available at: www.ph-eiti.org/#/EITI-Report/First-Country-Report.

31 Philippines Indigenous Peoples Links [PIPLINKS], 'Philippines: TVIRD Admits Fault and Performs Cleansing Ritual In Canatuan' (Gulang Gukom Press Release, 2011), available at: www.piplinks.org/Timuay+Jose+Boy+Anoy.html.

32 Cathal Doyle, 'Operational-level grievance mechanism and indigenous peoples' access to remedy', in Cathal Doyle (ed.), *Business and Human Rights: Indigenous Peoples' Experiences with Access to Remedy. Case Studies from Africa, Asia and Latin America* (Chiang Mai, Madrid and Copenhagen: AIPP, Almáciga, IWGIA, 2014), pp. 27–72, at pp. 52–6.

33 *Ibid.*

which would be even more challenging if the Subanon of Mt Canatuan sustained their public opposition to the Mt Canatuan project. Somewhat ironically therefore, the CERD urgent action, which was targeted towards the Government, resulted in a more significant (if largely self-serving) response from the company than the State. That said, CERD's engagement with the State in the context of the periodic report has led to some important observations and contributed towards some advances in indigenous rights protection in the context of extractive industries.

Philippines national context

Cognisant of the fact that addressing the underlying structural obstacles giving rise to the rights-denying reality with which they were confronted could only be resolved by tackling a range of institutional, policy and legal issues at the national level, the Subanon of Mt Canatuan requested that CERD encourage the State to submit its long overdue periodic report. A national network of indigenous peoples' organisations was established and a series of consultations held with indigenous communities throughout the country. The indigenous peoples' shadow report highlighted the dysfunctionality in the State's institutional apparatus and the associated ideological incoherence with the spirit and intent of the IPRA.[34]

By examining three of the key issues raised by the Philippine's indigenous peoples in this shadow report, and the corresponding recommendations of CERD, some insights can be gleaned into how the IPRA, a rights-affirming legal instrument – which embodies the core rights indigenous peoples have struggled to have recognised by States in the UN for over two decades – could effectively be turned against the very rights-holders its purpose was to empower. Essentially, this requires some consideration of the deficiencies inherent in the political, legal and institutional framework within which the law was adopted, subsequently interpreted, and ultimately amended in practice.[35] The first issue relates to the failure of the organs of the State to fully grasp the import of the inherent indigenous rights philosophy which underpins the IPRA.

In the years following the enactment of the 1987 Constitution, and prior to the adoption of the IPRA, a number of measures were

34 Philippine Indigenous Peoples, 'ICERD Shadow Report', Submission to CERD Seventy-fifth Session (3–28 August 2009).

35 Ponciano L. Bennagen, '"Amending" IPRA, negotiating autonomy, upholding the right to self-determination', in Gatmaytan, *Negotiating Autonomy Case Studies*, pp. 179–198, at pp. 181–3.

taken which afforded some degree of protection to indigenous peoples. The philosophy underpinning the associated instruments (such as the forest stewardship and ancestral domain claim certificates) was significantly different from that underpinning the IPRA. The latter is premised on recognising prior rights which have their source in customary law, and the right of all peoples to self-determination, while the former reflected State 'grants' of rights to indigenous peoples.[36] Furthermore, these pre-IPRA instruments leaned more towards the pursuit of environmental objectives than to indigenous emancipation and empowerment. Therefore, the legal framework prior to the adoption of the IPRA to a certain extent treated indigenous peoples' rights as more of a means towards an end, than an end in and of themselves. The IPRA's departure from this legal fiction of State 'granted' indigenous peoples' rights, is perhaps its most ground-breaking feature.

The full implications of this have yet to be fully appreciated by all three branches of government. One of the clearest manifestations of this is found in the 2000 Supreme Court's ruling on the constitutionality of the IPRA. The Act was challenged on the basis of its inconsistency with the Regalian doctrine, which holds that the State maintains 'full control' and ownership of natural resources. In that ruling, the Court held that 'there is nothing in the [IPRA] that *grants* to the Indigenous peoples ownership over the natural resources within their ancestral domains … [t]he IPRA does not therefore violate the Regalian doctrine' [emphasis added].[37] This rationale embodies the pre-IPRA conception of indigenous peoples' rights as 'grants' from the State, rather than 'inherent rights' which the law serves to recognise. Ironically, the Constitution itself is clear in this regard, stating that '[t]he State *recognizes* and promotes the rights of indigenous cultural communities'.[38]

Conceived of as State grants, indigenous peoples' resource ownership and control rights can be subordinated to the Regalian doctrine,[39] without necessitating an analysis of, or attempt to reconcile, the underlying definitional tensions between that doctrine and the concept of inherent rights and customary law based title over ancestral domains, which are also subject to constitutional protection. This is particularly

36 See Doyle, *Indigenous Peoples, Title to Territory, Rights and Resources*, pp. 112–17, for an overview of the sources of indigenous peoples' rights recognised under international law, including the recognition of 'indigenous peoples' as peoples vested with the right to self-determination; their customary tenure regimes, laws and legal systems; their unique and particular historical contexts; and their de facto inherent sovereignty, which predates the foundation of the State.

37 *Isagani Cruz and Cesar Europa* v. *Sec. of Environment and Natural Resources et al.*, GR No. 135385 (2000).

38 Constitution of the Philippines, Article II Section 22 and Article XII Section 5.

39 Affirmed under Article XII Section 2 of the Constutition.

problematic as the Regalian doctrine is highly discriminatory in its effect when applied in an undifferentiated manner to indigenous peoples, and is at odds with indigenous conceptions of ownership and the exercise of their self-determination and self-governance rights. This view has permeated the thinking and practices of those organs of the State engaging with indigenous peoples, and is particularly evident in the context of the State's implementation of the requirement for FPIC, which will be discussed further below.

Pointing to the need for a proper balancing of constitutionally recognised rights, in its Concluding Observations CERD stated that 'the Regalian doctrine as applied to indigenous property seems to run counter to the notion of inherent rights under the IPRA'.[40] It consequently called on the state to 'conduct an independent review, in consultation with indigenous peoples, of the legislative framework in relation to indigenous property, with particular regard to the question of consistency between the IPRA, its implementing guidelines, the Regalian doctrine and other related doctrines, as well as the Mining Act of 1995'.[41] Essentially, CERD was telling the Government that it needed to examine the underlying tenets of the Regalian doctrine to ensure consistency with the notion of indigenous peoples' inherent rights, as in this era of rights recognition the perpetuation of the archaic and fictional colonial rights-denying discourses is no longer logically justifiable or morally acceptable.

The second issue, which has been of major concern to the Subanon and other indigenous peoples, is the manner in which their rights are reconciled with, and in practice subordinated to, rights and concessions which are granted by the State to extractive companies. This issue in part relates to the fact that the IPRA itself was a product of negotiation and as a result has not escaped contradictory provisions and diverging interpretations.[42] Perhaps the IPRA's most controversial provision – and one which was repeatedly invoked by TVIRD, and unquestionably echoed by the NCIP – is its Section 56. It states that '[p]roperty rights within the ancestral domains already existing and/or vested upon effectivity of this Act, shall be recognized and respected'.[43] The discussions of the Congressional Commission responsible for the drafting of the IPRA indicate that this provision was intended to afford a degree of protection to the property rights of individuals residing within ancestral domains who already held property rights therein.[44]

40 CERD, 'Concluding Observations: Philippines' (2009), para. 22.

41 *Ibid.*

42 Bennagen, '"Amending" IPRA', p. 188.

43 Indigenous Peoples Rights Act 1997, Section 56.

44 Marvic Mario Victor F. Leonen, 'Weaving worldviews implications of constitutional challenges to the Indigenous Peoples Rights Act of 1997', *Philippine Natural*

This signals that the recognition of ancestral domains did not automatically negate these property rights. At the same time those rights would also be conditioned by respect for ancestral domain rights, including indigenous peoples' self-governance and decision-making rights. What was intended therefore was a balancing of rights.

Rather than engage in this balancing of rights, State agencies simply adopted the self-serving narrative put forward by mining industry actors, such as TVIRD, holding that the existence of a concession or mining agreement that pre-dates the IPRA implied that indigenous self-governance, and cultural, consent and property rights, no longer need to be safeguarded. Worse still, this argument applied irrespective of the rights-denying circumstances under which the concessions were obtained in the first place. Furthermore, the relative nature of the rights in question was not considered. As mining concessions or agreements do not constitute property rights, they do not automatically fall under its scope.[45] Nor does the provision imply that rights obtained by a mining company under agreements to use, exploit or develop resources are not subject to limitations based on the self-determination, cultural and territorial rights of indigenous peoples and the associated requirement to obtain their FPIC. However, a failure of the NCIP to interpret this provision from the perspective of indigenous peoples' inherent pre-existing rights meant that the entire body of rights recognised under the Constitution and the IPRA could simply be subordinated to a mining concession or agreement.

This precise point was emphasised by the UN Special Rapporteur on the rights of indigenous peoples, when commenting on the TVIRD case in 2002. He recommended that '[t]he idea of prior right being granted to a mining or other business company rather than to a community that has held and cared for the land over generations must be stopped, as it brings the whole system of protection of human rights of indigenous peoples into disrepute'.[46] CERD in turn requested that the Philippine Government report on how it was implementing the Special Rapporteur's recommendations.[47] In keeping with GR 23, which requires reparations for taking of indigenous property without

Resources Journal, 10:1 (2000), 3–44; Marvic Mario Victor F. Leonen, 'Seeking the norm: Reflections on land rights policy and indigenous peoples right', in Gatmaytan, *Negotiating Autonomy Case Studies*, pp. 37–66, at p. 53.

45 Leonen, 'Seeking the norm', p. 53.

46 United Nations, 'Report of the Special Rapporteur on the Situation of human rights and fundamental freedoms of indigenous people: Mission to Philippines (2002)', UN Doc. E/CN.4/2003/90/Add 3. (2003), para. 67e. While on his country mission to the Philippines in 2002, the Special Rapporteur was denied access to Mt Canatuan.

47 CERD, 'Concluding Observations: Philippines' (2009), para. 18.

their FPIC, irrespective of the national legislative framework in force at the time of the taking, CERD also repeatedly questioned the Government with regard to its compliance in the Subanon case with the requirement for FPIC under the IPRA, and affirmed that under no circumstances should indigenous peoples' rights be subordinated to mining activities.[48]

The third overarching issue relates to the political context within which indigenous peoples are seeking to assert their legally recognised rights. Since 1995, the Philippine Government has been actively promoting mining as a driver for economic growth and has implemented a range of legislation and policy measures aimed at attracting foreign investment in the sector.[49] It is estimated that in the region of 60 per cent of existing mining concessions are located in the lands of indigenous peoples, who in total comprise only 15 per cent of the country's population.[50] This disproportionate impact of mining is compounded by the fact that their identities and survival as peoples is intimately related to the maintenance of their relationship with, and control over, their ancestral territories.

In their efforts to protect their lands from widespread acquisition by mining companies, indigenous peoples succeeded in having certain provisions of the 1995 Mining Act declared unconstitutional in January 2004.[51] However, within ten months of this ruling – which had taken seven years to obtain – and following a concerted campaign by members of the Government together with the Chamber of Mines, the Supreme Court reversed its decision.[52] In its revised decision it acknowledged the potentially serious impacts of mining on indigenous peoples, their rights and existence, but nevertheless held that the Constitution 'should not be used to strangulate economic growth or to serve narrow, parochial interests'.[53] This subordination of the rights of indigenous peoples to economic interests

48 *Ibid.*, para. 22. See also CERD, Early Warning Urgent Action letters to the Government of the Philippines, 2007–12.

49 Philippine Indigenous Peoples, 'ICERD Shadow Report', p. 34; and Cathal Doyle, 'The effectiveness of legal and non-legal remedies for addressing the rights of Indigenous Peoples at Mindoro Island and elsewhere', in Forum for Development Cooperation with Indigenous Peoples, *Forum Conference 2010 Indigenous Participation in Policy-making: Ideals, Realities and Possibilities* (Tromso: University of Tromso, 2010), pp. 85–94, at p. 86.

50 Doyle, 'Effectiveness'.

51 *La Bugal-B'laan Tribal Association, Inc. et al* v. *DENR Secretary et al*, G.R. No. 127882 (2004).

52 Doyle *et al.*, 'Mining in the Philippines', p. 10.

53 *La Bugal-B'laan Tribal Association, Inc. et al* v. *DENR Secretary et al* and *Didipio Earth-Savers' Multi-Purpose Association, [DESAMA] Inc. et al.* v. *Elisea Gozun, et al*, G.R. No. 157882 (2006).

and political power is a pervasive phenomenon across the State's institutional apparatus.

This is exemplified by the weakening of the institutional capacity of the NCIP between 1998 and 2010 during which time it was passed around between various ministries, including the ministry responsible for mining,[54] and its administrative guidelines regulating the process for seeking FPIC were subject to the exigencies of the mining sector.[55] In light of the volume of evidence presented by indigenous communities as to how these FPIC guidelines conflicted with their customary laws and practices, CERD called on the Government to verify that 'the current structures and guidelines/procedures established to conduct FPIC are in accordance with the spirit and letter of the IPRA and set realistic time frames for consultation processes with indigenous peoples'.[56] This recommendation contributed to the conduct of an important revision and strengthening of the FPIC guidelines in 2012, which was carried out at the behest of and in cooperation with indigenous peoples.

A related issue affecting the independence of the NCIP is that the members of its *Commission en Banc* are appointed by the president, as opposed to being selected by indigenous peoples. The institutional legacy of the NCIP has also been a major debilitating factor. Its staff and ethos were inherited from previous governmental bodies which had a distinctly paternalistic approach towards indigenous peoples and lacked understanding or appreciation of these peoples' customs, institutions and practices. CERD's recommendation that the Government needs to address the lack of confidence of indigenous peoples in the NCIP is directly related to these issues.[57]

Reflections

While the direct impact of the Subanon engagement with CERD on the actions of the State and company is difficult to conclusively

54 The agency was moved to be under the Office of the President but indigenous peoples have argued that it should be constituted as an independent executive department to avoid it being passed from one government agency to another.

55 Emily Caruso, Marcus Colchester, Fergus McKay, Nick Hildyard and Geoff Nettleton, 'Extracting Promises Indigenous Peoples, Extractive Industries and the World Bank' (Manila: Tebtebba Foundation, 2005 / Washington, DC: Extractive Industries Review Report, 2003); Robert Goodland and Clive Wicks, 'The Philippines: Mining or food?' (London: Working Group on Mining in the Philippines, 2009), available at: www.piplinks.org/system/files/Mining+or+Food+Case+Study+4.pdf.

56 CERD, 'Concluding Observations: Philippines' (2009), para. 24.

57 *Ibid.*

demonstrate, the Subanon themselves believe that the Urgent Action procedure served to put pressure on both the Philippine Government and the company to address some of their issues. The international attention led to the overturning of the certification of ancestral domain title to the Subanon within months of the Urgent Action, and to a formal Government response to the allegations filed by the Subanon, including in 2009 an acknowledgement before the Committee by the CHRP that Subanon's FPIC had not been obtained. It also undoubtedly increased pressure on TVIRD – who went so far as to provide a detailed, and extremely inappropriate, response to the Subanon allegations – to recognise the leadership and authority of the Subanon Timuoy and the decision-making powers of the Subanon traditional body which he leads and to participate in the conduct of a Subanon ritual aimed at addressing the harms caused.

At the national level the engagement of the Subanon and other indigenous peoples of the Philippines triggered the submission of an overdue State party report and resulted in a series of constructive Concluding Observations by CERD addressing structural and philosophical issues which act as major constraints on the implementation of indigenous peoples' rights. Some of these recommendations have helped to empower indigenous peoples, as evidenced by the development – in genuine collaboration with indigenous peoples – of a set of NCIP FPIC implementing guidelines that are consistent with the IPRA's spirit and intent.

The significance of the collaborative work of indigenous peoples' organisations and networks to produce the CERD shadow report should likewise not be underestimated, particularly in a context where ideological divisions have tended to limit opportunities for such collaboration. In addition to providing an account of the implementation of the IPRA between 1997 and 2009 from the perspective of the concerned communities, the ensuing report and network also provided the platform for regular submissions of information to other UN processes, such as the Universal Periodic Review. In 2015, this network of indigenous organisations is being revitalised with the aim of developing a follow-up shadow report addressing if and how CERD's recommendations have been implemented, as well as other developments in the ensuing six years. Importantly, those recommendations also provide the basis for future advocacy on issues that are of fundamental importance to indigenous peoples for the foreseeable future. These include issues such as the applicability of the Regalian doctrine to their ancestral domain, the need for greater understanding of the source, content and implications of indigenous peoples' rights by all three branches of the Government, and the role which good faith consultations and customary law should play in FPIC processes and in the determination of culturally appropriate reparations.

Viewed from the perspective of the Subanon's initial demand that the project be halted and remediation ensured, an outside observer could conclude that little has been achieved as a result of the Subanon engagement with CERD. Indeed, as pointed out by the Subanon themselves, in their 2007 submission to CERD, the case demonstrates the potential for the perverse use by a mining company of national law and State institutions in order to subordinate and disempower indigenous peoples' customary law and institutions. Indeed, the role of the IPRA itself in supporting the Subanon struggle can be questioned – given that its controversial provision in relation to pre-existing rights and a distorted use of its FPIC provisions provided the basis upon which the corporation and the State sought to justify their unwanted presence in Subanon territories. The ultimate irony would be a scenario where not only did the Subanon CADT, and the landmark IPRA legislation underpinning it, fail to protect them from TVI's encroachment, but, instead contributed towards legitimising that non-consensual entry in the eyes of external actors.

However, to conclude that the IPRA is in some way responsible for the failure to uphold the Subanon rights would be to oversimplify a complex and multifaceted reality. What happened at Mt Canatuan, and indeed systematically throughout the Philippines, was that the integral relationship between the principle of FPIC and the territorial, cultural and self-determination rights of indigenous peoples recognised in the IPRA was brutally ruptured through the NCIP's bureaucratisation of FPIC, as reflected in its FPIC implementing guidelines. This was compounded by the facilitation of 'FPIC processes' in which the IPRA was considered as an instrument to be used whenever it proved favourable to the outcome desired by corporate actors, and to be avoided or reinterpreted when it was not. The IPRA was effectively trapped in the power struggle between government agencies in which the weak NCIP was transformed by more powerful actors into a facilitator of corporate access to indigenous peoples' lands, rather than an institution which helped to facilitate indigenous peoples in the exercise of their right to self-determination

This reality reveals that the post-IPRA relationship between indigenous peoples, the Philippine State and mining companies seeking to operate there, continues to be dominated by power rather than by law. The failure to implement the law in accordance with its spirit and intent is simply a reflection of the extent of the power imbalances in governance structures at local, national, regional and international levels, all of which act in favour of mining companies to the detriment of indigenous peoples' enjoyment of their rights. This power imbalance limits the role which the State can realistically be expected to play either as a neutral arbitrator or, more importantly, as a protector and facilitator of indigenous peoples' rights, irrespective of the legal framework that has been established.

In such contexts recommendations of bodies such as CERD can act as an important counter-balance to the status quo and force some degree of self-reflection on the part of the State and corporate actors, while amplifying the voices of the oppressed and powerless and the need for respect to be accorded to their customary law and institutions. However, even if the State's serious deficiencies in understanding and capacity in relation to indigenous peoples' rights are addressed, it may still be expecting too much of a law such as the IPRA to deliver on its emancipatory promise. As has been noted, some of these issues go beyond IRPA, as the 'contradictions [that are] inherent in the law [are] perhaps [inherent in] liberal theory' itself.[58] In this regard the assertion of indigenous customary law and the insistence on a genuine system of legal plurality take on even greater importance.

In its Concluding Observations CERD welcomed 'the recognition and the protection by the State party of traditional indigenous justice and conflict resolutions mechanisms' and its 'statements that it wishes to respect the customary practices … of the Subanon people'.[59] It has also placed considerable emphasis on the role of Subanon customary law in FPIC processes and in relation to ensuring culturally appropriate reparations. The focus which the Subanon experience has directed towards this central role which indigenous peoples' customary law can play in the pursuit of their rights, including FPIC and reparations, is one of the extremely important aspects of the case. It points to the need for genuine dialogue between the state and indigenous peoples as to how meaningful interfaces can be established between indigenous customary law and legal systems and the State's legal framework and systems. It also points to the need for corporate respect for indigenous peoples' customary practices and systems. The IPRA was envisaged as constituting a component of a pluralistic legal order that serves to create space for cultural diversity.[60] Compliance with the core recommendation of CERD, that consultations be held in accordance with Subanon custom in order to determine culturally appropriate reparations, would be nothing more than the fulfilment of the State's obligations under the IPRA, which requires that customary law have primacy

58 Leonen, 'Seeking the norm', p. 38.

59 CERD, 'Concluding Observations: Philippines' (2009), paras. 7 and 25.

60 Bennagen, '"Amending" IPRA', pp. 187–9; A. B. Gatmayan, 'Philippines indigenous peoples and the quest for autonomy: Negotiated or compromised?', in Gatmaytan, *Negotiating Autonomy Case Studies*, pp. 1–36, at p. 12.

within the ancestral domains in the context of dispute resolution.[61] By implementing this recommendation in good faith the Philippines would not only offer the world an example of landmark indigenous rights legislation, but also demonstrate how a core issue facing many of the world's indigenous peoples can be addressed in a meaningful and rights-respecting manner.

A range of other lessons also emerge from the Subanon case. Among these is the need for indigenous peoples to have greater control over the process of defining, establishing, governing and overseeing institutions, such as the NCIP, that are responsible for the facilitation of their rights. This relates directly to the issue of corporate control and influence over State institutions. The extent of the complicity between the State and TVIRD was abundantly clear in the state's submission of TVIRD's highly disparaging letter as part of its own submission to CERD. That letter also exposed the flow of information between the State organ responsible for upholding indigenous peoples' rights and the company alleged to have violated those rights – information which was not even provided to the Subanon themselves. The more recent portrayal by the state of TVIRD, as a responsible corporate actor in the context of the EITI, despite the ongoing vocal objections of Subanen communities in Midsalip and Bayog to its proposed mining operations in their territories, and the absence of any efforts to ensure effective remediation for the Subanon of Mt Canatuan, is indicative of the struggle which these communities will continue to face in a context where further State and corporate complicity in rights violations is foreseeable.

Another lesson which emerges from the Subanon experience is the need for more effective extraterritorial oversight and control of corporations by their home states. The Subanon case triggered a number of actions in Canada, including an investigation into the case and a national process to consider options for oversight of Canadian corporations. However, the outcome of these processes was grossly inadequate in light of the urgency of cases, such as that of the Subanon, and the degree of harm they involve. CERD's emphasis on extraterritorial responsibility in relation to indigenous peoples' rights – in particular that of home states of extractive companies such as Canada which it has urged to 'take appropriate legislative measures to prevent transnational corporations registered in Canada from carrying out activities that negatively impact on the enjoyment of rights of indigenous peoples in territories outside Canada, and hold them accountable'.[62]

---

61 Indigenous Peoples Rights Act 1997, Section 65.

62 CERD, 'Concluding Observations: Canada', UN Doc. CERD/C/CAN/CO/19–20 (2012), para. 14, and UN Doc. CERD/C/CAN/CO/18 (2007), para. 17. CERD

is an important development in this regard and should be the subject of active consideration by relevant UN bodies, such as the Working Group on Business and Human Rights. This is particularly relevant in contexts, such as the Philippines, where mining projects are associated with conflict and rights violations. In light of growing attention being directed towards the extraterritorial responsibilities of home States by other human rights treaty bodies, civil society and national courts (in particular in the context of tort cases),[63] systematically addressing the responsibilities of all home States in relation to the rights of indigenous peoples overseas is a practice that CERD could consider as part of its reporting procedure. Indeed, to that end the development of a general recommendation on the question of home State obligations under the Convention may well be opportune.

When viewed from the perspective of the Subanon, perhaps the core lesson emerging from their engagement with CERD is the fundamental importance of indigenous peoples being in control of the conduct of their own FPIC processes. Had this been the case at Mt Canatuan the Subanon would not be in the current situation whereby they are seeking reparations for violations of their fundamental rights. The imposition of State or corporate-determined FPIC processes stands in direct contradiction with the core principle of the IPRA that customary law and practices are to have primacy within ancestral domains in the context of dispute resolution.[64] Internal differences of opinion and disputes are inevitable when a project such as a large-scale mine is proposed by external actors. FPIC processes are the means through which the community can reach its decision through its own processes and in so doing resolves any differences that exist within the community.

The process through which the community takes this decision must therefore be determined by the community and not imposed from the outside. This may imply following customary decision-making

---

has made similar recommendations to other countries including the United States, Australia, the United Kingdom and Norway.

63 For a collation of this jurisprudence see Global Initiative for Economic, Social and Cultural Rights, 'Human Rights Law Sources: UN Pronouncements on Extra-Territorial Obligations, Concluding Observations, General Comments and Recommendations, Special Procedures, UPR Recommendations' (2015), available at: www.etoconsortium.org/nc/en/main-navigation/library/documents/?tx_drblob_pi1%5BdownloadUid%5D=163. For an overview of the developments in the area of extraterritorial responsibility, see Gwynne Skinner, 'Parent company accountability: Enhancing justice for human rights violations' (ICAR, 2015), available at: http://icar.ngo/wp-content/uploads/2015/06/ICAR-Parent-Company-Accountability-Project-Report.pdf.

64 This also implies the need to avoid control being exercised over FPIC processes through financial means. The required funding must be made available in a manner that ensures there is no sense of obligation or potential for undue influence.

processes, or it may result in the community developing alternative or hybrid decision-making processes. In this regard, respect for FPIC manifestos, policies, guidelines or protocols developed by indigenous themselves is essential.[65] Irrespective of the process they decide to follow, the fundamental principle is that FPIC is an autonomous decision-making right of indigenous peoples and communities and therefore the conduct of FPIC processes must be under community control.[66] As has been explained elsewhere in greater detail,

> FPIC is the mechanism through which indigenous peoples' operationalize their self-governance rights vis-à-vis external actors ... [It] is viewed by indigenous peoples as a principle which provides for their control over the future development of their territories, and as a manifestation of that control. [State and corporate actors] should accept that FPIC is a process which is to be defined and managed by the indigenous authorities and communities whose territories and futures are impacted by proposed mining projects.[67]

Consequently, when it comes to regulating activities such as mining, that are notorious for generating conflict and rights violations, the constant emphasis which CERD has placed on the importance of obtaining FPIC and ensuring respect for indigenous self-determined decision-making processes, in accordance with its GR 23, is of paramount importance.

Over the course of their engagement with CERD, the focus of the Subanon's requests evolved in accordance with the reality they were facing. Initially their hope was that the mine would be halted in light of the clear absence of their consent and the damage being caused to their sacred mountain. Once the mountain had been irreparably harmed, the Subanon shifted their focus to resolving the disunity which the project had caused within their community, with the goal of pursing a united self-determined future. A core component of realising this is that reparations for the destruction of their sacred mountain are guaranteed in accordance with the community's wishes, as has been repeatedly recommended by CERD. Mt Canatuan's gold has been exhausted and the mine operations stopped. For the Subanon, as for similarly impacted indigenous peoples throughout the world, the pursuit of their right to remedy and realising culturally appropriate reparations is now their major challenge.

---

65 Cathal Doyle and Jill Carino, *Making Free Prior and Informed Consent a Reality: Indigenous Peoples and the Extractive Sector* (London: Middlesex University, ECCR, PIPLinks, 2013), pp. 29–39.

66 *Ibid.*, p. 75.

67 *Ibid.*, pp. 68, 75.

CERD's GR 23 and the proactive and innovative approach which CERD was adopting in 2007 in relation to addressing indigenous issues were key factors in the Subanon decision to engage with its urgent action procedure, as opposed to taking a complaint under the optional protocol of the Human Rights Committee (HRC). The reduced burden of proof with regard to exhaustion of local remedies, and the less legalistic approach of the procedure, facilitated immediate engagement with the State on urgent substantive matters.[68] The body of recommendations and decisions in relation to the situation of numerous indigenous peoples which emerged under CERD's early warning urgent action procedure in the intervening years, and the relative silence of the HRC on indigenous issues during the same period, suggests that the Subanon selected wisely.

CERD engagement with the Subanon case has, without doubt, assisted the Mt Canatuan community in their struggle to assert their rights. However, if one were to identify a shortcoming in the process it would be CERD's reluctance to issue a final decision on the case. In 2010, it appeared inevitable that a decision would be forthcoming. The flaws in the arguments put forward by the State had been exposed, its collusion with the company was evident, and it had failed to convincingly refute the Subanon allegations of rights violations. However, just when a decision looked imminent, the State requested a closed-door meeting with CERD and presented 'new information' purportedly refuting the Subanon allegations. In light of this conflicting information CERD wrote to the State asking it to provide its account of events in writing. No response was provided by the State. However, the momentum to issue a decision appeared to be lost. Shortly afterwards, the Subanon decided that in light of their circumstances, negotiating with the company was their best option. The intensity of their engagement with CERD diminished somewhat, as their attendance at CERD sessions in Geneva became less feasible. They nevertheless maintain their request that CERD issue a final decision in relation to the need for the State to guarantee reparations and address the harms caused in a culturally appropriate manner.

Issuing such a decision would empower the Subanon of Mt Canatuan in their interaction with the state, which to date has not complied with CERD's recommendations. It would also be highly significant for other Subanen communities who have resisted, and continue to resist, the entry of TVIRD into their territories, and who along with

68 In making their choice the Subanon and those assisting them were in contact with representatives of other indigenous groups, such as the Western Shoshone, who had extensive experience with CERD's procedures and were aware of its potential and its limitations.

indigenous peoples across the country continue to denounce flawed FPIC processes facilitated by the State. Due to its limited capacity, CERD would simply be unable to engage with the sheer volume of such cases in the Philippines. A decision in relation to the Subanon of Mt Canatuan case would, however, resonate with their struggles and empower them to demand greater action on the part of State and corporate actors.

The issues which the Subanon have raised, and which have been the subject of CERD's recommendations, have their roots in centuries of colonialism and the associated predominant worldview which presents the disappearance of indigenous peoples as something predetermined and necessary for the realisation of the greater good. Individuals, State actors and corporate bodies are often unaware of the highly discriminatory nature of this homogenising worldview, and the structural discrimination which it serves to perpetuate. To expect such deep-rooted problems to be addressed within a decade or two by the enactment of legislation, the issuance of legal titles, or through recommendations issued by international bodies would be wishful thinking. That being said, indigenous peoples have survived centuries of oppression and their struggle at the international level over recent decades is beginning to bear some fruit. The Subanon experience, as one small component of this larger struggle, suggests that through sustained dialogue with the Government, and guided by the country's indigenous peoples, international human rights bodies such as CERD continue to have a constructive role to play in helping to shape a social and political context that is more conducive to the empowerment of indigenous peoples and the realisation of their right to self-determination in a non-discriminatory manner. This is ultimately the primary intent of the IPRA and the objective of CERD.

Chapter 10

ICERD in the post-conflict landscape: towards a transitional justice role

Lydia A. Nkansah

Introduction

The end of the twentieth century and the beginning of the twenty-first century have witnessed conflicts with untold suffering to humanity.[1] Ethnic conflicts have resulted in 'the denial of human rights, breakdown of political order, decline of economic performance and escalation into civil and regional wars'.[2] It is estimated that 'more than half of the world's thirty million refugees at the beginning of 1990 were fleeing from civil wars and repression which are the result of communally-based conflicts'.[3] Ethnic conflicts have economic consequences and have led to famine in places like Ethiopia and Sudan because interethnic warfare prevented farming.[4] There is an international dimension since it allows for military interventions by external 'powers'.[5] Deaths which have occurred as a result of ethnic conflicts 'vary widely, [with a] range of eleven to twenty million given for the period between 1945 and the early 1990s'.[6]

In consequence, peace-building efforts have been intensified over the past fifty years through various approaches.[7] Transitional justice is one of the peace-building mechanisms that transitional democracies

1 Lydia A. Nkansah, 'International Criminal Court in the trenches of Africa', *African Journal of International Criminal Justice*, 1:1 (2015), 8–36.
2 Rita Jalali and Seymour Martin Lipset, 'Racial and ethnic conflict: A global perspective', *Political Science Quarterly*, 107:4 (1992–93), 585–606, at 587.
3 Ted Robert Gurr, quoted in *ibid.*, 587.
4 *Ibid.*
5 *Ibid.*
6 Werner Bergmann and Robert D. Crutchfield, 'Introduction: Racial and ethnic conflict and violence', *International Journal of Conflict and Violence*, 3:2 (2009), 146–153, at 147.
7 Devon Curtis and Gwinyaye A. Dzinesa, *Peacebuilding, Power, and Politics in Africa* (Athens: Ohio University Press, 2013).

characterised by an abusive past caused by conflicts or oppressive political regimes use to address their turbulent past.[8] Transitional justice 'comprises the full range of processes and mechanisms associated with a society's attempts to come to terms with the legacy of large-scale past abuses, in order to ensure accountability, serve justice and achieve reconciliation'.[9] It is maintained that the success of transition from war to peace and stability is largely dependent on how effectively the affected countries address past human rights abuses.[10]

Transitional justice is expressed as both a backward- and forward-looking tool. As a backward-looking tool, it encapsulates 'punishing wrongdoers, compensating victims for their losses; forcing individuals to disgorge property that was wrongfully acquired; and revealing the truth about past events'.[11] In its forward-looking mode, transitional justice creates opportunities that allow the public to recapture lost traditions and institutions; it deprives former officials of political and economic influences that they could use to frustrate reform; it signals a commitment to property rights, the market and democratic institutions; and establishes constitutional precedents that are intended to deter future leaders from repeating the abuses of the old regime.[12]

Transitional justice is administered through mechanisms which are either restorative or retributive, or a combination of both, or traditional mechanisms like the Rwandan *gacaca*. Its frameworks are mostly based on international human rights and international humanitarian law. The International Convention on the Elimination of all Forms of Racial Discrimination (ICERD/the Convention), the foremost human rights convention that seeks to address racial discrimination, has not been part of the framework for analysing conflicts and human rights violations in transitional justice processes.[13] Yet available literature suggest that a major cause of some contemporary forms of conflict

---

8 Lydia A. Nkansah, *Transitional Justice: Perspectives on Truth, Justice and Reconciliation in Post-Conflict Sierra Leone* (Saarbruken: VDM Verlag, 2010).

9 United Nations, 'Report of the Secretary-General on the Rule of Law and Transitional Justice in Conflict and Post-Conflict Societies', UN Doc. S/2004/616 (2004), p. 4.

10 David Mendeloff, 'Truth-seeking, truth-telling and post-conflict peacebuilding; Curb the enthusiasm?' *International Studies Review*, 6:3 (2004), 355–80.

11 Eric A. Posner and Adrian Vermeule, 'Transitional justice as ordinary justice', *Harvard Law Review*, 117:3 (2004), 762–826, at 766.

12 *Ibid.*

13 See for example 'Truth and Reconciliation Commission of South Africa Report' (Cape Town, South Africa: Truth and Reconciliation Commission, 1999), available at: www.justice.gov.za/trc/report/index.htm and 'Truth and Reconciliation Commission of Liberia Final Report' (Monrovia, Liberia, 2008), available at: http://trcofliberia.org/reports/final-report – neither of which reference ICERD.

is inequalities based on racial discrimination as occurred in Rwanda, apartheid South Africa, and others.[14] Moreover, racial conflict persists in the United States, the Third World, Western Europe, the former Soviet Union and Eastern Europe.[15]

Against this background, the chapter argues first that there is a potential link between racial discrimination and some contemporary forms of conflicts, and that ICERD has the potential in averting future conflicts. Second, it seeks to identify and establish violations based on breaches of ICERD during armed conflict which transitional justice measures and processes should address and remedy. Third, it shows how ICERD could serve as a tool in laying the foundation for the rule of law in a new transitional order. Fourth, it suggests the role the Committee on the Elimination of Racial Discrimination (CERD/the Committee) could play in that regard.

ICERD and conflict prevention

ICERD was adopted by the United Nations in 1965 to address racial discrimination, coming into force in 1969 following the required number of ratifications. It was originally conceived to target colonialism and apartheid, hence white domination over other races,[16] but its provisions have always had a clear relevance to other situations of racial conflict and it has increased its sphere of operation as differing forms of racial conflict persist. This includes 'genocide, ethnic cleansing, pogroms, civil wars, and violent separatist movements', which may exhibit racial or ethnic dimensions.[17] Other more localised forms of racial conflicts are seen in rioting and hate crimes by individuals and small groups and others that are by-products of ethnic violence although they may not specifically target any population.[18] Racial conflicts exist and are a reality around the globe. In the Third World for example, Africa as a continent is plagued with serious, often large-scale racial conflicts – Rwanda, Congo, Darfur, Nigeria, Liberia, Kenya and others have experienced these.[19] Political instability in the Third World is attributed in part to ethnic violence. Elsewhere, there

---

14 Jalali and Lipset, 'Racial and ethnic conflict', 587; Bergmann and Crutchfield, 'Introduction', 147.

15 Jalali and Lipset, 'Racial and ethnic conflict'; Richard H. Pildes, 'Ethnic identity and democratic institutions: A dynamic perspective', in Sujit Choudhry (ed.), *Constitutional Design for Divided Societies: Integration or Accommodation?* (Oxford: Oxford University Press, 2008), pp. 173–201.

16 See ICERD, in particular Preamble, Article 3 and Article 15.

17 Bergmann and Crutchfield, 'Introduction', 147.

18 *Ibid.*

19 *Ibid.*

is racial conflict in the United States which forms part of the social fabric of that society.[20] In Europe, there are many historic racial/ethnic conflicts and the recent rising migrant populations are compounding the problem.[21] The role of ethnicity is also understood in an Asian context, seen in the conflict in Nepal or the political and civil violence in Myanmar, to name just two examples.

The perceived inability of ICERD to mitigate ethnic conflict is the result of varied factors. ICERD was adopted as a reaction against racial discrimination orchestrated by colonialism and apartheid, which in effect constitutes whites' discrimination against blacks.[22] Thus, once colonial polities gained independence and apartheid was disbanded it was perceived that ICERD had attained its core objectives and become, to a certain extent, redundant. Although the Committee from the early days recognised the inclusion of various groups across States parties, in particular ethnic or other groups not necessarily differentiated by skin colour, it was not an instrument designed to prevent conflict between such groups. It was only in more recent years that it has developed competence in that regard. The current wider understanding of groups under ICERD's remit, such as indigenous, ethno-religious, ethno-linguistic, as well as non-citizens, means that many more potential conflict situations now form part of the Convention's mandate.

The causes of racial conflict are partly due to the fact that States and especially modern States are multi-ethnic. Geographic boundaries of many states are not drawn on ethnic lines, to the extent that this is possible at all. Therefore, ethnic conflicts are a common phenomenon across continents.[23] Indeed, 'of a total of 132 contemporary states only 12 (19.1%) can be described as essentially homogenous from an ethnic view point. In some instances the number of groups within a state runs into the hundreds and in 53 states (40.2%) of the total), the population is divided into more than five significant groups'.[24] The global heterogeneous nature of States renders them prone to ethnic conflicts. As Richard H. Pildes asserts: 'The most urgent problem in the design of democratic institutions today is how best to design such institutions in the midst of seemingly profound internal heterogeneity, conflict, and group differences … This problem is central, not only to newly forming democracies over the last generation but also to more established democracies.'[25] In other words, the Committee's problems

20 Andrew Valls, 'Racial justice as transitional justice', *Polity*, 36:1 (2003), 53–71.
21 Jalali and Lipset, 'Racial and ethnic conflict', 585.
22 See ICERD, in particular Preamble, Article 3 and Article 15.
23 Bergmann and Crutchfield, 'Introduction', 147.
24 Walker Connan, quoted in Jalali and Lipset, 'Racial and ethnic conflict', 586.
25 Pildes, 'Ehnic identity and democratic institutions', p. 173.

in preventing conflict are wider problems of political stability in which the Convention needs to find a targeted role.

Overall the prevalence of racial conflicts globally suggests that ICERD is generally not being complied with by its 177 State parties. There is certainly a link between the elimination of racial discrimination and the prevention of conflict, and the general work of CERD is perceived as having an effect in reducing tension and the potential for conflict. However the Committee has also evolved specific tools to prevent conflict – the early warning/urgent action procedures. In 1993, the Committee adopted a working paper to guide it in dealing with possible measures to prevent, as well as to respond more effectively to, violations of the Convention.[26] The working paper noted that both early warning measures and urgent procedures could be used to try to prevent serious violations of the Convention. At its forty-fifth session in 1994, CERD decided that preventive measures including early warning and urgent procedures, should become part of its regular agenda. The measures are differentiated by CERD. Early warning measures are to be directed at preventing existing problems from escalating into conflicts and can also include confidence-building measures to identify and support whatever strengthens and reinforces racial tolerance, particularly to prevent a resumption of conflict where it has previously occurred. Urgent procedures are to respond to problems requiring immediate attention to prevent or limit the scale or number of serious violations of the Convention.[27]

Thus criteria for early warning measures could, for example, include the following situations: the lack of an adequate legislative basis for defining and prohibiting all forms of racial discrimination, as provided for in the Convention; inadequate implementation of enforcement mechanisms, including the lack of recourse procedures; the presence of a pattern of escalating racial hatred and violence, or racist propaganda or appeals to racial intolerance by persons, groups or organisations, notably by elected or other officials; a significant pattern of racial discrimination evidenced in social and economic indicators, and significant flows of refugees or displaced persons resulting from a pattern of racial discrimination or encroachment on the lands of minority communities. Criteria for initiating an urgent procedure could include, for example, the presence of a serious, massive or persistent pattern of racial discrimination; or a situation that is serious where there is a risk of further racial discrimination.[28]

---

26 CERD, 'Prevention of Racial Discrimination, including Early Warning and Urgent Procedures', UN Doc. A/48/18 (1993), Annex III.

27 CERD, 'Guidelines for the Early Warning and Urgent Action Procedure', UN Doc. A/62/18 (2007), Annex III.

28 *Ibid.*

Decisions, statements or resolutions have been adopted including further action taken by the Committee in relation to more than twenty States parties.[29] The Committee has, *inter alia*, conducted two field visits in connection with the procedure and has drawn the attention of the Secretary General, the Security Council or other relevant bodies in relation to six States parties.[30] For example, its most recent decision in relation to Iraq noted how the Committee was 'appalled by the massacres, atrocities and other human rights abuses against civilian populations, inter alia on ethnic and ethno-religious grounds, committed by the terrorist armed group calling itself the Islamic State (IS)', and urged the UN Secretary General to submit to the Security Council the suggestion to set up a UN peace force as a temporary emergency measure.[31]

Of the early warning/urgent action procedures, the former has been identified as having a role in post-conflict situations. Thus the International Movement Against All Forms of Discrimination and Racism (IMADR), in its summary of ICERD after fifty years, noted how '[u]rgent procedures address pressing issues to avoid or limit the scale of serious violations of the Convention', while 'early warning measures is designed to prevent ongoing issues from escalating into conflicts, which also function as confidence-building measures to promote racial tolerance and prevent conflicts especially in post-conflict countries'.[32] Yet this aspect of the Committee as a tool in post-conflict societies has not been investigated. While the role of the Convention in conflict prevention is growing through the more systematic use of these procedures by the Committee, its relevance in post-conflict mechanisms needs greater analysis.

ICERD and post-conflict mechanisms: international courts

ICERD and the ICJ

ICERD has been the subject of international adjudication in post-conflict setting but not in a sustained manner. First, under Article

29 See further CERD, 'Early Warning Measures and Urgent Procedures', available at: www.ohchr.org/EN/HRBodies/CERD/Pages/EarlyWarningProcedure.aspx.

30 *Ibid.*

31 CERD, 'Decision 1 (85): Iraq' (2014), unedited version, available at: www.ohchr.org/Documents/HRBodies/CERD/EarlyWarning/early-warningDecisionIraq.pdf.

32 International Movement Against All Forms of Discrimination and Racism (IMADR), 'Written Statement: Best Practices, Achievements and Challenges of the ICERD' (2015), available at: www.ohchr.org/Documents/HRBodies/CERD/50Years/IMADR.pdf.

22 States parties may seek recourse to the International Court of Justice (ICJ) to resolve disputes under the Convention. Article 22 reads: 'Any dispute between two or more States Parties with respect to the interpretation or application of this Convention, which is not settled by negotiation or by the procedures expressly provided for in this Convention, shall, at the request of any of the parties to the dispute, be referred to the International Court of Justice for decision, unless the disputants agree to another mode of settlement.' It has not proven an effective avenue in the context of post-conflict international justice. In *Democratic Republic of Congo (DRC)* v. *Republic of Rwanda*,[33] DRC made an allegation that Rwanda had committed breaches of human rights and international humanitarian law and cited ICERD as one of the international conventions that had been violated. However the ICJ held that it did not have jurisdiction over the matter by virtue of the fact that Rwanda had made a reservation to Article 22 of ICERD.[34] A number of other States parties have entered a similar reservation to Article 22.[35]

In *Georgia* v. *Russian Federation*,[36] following the conflict between the Russian Federation and the Georgian Region of Ossetia, Georgia instituted an action against Russia at the ICJ alleging that Russia had 'engaged in widespread and systematic discrimination against ethnic Georgians'.[37] Georgia submitted that Russia's alleged acts of discrimination included 'murder, torture, rape, deportation and forcible transfer, imprisonment, hostage taking, enforced disappearance, plunder, wanton destruction and unlawful appropriation of property not justified by military necessity'.[38] Georgia maintained that these constituted breaches of Russia's obligations under ICERD, calling on the ICJ to order Russia to comply with its obligations. Two days after the submission of Georgia's original proceedings, it applied to the ICJ for provisional measures against Russia. Georgia claimed this was necessary:

> to protect its citizens against violent discriminatory acts by Russian armed forces, acting in concert with separatist militia and foreign mercenaries,

---

33 See Armed Activities on the Territory of the Congo (New Application: 2002) (*Democratic Republic of the Congo* v. *Rwanda*), Jurisdiction and Admissibility, Judgment, I.C.J. Reports (2006), p. 6.

34 *Ibid.*, paras. 75–9.

35 United Nations Treaty Collection, 'Chapter IV (2): Human Rights, ICERD Status', available at: https://treaties.un.org/Pages/ViewDetails.aspx?src=IND&mtdsg_no=IV-2&chapter=4&lang=en.

36 See Cindy Galway Buys, 'Application of the International Convention on the Elimination of all Forms of Racial Discrimination (*Georgia v Russian Federation*)', *The American Journal of International Law*, 103:2 (2009), 294–99.

37 *Ibid.*, 294.

38 *Ibid.*, 295.

> including unlawful attacks against civilians and civilian objects, murder, forced displacement, denial of humanitarian assistance, and extensive pillage and destruction of towns and villages, in South Ossetia and neighboring regions of Georgia, and in Abkhazia and neighboring regions, under Russian occupation.

Russia objected to Georgia's application, arguing that it had not engaged in acts of discrimination, and that the acts complained of do not fall under ICERD, but within international humanitarian law. The fact that Georgia had not lodged a complaint directly to CERD suggested to Russia that Georgia did not believe that racial discrimination had occurred and that ICERD had been breached. Furthermore ICERD did not apply because the obligation was domestic in nature, Georgia had not complied with the procedural requirements of ICERD before submitting the matter before the ICJ, and the ICJ did not have jurisdiction in the matter.

In its decision on the application for provisional measures, the ICJ refuted Russia's objections and held that the fact that the matter complained of raised issues about international humanitarian law, which had not been pleaded by the applicants, did not preclude the ICJ from hearing the matter on ICERD. There was evidence of bilateral contact between the parties which did not resolve the dispute and both parties were members of ICERD, hence, there was no precondition to submit the matter before the Committee, before bringing it to the ICJ. As a result the ICJ asserted its jurisdiction and ordered provisional measures to be observed by both parties. This was the first time that the ICJ ruled to exercise jurisdiction over ICERD in respect of matters relating to the legality of the use of force. The decision was considered a positive direction on ICJ's jurisdiction over ICERD. Nevertheless, this decision was short-lived, for the ICJ in its subsequent and final decision on Russia's preliminary objections ruled that the ICJ did not have jurisdiction over the matter.[39]

The issue on the ICJ's jurisdiction hinged on Article 22. The Russian Federation argues that Article 22 imposes preconditions to the ICJ's jurisdiction on ICERD, the conditions being that the ICJ can only exercise jurisdiction on a dispute arising between ICERD State parties when the dispute has not been successfully resolved by negotiation or through procedures under ICERD. Georgia has not satisfied these preconditions, hence the ICJ cannot be seized with jurisdiction over the matter. Georgia for its part maintains that Article 22 of ICERD does not impose any definite obligation to negotiate a dispute or to resort to ICERD procedures before the ICJ can exercise jurisdiction over a

39 Application of the International Convention on the Elimination of All Forms of Racial Discrimination (*Georgia* v. *Russian Federation*), Preliminary Objections, Judgment, ICJ Reports (2011), p. 70.

matter. On the basis of the literal meaning of interpretation of Article 22, the ICJ in a majority held that Article 22 imposes definitive preconditions which must be met before the ICJ can exercise jurisdiction over ICERD. Under the circumstances Georgia has not complied with the procedural precondition, therefore, the ICJ does not have jurisdiction over the matter. By so doing the Court observed that whenever it has had to interpret treaties which contain similar provisions on other alternate forms of dispute resolutions, it has always held that they constitute preconditions to its jurisdiction.

The dissent considered the practical effect of Article 22 rather than its literal interpretation and held that Article 22 does not impose preconditions to the ICJ's jurisdiction, further, that the majority's position on preconditions does not emanate from recent cases of the ICJ and is not in consonance with its contemporary reasoning on the matter. In any case, the majority's decision in no way supports the literal meaning of Article 22 nor the *travaux preparatoires*. Assuming that procedural preconditions existed, Georgia had met the condition for unsuccessful negotiation of the dispute.

Commentators have opined that the ICJ by this decision limited the standards of earlier precedents on its jurisdiction over ICERD and other human rights instruments.[40] Georgia turned to the European Court of Human Rights (ECHR) for the resolution of the case which held that it had jurisdiction.[41] Thus with regard to Article 22, an ostensibly strong provision extending the resolution of the Convention's domain to the jurisdiction of the ICJ in case of dispute, in practice has not resulted in the international Court's adjudication of violations of the Convention. It remains an option and jurisdiction over the Russia–Georgia conflict should have been possible as demonstrated by the dissenting opinion in the case. Nevertheless, given the large number of reservations to Article 22, there appears to be little appetite among States parties to view the ICJ as the correct arbiter of violations of the treaty. Despite the promise of the two cases thus far, it appears that the ICJ will not play a significant role in providing adjudications by an international court on violations of the treaty.

ICERD and international criminal law

Ad hoc international criminal tribunals/courts have emerged as one of the tools for transitional justice to prosecute conflict-related crimes.

40 N. Lucak, 'Georgia v Russian Federation: A question of the jurisdiction of the International Court of Justice', *Maryland Journal of International Law* 27:1 (2012), 323–54.

41 See *Georgia* v. *Russia* (II), App No, 38263/08, Eur. Ct. H.R. Preliminary Objections (2011).

The Nuremberg and the Tokyo tribunals in 1945 for the abuses of the Second World War marked the beginning of international criminal justice. In 1992 the International Criminal Tribunal for the former Yugoslavia (ICTY) was established in response to the international crimes including genocide which took place in that country. The International Criminal Tribunal for Rwanda (ICTR) was established in 1994 for the Rwandan genocide. In 1998 the UN established the International Criminal Court (ICC).[42] There have also been domesticated international courts such as the Special Court for Sierra Leone (SCSL), the Special Tribunal for Cambodia, the Serious Crimes Investigation Unit (SCIU) in East Timor, and the Iraqi Special Tribunal.[43] The goals of international criminal justice in the context of conflict-related crimes are to:

- Provide justice to victims and prevent vigilante justice;
- Establish or re-establish the rule of law;
- Deter future crimes, by showing that those who have violated the law do not do so with impunity;
- Delegitimize those who committed crimes and diminish their potential to act as spoilers 'incapacitating' them through trial and sentences;
- Provide a bulwark against revisionism and the ensuing tension;
- Avoid demonization of social groups and facilitate reconciliation, by showing that individuals, not entire groups, bear criminal guilt;
- Provide a symbolic break with a violent past, by exposing and condemning past times.[44]

The ad hoc international tribunals/courts have prosecuted specific conflict-related offences under their enabling statutes. These are genocide,[45] crimes emanating from international humanitarian law,[46] and crimes enshrined in the Geneva Conventions of 1949 with their 1977 protocols.[47] Others are crimes against humanity which emerged from the Nuremberg trials and were incorporated into the Nuremberg

42 Lori F. Damrosch, Louis Henkin, Richard Crawford Pugh, Oscar Schachter and Hans Smit, *International Law: Cases and Materials* (St Paul: West Group, 2001).
43 Lydia A. Nkansah, 'International criminal justice in Africa: Some emerging dynamics', *Journal of Politics and Law*, 4:2 (2011), 74–84.
44 Sarah Nouwen, 'The International Criminal Court: A peacebuilder in Africa?', in Devon Curtis and Gwinyayi A. Dzinesa (eds), *Peacebuilding, Power and Politics in Africa* (South Africa: Wits University Press, 2013), pp. 171–92, at p. 173.
45 See Article 2 of the Statute of ICTR; Article 4 of the Statute of ICTY; Article 6 of the Rome Statute of the ICC.
46 See Article 3 of the Statute of ICTY; Article 4 of the Statute of SCSL.
47 See Article 3 of the of Statute of SCSL; Article 2 of the Statute of ICTY; Article 4 of Statute of ICTR; Article 8 of the Rome Statute of the ICC.

charter.[48] The hybrid tribunals such as that of the SCSL could prosecute crimes under Sierra Leonean law together with international crimes.[49]

Racial discrimination has not been created as an offence under the statutes of the international tribunal/courts; hence, ICERD has not been the basis for indictment by these tribunals. Thus, racial discrimination may constitute a context for the commission of offences like genocide or specific crimes against groups, but not a crime per se. For example, in *The Prosecutor* v. *Radislav Krstic*,[50] the ICTY cited ICERD to construe racial discrimination for the offence of genocide. In the same way, the ICTR cited Article 4 of ICERD to construe the crime of prohibited expressions in *The Prosecutor* v. *Simon Bikindi*.[51] Even though ICERD has found expression in the jurisprudence of these tribunals as part of the general international human rights instruments, it does not constitute the basis for prosecution. In *The Prosecutor* v. *Simon Bikindi* the prosecution made an allegation that the accused's 'music and speeches constitute a gross and blatant violation of international norms on incitement to discrimination and violence'. The ICTR emphasised the technical rather than general nature of the offences at issue: 'The Chamber … is not concerned with the violation of general international legal principles, but whether an accused has committed the crimes with which he has been charged, and over which the Tribunal has jurisdiction.'[52] The tribunals/courts only pursue those crimes within their jurisdiction as per their statutes.

In conflict situations there could be abuses or violations embedded or rooted in racial discrimination that cannot be prosecuted because such violations have not been criminalised. Just as ICERD member States have an obligation to criminalise and punish certain breaches of ICERD,[53] international criminal justice mechanisms can, in the same way, criminalise racial discrimination for prosecution and punishment given its inherent contradiction with international norms and indignities. However the trend to date has been to view racial discrimination as a causal factor in the commission of international crimes, but not as a criminal act itself. Hence the elimination of racial discrimination is an essential aim in the prevention of the commission of international

48 The concept of crimes against humanity has found expression in the statutes of the ICTR, ICTY, and Article 2 of SCSL; Article 7 of the Rome Statute of the ICC has widened the scope of crimes against humanity.

49 Article 5 of the Statute of SCSL.

50 *Prosecutor* v. *Radislav Krstic*, Case No. IT-98–33-T (2001).

51 *The Prosecutor* v. *Simon Bikindi*, Case No. ICTR-01–72-T (2008).

52 *Ibid.*, 96.

53 See ICERD Article 4(a) and (b).

crimes, but is not a part of the corpus of criminal acts except in the very narrow context of apartheid.

The role of ICERD is therefore to frame or contextualise the meaning of certain crimes, but not to form an element of those crimes themselves. Hence its role in international criminal law could be said to be explanatory, and the experience of citing ICERD in international criminal proceedings appears to emphasise its preventive rather than remedial role. It is a Convention designed to foster the conditions that prevent the outbreak of conflict, rather than responding to the commission of atrocities. Once international crimes have been committed, it may be too late for ICERD to play a meaningful role. While this holds true for procedures identifying and prosecuting individual actors for individual offences, the contextual elements that inform these crimes point to its potential within post-conflict situations as a tool for transitional justice mechanisms with wider aims of rebuilding societies, beyond the relatively narrow individualised remit of international criminal bodies.

ICERD and post-conflict mechanisms: truth commissions

Truth commissions are generally understood to be 'bodies set up to investigate a past history of violations of human rights in a particular country'.[54] Truth commissions offer a viable platform for justice and accountability for most conflict societies. This is because other policy options like trials may not be possible due to the political exigencies such as where a conflict has been peacefully negotiated and amnesty (blank or conditional) granted to perpetrators.[55] Even where trials are possible through the courts whether national, ad hoc international, or the ICC, only a small fraction of perpetrators are brought into accountability by the nature of the procedural requirements of a criminal process. Truth commissions therefore ensure wider accountability and reach out to victims and communities in a way that is not possible through trials.[56]

Truth commissions therefore offer restorative justice as opposed to retributive justice and therefore they do not conduct trials. A truth

54 Priscilla B. Hayner, 'Fifteen truth commissions – 1974 to 1994: A comparative study', *Human Rights Quarterly*, 16:4 (1994), 597–655, at 600; and Priscilla B. Hayner, *Unspeakable Truths* (New York: Routledge, 2001), p. 14.

55 Kader Asmal, 'Truth, reconciliation and justice: The South African experience in perspective', *The Modern Law Review*, 63:1 (2000), 1–24. See also Leslie Vinjamuri and Jack Snyder, 'Advocacy and scholarship in the study of international war crime tribunals and transitional justice', *Annual Review of Political Science*, 7:1 (2004), 345–62.

56 Lydia A. Nkansah, 'Restorative justice in transitional Sierra Leone', *Journal of Public Administration and Governance*, 1:1 (2011), 157–73.

process recognises the rights that have been violated with reparations offered in deserving cases. It also holds perpetrators accountable to the truth for their actions. However, at the same time, the perpetrator is offered the opportunity to say his/her part of the story and to explain his/her actions. An attempt is made to create an understanding of the conflict and measures adopted for the transformation of the society to avoid the occurrence of the conflict. It utilises what is referred to as 'process pluralism'. That means that there are not only two sides to a truth, as pertains in the adversarial processes. Truth commissions offer a legal process with a peculiar characteristic that recognises emotions in the administration of justice. The peculiar characteristic of emotions that makes it unique is what also attracts criticism, that the truth process is itself imperfect.[57] Here the animating purpose is reintegration into a community, rather than 'mere punishment, whether used for retributive or deterrent rationales'.[58]

From the foregoing, it is clear that the virtues of ICERD can be useful for attaining the objectives of truth commissions for enduring peace in post-conflict societies. However, racial discrimination has not featured as a violation acknowledged and determined by most truth commissions on the basis of ICERD, although racial discrimination is considered in the context of violations. This is even so with truth commissions of those countries that have been established in response to racial/ethnic conflicts, as took place in relation to South African apartheid, the Rwandan genocide, the Liberian civil wars and others. Yet ICERD could be mainstreamed in the various stages of the truth processes. This is possible where ICERD is conceptualised and operationalised as part of the human rights architecture of truth commissions.

Truth commissions are given specific mandates which include engaging with human rights law and international humanitarian law violations. At the preparatory stage of their work, truth commissions usually conceptualise and operationalise their mandates to give meaning to them. They frame what constitutes human rights and international humanitarian law among others by reference to specific international and/or national instruments as touchstones. A list of violations is created which guides in the determination of the violations which are processed and also in categorising various violations in their database.[59] Truth commissions have employed major international and national human rights instruments, but not ICERD. The following looks at how ICERD can be mainstreamed in the truth process.

57 Carrie Menkel-Meadow, 'Peace and justice: Notes on the evolution and purposes of legal processes', *Georgetown Law Journal*, 94 (2006), 553–80, at 576.

58 *Ibid.*

59 See for example; Section 3(1)(a) of the National Reconciliation Commission Act of Ghana (No. 611 of 2002); Section 4(a) of An Act to Establish the Truth and

First, ICERD may form part of the truth architecture of truth commissions. A major goal of transitional justice is to reveal the truth about past events. Truth in the context of truth process refers to the public acknowledgement of facts and information of past events as ascertained through the processes of truth commissions. Truth commissions carry out the process of truth seeking through statement(s)-taking from all those who are willing to give statements concerning their experiences of a conflict.[60] Statement-takers are usually given a list of violations to tick or look out for. This should include racial discrimination as understood by ICERD. Again, truth seeking is also ascertained through the hearings conducted by truth commissions. There are individual hearings, institutional and thematic hearings, and specialised hearings conducted sometimes in camera for women and children. The commissioners should be sensitised to recognise breaches of ICERD in the course of the hearings. This should include investigating relevant breaches of ICERD in the context of conflict.

Second, ICERD can feature in the report of truth commissions which serves as a critical peace architecture in the peace-building process of post-conflict societies. Truth reports also identify the causes of conflicts, and serve as the future road map for development such as institutional rebuilding. The report of the Truth and Reconciliation of Sierra Leone is said to be the best thing that ever happened to Sierra Leone. The Sierra Leone report has become a standard frame for evaluating government policies and actions, and a reference point to challenge government actions in Sierra Leone.[61] The report of the Truth and Reconciliation Commission of Liberia, for example, serves as part of the framework for the development agenda in Liberia guiding their journey to the desired future of 'One People, One Nation, United for Peace and Sustainable Development'.[62] There is a strong potential role for ICERD in informing the reports of truth commissions whose mandate includes fostering the conditions towards eradicating conflict. Its role needs greater understanding, on the part of truth commissioners, but also on the part of CERD, which needs to promote the treaty as an essential component in the post-conflict tools and architecture of truth and peace-building.

Reconciliation Commission of Liberia (2005); Section 5(a) of The Truth, Justice and Reconciliation Commission Act of Kenya (No.6 of 2008); Section (6)(1) and 7(1)(a) of the Truth And Reconciliation Commission Act of Sierra Leone (2000).

60 The Liberian TRC collected over 22,000 statements in Liberia and the diaspora in the United States of America, the United Kingdom and Ghana.

61 See further Nkansah, 'Restorative justice in transitional Sierra Leone'.

62 Statement by President of Liberia, Ellen Johnson Sirleaf, at a National Visioning Conference (2012). See futher: www.emansion.gov.lr/doc/EJS_National_Constitution_Conference_Liberia_March_30_2015.pdf.

Truth commissions reports have examined the status of human rights conventions with relevant recommendations for the new foundations for development. The role and status of ICERD in such reporting has not been sufficiently recognised, and it has a role as a key component in fostering the preventive conditions for the outbreak of further ethnic tensions and violence. While ICERD may not become a direct source of international criminal prosecutions, its strength lies in the creation of long-term conditions to incrementally eradicate inequalities between racial and ethnic groups reducing the causes of tension and violence. Truth commission reports should view the harmonisation of ICERD within the domestic legal system of post-conflict states as an essential tool.

Third, ICERD can be proclaimed and popularised as a human rights instrument on racial discrimination as a major part of the justice deliberation of truth commissions. By their nature, justice on the truth platform is encapsulated in linguistic symbolism and visual forms of communication. In South Africa,[63] Sierra Leone and Liberia, symbolic patterns of language were employed to articulate the mandate, vision and goals of the commissions. The Truth and Reconciliation Commission of Sierra Leone, for example, employed jingles on radio and television, banners and billboards, such as '*come clear your chest make peace sidon na Salone* [come and speak out so peace could sit down in Sierra Leone]' and '*there is no bad bush to throw away bad pikin* [There is no dumping ground for bad children]'.[64] The truth platform can be used to bring home the ills of racial discrimination and the need for peaceful co-existence among all segments of a post-conflict society as a way to prevent the re-occurrence of the ills of the past. This will require conscious efforts on the part of CERD and its affiliates to sensitise truth commissions to that effect.

Conclusion: ICERD in the post-conflict landscape

Racial conflicts prevail despite fifty years of ICERD. This is because to a certain extent, the aims and objects of ICERD are impossible to achieve fully; but also because ICERD has not been fully understood or operationalised by its States parties. The heterogeneous nature of modern societies makes it imperative for States to pay attention to their obligations under ICERD and put the necessary infrastructures in place, as guided by CERD, to guard against all forms of racial discrimination as a means of preventing racial conflicts. CERD needs to

63 Desmond Tutu, *No Future without Forgiveness: A Personal Overview of South Africa's Truth and Reconciliation Commission* (Johannesburg: Ride, 1999).
64 See Nkansah, 'Restorative justice in transitional Sierra Leone', 164.

commission research and facilitate movements in member States to create much greater awareness of the Convention. At present it is far too little understood or utilised by governments, policy-makers and specialist bodies, as well as grassroots organisations, and CERD needs to build momentum in that regard.

ICERD has begun to carve out a role for itself in conflict prevention. The early warning and urgent action procedures have become better understood and more systematised in the workings of the Committee. Furthermore, a range of human rights bodies are articulating the link between discrimination and conflict; and the denial of the rights of groups, such as minorities, indigenous peoples, and racial and ethnic groups, and the emergence of tensions that give rise to and fuel global conflicts. For example, speaking to the General Assembly in 2010, the (then) UN Independent Expert on Minority Issues, Gay McDougall, noted a clear link between minority rights violations and violent conflict.[65] The success of these prevention procedures will require much greater study, and analysing their efficacy will be a critical part of the Committee's future work.

While conflict prevention has begun to permeate the work of CERD, its role has not been invoked in post-conflict transitional justice and peace-building processes. CERD could facilitate the inclusion of ICERD in the work of truth commissions and related bodies through several avenues: development of guidelines on transitional justice; provision of technical support to truth commissions by way of training; or sensitisation programmes for staff especially at the preparatory stage of the truth process to incorporate ICERD in the operationalisation of human rights. ICERD may also contribute to building the capacity of the working groups of truth commissions. Furthermore, CERD can follow and engage with the proceedings of international criminal justice mechanisms and submit amicus curiae where these involve breaches of ICERD, even if the expected impact of such an intervention would be for an understanding of the treaty in the contextual analysis of a crime under the statute of the court or tribunal concerned.

In conclusion, ICERD has the potential to address racial discrimination in peacetime and facilitate peaceful co-existence in the heterogeneous world. Nevertheless, in the event of conflict, transitional justice processes offer a platform to invoke ICERD to address past abuses and also to serve as a forward-looking tool in addressing causal

65 United Nations, 'Effective promotion of the Declaration on the Rights of Persons Belonging to National or Ethnic, Religious and Linguistic Minorities: Report of the UN Independent Expert on Minority Issues', UN Doc. A/65/287 (2010), in particular paras. 17–28.

inequalities. This will require reflection by State parties, the Committee and the international community on how the treaty can best contribute to this emergent area. It may involve a coming together of the various stakeholders engaged in upholding the Convention's provisions – *inter alia* the Committee, States parties, NGOs and experts from the fields of international criminal law and transitional justice. As a focal point, CERD should consider a future general recommendation on its role in post-conflict societies.

Clearly, ICERD has within it both the seeds to prevent conflict, but also to resolve discrimination, inequality and injustice between groups that lie at the heart of many conflict situations. Its role in conflict prevention began in the 1990s, with recognised procedures and mechanisms now in place. But its role in post-conflict rebuilding needs greater definition and understanding, and has been neglected by comparison with conflict prevention. A thematic discussion could draw together these key actors to establish what would be the optimal role for CERD in a post-conflict landscape, with a view to a possible general recommendation outlining the role of racial discrimination in many global conflicts, and the consequent role for ICERD in their long-term resolution, furthering significantly the object and purpose of the treaty.

Part IV
Present and future of ICERD

Chapter 11

How effective has CERD been in protecting minorities?

Joshua Castellino

Introduction

The aspiration to protect the rights of the few from the tyranny of the many has great pedigree in the development of the law of nations. Early treaties such as the Promise of St. Louis of France of 1250[1] sought to establish that it was important for the powerful to stand up for the rights of groups that may be vulnerable due to their different religious (or ethnic or linguistic) identities.[2] The foundations of the human rights law edifice are built on the need to create robust institutions and mechanisms to prevent the violation of the rights of populations faced with authorities that seek to perpetrate atrocities against them.[3] This quest evolved from an initial approach based on the need to combat entrenched practices such as slavery,[4] genocide,[5] war crimes and crimes against humanity,[6] especially the disproportionate impact of these on populations far removed from sites of power. The end of the Second World War and the formation of the United Nations came with the promise that such practices would be eradicated, with the determination to build a human rights regime a strong

1 Charte de saint Louis, roi de France, donnée aux Maronites, à Saint-Jean-d'Acre, le 24 mai 1250 [Promise of St. Louis of France].

2 For more on such treaties see Patrick Thornberry, *International Law and the Rights of Minorities* (Oxford: Clarendon Press, 1991), pp. 25–37.

3 For a general reading on the human rights regime see Philip Alston and Ryan Goodman, *International Human Rights* (Oxford: Oxford University Press, 2012).

4 For more on slavery see Jean Allain, *Slavery in International Law: Of Human Exploitation and Trafficking* (The Hague: Brill, 2013). For a wider focus see Kevin Bales, *Understanding Global Slavery* (Berkeley: University of California Press, 2005).

5 For more on genocide see William Schabas, *Genocide in International Law: The Crime of Crimes* (Cambridge: Cambridge University Press, 2009).

6 For more on such atrocities see William Schabas, *Unimaginable Atrocities: Justice, Politics and Rights at the War Crimes Tribunals* (Oxford: Oxford University Press, 2012).

indicator of this aspiration.[7] Early discussions within the newly established Commission on Human Rights centred on the need to develop common standards that could become universal and binding, enshrining such protections into law. The bifurcation of human rights into civil and political, and economic, social and cultural, rights impeded the quest for the indivisibility of rights, but nonetheless established that the journey towards greater compliance for human rights would take place through robust legally enshrined mechanisms with a common three-fold focus: (1) the establishment of clear standards with regard to each human right enshrined in law (codification); (2) that States would endorse these standards and enact legislative, judicial and administrative measures within their jurisdictions to uphold these (implementation); and (3) that there would be a residual supervisory role for international bodies to oversee the extent to which the State parties adhered to their promises (monitoring).

This chapter discusses the effectiveness of one such monitoring body, the Committee on the Elimination of Racial Discrimination (CERD/the Committee), in protecting minority rights. The first section examines the initial marginalisation of minority rights questions within the UN system, highlighting how the mainstreaming of human rights provided early justification for not having titular standards devoted to protecting minorities and indigenous peoples. The second section focuses on why the International Convention on the Elimination of All Forms of Racial Discrimination (ICERD/the Convention)[8] is the only universal binding international standard for minority rights, on the basis of its remit against other related instruments, and its own aspiration to 'eliminate' racial discrimination in all forms. Arguing that the Convention is a 'minority and indigenous rights' treaty, the third section examines CERD's contribution to the advancement of such rights. It does so through a focus on how CERD has handled key questions such as the definition of 'racial discrimination', 'hate speech' and 'affirmative action', arguing that these are fundamental pillars to the protection of minority and indigenous rights. A brief conclusion comments on the effectiveness of CERD in furthering minority rights.

Minority issues and the UN human rights treaty regime

In the 1960s the Commission on Human Rights was engaged in complicated discussions concerning the extent to which an International

7 See William Schabas, *The Universal Declaration of Human Rights* (Cambridge: Cambridge University Press, 2013).

8 International Convention on the Elimination of All Forms of Racial Discrimination, GA Res. 2106 (XX), Annex, 20 UN GAOR Supp. (No. 14) at 47, UN Doc. A/6014 (1966), 660 UNTS 195, entered into force 4 January 1969.

Bill of Rights could be developed,[9] to realise the aspirations expressed in the Universal Declaration of Human Rights (1948). These discussions were caught in at least two specific ideological battles, the 'full belly argument' concerning the importance of socio-economic rights (South v. North),[10] and the extent to which the State needed to provide governance across the range of rights (East v. West).[11] These battles were put aside as States united to pass the Declaration on the Elimination of All Forms of Racial Discrimination (1963),[12] followed swiftly by a binding Convention (1965). The speed of the reaction – the International Bill of Rights was already over fourteen years in discussion – was motivated by the feared rise of anti-Semitism in Europe; concern from large 'sending' migrant States (e.g. Mexico, India) of the treatment of their nationals abroad; and by newly emerging post-colonial States' determination to construct what they considered would be a legally binding standard and statement against the complicated architecture of the apartheid regime which was becoming entrenched in South Africa.[13] Addressing fully these issues would, in the final analysis, be beyond the mandate of the Convention although the drive to create a robust regime against anti-Semitism remains visible in the strong provisions against hate speech.[14]

Being a Convention that works on the model of rights deriving within the social contract[15] between nationals and their territorial state, the issue of foreigners (the concern of 'sending' migrant States identified

9 Dominic McGoldrick, *The Human Rights Committee: Its Role in the Development of the International Covenant on Civil and Political Rights* (Oxford: Clarendon Press, 1994).

10 Rhoda E. Edward, 'The "full belly" thesis: Should economic rights take priority over civil and political rights? Evidence from Sub-Saharan Africa', *Human Rights Quarterly*, 5 (1983), 467–90.

11 Max M. Kampelman, *Three Years at the East-West Divide* (New York: Freedom House, 1983).

12 United Nations Declaration on the Elimination of All Forms of Intolerance and of Discrimination Based on Religion or Belief, GA res. 36/55, UN Doc. A/RES/36/55 (1981).

13 Theodore Meron, 'The meaning and reach of the International Convention on the Elimination of All Forms of Racist Discrimination', *American Journal of International Law*, 79 (1985), 283–318.

14 Notably in Article 4 ICERD, reinforced by CERD in: CERD, 'General Recommendation 7 on Measures to eradicate incitement to or acts of discrimination', UN Doc. A/40/18 at 120 (1985); 'General Recommendation 15 on Measures to eradicate incitement to or acts of discrimination', UN Doc. A/48/18 at 114 (1994); 'General Recommendation 35 on Combating racist hate speech', CERD/C/GC/35 (2013); and in the context of the situation of Roma in CERD, 'General Recommendation 27 on Discrimination against Roma', UN Doc. A/55/18, Annex V at 154 (2000).

15 Jean-Jacques Rousseau, *On the Social Contract* (London: J. M. Dent, 1913, translated by G. D. H. Cole).

above) is only briefly touched upon in the text of the Convention,[16] and has gradually become a dim focus, even though it is considerably stronger than in many of the other UN treaty mechanisms.[17] As for the Convention being a statement against South African apartheid, language towards this phenomenon is visible in Article 3,[18] alongside the development of a complaint mechanism (inter-State mechanism[19]). In practice, however, the development of human rights law, in particular its adherence to State sovereignty, relative to the structures of the international system under UN auspices (especially the Security Council) and the subsequent development of a binding Convention on apartheid,[20] diminished the importance of the Convention in this regard.

The early history of international law is replete with examples of treaties designed to protect minorities,[21] and a complex mechanism towards such protection was envisaged under the auspices of the League of Nations.[22] The failure of that system in protecting minorities from the ultimate existential threat they faced, genocide, dictated a changed approach at the end of the Second World War. While minorities featured heavily in preambles and discussions, there were relatively fewer mechanisms created to specifically address their situation. The Sub-Commission of experts working under the mandate of the Commission on Human Rights, named the Sub-Commission on Prevention of Discrimination and Protection of Minorities, clearly

16 ICERD, Articles 1(2) and 1(3).

17 CERD, 'General Recommendation 11 on Non-citizens', UN Doc. A/48/18 at 112 (1994); CERD, 'General Recommendation 30 on Discrimination against non-citizens', UN Doc. CERD/C/64/Misc.11/rev.3 (2004).

18 Article 3 calls on States to 'condemn racial segregation and apartheid and undertake to prevent, prohibit and eradicate all practices of this nature in territories under their jurisdiction'.

19 Article 11 reads: 'If a State Party considers that another State Party is not giving effect to the provisions of this Convention, it may bring the matter to the attention of the Committee.' There is also provision for reference to the International Court of Justice (Article 22), recently given effect in the Georgian referral to the ICJ over the Russian incursion in South Ossetia. See further: Application of the International Convention on the Elimination of All Forms of Racial Discrimination (*Georgia* v. *Russian Federation*), Preliminary Objections, Judgment, ICJ Reports (2011), p. 70.

20 International Convention on the Suppression and Punishment of the Crime of Apartheid, UN GAOR 3068 (XXVIII), 28 UN GAOR Supp. (No. 30) at 75, UN Doc. A/9030 (1974), 1015 UNTS 243, entered into force 18 July 1976.

21 Thornberry, *International Law and the Rights of Minorities*. See also Joshua Castellino, 'The protection of minorities and indigenous peoples in international law: A comparative temporal analysis', *International Journal on Minority and Group Rights*, 17:3 (2010), 393–422.

22 Mark Mazower, 'Minorities and the League of Nations in interwar Europe', *Daedalus*, 126:2 (1997), 47–65.

had a broadly defined remit in developing standards for human rights protection. Eventually its title changed to the Sub-Commission on the Promotion and Protection of Human Rights to reflect this reality, prior to the more sweeping changes wrought under the Human Rights Council. Rather than viewing this process as a relegation of minority rights from the headlines of the emerging system of human rights protection within the UN system, it could be seen as an ideological shift towards the need to create general human rights mechanisms that would benefit entire populations, rather than only those who differed from the rest by virtue of their ethnic, linguistic or religious identity. The argument, especially in the early years, was that the protection of human rights based on the inherent dignity and worth of *every* individual would create a sheltering umbrella, under which specific groups, far from the sites of power, may shelter.

While this approach is justifiable, the attempt at creating legally binding standards, persuading States to implement these, and maintaining a loose and reasonably respectful stance towards such States in monitoring, has been relatively unsuccessful in addressing the difference between the de facto persistence of inequality, and *de jure* guarantees against it. It could be argued that ICERD was the first to begin the process of unravelling the rhetoric of general human rights, setting a (re)-trend, subsequently replicated by other emergent mechanisms and bodies, in articulating the need for *lex specialis* regimes to protect specific categories of individuals who are classifiable as members of a definitive group. It is important to emphasise that this was not new – special regimes were designed in the past to protect women and children in the context of war,[23] and as noted, to protect minorities regarded as particularly vulnerable owing to their location within States that did not fully represent them.[24] The aim of such measures was always to create an extra layer of protection in a bid to overcome the difficulties of access to more general rights that members of such groups faced.[25]

Thus, despite the articulation of the modern agenda of human rights as rights applying *equally* to every individual, it was ICERD

---

23 There are forty-two provisions referring to women in the 1949 Geneva Conventions on the Laws of Wars and the 1977 Additional Protocols; see further Judith G. Gardam and Michelle J. Jarvis, *Women, Armed Conflict and International Law* (The Hague, London and Boston: Kluwer Law International, 2001). For an articulation of child rights during the League of Nations era, see Geneva Declaration of the Rights of the Child, adopted 26 September 1924, League of Nations.

24 See further Thornberry, *International Law and the Rights of Minorities*, especially Ch. I.

25 For more on access to justice which underpins this issue, see D. L. Rhode, *Access to Justice* (Oxford: Oxford University Press, 2004), pp. 1–19 and pp. 103–20.

that re-engaged recognition of *lex specialis* as an important tool in combating inequality and injustice when experienced collectively by individuals who belonged to an identifiable class of people. Among the pantheon of protections that have subsequently proliferated are instruments pertaining to indigenous peoples,[26] women,[27] children,[28] migrant workers (documented and undocumented),[29] refugees[30] and the disabled.[31] In each context, international documents have been signed and ratified containing a series of general human rights, a list of specific rights distinct to the class of persons in question (or at least an orientation of existing rights in that regard), and in some cases, an additional mechanism designed to overcome the problem of the groups' lack of access to general rights. Most recently, the trend has included the creation of non-identity based *lex specialis* for human rights defenders, on the grounds that their rights are particularly difficult to guarantee.[32]

Importantly, despite the extent to which the treatment of minorities has engaged and at times dominated world history, there is still no specific binding *lex specialis* at international level with 'minorities' in the title. There are two treaties that are legally binding and concern minorities: the Framework Convention on National Minorities[33] and the European Charter for Regional or Minority Languages.[34] Both documents, replete with (relatively) well-functioning monitoring mechanisms, work under the mandate of the Council of Europe. They are

26 Convention concerning Indigenous and Tribal Peoples in Independent Countries (ILO No. 169), 72 ILO Official Bull. 59, entered into force 5 September 1991.
27 Convention on the Elimination of All Forms of Discrimination against Women, GA Res. 34/180, 34 UN GAOR Supp. (No. 46) at 193, UN Doc. A/34/46, entered into force 3 September 1981.
28 Convention on the Rights of the Child, GA Res. 44/25, Annex, 44 UN GAOR Supp. (No. 49) at 167, UN Doc. A/44/49 (1989), entered into force 2 September 1990.
29 International Convention on the Protection of the Rights of All Migrant Workers and Members of Their Families, GA Res. 45/158, Annex, 45 UN GAOR Supp. (No. 49A) at 262, UN Doc. A/45/49 (1990), entered into force 1 July 2003.
30 Convention relating to the Status of Refugees, 189 UNTS 150, entered into force 22 April 1954.
31 International Convention on the Protection and Promotion of the Rights and Dignity of Persons with Disabilities, GA res. 61/106, Annex I, UN GAOR, 61st Sess., Supp. No. 49, at 65, UN Doc. A/61/49 (2006), entered into force 3 May 2008.
32 See for example Council of the European Union, 'Ensuring Protection: EU Guidelines On Human Rights Defenders' (Council of General Affairs, 2008), available at: www.consilium.europa.eu/uedocs/cmsUpload/GuidelinesDefenders.pdf.
33 Framework Convention for the Protection of National Minorities (ETS No. 157), entered into force 2 January 1998.
34 European Charter for Regional or Minority Languages (ETS No. 148), entered into force 3 January 1998.

however only binding on a small proportion of the world's States, and their geographic remit prevents them from being considered 'universal' standards. While this could not be said about 'indigenous peoples' due to the universalist nature of ILO Convention 169, the small number of States that have ratified the instrument means that indigenous peoples, too, have little access to a global binding instrument and mechanism that headlines their specific concerns. Two attempts at creating named universalist regimes for the protection of minorities,[35] and indigenous peoples,[36] have yielded declarations that articulate aspirational standards, but are not legally binding upon States.

The ambition, reality and development of the Convention by CERD

The ambition of ICERD, indicated in its title, potentially dooms any analysis of its effectiveness to failure. 'Eliminating' 'all forms of racial discrimination' may well be a utopian quest beyond reach, even without envisaging the possibility of it being achieved by unrepresentative States acting in narrow self-interest. It is equally clear however that creating a universal standard, making it legally binding, and cajoling States towards its adherence has yielded benefits in enhancing protection and moving towards the elimination of some, if not all, forms of racial discrimination. Thus adopting the language of socio-economic rights, the 'progressive realisation' of the elimination of racial discrimination, is more realistic than any sudden 'elimination', desirable as that is.

The lack of a named universally accepted legally binding standard governing the protection of minorities and indigenous peoples is offset by the existence of ICERD. It was described, in 1978, as:

> the international community's only tool in combatting racial discrimination, which is at one and the same time universal in reach, comprehensive in scope, legally binding in character and equipped with built-in measures of implementation.[37]

Legitimate questions could be posed as to whether eliminating 'racial discrimination' subsumes all of the needs of the protection of minority and indigenous peoples, and the current Declarations in both areas point to it having major shortcomings in that regard. But

---

35 United Nations, Declaration on the Rights of Persons Belonging to National or Ethnic, Religious or Linguistic Minorities, GA Res. 47/135, Annex, 47 UN GAOR Supp. (No. 49) at 210, UN Doc. A/47/49 (1993).

36 United Nations, Declaration on the Rights of Indigenous Peoples, GA Res. 61/295, UN Doc. A/RES/47/1 (2007).

37 CERD, 'Statement at the World Conference to Combat Racism and Racial Discrimination', 33 UN GAOR Supp. (No.18) at 108–9, UN Doc. A/33/18 (1989).

it is not the intention of the instrument to comprehensively articulate the meaning or range of minority or indigenous rights, but rather to provide protection to such groups within its ambit insofar as this is useful and practicable. It is argued here that the text of ICERD, the subsequent general recommendations passed by CERD, and the practice of the examination of State parties' performance all point to the Convention and its mechanism being in part a UN minority and indigenous peoples treaty, complementary to the more focused instruments in both spheres.

The Preamble of the Convention demonstrates its rationale, as seeking to overcome the gap between the *de jure* situation of the class (defined here as victims of racial discrimination) and their de facto position in society. The treaty articulates a series of general human rights available to all and, in addition, specific rights and mechanisms that need to be designed and implemented to ensure that those facing exclusion are effectively protected. The tension that inevitably exists with the regime is the extent to which these obligations can be realised without creating unfair discrimination against the rest of the population. This tension is best demonstrated in Article 2 of the Convention, which creates the obligation on States to design affirmative action measures that address the gap between those who face discrimination on racial grounds (identified as covering race, colour, descent, and national or ethnic origin),[38] and the rest of the population. Sub-article 2(2) states:

> States Parties shall, when the circumstances so warrant, take, in the social, economic, cultural and other fields, special and concrete measures to ensure the adequate development and protection of certain racial groups or individuals belonging to them, for the purpose of guaranteeing them the full and equal enjoyment of human rights and fundamental freedoms. These measures shall in no case entail as a consequence the maintenance of unequal or separate rights for different racial groups after the objectives for which they were taken have been achieved.[39]

To ensure that the systems created do not justify segregation such as apartheid,[40] Article 1(4) seeks to highlight that such rights can only be enshrined in a positive context. Thus:

---

38 ICERD, Article 1(1).

39 Article 2(2) *International Convention on the Elimination of All Forms of Racial Discrimination*. For more on the development of group rights by CERD, see Joshua Castellino, 'A re-examination of the International Convention for the Elimination of All Forms of Racial Discrimination', *Revista Iberoamericana de Derecho Humanos*, 2 (2006), 3–34.

40 For a discussion around segregation or 'Bantustanisation', see H. J. Richardson, 'Self-determination, international law and the South African Bantustan policy', *Columbia Journal of Transnational* Law, 17 (1978), 185–220.

> Special measures taken for the sole purpose of securing adequate advancement of certain racial or ethnic groups or individuals requiring such protection as may be necessary in order to ensure such groups or individuals equal enjoyment or exercise of human rights and fundamental freedoms shall not be deemed racial discrimination, provided, however, that such measures do not, as a consequence, lead to the maintenance of separate rights for different racial groups and that they shall not be continued after the objectives for which they were taken have been achieved.[41]

In recent years CERD has strengthened its mandate in protecting group rights by identifying specific categories of people as needing further protection, in particular through its general recommendations. Among these are: women facing multiple discrimination,[42] the Roma,[43] indigenous peoples,[44] 'descent-based' communities[45] and non-citizens.[46] The identification of these groups is underlined by their collective experience of discrimination, witnessed by individuals from these groups, on the basis of their membership of a particular subcategory of the population. By highlighting these communities CERD has not only furthered the agenda of collective rights in a system skewed towards individual rights protection, it has also highlighted the multiple intersectionalities that exist in discrimination. The approach towards articulating the rights of individuals belonging to communities that face collective violations of their enjoyment of human rights is maintained through Concluding Observations to various State parties, and is at present best studied through the 'List of Issues' attendant to the scrutiny of every reporting State in recent years. The issues identified inevitably commence with the need for greater implementation of the Convention, including the need to strengthen States' legal obligations in this regard. This is then often followed by a coherent identification of *inter alia* specific minorities or indigenous peoples in need of special protection.

CERD goes wider in its identification of issues than instruments focused on minorities and indigenous peoples, also highlighting for example violations faced by refugees, asylum-seekers and migrants. In this respect CERD has stayed true to the aspiration expressed above at

41 ICERD, Article 1(4). See further CERD, 'General Recommendation 32 on The meaning and scope of special measures in the ICERD', CERD/C/GC/32 (2009).

42 CERD, 'General Recommendation 25 on Gender-related dimensions of racial discrimination', UN Doc. A/55/18, Annex V at 152 (2000).

43 CERD, 'GR 27'.

44 CERD, 'General Recommendation 23 on Rights of indigenous peoples', UN Doc. A/52/18, Annex V at 122 (1997).

45 CERD, 'General Recommendation 29 on Discrimination based on descent', UN Doc. A/57/18 at 111 (2002).

46 CERD, 'GR 30'.

the birth of the Convention, attributed to Mexico and India, who were seeking greater protection for their nationals living within the jurisdiction of another State. This is also a significant enhancement of minority protection, which is usually restricted in traditional definitions and practice to individuals who are 'nationals of the State'.[47]

The protections offered by ICERD may be at times disappointing for certain long-standing minorities and indigenous peoples, in particular in relation to its ability to provide enhanced protection in areas such as cultural rights. That CERD may struggle to realise certain of the promises that exist or can be read into the treaty, may be as much a result of practical impediments and State intransigence as an absence of correct focus in the treaty's provisions. Similarly its practice views the realisation of rights for minority and indigenous, among other groups, as dependent on an effective and evolving dialogue with States parties. That dialogue can include oversight of stronger enforcement mechanisms, such as judgments of domestic courts, and is not intended as a substitute for these. The precise role of CERD warrants greater understanding, but to a certain extent it can be characterised as, if not the precise focus, then a custodian of minority and indigenous rights within the UN system.

Key tools in the protection of minority rights

ICERD is one of the briefest of the human rights treaties, with the specific content of rights limited to seven articles. Article 1 identifies the scope of the Convention; Article 2 stresses State obligations upon ratification; Article 3 makes reference to apartheid and other forms of segregation; Article 4 calls for States to eradicate 'hate speech'; Article 5 contains an inexhaustive listing of the rights that need to be accessed without discrimination; Article 6 underlines the notion of equality in law; Article 7 specifically deals with the field of education. These basic articles have been interpreted and clarified by CERD through general recommendations, developing the nature of State obligations and contributing to the growth of customary international law. In advancing the claim that CERD has been relatively effective in promoting minority and indigenous peoples rights, this section draws attention to its contribution in four specific spheres: (1) clarifying the wide scope of the Convention; (2) maintaining pressure on States to implement special

47 For instance the most widely used definition of a minority (Capotorti), includes the requirement that minorities are 'nationals' of the State from which they may seek protection. See Francesco Capotorti, 'Study on the Rights of Persons Belonging to Ethnic, Religious and Linguistic Minorities', UN Doc. E/CN.4/Sub.2/384/Rev.1 (1977).

measures to combat structural discrimination; (3) seeking to contain, regulate and ostracise hate speech against specific populations, usually minorities or those far from sites of power; and (4) developing innovative mechanisms that could, if given adequate weight within the international community, provide ideal protection against violations of minority and indigenous peoples' rights.

Clarification of scope

While the Convention was framed in response to anti-Semitism, its pertinence to contemporary times has sometimes been questioned. First, CERD inherited a Convention that uses the word 'race', itself socially constructed to categorise and dominate others. The lack of substance in the term 'race' required adoption of a pragmatic approach; while not defending the existence of 'race' it posited the need to combat the factual existence of racial discrimination. A second challenge arose under Article 1(2), which enabled differential treatment by a State of its citizens. While 1(2) was framed to enable States the prerogative of qualitative differences in treatment of its own citizens, it raised questions as to the scope of these and the extent to which non-citizens could be excluded from the Convention's protections. CERD addressed this through general recommendations, most notably GR 11, which stressed that the article did not absolve States from their obligation to report on matters concerning foreigners. It affirmed instead that 'State parties are under an obligation to report fully upon legislation on foreigners and its implementation', and further that the provisions 'must not be interpreted to detract in any way from the rights and freedoms recognised and enunciated in other instruments'.[48] The principle of non-discrimination and scope of Article 1 was also further clarified (Recommendation XIV), emphasising that the words 'based on' do not differ from 'on the grounds of' which appears in preambular paragraph 7, and that: 'A distinction is contrary to the Convention if it has either the purpose or the effect of impairing particular rights and freedoms.'[49] This is further confirmed by the State obligation identified in Article 2(1)(c).[50] A third challenge on scope arose as to the grounds of discrimination under its ambit, seen for example in the

48 CERD, 'GR 11'.

49 CERD, 'General Recommendation 14 on Definition of racial discrimination', UN Doc. A/48/18 at 114 (1994), para. 2.

50 Article 2(1)(c) states: 'Each State Party shall take effective measures to review governmental, national and local policies, and to amend, rescind or nullify any laws and regulations which have the effect of creating or perpetuating racial discrimination wherever it exists.'

issue of caste and descent discussed elsewhere in this volume.[51] Finally in terms of scope, the Committee also developed the issue of multiple discrimination, highlighting its salience for a regime seeking to eliminate discrimination.

Article 1(1) provides two avenues for the scope of this Convention. The first, a constitutive approach, contrasts with a second, 'effects' orientation. A constitutive approach would identify constituent elements that must be present for an action to be deemed 'racial discrimination'. CERD could then address the purpose or intent of these acts which are perpetrated for 'nullifying or impairing the recognition, enjoyment or exercise, on an equal footing, of human rights and fundamental freedoms in the political, economic, social, cultural or any other field of public life'.[52] By delineating grounds of 'racial discrimination', Article 1 could be said to be constitutive. CERD however has adopted a cautious, slightly wider approach, based on 'effects'.[53] This requires making the 'purpose or effect' as identified in Article 1, central to the scope of the Convention. Thus the grounds identified may be considered subsidiary to the effects of discrimination that results in the nullification or impairment of rights. This may allow the Convention to be extended to *all* situations of entrenched discrimination irrespective of whether this discrimination could be considered 'racial' in the sense identified in the first part of Article 1. By focusing on discrimination rather than its specific 'racial' guise, CERD could have endorsed the fact that 'race' is no more than a construct. But rather than go as far as that, CERD's cautious hybrid approach pays attention to the grounds for racial discrimination, steadily widening these, while remaining wary of construing the Convention as a general document challenging all discrimination.

Special measures as a legitimate tool in tackling structural inequality

ICERD clearly identifies special measures or affirmative action as a vital tool within human rights law. First, in combating historical grievances that have resulted in deep-rooted discrimination against particular groups,[54] such measures aim to provide groups that have faced

51 See also David Keane, *Caste Based Discrimination in International Human Rights Law* (Dartmouth: Ashgate, 2007), pp. 159–209.

52 The specific list of the categories of rights is contained in Article 5.

53 This approach may be contrasted with the discussion over several decades around the identification of minorities for the purposes of Article 27 of the International Covenant for Civil and Political Rights, 1966. See generally Timo Makkonen, *Identity, Difference and Otherness* (Helsinki: Erik Castren Institute, 2000).

54 For a general reading on affirmative action measures, see Michael Banton, *International Action Against Racial Discrimination* (Oxford: Oxford University

long-standing systemic discrimination with a means towards equal access to the fruits of human rights. This could be conceptualised as an *elevator mechanism* designed to raise a particular segment of the population that is at level zero (in terms of quantifiable indicators such as access to services, employment within the private and public sector, political participation, level of and access to education, and other civil, political, economic, social and cultural rights) to the level that the rest of the population enjoys, which can be conceptualised as level one.[55] The underlying cause for the difference between the target group and the rest of the population i.e. 'the gap', is often the result of past and present systemic invidious discrimination.[56] However rather than revising history, which is impossible and undesirable,[57] an *elevator mechanism* accepts the need for focusing on specific measures aimed at the alleviation of a particular disadvantage faced by a specific group. While not always successful, the attempt to seek redress has to be acknowledged as reasonable within societies that have perpetrated historical injustices towards segments of the population.

Second, CERD has consistently justified special measures as a legal guarantee through which power relationships within a system could be challenged. Thus special measures attempt to remedy existing social and structural discrimination, whether or not this has an identifiable 'history'.[58] While not tackling the prejudice that might exist in societies towards specific groups, these measures aim to create mechanisms to break down existing structural and institutional imbalances, whatever their cause.

Third, it attempts to diversify society through calls for proportional group representation.[59] While this may be criticised as tokenism, it nonetheless has the effect of creating new aspirations and expectations

---

Press, 1996) and G. Ezorsky, *Racism and Justice: The Case for Affirmative Action* (Ithaca, NY: Cornell University Press, 1991).

55 Castellino, 'A re-examination of the International Convention for the Elimination of All Forms of Racial Discrimination', 39, 19–24. For this discussion in the context of linguistic rights see Joshua Castellino, 'Affirmative action for the protection of linguistic rights: An analysis of international human rights legal standards in the context of the Irish language', *Dublin University Law Journal*, 25 (2004), 1–43.

56 See S. M. Cahn, *The Affirmative Action Debate* (New York: Routledge, 2002).

57 Some argue that affirmative action could be seen as a price for previous discrimination; see for example H. McGary, 'Justice and reparations', *Philosophical Forum*, 9 (1977–78), 250–63.

58 For an empirical study on the effect of affirmative action policies in the United States, see W. Bowen and D. Bok, *The Shape of the River: Long-Term Consequences of Considering Race in College and University Admissions* (Princeton: Princeton University Press, 1998).

59 Diversity as a justification for racial preference in higher education was discussed in *DeFunis* v. *Odegaard* 416 US 312 (1974). Also see *Regents of the University* v. *Bakke*

among minorities with a view towards fuller participation in all aspects of public life.[60] CERD's approach is also characterised by a social utilitarian argument, which stresses that society as a whole is better off with all its components participating in processes that affect them. This has the added potential impact of calming future social unrest as potentially antagonistic groups come into greater contact,[61] contributing to healthier 'nation-building',[62] through the emergence of multi-dimensional visions of the State.

Special measures could, of course, easily be used to promote privilege, and have been in certain contexts,[63] making it important for law to lay down conditions under which such measures may be justifiable. In looking through CERD's Concluding Observations and statements the following could be inferred as what emerges as the *necessary and sufficient conditions* for the articulation of such measures:[64]

a. The target group should be demonstrably disadvantaged;[65]
b. The aspiration for equality should be justified;[66]

---

483 US 265 (1978) and the commentary on this case in R. Post, 'Introduction: after *Bakke*', in R. Post and M. Rogin (eds), *Race and Representation: Affirmative Action* (New York: Zone Books, 1998), pp. 13–27.

60 By contrast, the argument of benefiting the 'creamy layer' (i.e. the elite among the target population) needs to be acknowledged. See J. Castellino and E. Domínguez Redondo, *Minority Rights in Asia: A Comparative Legal Analysis* (Oxford: Oxford University Press, 2006), Conclusion.

61 This is referred to in political science as the 'Contact Hypothesis'. See further H. D. Forbes, *Ethnic Conflict, Commerce, Culture, and the Contact Hypothesis* (New Haven: Yale University Press, 1997).

62 For an enunciation of the notion of state building, see K. Deutsch and W. Foltz, *Nation Building* (New York: Atherton Press, 1963).

63 The apartheid argument in South Africa was for 'separate' systems of development for each of the 'races' of South Africa. While never mooted as affirmative action, it was nonetheless a policy ostensibly designed with the 'capacities' of each 'race' in mind. Controversially in Malaysia, the privileged status of the majority Malay population is guaranteed by Article 153 of the Federal Constitution. For more on this, including an analysis of whether this can be justified as a measure of affirmative action, see Castellino and Redondo, *Minority Rights in Asia*, Ch. VI.

64 The discussion in US case law on the cases concerning restriction of affirmative action measures is also significant. See *Firefighters* v. *Stotts*, 467 US 561 (1984); *Wygant* v. *Jackson Board of Education*, 476 US 267 (1986); *Richmond* v. *J.A. Croson Co.*, 488 US 469 (1989) and *Adarand Constructors Inc.* v. *Pena*, 515 US 200 (1995).

65 This can be effectively measured through socio-economic statistical indicators such as access to education, birth rates, employment, health care, access to public housing, etc.

66 Important in the context where groups often construct themselves as desiring of special protection, when their aims may not necessarily be in keeping with the threshold required in a democratic society. For more on this issue see *Canada (Human Rights Commission)* v. *Taylor*, 3 S.C.R. (1990).

c. The measure should be designed to ensure closure of the gap;[67]
d. Empirical evidence should examine its success;[68]
e. The measures should not be unreasonably discriminatory towards the majority;[69]
f. The measures should cease on the achievement of equality;
g. The measures should cease should it be demonstrated that they are ineffective.

Commenting on its oversight of special measures, CERD reiterated in General Recommendation 14:

> a differentiation of treatment will not constitute discrimination if the criteria for such differentiation, judged against the objectives and purposes of the Convention, are legitimate or fall within the scope of article 1, paragraph 4, of the Convention. In considering the criteria that may have been employed, the Committee will acknowledge that particular actions have varied purposes. In seeking to determine whether an action has an effect contrary to the Convention, it will look to see whether that action has an unjustifiable disparate impact upon a group distinguished by race, colour, descent, or nationals or ethnic origin.[70]

Hate speech

The strong exhortations in ICERD on hate speech have been upheld and further developed by CERD. Article 4 of the Convention requires States to outlaw hate speech, with States not only required to condemn all organisations based on racial superiority, but also required to undertake 'to adopt immediate and positive measures designed to eradicate all incitement to, or acts of, such discrimination'. The provision and related general recommendations are discussed elsewhere in this volume, but the issue is central from a minority rights perspective and a key tenet in the 'protection' of minorities. From CERD's perspective, control over hate speech was identified as a central tool in eliminating racial discrimination,[71] but despite the unambiguous message of

67 Measures that are badly defined often affect the majority badly and generate angst against the minority. See S. Rothman, 'Racial diversity reconsidered', *Public Interest*, 151 (2003), 25–38.

68 This can be measured by recourse to statistics such as the level of education of the minority, per capita incomes, employment in the public and private sectors, degree of life expectancy and other such indicators.

69 If a measure proves generally discriminatory towards the majority it will fall foul of evolving human rights standards that seek equality as a basic guarantee of the legal system.

70 CERD, 'GR 14'.

71 'Race' in this context may be interpreted reasonably widely as including ethnicity, linguistic and other characteristics that are pertinent to minorities and under which

Article 4 only a relatively small proportion of States have legislation dealing with incitement to hatred. Several States have extended reservations to Article 4,[72] most along the lines of the well-known position of the United States, where the First Amendment to the Constitution is invoked to prevent laws being passed which infringe upon the right to freedom of expression.[73] As a result CERD is required to continue to exert pressure upon States to pass such legislation, evidenced in a range of GRs, most recently GR 35. These stress the nature of Article 4, and express concern at the large number of non-compliances with its provisions. It also regularly reiterates the importance of hate speech legislation:

> The proscription of the dissemination of ideas of racial superiority, and of organized activity likely to incite persons to racial violence, was properly regarded as crucial [at the signing of the Convention]. Since that time, the Committee has received evidence of organized violence based on ethnic origin and the political exploitation of ethnic difference. As a result, implementation of article 4 is now of increased importance.[74]

Clarifying the nature of State obligations, CERD states:

> To satisfy these obligations, States parties have not only to enact appropriate legislation but also to ensure that it is effectively enforced. Because threats and acts of racial violence easily lead to other such acts and generate an atmosphere of hostility, only immediate intervention can meet the obligations of effective response.[75]

In addressing hate speech legislation as a remedy to protect the rights of minorities and indigenous peoples the following points need to be emphasised. First, levels of racism in societies have risen on the back of patterns such as migration and forcible displacement of peoples, which has fostered ever more unequal contact between groups. This makes it crucial that freedom of expression is exercised with due restraint to prevent the instigation of hatred that might fester against vulnerable populations. Second, the civil libertarian view of the minimum

---

they may self-identify. See CERD, 'General Recommendation 8 on Membership of racial or ethnic groups based on self-identification', UN Doc. A/45/18 at 79 (1991). See also this principle in CERD, 'GR 11' and 'GR 30'.

72 United Nations Treaty Collection, 'Chapter IV (2): Human Rights, ICERD Status', available at: https://treaties.un.org/Pages/ViewDetails.aspx?src=IND&mtdsg_no=IV-2&chapter=4&lang=en.

73 See A. Adler, 'Inverting the First Amendment', *University of Pennsylvania Law Review*, 149:4 (2001), 921–1002; J. Goldsmith, 'Should international human rights law trump US domestic law?' *Chicago Journal of International Law*, 1:2 (2000), 327–39.

74 CERD, 'GR 15', para. 1.

75 *Ibid.*, para. 2.

restriction of the freedom of expression is clearly a throwback to common law rather than universal standards. Even NGOs campaigning for free speech such as Article 19 accept that it is inherent that such freedom is exercised with due constraint.[76] Third, rather than a pure individual rights based approach, modern human rights law includes group rights, and as a consequence the freedom of an individual (or group) to express sentiments that might cause physical or mental harm to another needs to be restricted. Fourth, unrestricted rights exercised by the powerful would violate the rights of those less able to assert their own rights.[77]

New mechanisms: early warning and urgent action

Mindful that persistent discrimination within society could lead to gross human rights violations, CERD developed the notion of an 'early warning mechanism'. The process of accepting such a mechanism within its operation began with the adoption of a working paper on the subject in 1993.[78] A year later CERD decided that 'early warning measures' and 'urgent procedures' could be used to prevent violations of the Convention, and adopted them as part of its regular agenda. Early warning mechanisms are directed against preventing escalation of persistent problems into conflicts, while urgent procedures are available once conflict has broken out, to prevent escalation and wide-scale violation of Convention norms. While both mechanisms are framed with a wide variety of situations in mind, their use remains limited, and they have not been sufficiently linked with the maintenance of international peace and security as overseen by the United Nations Security Council.

Since its inception such procedures have been used in relation to over twenty States but the decisions, statements and resolutions adopted have not merited adequate attention internationally, and as a result have had little effect. This is true, despite the Committee conducting field visits, and, specifically seeking to draw the attention of the Secretary General, Security Council and other relevant bodies to the grave situations of violations of the treaty.[79] Having failed to impact on such situations, CERD has indicated a willingness to set up

---

76 As indicated in Article 29(2) of the Universal Declaration for Human Rights 1948.

77 See for example J. Schlosberg, 'Judgment on "Nuremberg": An analysis of free speech and anti-abortion threats made on the internet', *Boston University Journal of Science and Technology Law*, 7 (2001), 52–79.

78 CERD, 'Prevention of Racial Discrimination, including Early Warning and Urgent Procedures', UN Doc. A/48/18 (1993), Annex III.

79 See further CERD, 'Early Warning Measures and Urgent Procedures', available at: www.ohchr.org/EN/HRBodies/CERD/Pages/EarlyWarningProcedure.aspx.

a working group to consider the status of implementation of its decisions and recommendations, to find ways of reactivating such mechanisms in a meaningful way.

While the mechanism has not been acted upon, it is clear that in developing it, CERD is seeking to highlight lessons learnt through history – that unchecked discrimination within society, when it occurs on the basis of differentiated identities, could lead to instability and war, with the potential for ethnic cleansing, war crimes, crimes against humanity and even genocide. Its latest 'decision', on Iraq, displays this fear as clearly as its attempted interventions in highlighting the dangers in Yugoslavia decades previously, after seeing early signs of the disaster about to befall that State.[80] The prescience of these warnings for the protection of minorities needs better understanding. To what extent and by what indicators have they been largely 'correct'? In which case arguments for greater access for CERD to global peace and security mechanisms can be premised.

Conclusion

This chapter sought to study the effectiveness of CERD in protecting minority rights. The Convention is the only universal and binding standard to protect minorities and indigenous peoples, and as such is a lynchpin in the UN mechanisms to protect these groups. However it is not an instrument that was designed with these groups specifically in mind, and so there are inherent limits in its provisions and in the practice of the Committee in realising the aims of different minority and indigenous groups. CERD's approach additionally protects a wider remit of groups than minorities and indigenous peoples. Nevertheless, these form a core of the Committee's work, and in this regard it operates as a custodian for the realisation of their rights through dialogue with States parties.

The chapter subsequently examined the aims and objectives of the text and the extent to which these had been developed by CERD. In addition to the furthering of group rights, which commenced through the will of the Convention's drafters, the chapter ended by articulating four features through which CERD has advanced the protection of the rights of minorities and indigenous peoples: clarifying the scope of the Convention, asserting the need for affirmative action measures in combating structural discrimination, insisting on the importance of hate speech against opposition, and generating a smarter mechanism

80 United Nations General Assembly, 'Report of the Committee for the Elimination of All Forms of Racial Discrimination', UN Doc. A/45/18 (1992), in particular paras. 194–205.

through which ethnic tensions within societies could be contained before they escalated to full-fledged crises.

CERD used to be considered a committee where States sent its diplomats to reward them for loyal service.[81] As a consequence many felt it would be unable to serve the needs of human rights, since diplomats were less likely to be harsh on States. Evidence suggests that these diplomats may have been as willing to construct a strong edifice of protection as any others, and over time the diplomats have been replaced by individuals of high standing and achievement, who have sought to further the cause of the elimination of all forms of racial discrimination. The breadth of that mandate probably means that they will never succeed, but for minorities and indigenous peoples CERD is likely to become ever more important in addressing their grievances.

81 K. Mechlem, 'Treaty bodies and the interpretation of human rights', *Vanderbilt Journal of International Law*, 42 (2009), 905–47, at 917.

Chapter 12

General Recommendation 35 on combating racist hate speech

Tarlach McGonagle[*]

Introduction

The central concern of General Recommendation 35 (2013) of the Committee on the Elimination of Racial Discrimination (CERD/ the Committee) is to figure out and set out how the 'resources' of the International Convention on the Elimination of All Forms of Racial Discrimination (ICERD/the Convention) can be optimally 'mobilised' for the purpose of combating racist hate speech. The term 'racist hate speech' does not actually appear in the text of the Convention, but the imperative of combating it falls squarely (but not exclusively) within the ambit of Article 4 *juncto* Article 5. GR 35 is CERD's fourth general recommendation that addresses (issues covered by) Article 4. Thus, to put it somewhat mischievously, at issue here are an unclear term that is alien to the Convention, but governed largely by the most convoluted and controversial article of the Convention, and a fourth structured attempt by CERD to elucidate the meaning of that article.

These observations provide a preview of some of the puzzles and complexities that are discussed in the present chapter. What is racist hate speech? How has ICERD been used to combat racist hate speech

* Note: full citations on file with author. This chapter draws in places on previous work by the present author: 'The Troubled Relationship between Free Speech and Racist Hate Speech: The Ambiguous Roles of the Media and Internet', Expert Paper, Day of Thematic Discussion 'Racist Hate Speech' (28 August 2012), UN Committee on the Elimination of Racial Discrimination, Eighty-first Session, Geneva, 6–31 August 2012; *Minority Rights, Freedom of Expression and of the Media: Dynamics and Dilemmas* (Antwerp: Intersentia, 2011) and 'The development of freedom of expression and information within the UN: Leaps and bounds or fits and starts?' in Tarlach McGonagle and Yvonne Donders (eds), *The United Nations and Freedom of Expression and Information: Critical Perspectives* (Cambridge: Cambridge University Press, 2015), pp. 1–51.

in the past? Why did CERD feel there was a need for a new GR to ameliorate the existing approach? What has been the initial impact of the new GR? What is its enduring impact likely to be?

This chapter sets out to provide some answers to these questions. First, it offers a brief reflection on the term 'racist hate speech'. It then introduces relevant provisions of ICERD, paying particular attention to Article 4, which has traditionally been the default provision for combating racist hate speech. Next, its focus fixes on GR 35 itself. It explains the context in which GR 35 was adopted, before examining its ambition and objectives, as well as its concrete provisions and textual emphases. Finally, it assesses the initial impact of GR 35 and offers a tentative prognosis of how it will fare in the future.

Racist hate speech: origins and meanings

Hate speech

The term 'hate speech' has been used widely and conventionally for quite some time now. The term has gained in familiarity and usage, despite the fact that it has never been defined in an authoritative, legally binding international instrument. Its appeal as a catchy shorthand term denoting a range of different types of hateful expression is obvious: more precise legal terminology is considerably more cumbersome and therefore unsuitable for use in a variety of (non-legal) contexts.

Nevertheless, the term's shorthand appeal should not detract from the need for legal precision and nuance in this regard. The term's straightforward appearance belies the great complexity of its actual scope. 'Hate speech' can actually be taken as referring to a whole spectrum of (extremely) negative discourse stretching from hatred and incitement to hatred; to abuse, vilification, insults and offensive words and epithets; and arguably also to extreme examples of prejudice and bias.[1] Robert Post has posited that a certain threshold of intensity must be reached before a particular expression can be qualified as hate speech.[2] He points to the *Oxford English Dictionary* entry for 'hate': 'an emotion of extreme dislike or aversion; detestation, abhorrence, hatred'.[3] For Post, the threshold or definitional

1 James B. Jacobs and Kimberley Potter, *Hate Crimes: Criminal Law and Identity Politics* (New York: Oxford University Press, 1998), p. 11.

2 Robert Post, 'Hate speech', in Ivan Hare and James Weinstein (eds), *Extreme Speech and Democracy* (New York: Oxford University Press, 2009), pp. 123–38, at 123.

3 *Ibid.*

prerequisite is the qualification, 'extreme', because ordinary 'intolerance and dislike are necessary human emotions which no legal order could pretend to abolish'.[4] Similarly, for Jeremy Waldron, the threshold lies beyond expression that offends people and rather concerns expression that attacks their dignity.[5] He notes in this connection that hate speech aims to 'compromise the dignity of those at whom it is targeted, both in their own eyes and in the eyes of other members of society'.[6]

From a legal perspective, the spectrum of negative discourse stretches from types of expression that are not entitled to protection under international human rights law (e.g. incitement to hatred), through types of expression that may or may not be entitled to protection, depending on a number of 'contextual variables'[7] (e.g. *gravely* offensive expression), to types of expression that presumptively would be entitled to protection, despite their objectionable character (e.g. negative stereotyping of minorities). This is essentially the approach that is recommended by the Rabat Plan of Action on the prohibition of advocacy of national, racial or religious hatred that constitutes incitement to discrimination, hostility or violence:

> In terms of general principles, a clear distinction should be made between three types of expression: expression that constitutes a criminal offence; expression that is not criminally punishable but may justify a civil suit or administrative sanctions; expression that does not give rise to criminal, civil or administrative sanctions but still raises a concern in terms of tolerance, civility and respect for the rights of others.[8]

Different types of hate speech are 'neither equally harmful nor performative'.[9] It is therefore important to differentiate between the various types of expression on the hate speech spectrum: they vary in

4 *Ibid.*

5 Jeremy Waldron, *The Harm in Hate Speech* (Cambridge, MA and London: Harvard University Press, 2012), pp. 5, 15 and, in more detail, 105–43.

6 *Ibid.*, p. 5.

7 Michael Rosenfeld, 'Hate speech in constitutional jurisprudence: A comparative analysis', *Cardozo Law Review*, 24:4 (2003), 1523–67, at 1565.

8 Rabat Plan of Action on the prohibition of advocacy of national, racial or religious hatred that constitutes incitement to discrimination, hostility or violence, 5 October 2012.

9 Jean-Francois Gaudreault-DesBiens, 'From Sisyphus's dilemma to Sisyphus's duty? A meditation on the regulation of hate propaganda in relation to hate crimes and genocide', *McGill Law Journal*, 46:4 (2001), 1117–37, at 1130. See also in this connection, Bikhu Parekh, 'Is there a case for banning hate speech?', in Michael Herz and Peter Molnar (eds), *Content and Context: Rethinking Regulation and Remedies for Hate Speech* (New York: Cambridge University Press, 2012), pp. 37–56, at 54–5.

terms of the intent of the speaker,[10] the intensity of the expression, the severity of its impact, etc. Further differentiation can usefully be made between hate speech that is 'direct (sometimes called "specific") or indirect; veiled or overt; single or repeated; backed by power, authority, or threat, or not'.[11] These types of differentiation are crucial when attempting to gauge the impact of racist hate speech on its targets/victims in a variety of contexts.

The purpose of regulating hate speech is to prevent interference with other rights and to prevent the occasioning of certain harms.[12] In the first place, hate speech can interfere with other human rights or 'operative public' values:[13] dignity, non-discrimination and equality, (effective) participation in public life (including public discourse),[14] freedom of expression, association, religion, etc. These rights and values are essential elements of what Waldron has described as 'a sort of public good of inclusiveness that our society sponsors and that it is committed to'.[15] Second, the prevention of particular harms suffered by individual victims should also be considered: psychological harm, damage to self-esteem, inhibited self-fulfilment, etc.[16]

---

10 In this connection, Jogchum Vrielink usefully distinguishes three categories of perpetrators of racist hate speech: offenders by conviction, activists/instrumentalists and incidentalists: Jogchum Vrielink, *Van haat gesproken? Een rechtsantropologisch onderzoek naar de bestrijding van rasgerelateerde uitingsdelicten in België* (Antwerp: Maklu, 2011), pp. 466 *et seq*.

11 Richard Delgado and Jean Stefancic, 'Four observations about hate speech', *Wake Forest Law Review*, 44:2 (2009), 353–70, at 361. See also: Richard Delgado and Jean Stefancic, *Understanding Words That Wound* (Boulder: Westview Press, 2004), pp. 11–12.

12 See further: Kevin Boyle and Anneliese Baldaccini, 'A critical evaluation of international human rights approaches to racism', in Sandra Fredman (ed.), *Discrimination and Human Rights: The Case of Racism* (New York: Oxford University Press, 2001), pp. 135–91, at 152.

13 Operative public values are those values 'that a society cherishes as part of its collective identity and in terms of which it regulates the relations between its members', and which 'constitute the moral structure of its public life and give it coherence and stability': Bikhu Parekh, *Rethinking Multiculturalism: Cultural Diversity and Political Theory* (New York: Palgrave Macmillan, 2nd edn, 2006), p. 363.

14 For an expansive analysis of this topic, see: Robert C. Post, 'Racist speech, democracy, and the First Amendment', *William and Mary Law Review*, 32:2 (1991), 267–327.

15 Waldron, *The Harm in Hate Speech*, p. 4.

16 See generally, Mari J. Matsuda, Charles R. Lawrence III, Richard Delgado and Kimberle Williams Crenshaw (eds), *Words That Wound: Critical Race Theory, Assaultive Speech, and the First Amendment* (Boulder, San Francisco and Oxford: Westview Press, 1993) and more recently, Katharine Gelber and Luke McNamara, 'Evidencing the harms of hate speech', *Social Identities – Journal for the Study of Race, Nation and Culture* (2015), 1–18.

All in all, the range of harms to be prevented is varied and complex. The challenge is therefore to identify 'which criteria allow us to distinguish between harms that justify restrictions and those that do not'.[17] Those criteria should then guide relevant regulatory approaches to hate speech. Whereas some types of racist hate speech – the most egregious forms – may be best dealt with by prohibitions and criminal law measures, others are more suitably dealt with by civil law measures and others still by educational, cultural, informational and other non-regulatory measures. As affirmed in the Rabat Plan of Action, '[W]hile a legal response remains important, legislation is only part of a larger toolbox to respond to the challenges of hate speech'.[18] The regulatory framework to counter racist hate speech should be holistic, in recognition of the fact that racist hate speech covers a range of different types of expression. But it is not enough for that regulatory framework to be holistic: the approaches it sets out must also be differentiated. The 'horses for courses' principle applies.

Racist hate speech

In order to distinguish between different sub-sets of hate speech, various qualifiers can be prefixed to the generic term. For instance, 'racist' hate speech specifies that the particular motive for the hate speech is racist in nature. Qualifiers like 'sexist' or 'misogynist', 'homophobic' and 'religious' perform similar functions. While the use of such qualifiers does not alter the meaning of the term hate speech, it does facilitate a more precise classification of different types of hate speech according to their dominant characteristics. This can help to identify the legal instrument that is best suited for combating the particular type of hate speech in question. At the same time, though, as Nazila Ghanea has cautioned, the propagators of hate speech 'need to be taken seriously regardless of the exact human rights classification we can "pigeon hole" them into'.[19]

GR 35 has helped to cement the status and familiarity of the term, 'racist hate speech', by incorporating it into its titular and substantive focuses. In practice, CERD had already been using the term prior to the adoption of GR 35.

17 David Kretzmer, 'Freedom of speech and racism', *Cardozo Law Review*, 8:3 (1987), 445–513, at 478.

18 Rabat Plan of Action, para. 23.

19 Nazila Ghanea, 'Intersectionality and the spectrum of racist hate speech: Proposals to the UN Committee on the Elimination of Racial Discrimination', *Human Rights Quarterly*, 35:4 (2013), 935–54, at 953–4.

ICERD and racist hate speech

Over the years, ICERD has been widely – and correctly – perceived as an outlier among other international human rights treaties that contain provisions governing the relationship between freedom of expression and hate speech, insofar as Article 4 of ICERD creates more far-reaching obligations for States parties than comparable provisions in other treaties. Article 4 requires States to render several types of expression *punishable* by law, whereas Article 20 of the International Covenant on Civil and Political Rights (hereafter, 'ICCPR') requires that a narrower range of types of expression be *prohibited* by law. Moreover, the complex and somewhat confusing provisions in ICERD concerning racist hate speech, and the strict manner in which they have traditionally been interpreted by CERD,[20] both underscore the need for insightful clarification of key phrases and qualification of key offences.

Article 4 reads in full:

> States Parties condemn all propaganda and all organizations which are based on ideas or theories of superiority of one race or group of persons of one colour or ethnic origin, or which attempt to justify or promote racial hatred and discrimination in any form, and undertake to adopt immediate and positive measures designed to eradicate all incitement to, or acts of, such discrimination and, to this end, with due regard to the principles embodied in the Universal Declaration of Human Rights and the rights expressly set forth in article 5 of this Convention, inter alia:

(a) Shall declare an offence punishable by law all dissemination of ideas based on racial superiority or hatred, incitement to racial discrimination, as well as all acts of violence or incitement to such acts against any race or group of persons of another colour or ethnic origin, and also the provision of any assistance to racist activities, including the financing thereof;
(b) Shall declare illegal and prohibit organizations, and also organized and all other propaganda activities, which promote and incite racial discrimination, and shall recognize participation in such organizations or activities as an offence punishable by law;
(c) Shall not permit public authorities or public institutions, national or local, to promote or incite racial discrimination.

---

20 For detailed analysis, see: Patrick Thornberry, 'Forms of hate speech and the Convention on the Elimination of all Forms of Racial Discrimination', *Religion and Human Rights*, 5:2 (2010), 97–117; Patrick Thornberry, 'Confronting racial discrimination: A CERD perspective', *Human Rights Law Review*, 5:2 (2005), 239–69; Tarlach McGonagle, *Minority Rights, Freedom of Expression and of the Media: Dynamics and Dilemmas* (Antwerp: Intersentia, 2011), pp. 280–90.

Article 4 has been described as 'one of the most difficult and controversial' articles of the entire Convention.[21] It explicitly creates a range of obligations for States parties which entail far-reaching interference with the right to freedom of expression (in particular) and other human rights. This explains why Article 4 presented 'many difficulties in all stages of its drafting';[22] why it has been 'contested *ab initio*'[23] and why it is the subject of a relatively high number of reservations (see further, below). The complexity of the article is underscored by the varying nature of the obligations it creates.

The so-called 'due regard' clause was inserted into the Convention in order to assuage widely held fears among (especially Western) delegates that the envisaged State obligations would unduly encroach on the right to freedom of expression (and freedom of association). Without the 'due regard' clause in Article 4's chapeau paragraph, most of the enumerated measures would have been deemed incompatible with the right to freedom of opinion and expression, which is specifically mentioned in Article 5(d)(viii).

Another factor that has contributed to ICERD's outlier status among international human rights treaties, from the perspective of freedom of expression guarantees, is that Article 4 requires that States render the dissemination of ideas based on racial superiority or racial hatred – without further explicit qualification – offences punishable by law. There is no explicit requirement of intent, nor is there any requirement that harm or other concrete consequences would flow from the dissemination of such ideas. Explicit references to other contextual factors that could influence the interpretation of the envisaged offences are also lacking in the text of Article 4. In the absence of such qualifications, there has been a notable tendency towards literalist interpretations of Article 4.[24]

Besides Article 4 and its linkage to Article 5, another provision of the Convention, Article 7, is particularly relevant to CERD's engagement with racist hate speech. It reads:

---

21 Natan Lerner, *The U.N. Convention on the Elimination of all Forms of Racial Discrimination* (Alphen aan den Rijn: Sijthoff & Noordhoff, 2nd edn, 1980), p. 43.

22 *Ibid.*, p. 47. In that respect, it was no different to the corresponding article in the earlier UN Declaration on the Elimination of All Forms of Racial Discrimination, United Nations General Assembly Resolution 1904 (XVIII), 20 November 1963.

23 Patrick Thornberry, 'International Convention on the Elimination of All Forms of Racial Discrimination: The prohibition of "racist hate speech"', in McGonagle and Donders, *The United Nations and Freedom of Expression and Information*, pp. 121–44, at 125.

24 For detailed analysis, see McGonagle, *Minority Rights, Freedom of Expression and of the Media*, pp. 280–90.

> States Parties undertake to adopt immediate and effective measures, particularly in the fields of teaching, education, culture and information, with a view to combating prejudices which lead to racial discrimination and to promoting understanding, tolerance and friendship among nations and racial or ethnical groups, as well as to propagating the purposes and principles of the Charter of the United Nations, the Universal Declaration of Human Rights, the United Nations Declaration on the Elimination of All Forms of Racial Discrimination, and this Convention.

As Article 4 has traditionally been the 'principal vehicle'[25] for CERD's engagement with racist hate speech, Article 7 has been somewhat underused and its potential somewhat understated. This has led to the suggestion that it is the Convention's 'neglected pillar'.[26]

General Recommendation 35

ICERD and general recommendations

CERD's general recommendations (GRs), like general comments or recommendations adopted by other treaty-monitoring bodies, focus on one or more specific themes or provisions within ICERD. They are usually regarded as the leading source of interpretive guidance for the Convention.[27] These GRs typically reflect CERD's accumulated experience and expertise on the subject matter of the GR in question. Sometimes the focus of a GR will be revisited in a subsequent GR, e.g. to reflect developments in CERD's practice or thinking, or to explore the same focus from an alternative angle.

CERD adopted its GR 35 entitled 'Combating Racist Hate Speech' during its eighty-third session in August 2013.[28] GR 35 is CERD's most explicit and detailed engagement with racist hate speech to date, but it is not the first GR to have a main focus on Article 4.[29] GR 1

---

25 CERD, 'GR 35', para. 8.

26 Stephanie Farrior, 'The neglected pillar: The "teaching tolerance" provision of the International Convention on the Elimination of All Forms of Racial Discrimination', *ILSA Journal of International and Comparative Law*, 5:2 (1999), 291–9.

27 See further, Philip Alston, 'The historical origins of the concept of "General Comments" in human rights law', in Laurence Boisson De Charzournes and Vera Gowlland-Debbas (eds), *The International Legal System in Quest of Equity and Universality* (Leiden: Martinus Nijhoff Publishers, 2001), pp. 763–76.

28 CERD, 'General Recommendation 35 on Combating racist hate speech', UN Doc. CERD/C/GC/35 (2013).

29 CERD, 'General Recommendation 1 on States parties' obligations', UN Doc. A/87/18 (1972); CERD, 'General Recommendation 7 on Measures to eradicate incitement to or acts of discrimination to the implementation of article 4', UN

(1972), GR 7 (1985) and GR 15 (1993) all focus on different aspects of Article 4, while other GRs also deal with issues relating to racist hate speech in a less direct or detailed fashion.[30]

Day of thematic discussion

CERD regularly holds thematic discussions on issues relating to racial discrimination and ICERD, which enables it to hear the views of a wide variety of stakeholders on the selected themes.[31] CERD's eighty-first session in Geneva in August 2012 included a Day of Thematic Discussion on 'Racist Hate Speech'.[32] It focused on the following themes:

1 the concept of racist hate speech and its evolution over time;
2 combating racist hate speech: the work of the Committee on the Elimination of Racial Discrimination;
3 racist hate speech and freedom of opinion and expression;
4 racist hate speech in political life, and in the media including the internet.

Each of these themes, as will be seen below, would feature centrally in GR 35, which CERD adopted a year later. In October 2012 – shortly after the Day of Thematic Discussion was held – the Rabat Plan of Action was adopted.[33] The Rabat Plan of Action comprises the conclusions and recommendations of four regional expert workshops on the same topics, which were organised by the Office of the High Commissioner for Human Rights in 2011. Its influence on some of GR 35's focuses has been explicitly acknowledged.[34]

Challenges and ambition

CERD decided to draft a new GR on racist hate speech in order 'to provide guidance on the requirements of the Convention in the area of racist hate speech in order to assist States parties in discharging

---

Doc. A/40/18 (1985); CERD, 'General Recommendation 15 on Measures to eradicate incitement to or acts of discrimination', UN Doc. A/48/18 (1993).

30 For details, see para. 3 of GR 35.

31 For more information on this practice, as well as an overview of previous thematic discussions, see: www.ohchr.org/EN/HRBodies/CERD/Pages/Discussions.aspx.

32 28 August 2012, for an overview and documentation, see: www.ohchr.org/EN/HRBodies/CERD/Pages/Racisthatespeech.aspx.

33 For commentary, see Sejal Parmar, 'The Rabat Plan of Action: A global blueprint for combating "hate speech"', *European Human Rights Law Review*, 1 (2014), 21–31.

34 See, in particular, para. 15 (fn. 17), but also paras. 15 (fn. 18) and 29 (fn. 26).

their obligations, including reporting obligations'.[35] It did so knowing that the project would have to overcome several significant challenges. Those challenges, a number of which were identified and explored during the Day of Thematic Discussion, included:

1 the challenge of rendering CERD's interpretation of Article 4 *juncto* 5 more consonant with contemporary interpretations of the freedom of expression guarantees in other international human rights standards;
2 the challenge of (re-)aligning the term, racist hate speech, with all relevant provisions of the Convention (and not only Article 4);
3 the challenge of differentiating between various types of racist hate speech;
4 the challenge of appreciating and reflecting the roles that the media, the Internet and public debate can play in combating racist hate speech.

Textual provisions and emphases[36]

One of GR 35's major accomplishments is that it manages to articulate a hitherto under-appreciated proximity between ICERD's provisions that touch on freedom of expression and those of other international legal standards, in particular Articles 19 and 20, ICCPR. As already mentioned, ICERD has traditionally had an outlier status among international human rights treaties in respect of freedom of expression because of its heavy reliance on the prohibition and/or criminalisation of (certain types of) expression in order to combat racism. It should be noted that if GR 35 did not differentiate between different types of racist hate speech and the consequent need for tailored responses (see further, below), it would have been very difficult for CERD to assert that the relationship between relevant provisions of ICERD and ICCPR is proximate. In this respect, GR 35 provides crucial guidance for the interpretation and implementation of Article 4 that is absent from the lapidary text of the provision itself.

GR 35 recognises that ICERD is a living instrument and that it must be better synchronised with other international human rights treaties and informed by contemporary understandings of the right to freedom of opinion and expression. To these ends, GR 35 is right to choose Article 19 *juncto* 20 ICCPR and the Human Rights

35 CERD, 'GR 35', para. 2.
36 For excellent analysis, see Thornberry, 'International Convention on the Elimination of All Forms of Racial Discrimination', pp. 121–44.

Committee's General Comment No. 34,[37] which provides a synthesised update of the Committee's interpretation of Article 19, as its key points of reference. How GR 35 expresses that recognition of the importance of inter-treaty awareness reveals a very deep understanding of the Convention and its place in the broader canon of international human rights standards:

> By virtue of its work in implementing the Convention as a living instrument, the Committee engages with the wider human rights environment, awareness of which suffuses the Convention. In gauging the scope of freedom of expression, it should be recalled that the right is integrated into the Convention and is not simply articulated outside it: the principles of the Convention contribute to a fuller understanding of the parameters of the right in contemporary international human rights law. The Committee has integrated this right to freedom of expression into its work on combating hate speech, commenting where appropriate on its lack of effective implementation and, where necessary, drawing upon its elaboration in sister human rights bodies.[38]

This paragraph has an important iterative function as it articulates CERD's approach with a clarity of purpose that cannot be gleaned from a literalist reading of the text of the Convention. Moreover, while stressing that CERD embraces developments outside of the Convention, in particular concerning the evolution of the right to freedom of expression, it also points out that relevant principles of the Convention also contribute to the broader shaping of the right to freedom of expression in international human rights law.[39] This is a very valid – if seldom heard – observation. It demonstrates a confidence in the principles of the Convention, as revisited in GR 35, and an awareness of the broader relevance of those principles beyond the Convention.

GR 35 meets the second challenge, that of (re-)aligning the term, racist hate speech, with all relevant provisions of the Convention (and not only Article 4), head-on. Indeed, the structure of the GR creates ample space to engage with this challenge. Part III, entitled 'Resources of the Convention', deals extensively with Articles 4, 5 and 7 in turn. At the textual level, besides the titular reference in Part III, there are various references to the fact that the Convention's

37 Human Rights Committee, 'General Comment 34: Article 19 (Freedoms of Opinion and Expression)', UN Doc. CCPR/C/GC/34 (2011). For commentary, see Michael O'Flaherty, 'International Covenant on Civil and Political Rights: Interpreting freedom of expression and information standards for the present and the future', in McGonagle and Donders, *The United Nations and Freedom of Expression and Information*, pp. 55–88.

38 CERD, 'GR 35', para. 4.

39 See also para. 46.

approach to racist hate speech is shaped by a number of its provisions: 'the resources of' ICERD, 'the full span of procedures under the Convention', the 'mobilization of the full normative and procedural resources of the Convention', 'the ensemble of Convention provisions', etc. These repeated references underscore CERD's vision of the Convention as a coherent, integrated whole, and thereby serve to fend off criticisms that CERD's interpretation of ICERD in relation to racist hate speech has tended in the past to be over-reliant on Article 4.

In keeping with this line of thinking, the GR explores a range of strategies against racist hate speech other than the criminalisation of expression, i.e. civil and administrative law measures, as well as non-legal measures. It acknowledges that there is inherent differentiation within the notion of 'racist hate speech', which means that different remedies and responses are appropriate. The multiple and differentiated measures envisaged by the Convention for combating racist hate speech include teaching, education, culture and information, all of which are provided for by Article 7.[40] GR 35 affirms that Article 7's 'broadly educational approach to eliminating racial discrimination is an indispensable complement to other approaches to combating racial discrimination'.[41] In this respect, it can be said to have rediscovered the 'neglected pillar'[42] of ICERD.

As the provisions of Article 4 are not self-executing, CERD recommends that 'the States parties declare and effectively sanction as offences punishable by law':

(a) All dissemination of ideas based on racial or ethnic superiority or hatred, by whatever means;
(b) Incitement to hatred, contempt or discrimination against members of a group on grounds of their race, colour, descent, or national or ethnic origin;
(c) Threats or incitement to violence against persons or groups on the grounds in (b) above;
(d) Expression of insults, ridicule or slander of persons or groups or justification of hatred, contempt or discrimination on the grounds in (b) above, when it clearly amounts to incitement to hatred or discrimination;
(e) Participation in organizations and activities which promote and incite racial discrimination.[43]

---

40 See also: *ibid.*, paras. 8 and 9.
41 *Ibid.*, para. 30.
42 Farrior, 'The neglected pillar'.
43 CERD, 'GR 35', para. 13.

It then goes on to recommend that 'public denials or attempts to justify crimes of genocide and crimes against humanity, as defined by international law, should be declared as offences punishable by law, provided that they clearly constitute incitement to racial violence or hatred'.[44] It additionally stresses that '"the expression of opinions about historical facts" should not be prohibited or punished'.[45] In this respect, CERD takes its cue from the Human Rights Committee's General Comment No. 34 and these qualifications constitute very important safeguards for the right to freedom of expression.

In an exemplary exercise of critical self-reflection, CERD acknowledges that while Article 4 'requires that certain forms of conduct be declared offences punishable by law, it does not supply detailed guidance for the qualification of forms of conduct as criminal offences'.[46] This lacuna has arguably contributed in the past to CERD's tendency to interpret Article 4 strictly. In a very commendable attempt to fill this lacuna, CERD emphasises the need to examine contextual factors, such as the content and form of the speech, the economic, social and political climate in which the speech takes place, the position or status of the speaker, the reach of the speech and the objectives of the speech,[47] when determining what sort of remedies or responses are best suited to combating particular types of racist hate speech. Two further contextual factors are addressed: the intent of the speaker and the 'imminent risk or likelihood that the conduct desired or intended by the speaker will result from the speech in question'.[48] All of these contextual factors have been adapted from the Rabat Plan of Action.[49]

It is against this background that the GR's media-specific provisions have been crafted. The GR stresses that 'informed, ethical and objective media, including social media and the Internet, have an essential role in promoting responsibility in the dissemination of ideas and opinions'.[50] States should therefore put in place 'appropriate legislation for the media in line with international standards' and 'encourage the public and private media to adopt codes of professional ethics and press codes that incorporate respect for the principles of the Convention and other fundamental human rights standards'.[51]

It states that 'media representations of ethnic, indigenous and other groups ... should be based on principles of respect, fairness and the

44 *Ibid.*, para. 14.
45 *Ibid.*
46 *Ibid.*, para. 15.
47 *Ibid.*
48 *Ibid.*, para. 16.
49 Rabat Plan of Action, para. 22.
50 CERD, 'GR 35', para. 39.
51 *Ibid.*

avoidance of stereotyping'.[52] The media should furthermore 'avoid referring unnecessarily to race, ethnicity, religion and other group characteristics in a manner that may promote intolerance'.[53] It recognises that 'local empowerment through media pluralism facilitates the emergence of speech capable of countering racist hate speech'.[54] For that reason, it advocates 'facilitation of access to and ownership of media by minority, indigenous and other groups … including media in their own languages'.[55] It also 'encourages self-regulation and compliance with codes of ethics by Internet service providers'.[56]

This philosophy of empowerment through access to the media and the internet is very much in line with a growing body of scholarship focusing on 'counter-speech'[57] as a strategy for combating racist hate speech in practice.[58] Counter-speech is not only reactionary in character: it can have many ramifications. For instance, it embraces strategies of 'social contact' and 'confrontation' alike.[59] This means that it is both about inter-group communication or dialogue designed to foster tolerance and understanding and about empowering specific groups that are targeted by racist hate speech 'so that they can "talk back" at their oppressors'.[60]

The relevance of counter-speech for combating racist hate speech rests on a growing appreciation of the positive role that the right to freedom of opinion and expression can generally play in countering racist and other forms of hate speech. That role has been acknowledged and teased out in, *inter alia*, GR 35;[61] the Declaration and Programme of Action of the World Conference against Racism, Racial

52 *Ibid.*, para. 40.
53 *Ibid.*
54 *Ibid.*, para. 41.
55 *Ibid.*
56 *Ibid.*, para. 42.
57 For a rich theoretical exposition of counter speech and the question of its suitability as a remedy for hate speech, see: Katharine Gelber, *Speaking Back: The Free Speech Versus Hate Speech Debate* (Amsterdam and Philadelphia: John Benjamins Publishing Company, 2002) and Katharine Gelber, 'Reconceptualizing counter-speech in hate speech policy (with a focus on Australia)', in Herz and Molnar, *Content and Context*, pp. 198–216. See also: Ignio Gagliardone, Danit Gal, Thiago Alves and Gabriela Martinez, *Countering Online Hate Speech* (Paris: UNESCO Publishing, 2015). Surprisingly, this study fails to mention GR 35, even though it does purport to set out ICERD's approach to hate speech.
58 James Bartlett and Alex Krasodomski-Jones, *Counter-speech: Examining Content that Challenges Extremism Online* (London: Demos, October 2015).
59 Richard Delgado and Jean Stefancic, 'Hate speech in cyberspace', *Wake Forest Law Review*, 49:2 (2014), 319–43, at 334 *et seq*.
60 Thornberry, 'International Convention on the Elimination of All Forms of Racial Discrimination', p. 136.
61 CERD, 'GR 35', para. 27.

Discrimination, Xenophobia and Related Intolerance (the 'Durban Conference', 2001);[62] the Durban Review Conference (2009),[63] and the Camden Principles on Freedom of Expression and Equality, adopted by the free-speech NGO, ARTICLE 19.[64]

Finally, it is important to note that GR 35 points out that indirect hate speech also falls within the scope of ICERD. Thus, where racism and other grounds of discrimination (e.g. religion or gender) intersect or overlap, they should not be regarded as falling outside the scope of the Convention.[65] These concerns were already raised in the discussion, above, of the desirability of specifying or classifying sub-sets of hate speech.

Initial (impact) assessment

GR 35 was adopted at the eighty-third session of CERD in August 2013. It has not yet been cited in an Individual Communication, but it has been systematically relied upon in Concluding Observations. Table 12.1 provides an overview of the state reports considered by CERD since the adoption of GR 35. The Concluding Observations adopted in respect of those thirty-five State reports will form the basis of the assessment of GR 35's initial impact.

---

62 See: Report of the World Conference against Racism, Racial Discrimination, Xenophobia and Related Intolerance, Durban, 31 August – 8 September 2001, UN Doc. A/CONF.189/12.

63 Outcome document of the Durban Review Conference, 24 April 2009. For analysis of the relevance of the Durban Conference and the Durban Review Conference for issues relating to freedom of expression and the media, see: McGonagle, *Minority Rights, Freedom of Expression and of the Media*, pp. 291–3. On the Durban Review Conference specifically, see: Corinne Lennox, 'Reviewing Durban: Examining the outputs and review of the 2001 World Conference against Racism', *Netherlands Quarterly of Human Rights Law Review*, 27:2 (2009), 191–235; Dimitrina Petrova, '"Smoke and mirrors": The Durban Review Conference and human rights politics at the United Nations', *Human Rights Law Review*, 10:1 (2009), 129–50.

64 ARTICLE 19, 'The Camden Principles on Freedom of Expression and Equality', April 2009.

65 For a fuller discussion of the complex range of 'intersectionality' issues in the context of ICERD, see generally: Ghanea, 'Intersectionality and the spectrum of racist hate speech'; Stephanie E. Berry, 'Bringing Muslim minorities within the International Convention on the Elimination of All Forms of Racial Discrimination: Square peg in a round hole?', *Human Rights Law Review*, 11:3 (2011), 423–50; See also: David Keane, 'Addressing the aggravated meeting points of race and religion', *University of Maryland Law Journal of Race, Religion, Gender and Class*, 6:2 (2006), 367–406, at 398 *et seq.*; Jose Augusto Lindgren Alves, 'Race and religion in the United Nations Committee on the Elimination of Racial Discrimination', *University of San Francisco Law Review*, 42:4 (2008), 941–82, at 951–2 and 974–7.

Table 12.1 Overview of State reports since the adoption of GR 35

Session	Dates	Countries
88	23/11/2015–11/12/2015	Egypt, the Holy See, Lithuania, Mongolia, Slovenia, Turkey
87	03/08/2015–28/08/2015	Colombia, Costa Rica, Czech Republic, the Netherlands, Niger, Norway, Suriname, the former Yugoslav Republic of Macedonia
86	27/04/2015–15/05/2015	Bosnia and Herzegovina, Denmark, France, Germany, Guatemala, Sudan
85	11/08/2014–29/08/2014	Cameroon, El Salvador, Estonia, Iraq, Japan, Peru, United States of America
84	03/02/2014–21/02/2014	Belgium, Honduras, Kazakhstan, Luxembourg, Montenegro, Poland, Switzerland, Uzbekistan

With the exception of the Concluding Observations on Montenegro, all of the above Concluding Observations have referenced GR 35 in one way or another. This shows that GR 35 has instantly become a standard reference point for CERD in its engagement with the issues addressed by Article 4 (*juncto* Article 5). References to GR 35 are typically made under the heading 'Concerns and recommendations', but they have also featured under the heading 'Positive aspects/measures'.[66] For instance, CERD has drawn attention to the 'numerous forceful statements of the Pope condemning racism and fostering intercultural and interreligious understanding and tolerance, including statements in support of refugees and migrants'.[67] Referencing GR 35, CERD 'underscore[d] the importance of such statements by high-level officials to promote a culture of tolerance and respect and to combat xenophobia and racist discourse'.[68] GR 35 has also been mentioned under the heading, 'Other recommendations', for example when CERD recommended that Germany 'act upon and provide information on follow-up measures to give effect to' CERD's recommendations in its Communication on *TBB-Turkish Union in Berlin/Brandenburg* v. *Germany*.[69] CERD reminded Germany of 'the

66 CERD, 'Concluding Observations: The Holy See', CERD/C/VAT/CO/16–23 (2016), para. 4(d).

67 *Ibid.*

68 *Ibid.*

69 CERD, 'Concluding Observations: Germany', CERD/C/DEU/CO/19–22 (2015), para. 20. The *TBB-Turkish Union in Berlin/Brandenburg* v. *Germany* case concerned statements that 'amounted to dissemination of ideas based upon racial superiority or hatred and contained elements of incitement to racial discrimination': CERD, *TBB-Turkish Union in Berlin/Brandenburg* v. *Germany*, Communication No. 48/

need for effective responses to racist hate speech in accordance with' GR 35.[70]

By clarifying and consolidating CERD's approach to racist hate speech, GR 35 has facilitated a more systematic engagement by CERD with substantive issues covered by Article 4 *juncto* 5 and by Article 7. The language used in the GR has often been replicated, sometimes verbatim, in relevant sections of the Concluding Observations analysed here.[71]

A few reflections on the main lines of CERD's engagement with the troubled relationship between freedom of expression and racist hate speech in these Concluding Observations are now in order. First, CERD continues to insist on the preventive and mandatory character of the offences to be declared punishable by law under Article 4.[72] This is an important continuation of CERD's consistent interpretation of Article 4, as re-affirmed in GR 35. It is important because for all of GR 35's 'refreshing' of CERD's *acquis* in respect of Article 4, the central tenets of that *acquis* remain unchanged. What has been enhanced is rather the clarification of the relevance of complementary provisions in the Convention and the relevance of other international human rights standards. This 'refreshing' exercise can be detected in some – but only some – Concluding Observations, in the guise of references to the importance of avoiding 'unnecessary or disproportionate interference' with the right to freedom of expression and the need to calibrate responses to racist hate speech in accordance with their seriousness.[73]

Linked to this is a second observation, re-iterated in GR 35:

> it is not enough to declare the forms of conduct in article 4 as offences; the provisions of the article must also be effectively implemented. Effective implementation is characteristically achieved through investigations of offences set out in the Convention and, *where appropriate*, the prosecution

---

2010, CERD/C/82/D/48/2010 (2013), para. 12.8. See also the Individual opinion of Committee member Mr Carlos Manuel Vazquez (dissenting), CERD/C/82/3, 5 April 2013.

70 *Ibid.*

71 It is beyond the scope of the present chapter to examine the extent to which the language used by CERD since the adoption of GR 35 is consistent with that used prior to its adoption.

72 See, for example: CERD, 'Concluding Observations: Belgium', CERD/C/BEL/CO/16–19 (2014); CERD, 'Concluding Observations: Luxembourg', CERD/C/LUX/CO/14–17 (2014); CERD, 'Concluding Observations: The former Yugoslav Republic of Macedonia', CERD/C/MKD/CO/8–10 (2015); CERD, 'Concluding Observations: Norway', CERD/C/NOR/CO/21–22 (2015).

73 See, for example, CERD, 'Concluding Observations: Kazakhstan', CERD/C/KAZ/CO/6–7 (2014), para. 13 and CERD, 'Concluding Observations: Mongolia', CERD/C/MNG/CO/19–22 (2016), para. 15.

> of offenders. The Committee recognizes *the principle of expediency* in the prosecution of alleged offenders, and observes that it must *in each case be applied in the light of the guarantees laid down in the Convention and in other instruments of international law*.[74]

This appropriately circumspect wording shows a degree of deference to relevant safeguards recognised under international human rights law against abuses of the judicial and in particular penal process. Similar wording is used in a number of the Concluding Observations surveyed.[75] Relatedly, CERD recommends that 'racist motive be recognized as a general aggravating circumstance for all offences and crimes', or words to that effect.[76]

The added value of GR 35 can be gleaned *inter alia* from its articulation of CERD's awareness that 'broad or vague restrictions' on the right to freedom of expression are susceptible to abuse and moreover 'have been used to the detriment of groups protected by the Convention'.[77] This calls for the precise formulation of any restrictions on the right to freedom of expression. CERD therefore 'stresses that measures to monitor and combat racist speech should not be used as a pretext to curtail expressions of protest at injustice, social discontent or opposition'.[78] This language has been used in a number of Concluding Observations.[79]

An interesting feature of GR 35 is how it links Article 4(c), regarding public authorities or public institutions, and Article 7. In respect of the former provision, 'racist expressions emanating from such authorities or institutions are regarded by the Committee as of particular concern, especially statements attributed to high-ranking officials'.[80] CERD's 'particular concern' can be explained by the additional power acquired by racist hate speech when it has, or is perceived as having,

---

74 CERD, 'GR 35', para. 17 (emphasis added).

75 CERD, 'Concluding Observations: Germany' (2015), para. 9(b); CERD, 'Concluding Observations: Turkey', CERD/C/TUR/CO/4–6 (2016), para. 24(b).

76 CERD, 'Concluding Observations: Costa Rica', CERD/C/CRI/CO/19–22 (2015), para. 20; CERD, 'Concluding Observations: Egypt', CERD/C/EGY/CO/17–22 (2016), paras. 11 and 12; CERD, 'Concluding Observations: Peru', CERD/C/PER/CO/18–21 (2014), para. 10; CERD, 'Concluding Observations: Slovenia', CERD/C/SVN/CO/8–11 (2016), para. 96; CERD, 'Concluding Observations: Turkey' (2016), para. 22 and CERD, 'Concluding Observations: Uzbekistan', CERD/C/UZB/CO/8–9 (2014), para. 6(b).

77 CERD, 'GR 35', para. 20.

78 *Ibid.*

79 See, for example: CERD, 'Concluding Observations: Egypt' (2016), para. 12; CERD, 'Concluding Observations: Japan', CERD/C/JPN/CO/7–9 (2014), para. 11; CERD, 'Concluding Observations: The Niger', CERD/C/NER/CO/15–21 (2015), para. 7(a) and CERD, 'Concluding Observations: Turkey' (2016), para. 22.

80 CERD, 'GR 35', para. 22.

official or institutional backing. Recalling that para. (c) is governed by Article 4's chapeau paragraph, which refers to 'immediate and positive measures', CERD states that such measures 'may additionally include measures of a disciplinary nature, such as removal from office, where appropriate, as well as effective remedies for victims'.[81] In respect of Article 7, CERD states: '[F]ormal rejection of hate speech by high-level public officials and condemnation of the hateful ideas expressed play an important role in promoting a culture of tolerance and respect.'[82] These concerns and/or recommendations to address them are voiced in several Concluding Observations and have also been directed *mutatis mutandis* at politicians generally (i.e. not only those with official functions).[83] In its Concluding Observations on Slovenia, CERD has specifically called for the adoption of a code of conduct for Members of Parliament that would include 'provisions stressing the importance of avoiding and condemning racist and xenophobic discourse'.[84]

The various references in the Concluding Observations to the ambiguous roles of the media and internet in countering and facilitating the dissemination of racist hate speech are not yet, on the whole, very insightful. They do not really address the dynamics of the media and tend to limit themselves to stressing the need to combat racist hate speech in the media or on the internet. Some expressly mention the relevance of the right to freedom of expression,[85] whereas others limit themselves to cursory references to ('appropriate') measures.[86] CERD encourages the promotion of ethical journalism and only one of the Concluding Observations[87] reiterates GR 35's call on States to put in place 'appropriate legislation for the media in line with international

81 *Ibid.*
82 *Ibid.*, para. 37.
83 CERD, 'Concluding Observations: The Czech Republic', CERD/C/CZE/CO/10–11 (2015), para. 14; CERD, 'Concluding Observations: France', CERD/C/FRA/CO/20–21 (2015), para. 8(a); CERD, 'Concluding Observations: Germany' (2015), para. 9(a); CERD, 'Concluding Observations: Japan' (2014), para. 11(d); CERD, 'Concluding Observations: Kazakhstan' (2014), para. 11; CERD, 'Concluding Observations: Lithuania', CERD/C/LTU/CO/6–8 (2016), para. 15(a); CERD, 'Concluding Observations: the Netherlands', CERD/C/NLD/CO/19–21 (2015), para. 12; CERD, 'Concluding Observations: Norway', CERD/C/NOR/CO/21–22 (2015), para. 16(a); CERD, 'Concluding Observations: Switzerland', CERD/C/CHE/CO/7–9 (2014), para. 12(d) and CERD, 'Concluding Observations: Turkey' (2016), para. 24(a).
84 CERD, 'Concluding Observations: Slovenia' (2016), para. 9(c).
85 CERD, 'Concluding Observations: Denmark', CERD/C/DNK/CO/20–21 (2015), para. 10.
86 CERD, 'Concluding Observations: Germany' (2015), para. 9(c); CERD, 'Concluding Observations: Poland', CERD/C/POL/CO/20–21 (2014), paras. 10(b) and (c).
87 CERD, 'Concluding Observations: the Czech Republic' (2015), para. 14(c).

standards'.[88] However, in doing so, it problematically conflates the putting in place of legislation and the promotion of ethical standards. The two are deliberately styled as complementary in GR 35, reflecting the important distinction between legal and ethical standards.[89] The scattered references in the surveyed Concluding Observations to the internet are laconic and unimaginative and when CERD takes the somewhat unusual step of recommending that Estonia ratify the Additional Protocol to the [Council of Europe's] Convention on Cybercrime, concerning the criminalisation of acts of a racist and xenophobic nature committed through computer systems, it makes a mistake in the title it gives for the Additional Protocol.[90]

GR 35's emphasis on the need to tackle the root causes of racist hate speech can be found explicitly[91] in a number of Concluding Observations and in different guises in others, e.g. in references to the importance of awareness-raising measures for countering racist hate speech,[92] the importance of fostering tolerance and (intercultural) understanding,[93] and the importance of training public officials.[94]

GR 35 is also relevant for CERD's overtures to States which have entered reservations to Article 4 of the Convention. In the context of ICERD, there is a relatively high incidence of State reservations

88 CERD, 'GR 35', para. 39.

89 *Ibid.*

90 It erroneously adds 'and in the media' to the end of the title of the Additional Protocol: CERD, 'Concluding Observations: Estonia', CERD/C/EST/CO/10–11 (2014), para. 7(b).

91 CERD, 'Concluding Observations: Japan' (2014), para. 11(e); CERD, 'Concluding Observations: Mongolia' (2016), para. 15; CERD, 'Concluding Observations: The Netherlands' (2015), para. 12(a).

92 CERD, 'Concluding Observations: Bosnia and Herzegovina', CERD/C/BIH/CO/9–11 (2015), para. 12; CERD, 'Concluding Observations: France' (2015), paras. 8(c) and 9(a); CERD, 'Concluding Observations: Lithuania' (2016), para. 15(d); CERD, 'Concluding Observations: Norway' (2015), para. 16(d); CERD, 'Concluding Observations: Peru' (2014), para. 24(c); CERD, 'Concluding Observations: Switzerland' (2014), para. 12(a) and CERD, 'Concluding Observations: Turkey' (2016), para. 24(d).

93 CERD, 'Concluding Observations: Bosnia and Herzegovina' (2015), para. 12; CERD, 'Concluding Observations: Denmark' (2015), para. 10(a); CERD, 'Concluding Observations: El Salvador', CERD/C/SLV/CO/16–17 (25 September 2014), para. 12; CERD, 'Concluding Observations: France' (2015), paras. 8(c) and 9(a); CERD, 'Concluding Observations: Germany' (2015), para. 9; CERD, 'Concluding Observations: Japan' (2014), para. 11(e); CERD, 'Concluding Observations: Kazakhstan' (2014), para. 11 and CERD, 'Concluding Observations: Peru' (2014), para. 24.

94 CERD, 'Concluding Observations: Switzerland' (2014) (legal personnel, including the judiciary: para. 12(c)); CERD, 'Concluding Observations: Turkey' (2016) (law-enforcement officials: para. 24(d)).

to Article 4, most of which concern the often frictional relationship between the obligations created by that article and the right to freedom of opinion and expression. Nineteen of the 177 States parties to ICERD have entered (interpretive) declarations or reservations concerning Article 4.[95]

GR 35 has deliberately furnished CERD with the basis for a new strategy to persuade Contracting Parties which had entered reservations in respect of Article 4 to withdraw or narrow those reservations.[96] GR 35's nuanced, 'more fully realized account of the letter and spirit of Article 4 and related articles',[97] could serve to allay the fears behind such reservations. Those fears are generally that national constitutional protection for the right to freedom of expression would be undermined by Article 4's predominant emphasis on the criminalisation of certain types of expression.

Such a new strategy is not merely notional; it has already been employed by CERD in its Concluding Observations on France and the USA. CERD, perhaps somewhat diffidently, 'invite[d]' the French authorities to 'consider withdrawing' their reservation[98] to Article 4, 'bearing in mind' GR 35.[99] However, it adopted a more overtly persuasive approach when it 'recommend[ed]' that the USA '[c]onsider withdrawing or narrowing its reservation[100] to article 4 of the Convention, taking into account the Committee's General Recommendation No. 35 (2013) on Combating Racist Hate Speech, which outlines diverse

95 Antigua and Barbuda, Australia, Austria, Bahamas, Barbados, Belgium, France, Grenada, Ireland, Italy, Japan, Malta, Nepal, Papua New Guinea, Switzerland, Thailand, Tonga, the United Kingdom and the United States. Monaco has submitted an interpretive declaration pertaining to Article 5 which is of relevance to Article 4, but without expressly mentioning the latter article. Source: UN Treaty Database: overview of declarations and reservations to ICERD, d.d. 1 March 2016.

96 CERD, 'GR 35', para. 23.

97 Thornberry, 'International Convention on the Elimination of All Forms of Racial Discrimination', p. 124.

98 French reservation (extract): 'With regard to article 4, France wishes to make it clear that it interprets the reference made therein to the principles of the Universal Declaration of Human Rights and to the rights set forth in article 5 of the Convention as releasing the States Parties from the obligation to enact anti-discrimination legislation which is incompatible with the freedoms of opinion and expression and of peaceful assembly and association guaranteed by those texts.'

99 CERD, 'Concluding Observations: France' (2015), para. 7.

100 (footnote inserted by author) US reservation (extract) entered upon ratification: '(1) That the Constitution and laws of the United States contain extensive protections of individual freedom of speech, expression and association. Accordingly, the United States does not accept any obligation under this Convention, in particular under articles 4 and 7, to restrict those rights, through the adoption of legislation or any other measures, to the extent that they are protected by the Constitution and laws of the United States.'

measures to effectively combat racist hate speech while protecting the legitimate right to freedom of expression'.[101]

Prognosis

The task of drafting GR 35 provided CERD with an ideal opportunity to mount a critical examination of its own positioning on relevant issues in the past. This called for the identification of consistency (and divergence) in existing interpretive patterns and the consolidation of previous experience, with a view to facilitating more systematic engagement with relevant issues in the future. What emerged from the drafting exercise was a new GR that 'presents itself as a rounded articulation of the Convention, subsuming elements of earlier readings by the Committee into a fresh normative synthesis, upgrading the anti-racist currency through clearer integration with libertarian speech principles, understood as both within and without the Convention'.[102]

GR 35 benefits from the clear narrative that permeates the text. It explains, patiently and persuasively, what it is doing, why it is doing it and how it is doing it. One of the GR's fortes is the explanatory power of that narrative. Patrick Thornberry, who was CERD's Rapporteur for the drafting of the GR, has provided very insightful academic analysis of GR 35, which enhances our understanding of the GR even further.[103] While recognising the importance of GR 35 and in particular the 'fresh conceptualization' of Article 4 that it provides,[104] Thornberry remains clear-sighted about the limitations of its potential due to the complexities of combating racist hate speech in a globalised and networked multi-media world.[105]

Another of GR 35's fortes is that it recognises and appreciates the multi-level differentiation that is needed in order to effectively combat racist hate speech while *truly* having 'due regard' for the right to freedom of expression. This includes differentiation in the types of expression that could be categorised as racist hate speech, their intensity, the nature of the harms they occasion and the nature of the regulatory and other responses that those harms elicit. The protection of human rights and public values also calls for differentiated strategies for combating racist hate speech, including regulatory, educational,

---

101 CERD, 'Concluding Observations: The United States of America', CERD/C/USA/CO/7–9 (2014), para. 9(a).

102 Thornberry, 'International Convention on the Elimination of All Forms of Racial Discrimination', p. 139.

103 *Ibid.*

104 *Ibid.*, p. 131.

105 *Ibid.*, pp. 138–41.

cultural and informational measures. All of these levels of differentiation remain relevant in an online context.

It is too early to draw any firm conclusions from the incipient impact of GR 35. It is clear, however, that CERD is already referencing it systematically in its Concluding Observations on State reports. While this is welcome, because GR 35 frames and recalibrates CERD practice with a clarity of purpose that was previously lacking, referencing GR 35 should not become a mere *pro-forma* exercise. CERD must also, besides systematically recalling GR 35, turn the nuance and detail of the GR to good use. In any case, GR 35 provides CERD with a coherent conceptual framework, explicitly embracing Articles 4, 5 and 7 of the Convention, for its future practice. It also provides CERD with consistent language, which should ensure a heightened consistency of engagement by CERD with relevant issues in its future practice.

While preparing GR 35, CERD had to reconcile formal (but imperfect and somewhat underused) treaty provisions and objectives with a sensitivity to contextual variables, such as the complex operational dynamics of the media and internet. This has led, in the first place, to a sharper inward focus on the relevant provisions of the Convention and their interplay. That focus is complemented by a more outward-looking stance and receptiveness to extraneous human rights standards and developments than heretofore. All of this has led to CERD having a clearer, stronger sense of its own position on racist hate speech, and of how that position relates to the broader international human rights framework. GR 35 appears to exude a new-found confidence in CERD's practice, suggesting that it does not intend to have a shrinking violet status in respect of international human rights law's engagement with (racist) hate speech.

In the future, it will be important for CERD to move beyond its own experiential horizons when addressing media- and internet-related issues. The Committee will have to continue to re-assess and expand its prior experience of such issues in light of the increasing complexity and continued ambiguity in the roles played by the media and internet in spreading and countering racist hate speech. It will also be important for the Committee to continue to engage with issues of intersectionality and remain attentive to the important role that the Convention can play in combating hybrid types of hate speech that comprise racist and other elements.

Chapter 13

ICERD: the next fifty years

Ion Diaconu

As with all international treaties, the International Convention on the Elimination of All Forms of Racial Discrimination (ICERD/the Convention) reflects the historic context of the time of its adoption. As shown above, racism was equated with colonialism and apartheid, and many States gave in the beginning a narrow meaning to racial discrimination.[1]

Evolution after the adoption of the Convention

The evolution in the world since the adoption of ICERD shows that discrimination on grounds of race, colour, descent, national or ethnic origin, as provided for in the definition given by ICERD, continues to take place, albeit in different forms from what was perceived initially, and certainly not to the same extent. Racism is no longer institutionalised, nor an official policy in some States, but nevertheless it is still a reality and takes new forms and nuances, concerning in some States important segments of the population.

Therefore, the Convention, to which 177 States are today parties, remains a topical instrument of protection of human rights, and responds to social needs. It enshrines principles and concepts comprehensive enough to be interpreted and applied so as to cover new aspects of the struggle against racial discrimination. The Convention aims at the elimination of racial discrimination; as has been noted, this objective may be impossible to achieve 100 per cent, but any progress towards it is a welcome step. As a rule, norms of general international law do not have a deadline, and remain valid as long as the facts they regulate continue to occur.

1 On the history and significance of the Convention, see Michael Banton, *International Action Against Racial Discrimination* (Oxford: Clarendon Press, 1996).

The activity of States parties and of the Committee on the Elimination of Racial Discrimination (CERD/the Committee) shows that the application of the Convention is a process responding to social needs as they surface; concerns for discrimination against groups such as indigenous peoples, Roma, persons of African descent, as well as those based on caste and descent, have retained the attention of States and of CERD at the end of the 1990s and into the first decades of the twenty-first century. The 2001 UN World Conference Against Racism, Racial Discrimination, Xenophobia and Related Intolerance held in Durban provided a review of the situation and established an agenda for further efforts in this field.

Periodic reports of States parties and Concluding Observations of the Committee reveal undoubtedly an important and continuous evolution in the application of ICERD. The Convention is the object of dynamic activity of State parties and of the Committee combined, which has made it possible to extend the dialogue with States parties, to approach constructively new aspects of the struggle against racial discrimination and to adopt new general recommendations. The dialogue with States parties remains the most important way to improve the implementation of the Convention worldwide.

An important evolution has to be noted with regard to the concept of race; the Convention forbids racial discrimination and refers to race as one of the grounds on which any act of discrimination is forbidden. Scientific studies have proven that there are no races and all human beings belong to the same species; universal conscience rejects the existence of human races. To reflect this evolution, some States parties refer in their reports and in the dialogue with the Committee to 'supposed race' or 'attributed race'.[2] Nevertheless, in human conscience or sub-conscience, prejudices based on race continue to exist, leading to racist attitudes and to racial discrimination. Moreover, in some States parties the history of massive and flagrant discrimination based on race is still vivid and racial prejudice is still extensive. Therefore, it would be unacceptable to question the rationale to continue the application of the Convention.

According to a general norm accepted in all instruments on human rights, the interdiction of discrimination on the ground of race concerns all human beings, wherever they may be situated. The definition given to racial discrimination in Article 1(1) of the Convention reflects this general norm. Nevertheless, the Committee was confronted with the provision, drafted in general terms in Article 1(2), according to which the Convention will not apply to distinctions between citizens

---

2 Ion Diaconu, *Racial Discrimination* (The Hague: Eleven International Publishing, 2011), pp. 51–60.

and non-citizens. The Committee had to interpret this in the context of all other provisions of the Convention, mainly those of Article 5, which forbids discrimination based on race, colour, national or ethnic origin, with regard to a non-exhaustive list of human rights in all fields and makes no distinction based on citizenship; and in the light of other human rights instruments, in particular the International Covenant on Civil and Political Rights of 1966, which reserves political rights and some related rights only to citizens. A clear distinction is now accepted by CERD and the States parties between discrimination based on race, colour, descent, or national or ethnic origin, which is not acceptable against any person, and difference of treatment in favour of citizens with regard to the right to vote, to be elected, and to accede to public functions, as well as the right to enter one's own country. It is obvious that a different interpretation would have restricted very much the ambit of the Convention.

Challenges and reponses

The Convention refers to discrimination against individuals and against groups, on grounds of race, colour, descent, and national or ethnic origin (Article 2(1)(a), 2(2) and 2(4)(a)). As is well-known, some States do not recognise the existence of minorities on their territories. The Committee started from the grounds of discrimination under the definition given in Article 1(1), that is race, colour, descent and national or ethnic origin, and considered the situation in all States parties leaving aside the issue of existence of minorities in the respective States. Difficulties appeared also with regard to the absence of data about the number of people concerned experiencing wrongly differential treatment; as it is known, for different reasons, many States do not officially collect data based on race or ethnic origin. But the absence of data makes it difficult for a State party to define an adequate policy in different regulated fields of life in order to avoid discrimination, and of course for the Committee to evaluate the situation. Therefore, the Committee asks the respective States to provide estimates based on unofficial inquiries and research, based on self-identification, but allowing for anonymity and confidentiality where necessary.

The concerns with regard to discrimination based on descent began with States parties in South Asia; but the evolution of the activity of the Committee, the reports of States parties and the information received from non-governmental organisations (NGOs) showed that the problem exists also in other areas, mainly in Africa, and was even displaced by migrants in countries of Western Europe. Even if some States parties consider that it is not a case of racial discrimination, but a social problem, the Committee continues to give great attention to such situations. It takes into account the provision of Article 1 of the Convention and the definition given in its General Recommendation 29 of 2002 to discrimination based on descent,[3] as discrimination against members of communities based on forms of social stratification such as caste and analogous systems of inherited status which nullify or impair their equal enjoyment of human rights. It is submitted that such a social stratification created in time a practice of discrimination against a distinct group of persons.[4]

The provisions of the Convention concerning special measures, one defining such measures in Article 1(4) and the second in Article 2(2) enouncing the obligation of States parties to take such measures when and as long as they are necessary to ensure the adequate development and protection to disadvantaged groups or individuals,[5] were met from the beginning with some adverse positions. Some States parties do not accept the idea in principle, although they adopt such measures, while others reject it fully. However, the Convention is clear; States should decide when the circumstances warrant taking such measures, whose purpose is to guarantee to the respective groups and individuals the full and equal enjoyment of human rights. This does not mean that the State party is allowed to avoid taking into account the situation of such groups and individuals and to deny the application of the provisions of the Convention in general. In order to contribute to the clarification of the respective provisions and obligations of States parties, the Committee adopted General Recommendation 32 of 2009 on the meaning and scope of special measures under the Convention.[6] The Committee will continually insist on an extended application of these provisions, taking into account the legal meaning of special measures to ensure equality in the exercise of human rights.

Commitments of States parties

One of the main obligations of States parties is to adopt policies and practices for the elimination of racial discrimination (Article 2(1)). This is the first and foremost step towards the application of the Convention. Most of the States parties adopt such policies, either by stating them officially or in particular by adopting constitutional and other legislative provisions to this effect. The Committee is not

---

3 CERD, 'General Recommendation 29 on Discrimination based on descent', UN Doc. A/57/18 at 111 (2002).

4 *Ibid.*

5 Ion Diaconu, 'Racial discrimination: Using special measures for promoting equal human rights', *East African Journal of Peace and Human Rights*, 18:1 (2012), 1–17.

6 CERD, 'General Recommendation 32 on The meaning and scope of special measures in the ICERD', CERD/C/GC/32 (2009).

faced with legal provisions openly allowing racial discrimination or with official policies promoting it. But this is not enough; there are still cases where public authorities and officials are involved in such acts and in particular States do not always prohibit and sanction racial discrimination by private persons, groups and organisations. Societal developments mean that private actors are now fulfilling more and more activities and services, including public services. The policies of States should also include the activities of private actors which may practice or accept wrongful differences of treatment, including on the grounds for which such differential treatment is forbidden under the Convention; it is unacceptable that in fields such as education, health care, labour, which are essential for human life, such practices are allowed because the State does not overtly control them. The Committee has given more attention to the operative provisions of the Convention (Articles 3–7) and less to this general obligation, which, if better understood and implemented, may be conducive to improvement of the application of all other provisions.

In the beginning, States parties gave most attention to policies of apartheid, condemning and declaring that they did not support them. It was only later in the life of the Convention that racial segregation in general became a subject of attention, and the Committee underlined that it is not always the result of State policies or actions, but also that of individual decisions and trends to group together by language or ethnic affinities. The Committee insisted that even in such cases, the State has to define policies and take adequate measures in order to avoid segregation on grounds including race or ethnicity, which leads usually to isolation, rejection and discrimination, and to promote multi-ethnic and multicultural communities.

The Committee has always given particular attention to the criminalisation of dissemination of ideas based on racial superiority or hatred, to incitement to racial discrimination, to acts of violence, or incitement to such acts against any race or group of persons of another colour or ethnic origin, and to acts of assistance to racist activities, including financial assistance (Article 4(a) and (c)).[7] The Convention also asked States parties to declare illegal and to prohibit organisations and organised activities promoting or inciting racial discrimination and to consider participation in such activities as an offence (Article 4(b)). The Committee has adopted several general recommendations on these provisions underlining their mandatory nature

7 Karl Joseph Partsch, 'Racial speech and human rights: Article 4 of the Convention on the Elimination of All Forms of Racial Discrimination', in Sandra Coliver (ed.), *Striking a Balance: Hate Speech Freedom of Expression and Non-Discrimination* (London: Article 19, 1992), pp. 21–8.

and asking States to include in their legislation adequate provisions as requested by the Convention. In spite of reservations to these provisions entered by several States, and the maintenance of a restrictive position by some of them, the Committee noted progress in the legislation of others, asking States to consider withdrawing their reservations and continuing to insist that the evolution in the field of human rights makes it necessary to protect persons against such acts. The most recent General Recommendation 35 on combating racist hate speech,[8] taking into account some developments, asks States parties again to declare and effectively sanction as offenses punishable by law clearly specified categories of such acts, as well as denials or attempts to justify crimes of genocide or crimes against humanity as defined by international law. The Committee makes it clear that criminalisation of forms of racist expression should be reserved for serious cases, while less serious cases should be addressed by other means. The Committee is also defining the contextual factors that should be taken into account in the qualification of facts as offences under this article. No doubt, these provisions should remain central to the activity of States parties and of the Committee, and the new general recommendation should give a new opportunity to review the situation and improve the application of the Convention.

Consideration of periodic reports

With regard to the obligations of States parties to prohibit and eliminate racial discrimination and to guarantee the right of everyone, without distinction as to race, colour, descent, or national or ethnic origin, to equality before the law in the exercise of the long non-exhaustive list of human rights enounced in Article 5, States parties usually present long reports, focussing mainly on legislative provisions and less on the real enjoyment of such rights. The Committee has focused, in its dialogue and in the recommendations addressed individually to States parties, on those human rights which, according to information received, were the object of racial discrimination. The starting point was the situation of vulnerable groups, such as persons belonging to minorities, indigenous peoples,[9] persons of African descent, migrants, asylum seekers, women, and children, in cases of double or often multiple discrimination in various States parties. The Committee usually asked for data on the enjoyment mainly of economic, social and cultural rights by

8 CERD, 'General Recommendation 35 on Combating racist hate speech', CERD/C/GC/35 (2013).

9 See further Patrick Thornberry, *Indigenous Peoples and Human Rights* (Manchester: Manchester University Press, 2002).

those groups, and sometimes on the use of resources for the development of different areas of specific territories of States. Due to the variety of types of discrimination considered, Concluding Observations are very different for the range of States parties; the Committee will increase its efforts to focus on and promote this practical implementation of all human rights without racial discrimination. General recommendations adopted with regard to discrimination against indigenous peoples, Roma, non-citizens, and Afro-descendants, give a more pointed approach on what the Committee is expecting from the States parties with regard to the realisation of the range of rights in Article 5 without racial discrimination.

In considering the periodic report of each State, the Committee is also interested to see what are the remedies assured to victims of acts of racial discrimination, which according to the Convention have to be effective and offer the right to seek just and adequate reparation or satisfaction for any damage suffered (Article 6). Judicial systems are different and the practice of States is not uniform. The periodic reports of States parties present usually legal provisions about such remedies, but not cases of their use and solutions adopted, omitting the practice of the application of Article 6 of the Convention. The Committee insists upon the right of individuals to address courts or institutions having the competence to take or to promote effective solutions to cases of racial discrimination and to offer reparation or satisfaction for damages. The Committee also adopted General Recommendation 31 on the prevention of racial discrimination in the administration and functioning of the criminal justice system,[10] taking into account the special need to protect human rights in the criminal justice system.

Understanding that nobody is born racist and that the societal context is the main factor in racist conduct, the Convention asked States to adopt immediate and effective measures in the fields of teaching, education, culture and information with the view to combating prejudices and to promoting understanding, tolerance and friendship among nations and racial and ethnical groups (Article 7). Reports presented by States parties include extended information about education and cultural activities, and education in the spirit of respect for human rights in general, and for preventing racial discrimination; the Committee also provides comments and recommendations on the use of media for this purpose. The Committee is concerned not only about education in schools, but also about the training of police, judges, prosecutors and all those involved in law enforcement for combating

10 CERD, 'General Recommendation 31 on The prevention of racial discrimination in the administration and functioning of the criminal justice system', UN Doc. A/60/18 (2005).

prejudice and avoiding racial discrimination. Due attention should be given constantly to this field of implementation of the Convention, given its importance for preventing prejudice and discrimination.

Difficulties and solutions

The Convention is not a perfect document; it contains notions which are not clear or leave room for interpretation. There are also many reservations entered by States parties to the Convention, mainly to Article 4, which are invoked by some States in order not to adopt legislation forbidding hate speech or the existence of organisations promoting racial discrimination.[11] Other reservations are so general as to exclude the application of many provisions of the Convention to the respective States. The provision of the Convention (Article 20(2)) indicating how to deal with such reservations (consider them invalid if two-thirds of the States parties consider them inadmissible) is not practical. Other human rights treaty bodies adopted the practice to consider as inadmissible such reservations and to ask the States parties to fulfil the respective obligations. The Committee is also faced with the absence of periodic reports from many States parties for more than five or even ten years, mainly from States confronted with internal conflicts, where the potential for racial discrimination is greater. The Committee should continue to look for ways and means to engage all States parties in the dialogue on the application of the Convention, even if they are late with presenting their periodic reports. It is also a fact that less than one-third of the States parties have made the declaration of acceptance of the competence of the Committee to receive and consider individual communications about alleged violations under Article 14;[12] the Committee receives only a limited number of communications and from a small number of States parties. The Committee should continue to insist on raising awareness about the importance of this procedure and the need to make it known to the public. The experience of the Human Rights Committee should be considered.

The Committee is also faced with events which, according to the information received, involve serious acts of discrimination concerning usually vulnerable groups, which happen in the period between the consideration of periodic reports of the respective States and which may

11 On reservations to Article 4, see Vera Gowlland-Debbas, 'Effects of reservations to Article 4 of ICERD on the fight against racism and racial discrimination', Background paper presented at the UN Seminar to assess the implementation of ICERD, 9–11 September 1996 (on file with author).

12 Theo van Boven, 'The petition system under the International Convention on the Elimination of All Forms of Racial Discrimination: A sobering balance sheet', *Max Planck Yearbook of United Nations Law*, 4 (2000), 271–87.

require immediate action. To deal with such cases, taking into account that they may develop into ethnic conflicts and lead to extended violations of human rights, CERD has developed early warning and urgent action procedures, considering such information and engaging States parties in a dialogue; it has also developed indicators of patterns of violations making it necessary to initiate an urgent procedure, as well as indicators of patterns of systematic and massive racial discrimination which may lead to conflict and genocide. Solutions can be found for the application of such urgent procedures even between the sessions of the Committee, involving the bureau and the working group considering such cases, under the control of the Committee. The Committee has also developed a follow-up procedure for the recommendations addressed in its Concluding Observations and is trying to combine it with the urgent procedure and with the results of the consideration of individual communications. This should also be given more time and be better used to improve the dialogue with States parties.

The Committee should continue to seek solutions to these and potentially new problems, in conformity with the purpose and the object of the Convention, to improve its methods of work, mainly the dialogue with States parties, inclusive of representative bodies such as national human rights institutions and NGOs. It should find the time and the way to consider the situation of States parties that are late reporting by more than 5–10 years. It should continue to adopt general recommendations, after careful consideration and consultations with States parties and NGOs, as well as other UN actors and experts. As an overall preoccupation, it should involve more States parties in the consideration and the clarification of issues of application of the Convention.

The Committee should follow carefully the new social trends, like for instance the increase of the significance of cultural identities, of the diversity of cultures, and diversity in general, and consequently of the need to respect them in societies increasingly more diverse and multicultural. Another trend is the motivation of racist attitudes by cultural differences, considered unacceptable and insurmountable, which leads to new forms of racial discrimination based on cultural differences. The evolution of global issues like limited resources of energy, water and food, as well as dramatic climate change, may lead to new conflicts and to the need to strengthen the application of the Convention in more specific cases.

New standards and developments

The issue of adopting new standards and amending the Convention has been considered by a UN working group, without a tangible result. On this issue, members of the Committee refer often to procedural aspects, like the possibility to initiate visits *in situ* when considered necessary, with the agreement of the State party. Of course, the Convention, as part of the UN system of protection of human rights, may still evolve and even be modified. The Committee itself may develop ways and means to expand the application of the Convention by adopting new general recommendations thereby drawing in new groups or points of focus (as in the past in relation to indigenous peoples, gender related dimensions of racial discrimination, Roma, descent, non-citizens, special measures and Afro-descendants) and constantly improving the dialogue with State parties and its working methods. One has to note also statements adopted by the Committee having significant or substantial content, such as the 'Statement on racial discrimination and measures to combat terrorism' of 2002, the 'Statement on the situation in Iraq' of 2014, and the 'Statement on the recent migrant crises' of 2015.

The application of the Convention can also benefit from developments in other human rights treaty bodies and UN organs; for example, the Committee is already consistently using in its activities the UN Declaration on the Rights of Persons Belonging to National or Ethnic, Religious and Linguistic Minorities (1992), the UN Declaration on the Rights of Indigenous Peoples (2007), and regional instruments related to the combat against racial discrimination, as well as general recommendations and comments adopted by other human rights treaty bodies. The activity of codification of international law, undertaken by the International Law Commission, is also relevant; for instance, the draft articles adopted by the Commission in 2007 on diplomatic protection (recommended to the States by the resolution of the General Assembly no. 62/67 of 6 December 2007), connecting diplomatic protection with State responsibility, is clarifying some aspects concerning the protection of human rights; similarly, the Guide concerning reservations to multilateral treaties, submitted to the General Assembly in 2011, includes some very important rules concerning multilateral human rights treaties, mainly the presumption of separability of reservations to such treaties which are not compatible with the object and the purpose of the treaty, from the ratification of the treaty by the respective State. The jurisprudence of the International Court of Justice, of regional courts on human rights, and of other international tribunals is also important, giving impetus to the formation of a general practice and leading to customary rules of international law in the area of the elimination of racial discrimination.

Progress in the application of the Convention may also be obtained through the evolution of the protection of some vulnerable groups by other ways and instruments (including ethnic and other minorities, indigenous peoples, Afro-descendants, migrants and others) and by other human rights treaty bodies. The Committee can receive input from the activity of all other human rights treaty bodies dealing with issues of discrimination on different grounds, including when there is intersectionality of grounds of discrimination (gender and race or ethnicity, religion and race or ethnicity, or other forms).

The international community has reached such a level of standards of protection of human rights, including against racial discrimination, and a corresponding level of social conscience, that it should not accept less. The Convention and the system developed around it could be, when the international community will decide, a starting point for a system of more precise norms and improved mechanisms of protection. The prohibition of racial discrimination will remain as a generally accepted norm of international law. As a part of the system of protection of human rights as a whole, universal and indivisible as they are, it will benefit from all evolutions and developments achieved.

Conclusion

David Keane and Annapurna Waughray

> The United Nations does not seek a world cut after a single pattern, nor does it consider this desirable. The United Nations seeks only unity, not uniformity, out of the world's diversity.
>
> – Ralph Bunche, Nobel Lecture (1950)[1]

The collection has charted the forces behind the drafting and entry into force of the International Convention on the Elimination of All Forms of Racial Discrimination (ICERD) in 1965, and in the fifty years of its implementation under the aegis of the Committee on the Elimination of Racial Discrimination (CERD), its evolution from a narrow focus on colonialism and apartheid to an instrument governing a wide range of groups and themes. The number of ratifications means that the obligations found in the treaty are near-universal in reach. Its provisions at times betray their age but have nevertheless proven very capable of application to contemporary aspects of racial discrimination. The title of this collection has ensured a focus on the treaty as a 'living instrument', but this does not always entail dynamic or evolutive interpertation. Complex questions of treaty interpretation coexist with straightforward applications of clear provisions to contemporary situations that confront the Committee. The text of ICERD has not changed since 1965; there are no protocols to the instrument. Its text has proven capable of a remarkable array of applications, and has framed the development of an in-depth corpus of international standards on the elimination of all forms of racial discrimination.

The chapters in this collection provide examples of many of these applications, and the motivations that lie behind their entry into the international sphere. This includes the meaning and relevance of CERD measures to the range of actors that engage with the Committee and

1 Ralph Bunche, 'Some Reflections on Peace in Our Time', Nobel Lecture, 11 December 1950, available at: www.nobelprize.org/nobel_prizes/peace/laureates/1950/bunche-lecture.html.

ICERD, in particular States parties, NGOs, UN and other experts, and victims of racial discrimination. The chapters are not exhaustive and gaps can be readily identified, partly the result of hazards of the editing process, partly a lack of foresight on the part of editors, partly a lack of space, partly a lack of available expertise, among other factors. A point that the editing of this collection brought through, however, is the need for more scholarship and engagement on CERD and ICERD. It is apparent that a large body of the writing on CERD is by (current or former) CERD members themselves. This is certainly not a criticism; it is clear that several authors and Committee members who appear frequently in these pages, such as Banton, Thornberry or others, have not only been central in bringing the instrument to a range of groups and themes, but have documented and presented the legal and other aspects that have informed this process. Yet the current volume is the first book on ICERD by non-CERD members since Lerner's work of 1970.[2] It is one of only two publications to mark the fiftieth anniversary of the treaty, in conjunction with Thornberry's commentary.[3] In fact it is the very first edited collection on ICERD in its fifty years, and the first time that authors from CERD and outside of CERD have discussed the treaty in the same volume. There are of course a range of publications in journals and other sources that examine many aspects of the treaty, but by comparison with the interest in other international and regional human rights instruments, it appears if not neglected, at least under-researched.

It is clear that in particular, the international legal character of ICERD and its obligations needs greater analysis and discussion. At times it appears like a sleight of hand to convert issues that States traditionally struggle to engage with at the international level, or outright oppose – such as minority rights, indigenous peoples, difficult questions of ethnic or analogous groups and their access to civil, political, economic, social and cultural rights – and call it something that all States ostensibly agree on, the elimination of all forms of racial discrimination. But this is to ignore the critical input of NGOs and other groups who have brought the Committee closer to local activists and issues, and the experience of racial discrimination on the ground. That has created a picture of the diversity of racial discrimination that is in tandem with the diversity of the world, and the Committee has clearly felt compelled to respond, in line with its mandate to address 'all forms of' such discrimination. Additionally its work is underpinned by legal

2 Natan Lerner, 'The UN Convention on the Elimination of All Forms of Racial Discrimination: A commentary' (A.W. Sijthoff, Leyden, 1970, reprinted 2015).

3 Patrick Thornberry, *The International Convention on the Elimination of All Forms of Raial Discrimination: A Commentary* (Oxford: Oxford University Press, 2016).

doctrine, including the text of the treaty, the wording and dialogue in its Concluding Observations, the interpretations and guidance found in its general recommendations, as well as the international legal character assigned to its innovation in procedures in line with an evolving United Nations human rights machinery.

The present collection has sought to identify the 'living instrument' doctrine as capturing the totality of this approach. In the editors' view, what emerges is a distinct CERD understanding of the living instrument doctrine that can now be discerned, but continues to evolve. It is distinct because it differs in its approach from other instruments and their monitoring bodies, regional and international. It is located principally in the dialogue with States parties and Concluding Observations that grow the State party's obligations incrementally, the guiding and interpretive general recommendations that at times stretch the provisions of the treaty, the innovations in procedure that indicate that the monitoring process itself is subject to the doctrine, the integration of civil society voices at local and international organisational level at times leading the agenda, the identification of particular groups or themes previously without a 'home' in international human rights bodies, and the autonomous meaning of special measures in the treaty tied to disaggregated data obligations.

Some of these traits are common to international human rights law in general, but there is perhaps no treaty body that displays such an evolution between its initial founding mandate, or at least the perception of that mandate by States parties, and its current sphere of operation. Although there are contestations and challenges as this volume attests, the contemporary meaning and reach of ICERD, as articulated by the Committee, is not fundamentally questioned by States parties. CERD will continue to offer a voice at the international level for victims of all forms of racial discrimination, which will drive more in-depth implementation of its standards. But it is also not just about victims, but rather full representation of the diversity of the world's peoples from the local to the international level and back again. If, as indicated in the opening quote to the collection by Ralph Bunche, the United Nations is to be a vehicle for change, even radical change, the processes and recommendations of ICERD as a living instrument need greater understanding and realisation.

Select bibliography

Primary sources

I. CERD standards

Declaration on the Elimination of All Forms of Racial Discrimination, GA res. 1904 (XVIII), at 35 (1963)

International Convention on the Elimination of All Forms of Racial Discrimination, GA Res. 2106 (XX), Annex, 20 UN GAOR Supp. (No. 14) at 47, UN Doc. A/6014 (1966), 660 UNTS 195, entered into force 4 January 1969 (1965)

CERD, 'Communication', UN Doc. CERD/C/R.12 (1970)

CERD, 'Report of the CERD', General Assembly Official Records, UN Doc. A/9618 (1974); UN Doc. A/31/18 (1976); UN Doc. A/35/18 (1980); UN Doc. A/38/18 (1983); UN Doc. A/39/18 (1984); UN Doc. A/45/18 (1990); UN Doc. A/47/18 (1992); CERD/C/70/Rev.3 (1993)

CERD, 'Prevention of Racial Discrimination, including Early Warning and Urgent Procedures', UN Doc. A/48/18, Annex III (1993)

CERD, 'Letter of transmittal', Report of the Committee on the Elimination of Racial Discrimination, Forty-ninth Session, UN Doc. A/49/18 (1994)

CERD, 'Declaration on the Prevention of Genocide', CERD/C/66/1 (1995)

CERD, 'Decision on Follow-up to the Declaration on the Prevention of Genocide: Indicators of Patterns of Systematic and Massive Racial Discrimination', CERD/C/67/1 (2005)

CERD, 'Guidelines for the CERD-specific document to be submitted by States parties', CERD/C/2007/1 (2007)

CERD, 'Guidelines for the Early Warning and Urgent Action Procedure', UN Doc. A/62/18, Annex III (2007)

II. CERD General Recommendations

CERD, 'General Recommendation 1 on States parties' obligations', UN Doc. A/87/18 (1972)

CERD, 'General Recommendation 2 on States' parties obligations', UN Doc. A/8718 at 38 (1972)

CERD, 'General Recommendation 4 on Information on the demographic composition of the population', UN Doc. A/9018 at 106 (1973)
CERD, 'General Recommendation 7 on Measures to eradicate incitement to or acts of discrimination', UN Doc. A/40/18 at 120 (1985)
CERD, 'General Recommendation 8 on Membership of racial or ethnic groups based on self-identification', UN Doc. A/45/18 at 79 (1991)
CERD, 'General Recommendation 11 on Non-citizens', UN Doc. A/48/18 at 112 (1994)
CERD, 'General Recommendation 14 on Definition of racial discrimination', UN Doc. A/48/18 at 114 (1994)
CERD, 'General Recommendation 15 on Measures to eradicate incitement to or acts of discrimination', UN Doc. A/48/18 at 114 (1994)
CERD, 'General Recommendation 19 on The prevention, prohibition and eradication of racial segregation and apartheid', UN Doc. A/50/18 at 140 (1995)
CERD, 'General Recommendation 23 on Rights of indigenous peoples', UN Doc. A/52/18, Annex V at 122 (1997)
CERD, 'General Recommendation 24 on Information on the demographic composition of the population', UN Doc. A/54/18, Annex V at 103 (1999)
CERD, 'General Recommendation 25 on Gender-related dimensions of racial discrimination', UN Doc. A/55/18, Annex V at 152 (2000)
CERD, 'General Recommendation 26 on The right to seek just and adequate reparation or satisfaction', UN Doc. A/55/18, Annex V at 153 (2000)
CERD, 'General Recommendation 27 on Discrimination against Roma', UN Doc. A/55/18, Annex V at 154 (2000)
CERD, 'General Recommendation 29 on Discrimination based on descent', UN Doc. A/57/18 at 111 (2002)
CERD, 'General Recommendation 30 on Discrimination against non-citizens', CERD/C/64/Misc.11/rev.3 (2004)
CERD, 'General Recommendation 31 on The prevention of racial discrimination in the administration and functioning of the criminal justice system', UN Doc. A/60/18 (2005)
CERD, 'General Recommendation 32 on The meaning and scope of special measures in the ICERD', CERD/C/GC/32 (2009)
CERD, 'General Recommendation 33 on Follow-up to the Durban Review Conference', CERD/C/GC/33 (2009)
CERD, 'General Recommendation 34 on Racial discrimination against people of African descent', CERD/C/GC/34 (2011)
CERD, 'General Recommendation 35 on Combating racist hate speech', CERD/C/GC/35 (2013)

III. CERD individual communications

Anna Koptova v. *Slovakia*, CERD Communication No. 13/1998, CERD/C/57/D/13/1998 (2000)
Miroslav Lacko v. *Slovakia*, CERD Communication No. 11/1998, CERD/C/59/D/11/1998 (2001)
Stephen Hagan v. *Australia*, CERD Communication No. 26/2002, CERD/C/62/D/26/2002 (2003)
L.R. et al. v. *Slovakia*, CERD Communication No. 31/2003, CERD/C/66/D/31/2003 (2005)

Dragan Durmic v. Serbia and Montenegro, Communication No. 29/2003, CERD/C/68/D/29/2003 (2006)
Zentralrat Deutscher Sinti und Roma et al. v. *Germany*, CERD Communication No. 38/2006, CERD/C/72/D/38/2006 (2008)
A.S. v. *Russian Federation*, CERD Communication No. 45/2009, CERD/C/79/D/45/2009 (2011)
TBB-Turkish Union in Berlin/Brandenburg v. *Germany*, Communication No. 48/2010, CERD/C/82/D/48/2010 (2013)

IV. CERD Concluding Observations

CERD, 'Concluding Observations: Rwanda', UN Doc. A/49/18 (1994)
CERD, 'Concluding Observations: Peru', UN Doc. A/50/18 (1995)
CERD, 'Concluding Observations: Brazil', CERD/C/304/Add.11 (1996)
CERD, 'State Report: India', CERD/C/299/Add.3 (1996)
CERD, 'Concluding Observations: India', UN Doc. A/51/18 (1996)
CERD, 'Concluding Observations: Philippines', CERD/C/304/Add.34 (1997)
CERD, 'Concluding Observations: Czech Republic', CERD/C/304/Add.47 (1998)
CERD, 'Concluding Observations: Peru', CERD/C/304/Add.69 (1999)
CERD, 'Concluding Observations: Canada', UN Doc. A/57/18 (2002)
CERD, 'Concluding Observations: Bolivia', CERD/C/63/CO/2 (2003)
CERD, 'Concluding Observations: Ecuador', CERD/C/62/CO/2 (2003)
CERD, 'Concluding Observations: Brazil', CERD/C/64/CO/2 (2004)
CERD, 'Concluding Observations: Laos', CERD/C/LAO/CO/15 (2005)
CERD, 'Concluding Observations: Canada', CERD/C/CAN/CO/18 (2007)
CERD, 'Concluding Observations: Democratic Republic of Congo', CERD/C/COD/CO/15 (2007)
CERD, 'Concluding Observations: India', CERD/C/IND/CO/19 (2007)
CERD, 'Concluding Observations: Venezuela, CERD/C/VEN/CO/18 (2007)
CERD, 'Concluding Observations: Russian Federation', UN Doc. A/63/18 (2008)
CERD, 'Concluding Observations: United States', UN Doc. A/63/18 (2008)
CERD, 'Concluding Observations: Colombia', CERD/C/COL/CO/14 (2009)
CERD, 'Concluding Observations: Philippines', CERD/C/PHL/CO/20 (2009)
CERD, 'Concluding Observations: France', CERD/C/FRA/CO/17–19 (2010)
CERD, 'Concluding Observations: Bolivia', CERD/C/BOL/CO/17–20 (2011)
CERD, 'Concluding Observations: Moldova', CERD/C/MDA/CO/8–9 (2011)
CERD, 'Concluding Observations: Paraguay', CERD/C/PRY/CO/1–3 (2011)
CERD, 'Concluding Observations: Rwanda', CERD/C/RWA/CO/13–17 (2011)
CERD, 'Concluding Observations: Spain', CERD/C/ESP/CO/18–20 (2011)
CERD, 'State Report: United Kingdom', CERD/C/GBR/18–21 (2011)
CERD, 'Concluding Observations: Belize', CERD/C/BLZ/CO/1 (2012)
CERD, 'Concluding Observations: Canada', CERD/C/CAN/CO/19–20 (2012)
CERD, 'Concluding Observations: Mexico', CERD/C/MEX/CO/16–17 (2012)
CERD, 'Concluding Observations: Norway', UN Doc. A/66/18 (2012)
CERD, 'Concluding Observations: United Kingdom', UN Doc. A/66/18 (2012)
CERD, 'Concluding Observations: Belarus', CERD/C/BLR/CO/18–19 (2013)
CERD, 'Concluding Observations: Burkina Faso', CERD/C/BFA/CO/12–19 (2013)
CERD, 'Concluding Observations: Slovakia', CERD/C/ SVK/CO/9–10 (2013)
CERD, 'Concluding Observations: Belgium', CERD/C/BEL/CO/16–19 (2014)

CERD, 'Concluding Observations: Cameroon', CERD/C/CMR/CO/19–21 (2014)
CERD, 'Concluding Observations: El Salvador', CERD/C/SLV/CO/16–17 (2014)
CERD, 'Concluding Observations: Estonia', CERD/C/EST/CO/10–11 (2014)
CERD, 'Concluding Observations: Honduras', CERD/C/HND/CO/1–5 (2014)
CERD, 'Concluding Observations: Iraq', CERD/C/IRQ/CO/15–21 (2014)
CERD, 'Concluding Observations: Japan', CERD/C/JPN/CO/7–9 (2014)
CERD, 'Concluding Observations: Kazakhstan', CERD/C/KAZ/CO/6–7 (2014)
CERD, 'Concluding Observations: Luxembourg', CERD/C/LUX/CO/14–17 (2014)
CERD, 'Concluding Observations: Montenegro', CERD/C/MNE/CO/2–3 (2014)
CERD, 'Concluding Observations: Peru', CERD/C/PER/CO/18–21 (2014)
CERD, 'Concluding Observations: Poland', CERD/C/POL/CO/20–21 (2014)
CERD, 'Concluding Observations: Switzerland', CERD/C/CHE/CO/7–9 (2014)
CERD, 'Concluding Observations: United States of America', CERD/C/USA/CO/7–9 (2014)
CERD, 'Concluding Observations: Uzbekistan', CERD/C/UZB/CO/8–9 (2014)
CERD, 'Concluding Observations: Bosnia and Herzegovina', CERD/C/BIH/CO/9–11 (2015)
CERD, 'Concluding Observations: Colombia', CERD/C/COL/CO/15–16 (2015)
CERD, 'Concluding Observations: Costa Rica', CERD/C/CRI/CO/19–22 (2015)
CERD, 'Concluding Observations: Czech Republic', CERD/C/CZE/CO/10–11 (2015)
CERD, 'Concluding Observations: Denmark', CERD/C/DNK/CO/20–21 (2015)
CERD, 'Concluding Observations: France', CERD/C/FRA/CO/20–21 (2015)
CERD, 'Concluding Observations: Germany', CERD/C/DEU/CO/19–22 (2015)
CERD, 'Concluding Observations: Guatemala', CERD/C/GTM/CO/14–15 (2015)
CERD, 'Concluding Observations: (former Yugoslav Republic of) Macedonia', CERD/C/MKD/CO/8–10 (2015)
CERD, 'Concluding Observations: Netherlands', CERD/C/NLD/CO/19–21 (2015)
CERD, 'Concluding Observations: Niger', CERD/C/NER/CO/15–21 (2015)
CERD, 'Concluding Observations: Norway', CERD/C/NOR/CO/21–22 (2015)
CERD, 'Concluding Observations: The Sudan', CERD/C/SDN/CO/12–16 (2015)
CERD, 'Concluding Observations: Suriname', CERD/C/SUR/CO/13–15 (2015)
CERD, 'Concluding Observations: Egypt', CERD/C/EGY/CO/17–22 (2016)
CERD, 'Concluding Observations: Holy See', CERD/C/VAT/CO/16–23 (2016)
CERD, 'Concluding Observations: Lithuania', CERD/C/LTU/CO/6–8 (2016)
CERD, 'Concluding Observations: Mongolia', CERD/C/MNG/CO/19–22 (2016)
CERD, 'Concluding Observations: Slovenia', CERD/C/SVN/CO/8–11 (2016)
CERD, 'Concluding Observations: Turkey', CERD/C/TUR/CO/4–6 (2016)

V. CERD decisions

CERD, 'Decision 1(45): Rwanda', UN Doc. A/49/18 (1994)
CERD, 'Decision 1(54): Australia', UN Doc A/53/18 (1998)
CERD, 'Decision 2(54): Australia', UN Doc. A/54/18 (1999)
CERD, 'Decision 1(66): New Zealand', CERD/C/DEC/NZL/1 (2005)
CERD, 'Decision 2(66): Situation in Darfur', CERD/C/DEC/SDN/1 (2005)
CERD, 'Decision 1(67): Suriname', CERD/C/DEC/SUR/2 (2005)
CERD, 'Decision 1(69): Suriname', CERD/C/DEC/SUR/3 (2006)
CERD, 'Decision 1(85): Iraq' (2014)

VI. Regional and international standards

Council of Europe, Convention for the Protection of Human Rights and Fundamental Freedoms (European Convention on Human Rights, as Amended) (ECHR) Art. 3 (1950)
Council of Europe, Framework Convention for the Protection of National Minorities, 1 February 1995, ETS 157 (1995)
Organisation of American States, American Convention on Human Rights, OAS Treaty Series No. 36; 1144 UNTS 123; 9 ILM 99 (1969)
Organization of African Unity, African Charter on Human and Peoples' Rights CAB/LEG/67/3 rev. 5, 21 ILM 58 (1981)
Covenant of the League of Nations, [1919] UKTS 4 (Cmd. 153)/ [1920] ATS 1/ [1920] ATS 3 (1919)
Charter of the United Nations, 26 June 1945, 59 Stat. 1031, T.S. 993, 3 Bevans 1153, entered into force 24 October 1945 (1945)
UN General Assembly Resolution 103(1), 'Persecution and discrimination' (1946)
Universal Declaration of Human Rights, GA Res. 217A (III), UN Doc A/810 at 71 (1948)
Convention on the Prevention and Punishment of the Crime of Genocide, 78 UNTS 277, entered into force 12 January 1951 (1948)
Declaration on the Granting of Independence to Colonial Countries and Peoples, GA Res. 1514 (XV), 15 UN GAOR Supp. (No. 16) at 66, UN Doc. A/4684 (1961)
UNESCO, 'Four Statements on the Race Question', Com.69/II.27/A (1969)
Vienna Convention on the Law of Treaties, 1155 UNTS 331, 8 ILM 679, entered into force 27 January 1980 (1980)
United Nations Declaration on the Elimination of All Forms of Intolerance and of Discrimination Based on Religion or Belief, GA res. 36/55, UN Doc. A/RES/36/55 (1981)
UN Sub-Commission on the Prevention of Discrimination and the Protection of Minorities, 'Revised and Updated Report on the Question of the Prevention and Punishment of the Crime of Genocide', UN Doc. E/CN.4/Sub.2/1985/6 (1985)
UN Security Council Resolution 1325 (2000), 'Women, Peace and Security', UN Doc. S/RES/1325 (2000)
United Nations, 'Report of the International Commission of Inquiry on Violations of International Humanitarian Law and Human Rights Law in Darfur', UN Doc. S/2005/60 (2005)
Inter-Committee Technical Working Group, 'Harmonized guidelines on reporting under the international human rights treaties', HRI/MC/2006/3 (2006)
United Nations, 'Declaration and Programme of Action: World Conference Against Racism, Racial Discrimination, Xenophobia and Related Intolerance', UN Doc. A/CONF.189/12 (2002)
UN General Assembly, 'Programme of activities for the implementation of the International Decade for People of African Descent', UN Doc. A/RES/69/16 (2014)
Human Rights Council, 'Mandate of the Working Group of Experts on People of African Descent', UN Doc. A/HRC/27/25 (2014)

VII. Regional and international caselaw

Tyrer v. *United Kingdom* 58 ILR 339, 353 (1978)

Nachova and Others v. *Bulgaria* (Application nos. 43577/98 and 43579/98), Judgment (Grand Chamber) (2005)
Oršuš and Others v. *Croatia* (Application no. 15766/03), Judgment (Grand Chamber) (2010)
Georgia v. *Russia* (II), App No, 38263/08, Eur. Ct. H.R. Preliminary Objections (2011)
The Mayagna (Sumo) Awas Tingni Community v. *Nicaragua*, Judgment of 31 August 2001, Inter-Am. Ct. H.R. (Ser. C) No. 79 (2001)
Sawhoyamaxa Indigenous Community v. *Paraguay*, Judgment of 29 March 2006, Inter-Am. Ct. H.R. (Ser. C), No. 146 (2006)
Inter-American Commission on Human Rights (IACHR), 'The Situation of People of African Descent in the Americas', OEA/Ser.L/V/II, Doc. 62 (Washington, DC: Organization of American States, 2011)
Centre for Minority Rights Development (Kenya) and Minority Rights Group (on behalf of Endorois Welfare Council) v. *Kenya*, 276/03 (2009)
Prosecutor v. *Krstić* (IT-98–33-T), Judgment (2001)
Prosecutor v. *Tadić* (IT-94–1-AR72), Decision on the Defence Motion for Interlocutory Appeal on Jurisdiction (1995)
Prosecutor v. *Akayesu* (ICTR-96–4-T), Judgment (1998)
Prosecutor v. *Rutaganda* (ICTR-96–3-T), Judgment and Sentence (1999)
Prosecutor v. *Musema* (ICTR-96–13-T), Judgment and Sentence (2000)
Prosecutor v. *Bikindi* (ICTR-01–72-T), Judgment (2008)
Armed Activities on the Territory of the Congo (New Application: 2002) (*Democratic Republic of the Congo* v. *Rwanda*), Jurisdiction and Admissibility, Judgment, ICJ Reports (2006)
Application of the International Convention on the Elimination of All Forms of Racial Discrimination (*Georgia* v. *Russian Federation*), Preliminary Objections, Judgment, ICJ Reports (2011)

Secondary sources

I. Books

Allain, Jean, *Slavery in International Law: Of Human Exploitation and Trafficking* (The Hague: Brill, 2013)
Alston, Philip and Goodman, Ryan, *International Human Rights* (Oxford: Oxford University Press, 2012)
Anaya, James, *Indigenous Peoples in International Law* (Oxford: Oxford University Press, 2004)
Anderson, Benedict, *Imagined Communities* (revised edn) (London: Verso, 1991)
Andrews, George Reid, *Afro-Latin America, 1800–2000* (Oxford: Oxford University Press, 2004)
Bales, Kevin, *Understanding Global Slavery* (Berkeley: University of California Press, 2005)
Banton, Michael, *Race Relations* (London: Tavistock Publications, 1967)
Banton, Michael, *International Action against Racial Discrimination* (Oxford: Oxford University Press, 1996)

Banton, Michael, *The International Politics of Race* (Oxford: Blackwell, 2002)

Banton, Michael, *What We Now Know About Race and Ethnicity* (New York and Oxford: Berghahn Books, 2015)

Bassiouni, M. Cherif, *The Legislative History of the International Criminal Court: Introduction, Analysis and Integrated Text*, Vol. I (Ardsley: Transn ational, 2005)

Bayly, Susan, *Caste, Society and Politics in Modern India from the Eighteenth Century to the Modern Age* (Cambridge: Cambridge University Press, 1998)

Bjorge, Eirik, *The Evolutionary Interpretation of Treaties* (Oxford: Oxford University Press, 2014)

Carmona, Magdalena Sepulveda, *Nature of the Obligations under the International Covenant on Economic, Social and Cultural Rights* (Cambridge: Intersentia, 2003)

Castellino, J. and Domínguez Redondo, E., *Minority Rights in Asia: A Comparative Legal Analysis* (Oxford: Oxford University Press, 2006)

Clark, Joshua, *The Global Fight against Racial Discrimination: Counting, Representation, and Responsibility in Costa Rica and at the United Nations* (PhD dissertation, University of California, Irvine, 2016)

Cooper, John, *Raphael Lemkin and the Struggle for the Genocide Convention* (Basingstoke: Palgrave Macmillan, 2008)

Curtis, Devon and Dzinesa, Gwynyayi A., *Peacebuilding, Power, and Politics in Africa* (Athens: Ohio University Press, 2013)

Damrosch, Lori. F., Henkin, Louis, Pugh, Richard Crawford, Schachter, Oscar and Smit, Hans, *International Law: Cases and Materials* (St Paul: West Group, 2001)

Delgado, Richard and Stefancic, Jean, *Understanding Words That Wound* (Boulder: Westview Press, 2004)

Diaconu, Ion, *Racial Discrimination* (The Hague: Eleven International Publishing, 2011)

Doyle, Cathal, *Indigenous Peoples, Title to Territory, Rights and Resources: The Transformative Role of Free Prior and Informed Consent* (London: Routledge, 2015)

Doyle, Cathal and Whitmore, Andrew, *Indigenous Peoples and the Extractive Industries: Towards Rights Respecting Engagements* (Manila and London: Tebtebba, Middlesex University, PIPLinks, 2014)

Drost, Pieter N., *Genocide, United Nations Legislation on International Criminal Law* (Leiden: A. W. Sythoff, 1959)

Ezorsky, G., *Racism and Justice: The Case for Affirmative Action* (Ithaca, NY: Cornell University Press, 1991)

Forbes, H. D., *Ethnic Conflict, Commerce, Culture, and the Contact Hypothesis* (New Haven: Yale University Press, 1997)

Fraser, Angus, *The Gypsies* (Oxford: Blackwell, 1992)

Freyre, Gilberto, *The Masters and the Slaves* (New York: Knopf, 1946), first published in 1933 as *Casa Grande & Senzala*

Gardam, Judith G. and Jarvis, Michelle J., *Women, Armed Conflict and International Law* (The Hague, London and Boston: Kluwer Law International, 2001)

Gates Jr., Henry, *Black in Latin America* (New York and London: New York University Press, 2011)

Gelber, Katharine, *Speaking Back: The Free Speech Versus Hate Speech Debate* (Amsterdam and Philadelphia: John Benjamins Publishing Company, 2002)

Gilbert, Jérémie, *Indigenous Peoples' Land Rights under International Law: From Victims to Actors* (Leiden, Boston and Tokyo: Brill, 2nd edn, 2016)

Guillaumin, Colette, *Racism, Sexism, Power and Ideology* (London: Routledge, 1995)

Hanchard, Michael George, *Orpheus and Power: The Movimento Negro of Rio de Janeiro and São Paulo, Brazil, 1945–1988* (Princeton: Princeton University Press, 1994)

Hayner, Priscilla B., *Unspeakable Truths* (New York: Routledge, 2001)

Jacobs, James B. and Potter, Kimberley, *Hate Crimes: Criminal Law and Identity Politics* (New York: Oxford University Press, 1998)

Jaffrelot, Christophe, *Dr Ambedkar and Untouchability: Analysing and Fighting Caste* (New Delhi: Permanent Black, 2005)

Jodhka, Surinder, *Oxford India Short Introductions: Caste* (New Delhi: Oxford University Press India, 2012)

Kampelman, Max M., *Three Years at the East-West Divide* (New York: Freedom House, 1983)

Keane, David, *Caste-based Discrimination in International Human Rights Law* (Surrey: Ashgate/Routledge, 2007)

Kenrick, Donald and Puxon, Grattan, *Gypsies under the Swastika* (Hertfordshire: University of Hertfordshire Press, 1995)

Kephart, William M., *Extraordinary Groups: The Sociology of Unconventional Life-Styles* (New York: St. Martin's Press, 1982, 2nd edn)

Lemkin, Raphael, *Axis Rule in Occupied Europe* (New York: Carnegie Endowment for World Peace, 1944)

Lenzerini, Federico, *The Culturalization of Human Rights Law* (Oxford: Oxford University Press, 2014)

Lerner, Natan, *The UN Convention on the Elimination of All Forms of Racial Discrimination: A Commentary* (Leiden: A. W. Sijthoff, 1970)

Lester, Anthony and Bindman, Geoffrey, *Race and Law* (Harmondsworth: Penguin, 1972)

Makkonen, Timo, *Identity, Difference and Otherness* (Helsinki: Erik Castren Institute, 2000)

Marushiakova, Elena and Popov, Vesselin, *The Gypsies in the Ottoman Empire* (Hatfield: University of Hertfordshire Press, 2001)

Matras, Yaron, *Romani: A Linguistic Introduction* (Cambridge: Cambridge University Press, 2002)

Matsuda, Mari J., Lawrence III, C. R., Delgado, Richard and Williams Crenshaw, Kimberle (eds), *Words That Wound: Critical Race Theory, Assaultive Speech, and the First Amendment* (Boulder, San Francisco and Oxford: Westview Press, 1993)

May, Larry, *Genocide, A Normative Account* (New York: Cambridge University Press, 2010)

McGoldrick, Dominic, *The Human Rights Committee: Its Role in the Development of the International Covenant on Civil and Political Rights* (Oxford: Clarendon Press, 1994)

McGonagle, Tarlach, *Minority Rights, Freedom of Expression and of the Media: Dynamics and Dilemmas* (Antwerp: Intersentia, 2011)

Mendelsohn, Oliver and Vicziany, Marika, *The Untouchables: Subordination, Poverty and the State in Modern India* (Cambridge: Cambridge University Press, 1998)

Mettraux, Guénaël, *International Crimes and the Ad Hoc Tribunals* (Oxford: Oxford University Press, 2005)

Moller, Jakob and de Zayas, Alfred, *The United Nations Human Rights Committee Case Law 1977–2008* (Kehl/Strasbourg: N. P. Engel, 2009)

Mugwanya, George William, *The Crime of Genocide in International Law: Appraising the Contribution of the UN Tribunal for Rwanda* (London: Cameron May, 2007)

Natrajan, Balmurli, *The Culturalisation of Caste in India: Identity and Inequality in a Multicultural Age* (Abingdon: Routledge, 2012)

Nersessian, David L., *Genocide and Political Groups* (Oxford: Oxford University Press, 2010)

Nkansah, Lydia A., *Transitional Justice: Perspectives on Truth, Justice and Reconciliation in Post-Conflict Sierra Leone* (Saarbruken: VDM Verlag, 2010)

Parekh, Bikhu, *Rethinking Multiculturalism: Cultural Diversity and Political Theory* (New York: Palgrave Macmillan, 2nd edn, 2006)

Pedersen, Susan, *The Guardians: The League of Nations and the Crisis of Empire* (Oxford: Oxford University Press, 2015)

Pietila, Hilkka and Vickers, Jeanne, *Making Women Matter: The Role of the United Nations* (London: Zed Books, 1990)

Reichmann, Rachel, *Race in Contemporary Brazil: From Indifference to Inequality* (Philadelphia: Pennsylvania State University Press 1999)

Rhode, D. L., *Access to Justice* (Oxford: Oxford University Press, 2004)

Rooker, Marcia, *The International Supervision of the Protection of Romany People in Europe* (Nijmegen: Nijmegen University Press, 2002)

Rousseau, Jean-Jacques, *On the Social Contract* (London: J. M. Dent, 1913, translated by G. D. H. Cole)

Sachs, Albie, *Protecting Human Rights in a New South Africa* (Cape Town: Oxford University Press, 1990)

Schabas, William, *Genocide in International Law: The Crime of Crimes* (Cambridge: Cambridge University Press, 2009)

Schabas, William, *Unimaginable Atrocities: Justice, Politics and Rights at the War Crimes Tribunals* (Oxford: Oxford University Press, 2012)
Schabas, William, *The Universal Declaration of Human Rights* (Cambridge: Cambridge University Press, 2013)
Sieder, Rachel, *Multiculturalism in Latin America: Indigenous Rights, Diversity and Democracy* (Basingstoke: Palgrave Macmillan, 2002)
Telles, Edward, *Race in Another America: The Significance of Skin Color in Brazil* (Princeton: Princeton University Press, 2004)
Thornberry, Patrick, *International Law and the Rights of Minorities* (Oxford: Clarendon Press, 1991)
Thornberry, Patrick, *Indigenous Peoples and Human Rights* (Manchester: Manchester University Press, 2002)
Thornberry, Patrick, *The International Convention on the Elimination of All Forms of Raial Discrimination: A Commentary* (Oxford: Oxford University Press, 2016)
Tutu, Desmond, *No Future without Forgiveness: A Personal Overview of South Africa's Truth and Reconciliation Commission* (Johannesburg: Ride, 1999)
Urton, Gary, *The Social Life of Numbers: A Quechua Ontology of Numbers and Philosophy of Arithmetic* (Austin: University of Texas Press, 1997)
Viorel, Achim, *The Roma in Romanian History* (Budapest: Central European University Press, 2004)
Viswanath, Rupa, *The Pariah Problem: Caste, Religion, and the Social in Modern India* (New York: Columbia University Press, 2014)
Wade, P., *Race and Ethnicity in Latin America* (London and Chicago: Pluto Press, 1997)
Waldron, Jeremy, *The Harm in Hate Speech* (Cambridge, MA and London: Harvard University Press, 2012)
Waughray, Annapurna, *Capturing Caste in Law: The Legal Regulation of Caste-based Discrimination* (Routledge, 2018, forthcoming)
Zelliot, Eleanor, *From Untouchable to Dalit: Essays on the Ambedkar Movement* (New Delhi: Manohar, 1998).

II. Book chapters and edited collections

Alston, Philip, 'The historical origins of "General Comments" in human rights law', in L. Boisson de Chazournes and V. Gowlland-Debbas (eds), *The International Legal System in Quest of Equity and Universality* (The Hague: Martinus Nijhoff, 2001), pp. 763–76
Banton, Michael, 'Political motives as grounds of racial discrimination', in F. Coomans, F. Grünfeld, I. Westendorp and J. Willems (eds), *Rendering Justice to the Vulnerable: Liber Amicorum in Honour of Theo van Boven* (The Hague: Kluwer, 2000), pp. 61–8
Banton, Michael, 'Decision-taking in the Committee on the Elimination of Racial Discrimination', in P. Alston and J. Crawford (eds), *The Future of*

UN Human Rights Treaty Monitoring (Cambridge: Cambridge University Press, 2000), pp. 55–78

Banton, Michael, 'Ethnic monitoring in international law: The work of CERD', in Andrea Krizsán (ed.), *Ethnic Monitoring and Data Protection: The European Context* (Budapest: Central European University Press, 2001), pp. 62–85

Banton, Michael, 'Colour as a ground of discrimination', in N. Ghanea and A. Xanthaki (eds), *Minorities, Peoples and Self-Determination: Essays in Honour of Patrick Thornberry* (Leiden: Martinus Nijhoff, 2004), pp. 237–47

Bazilli, Susan, 'Introduction', in S. Bazili (ed.), *Putting Women on the Agenda* (Johannesburg: Raven Press, 1992), pp. 1–26

Bennagen, Ponciano L., '"Amending" IPRA, negotiating autonomy, upholding the right to self-determination', in A. B. Gatmaytan (ed.), *Negotiating Autonomy Case Studies on Philippines Indigenous Peoples' Land Rights* (Quezon City and Cogenhagen: IWGIA, LRC-KsK/FOE-Phils, 2007), pp. 179–98

Boyle, Kevin and Baldaccini, Annaliese, 'International human rights approaches to racism', in S. Fredman (ed.), *Discrimination and Human Rights* (Oxford: Oxford University Press (Academy of European Law), 2001), pp. 135–91

Cahn, Claude, 'Roma and racial discrimination: The jurisprudence of the European Court of Human Rights', in D. Bigo, S. Carrera and E. Guild (eds), *Foreigners, Refugees and Minorities? Rethinking People in the Context of Border Controls and Visas* (Farnham: Ashgate, 2013), pp. 55–73

Doyle, Cathal, 'The effectiveness of legal and non-legal remedies for addressing the rights of Indigenous Peoples at Mindoro Island and elsewhere', in Forum for Development Cooperation with Indigenous Peoples, *Forum Conference 2010 Indigenous Participation in Policy-making: Ideals, Realities and Possibilities* (Tromso: University of Tromso, 2010), pp. 85–94

Doyle, Cathal, 'Operational-level grievance mechanism and indigenous peoples' access to remedy', in C. Doyle (ed.), *Business and Human Rights: Indigenous Peoples' Experiences with Access to Remedy. Case studies from Africa, Asia and Latin America* (Chiang Mai, Madrid and Copenhagen: AIPP, Almáciga, IWGIA, 2014), pp. 27–72

Dulitzky, Ariel, 'A region in denial: Racial discrimination and racism in Latin America', in A. Dzidzienyo and S. Oboler (eds), *Neither Enemies nor Friends: Latinos, Blacks, Afro-Latinos* (New York: Palgrave Macmillan, 2005), pp. 39–60

Frieze, Donna-Lee (ed.), *Totally Unofficial: The Autobiography of Raphael Lemkin* (New Haven and London: Yale University Press, 2013)

Gatmayan, Augusto B., 'Philippines indigenous peoples and the quest for autonomy: Negotiated or compromised?', in A. B. Gatmaytan (ed.), *Negotiating Autonomy Case Studies on Philippines Indigenous Peoples' Land Rights* (Quezon City and Cogenhagen: IWGIA, LRC-KsK/FOE-Phils, 2007), pp. 1–36

Gelber, Katharine, 'Reconceptualizing counterspeech in hate speech policy (with a focus on Australia)', in M. Herz and P. Molnar (eds), *Content and Context: Rethinking Regulation and Remedies for Hate Speech* (New York: Cambridge University Press, 2012), pp. 198–216

Gorringe, Hugo, 'Dalit Politics: Untouchability, identity and assertion' in A. Kohli and P. Singh (eds), *Routledge Handbook of Indian Politics* (London: Routledge, 2012), pp. 119–28

Hacking, Ian, 'Making up people', in T. C. Heller, M. Sosna and D. E. Wellbery (eds), *Reconstructing Individualism* (Stanford: Stanford University Press, 1986), pp. 222–36

Hasenbalg, Carlos, 'Racial inequalities in Brazil and throughout Latin America: Timid responses to disguised racism', in E. Jelin and E. Hersheberg (eds), *Constructing Democracy: Human Rights, Citizenship, and Society in Latin America* (Boulder: Westview Press, 1996), pp. 161–76

Keane, David and Castellino, Joshua, 'Is ICERD the *de facto* minority rights treaty?' in C. Buckley, A. Donald and P. Leach (eds), *Towards Convergence in International Human Rights Law: Approaches of Regional and International Systems* (Leiden: Martinus Nijhoff, 2016), pp. 275–95

Leonen, Marvic Mario Victor F., 'Seeking the norm: Reflections on land rights policy and indigenous peoples right', in A. B. Gatmaytan (ed.), *Negotiating Autonomy Case Studies on Philippines Indigenous Peoples' Land Rights* (Quezon City and Cogenhagen: IWGIA, LRC-KsK/FOE-Phils, 2007), pp. 37–66

Letsas, George, 'The ECHR as a living instrument: Its meaning and legitimacy', in A. Follesdahl, B. Peters and G. Ulfstein (eds), *Constituting Europe: The European Court of Human Rights in a National, European and Global Context* (Cambridge: Cambridge University Press, 2013), pp. 106–41

Mackay, Fergus, 'Indigenous peoples' rights and the UN Committee on the Elimination of Racial Discrimination', in S. Dersso (ed.), *Perspectives on the Rights of Minorities and Indigenous Peoples in Africa* (Pretoria: Pretoria University Law Press, 2010), pp. 155–202

McGonagle, Tarlach, 'The development of freedom of expression and information within the UN: Leaps and bounds or fits and starts?', in T. McGonagle and Y. Donders (eds), *The United Nations and Freedom of Expression and Information: Critical Perspectives* (Cambridge: Cambridge University Press, 2015), pp. 1–51

Morrison, Judith, 'Social movements in Latin America: The power of regional and national networks', in K. Dixon and J. Burdick (eds), *Comparative Perspectives on Afro-Latin America* (Gainesville: University Press of Florida, 2012), pp. 243–63

Murray, Christine and O'Regan, Catherine, 'Putting women into the constitution', in S. Bazili (ed.), *Putting Women on the Agenda* (Johannesburg: Ravan Press, 1992), pp. 33–55

Nouwen, Sarah, 'The International Criminal Court: A peacebuilder in Africa?', in Devon Curtis and Gwinyayi A. Dzinesa (eds), *Peacebuilding,*

Power and Politics in Africa (South Africa: Wits University Press, 2013), pp. 171–92
O'Flaherty, Michael, 'International Covenant on Civil and Political Rights: Interpreting freedom of expression and information standards for the present and the future', in T. McGonagle and Y. Donders (eds), *The United Nations and Freedom of Expression and Information: Critical Perspectives* (Cambridge: Cambridge University Press, 2015), pp. 55–88
Parekh, Bikhu, 'Is there a case for banning hate speech?', in M. Herz and P. Molnar (eds), *Content and Context: Rethinking Regulation and Remedies for Hate Speech* (New York: Cambridge University Press, 2012), pp. 37–56.
Partsch, Karl Joseph, 'Racial speech and human rights: Article 4 of the Convention on the Elimination of All Forms of Racial Discrimination', in S. Coliver (ed.), *Striking a Balance: Hate Speech Freedom of Expression and Non-Discrimination* (London: Article 19, 1992), pp. 21–28
Partsch, Karl Josef, 'The Committee on the Elimination of Racial Discrimination', in P. Alston (ed.), *The United Nations and Human Rights: A Critical Appraisal* (Oxford: Oxford University Press, 1992), pp. 339–68
Pildes, Richard H., 'Ethnic identity and democratic institutions: A dynamic perspective', in S. Choudhry (ed.), *Constitutional Design for Divided Societies: Integration or Accommodation?* (Oxford: Oxford University Press, 2008), pp. 173–201
Post, Robert, 'Hate speech', in I. Hare and J. Weinstein (eds), *Extreme Speech and Democracy* (New York: Oxford University Press, 2009), pp. 123–38
Pradhan-Malla, Sapana, 'Racism and gender', in United Nations, *Dimensions of Racism* (New York and Geneva: United Nations, 2005), pp. 179–91
Prouvez, Nathalie, 'Committee on the Elimination of Racial Discrimination: Confronting racial discrimination and Inequality in the enjoyment of economic, social and cultural rights', in M. Langford (ed.), *Social Rights Jurisprudence: Emerging Trends in International and Comparative Law* (Cambridge: Cambridge University Press, 2008), pp. 517–37
Rovillos, Raymundo D. and Tauli-Corpuz, Victoria, 'Development power and identity politics in the Philippines', in S. Sawyer and E. T. Gome (eds), *The Politics of Resource Extraction: Indigenous Peoples, Multinational Corporations and the State* (London: Palgrave Macmillan, 2012), pp. 129–52
Sanz, Penelope, 'The politics of consent: The State, multinational capital and the Subanon of Canatuan', in A. B. Gatmaytan (ed.), *Negotiating Autonomy Case Studies on Philippines Indigenous Peoples' Land Rights* (Quezon City and Cogenhagen: IWGIA, LRC-KsK/FOE-Phils, 2007), pp. 109–37
Schlutter, Birgit, 'Aspects of human rights interpretation by the UN Treaty bodies', in H. Keller and G. Ulfstein (eds), *UN Human Rights Treaty Bodies: Law and Legitimacy* (Cambridge: Cambridge University Press, 2015), pp. 261–319
Thornberry, Patrick, 'Race, descent and caste under ICERD', in K. Nakano, M. Yutzis and R. Onoyama (eds), *Peoples for Human Rights*, Vol. 9,

'Descent-based Discrimination' (Tokyo: International Movement Against all Forms of Discrimination and Racism, 2004)

Thornberry, Patrick, 'The Convention on the Elimination of Racial Discrimination, indigenous peoples, and caste/descent-based discrimination', in J. Castellino and N. Walsh (eds), *International Law and Indigenous Peoples* (Leiden: Martinus Nijhoff, 2005), pp. 17–53

Thornberry, Patrick, 'International Convention on the Elimination of All Forms of Racial Discrimination: The prohibition of "racist hate speech"', in T. McGonagle and Y. Donders (eds), *The United Nations and Freedom of Expression and Information: Critical Perspectives* (Cambridge: Cambridge University Press, 2015), pp. 121–44.

Van Boven, Theo, 'Racial and religious discrimination', in R. Wolfrum (ed.), *The Max Planck Encyclopedia of Public International Law*, Vol. VIII (Oxford: Oxford University Press, 2012), pp. 608–17

Von Hebel, Herman and Robinson, Darryl, 'Crimes within the jurisdiction of the Court', in R. S. Lee (ed.), *The International Criminal Court: The Making of the Rome Statute, Issues, Negotiations, Results* (The Hague, London and Boston: Kluwer Law International, 1999), pp. 79–126

Wolfrum, Rudiger, 'The elimination of racial discrimination: Achievements and challenges', in The United Nations Educational, Scientific and Cultural Organization, *United to Combat Racism: Selected Articles and Standard-setting Instruments* (Paris: UNESCO, 2001)

III. Journals

Adler, A., 'Inverting the First Amendment', *University of Pennsylvania Law Review*, 149:4 (2001), 921–1002

Alves, Jose A. Lindgren, 'Race and religion in the United Nations Committee on the Elimination of Racial Discrimination', *University of San Francisco Law Review*, 42 (2007–8), 941–82

Anderson, Mark, 'When Afro becomes (like) indigenous: Garifuna and Afro-indigenous politics in Honduras', *Journal of Latin America and Caribbean Anthropology*, 12:2 (2007), 384–413

Andrews, George Reid, 'Brazilian racial democracy, 1900–90', *Journal of Contemporary History*, 31 (1996), 483–507

Asad, Talal, 'Ethnographic representation, statistics and modern power', *Social Research*, 61 (1994), 55–88

Asmal, Kader, 'Truth, reconciliation and justice: The South African experience in perspective', *The Modern Law Review*, 63:1 (2000), 1–24

Banton, Michael, 'States and civil society in the campaign against racial discrimination', *Nationalism and Ethnic Politics*, 18:4 (2012), 385–405

Bergmann, Werner and Crutchfield, Robert D., 'Introduction: Racial and ethnic conflict and violence', *International Journal of Conflict and Violence*, 3:2 (2009), 146–153

Berry, Stephanie E., 'Bringing Muslim minorities within the International Convention on the Elimination of All Forms of Racial Discrimination: square peg in a round hole?', *Human Rights Law Review*, 11:3 (2011), 423–50

Brazta, Nicolas, 'Living instrument or dead letter: The future of the European Convention on Human Rights', *European Human Rights Law Review*, 2 (2014), 116–28

Bob, Clifford, '"Dalit Rights are Human Rights": Caste discrimination, international activism and the construction of a new human rights issue', *Human Rights Quarterly*, 29 (2007), 167–93

Bourdieu, Pierre, 'Rethinking the state: Genesis and structure of the bureaucratic field' (Wacquant, L. J. D., and Farage, S., trans.), *Sociological Theory*, 12 (1994), 1–18

Buergenthal, Thomas, 'Implementing the UN racial convention', *Texas International Law Journal*, 12 (1977), 187–221

Buergenthal, Thomas, 'The UN Human Rights Committee', *Max Planck Yearbook of United Nations Law*, 5 (2001), 341–98

Buys, Cindy Galway, 'Application of the International Convention on the Elimination of all Forms of Racial Discrimination (*Georgia v Russian Federation*)', *The American Journal of International Law*, 103:2 (2009), 294–9

Cahn, Claude, 'Birth of a nation: Kosovo and the persecution of pariah minorities', *German Law Journal*, 8:1 (2007), 81–94

Castellino, Joshua, 'Affirmative action for the protection of linguistic rights: An analysis of international human rights legal standards in the context of the Irish language', *Dublin University Law Journal*, 25 (2004), 1–43

Castellino, Joshua, 'A re-examination of the International Convention for the Elimination of All Forms of Racial Discrimination', *Revista Iberoamericana de Derecho Humanos*, 2 (2006), 3–34

Castellino, Joshua, 'The protection of minorities and indigenous peoples in international law: A comparative temporal analysis', *International Journal on Minority and Group Rights*, 17:3 (2010), 393–422

Collier, Jane, Maurer, Bill and Suárez-Navaz, Liliana, 'Sanctioned identities: Legal constructions of modern personhood', *Identities*, 2 (1995), 1–27.

Cottrol, Robert, J., 'The long, lingering shadow: Law, liberalism, and cultures of hierarchy and identity in the Americas', *Tulane Law Review*, 76 (2001), 11–80

De la Rey, Cheryl, 'South African feminism, race, and racism', *Agenda*, 32 (1997), 6–10

Delgado, Richard and Stefancic, Jean, 'Four observations about hate speech', *Wake Forest Law Review*, 44:2 (2009), 353–70

Delgado, Richard and Stefancic, Jean, 'Hate speech in cyberspace', *Wake Forest Law Review*, 49:2 (2014), 319–43

Desrosières, Alain, 'How real are statistics? Four possible attitudes', *Social Research*, 68 (2001), 339–55

Diaconu, Ion, 'Racial discrimination: Using special measures for promoting equal human rights', *East African Journal of Peace and Human Rights*, 18:1 (2012), 1–17

Doyle, Cathal, 'Indigenous peoples and the Millennium Development Goals: "Sacrificial lambs" or equal beneficiaries?', *The International Journal of Human Rights*, 13:1 (2009), 44–71

Edward, Rhoda E., 'The "full belly" thesis: Should economic rights take priority over civil and political rights? Evidence from Sub-Saharan Africa', *Human Rights Quarterly*, 5 (1983), 467–90

Espeland, Wendy Nelson and Stevens, Mitchell, 'A sociology of quantification', *European Journal of Sociology*, 49 (2008), 401–36

Farrior, Stephanie, 'The neglected pillar: The "teaching tolerance" provision of the International Convention on the Elimination of All Forms of Racial Discrimination', *ILSA Journal of International and Comparative Law*, 5:2 (1999), 291–9

French, Jan Hoffman, '*Mestizaje* and law making in indigenous identity formation in northeastern Brazil', *American Anthropologist*, 106 (2004), 663–74

Gaudreault-DesBiens, Jean-Francois, 'From Sisyphus's dilemma to Sisyphus's duty? A meditation on the regulation of hate propaganda in relation to hate crimes and genocide', *McGill Law Journal*, 46:4 (2001), 1117–37

Gelber, Katharine and McNamara, Luke, 'Evidencing the harms of hate speech', *Social Identities – Journal for the Study of Race, Nation and Culture* (2015), 1–18

Ghanea, Nazila, 'Intersectionality and the spectrum of racist hate speech: Proposals to the UN Committee on the Elimination of Racial Discrimination', *Human Rights Quarterly*, 35:4 (2013), 935–54

Gilbert, Jérémie, 'Indigenous rights in the making: The United Nations Declaration on the Rights of Indigenous Peoples', *International Journal on Minority and Group Rights*, 14(2/3) (2007), 207–30

Gilbert, Jérémie, 'The right to freely dispose of natural resources: Utopia or forgotten right?', *Netherlands Quarterly of Human Rights*, 31(2) (2013), 314–41

Gilbert, Jérémie, 'Land rights as human rights: The case for a specific right to land', *SUR Journal on Human Rights*, 18 (2014), 114–35

Goldsmith, J., 'Should international human rights law trump US domestic law?' *Chicago Journal of International Law*, 1:2 (2000), 327–39

Guyer, Jane I., Khan, Naveeda and Obarrio, Juan, *et al.*, Special section: 'Number as inventive frontier', *Anthropological Theory*, 10 (2010), 36–197

Hayner, Priscilla B., 'Fifteen truth commissions – 1974 to 1994: A comparative study', *Human Rights Quarterly*, 16:4 (1994), 597–655

Hetherington, Kregg, 'Waiting for the surveyor: Development promises and the temporality of infrastructure', *Journal of Latin American and Caribbean Anthropology*, 19 (2014), 195–211.

Hooker, Juliet, 'Indigenous inclusion, black exclusion: Race, ethnicity and multicultural citizenship in Latin America', *Journal of Latin American Studies*, 37:2 (2005), 285–310

Htun, Mala, 'From racial democracy to affirmative action: Changing state policy on race in Brazil', *Latin American Research Review*, 39:1 (2004), 60–89

Jalali, Rita and Lipset, Seymour Martin, 'Racial and ethnic conflict: A global perspective, *Political Science Quarterly*, 107:4 (1992–3), 585–606

Keane, David, 'Addressing the aggravated meeting points of race and religion', *University of Maryland Law Journal of Race, Religion, Gender and Class*, 6 (2006), 353–91

Kingsbury, Benedict, 'Indigenous peoples in international law: A constructivist approach to the Asian controversy', *American Journal of International Law* 92 (1998), 414–57

Kretzmer, David, 'Freedom of speech and racism', *Cardozo Law Review*, 8:3 (1987), 445–513

Lampland, Martha, 'False numbers as formalizing practices', *Social Studies of Science*, 40 (2010), 377–404

Lennox, Corinne, 'Reviewing Durban: Examining the outputs and review of the 2001 World Conference against Racism', *Netherlands Quarterly of Human Rights*, 27:2 (2009), 209–13

Lennox, Corinne and Minott, Carlos, 'Inclusion of Afro-descendants in ethnic data collection: Towards visibility', *International Journal on Minority and Group Rights*, 18 (2011), 257–75.

Leonen, Marvic Mario Victor F., 'Weaving worldviews implications of constitutional challenges to the Indigenous Peoples Rights Act of 1997', *Philippine Natural Resources Journal*, 10:1 (2000), 3–44

Lerche, Jens, 'Transnational advocacy networks and affirmative action for Dalits in India', *Development and Change*, 39:2 (2008), 239–61

Lovelace Jr., Timothy, 'Making the world in Atlanta's image: The Student Nonviolent Coordinating Committee, Morris Abram, and the legislative history of the United Nations Race Convention', *Law and History Review*, 32:2 (2014), 385–429

Lucak, Natalia, 'Georgia v Russian Federation: A question of the jurisdiction of the International Court of Justice', *Maryland Journal of International Law*, 27:1 (2012), 323–54

Mazower, Mark, 'Minorities and the League of Nations in interwar Europe', *Daedalus*, 126:2 (1997), 47–65

McGary, H., 'Justice and reparations', *Philosophical Forum*, 9 (1977–78), 250–63

McVeigh, Robbie, '"Ethnicity denial"' and racism: The case of the Government of Ireland against Irish Travellers', *Translocations*, 2:1 (2007), 90–133

Mechlem, K., 'Treaty bodies and the interpretation of human rights', *Vanderbilt Journal of International Law*, 42 (2009), 905–47

Mendeloff, David, 'Truth-seeking, truth-telling and post-conflict peacebuilding: Curb the enthusiasm?' *International Studies Review,* 6:3 (2004), 355–80

Menkel-Meadow, Carrie, 'Peace and justice: Notes on the evolution and purposes of legal processes', *Georgetown Law Journal*, 94 (2006), 553–80

Meron, Theodor, 'The meaning and reach of the International Convention on the Elimination of All Forms of Racist Discrimination', *American Journal of International Law*, 79 (1985), 283–318

Merry, Sally Engle, 'Measuring the world: Indicators, human rights, and global governance', *Current Anthropology*, 52:3 (2011), s83–s95 ["s" = supplement]

Morning, Ann, 'Ethnic classification in global perspective', *Population Research and Policy Review*, 27 (2008), 239–72

Nkansah, Lydia A., 'International criminal justice in Africa: Some emerging dynamics', *Journal of Politics and Law*, 4:2 (2011), 74–84

Nkansah, Lydia A., 'Restorative justice in transitional Sierra Leone', *Journal of Public Administration and Governance*, 1:1 (2011), 157–73

Nkansah, Lydia A., 'International Criminal Court in the trenches of Africa', *African Journal of International Criminal Justice*, 1:1 (2015), 8–36

Parmar, Sejal, 'The Rabat Plan of Action: A global blueprint for combating "hate speech"', *European Human Rights Law Review*, 1 (2014), 21–31

Partsch, Karl Josef, 'Elimination of racial discrimination in the enjoyment of civil and political rights: A study of Article 5, subparagraphs (a) to (d), of the International Convention on the Elimination of All Forms of Racial Discrimination', *Texas International Law Journal*, 14 (1979), 191–250

Petrova, Dimitrina, '"Smoke and mirrors": The Durban Review Conference and human rights politics at the United Nations', *Human Rights Law Review*, 10:1 (2009), 129–50

Posner, Eric A. and Vermeule, Adrian, 'Transitional justice as ordinary justice', *Harvard Law Review*, 117:3 (2004), 762–826

Post, Robert C., 'Racist speech, democracy, and the First Amendment', *William and Mary Law Review*, 32:2 (1991), 267–327

Richardson, H. J., 'Self-determination, international law and the South African Bantustan policy', *Columbia Journal of Transnational* Law, 17 (1978), 185–220

Romany, Celina and Culliton, Katherine 'The UN World Conference against Racism: A race–ethnic and gender perspective', *Human Rights Brief*, 9:2 (2002)

Rosenfeld, Michael, 'Hate speech in constitutional jurisprudence: A comparative analysis', *Cardozo Law Review*, 24:4 (2003), 1523–67

Rosga, AnnJanette and Satterthwaite, Margaret, 'The trust in indicators: Measuring human rights', *Berkeley Journal of International Law*, 27 (2009), 253–315

Rothman, S., 'Racial diversity reconsidered', *Public Interest*, 151 (2003), 25–38

Safa, Helen, 'Race and national identity in the Americas', *Latin American Perspectives*, 25:3 (1998), 3–12

Salas, Jesus Maria Herrera, 'Ethnicity and revolution: The political economic of racism in Venezuela', *Latin America Perspectives*, 32:2 (2005), 72–91

Saunders, Pammela, 'The integrated enforcement of human rights', *New York University Journal of International Law and Politics*, 45 (2012), 97–174

Schlosberg, J., 'Judgment on "Nuremberg": An analysis of free speech and anti-abortion threats made on the internet', *Boston University Journal of Science and Technology Law*, 7 (2001), 52–79

Schwelb, Egon, 'The International Convention on the Elimination of All Forms of Racial Discrimination', *International and Comparative Law Quarterly*, 15:4 (1966), 996–1068

Thornberry, Patrick, 'Confronting racial discrimination: A CERD perspective', *Human Rights Law Review*, 5:2 (2005), 239–69

Thornberry, Patrick, 'Forms of hate speech and the Convention on the Elimination of all Forms of Racial Discrimination', *Religion and Human Rights*, 5:2 (2010), 97–117

Thorne, Eva, 'Land rights and Garifuna identity', *North American Congress on Latin America*, 38:2 (2004), 21–5

Turner, Michael J., 'The road to Durban – and back', *NACLA Report on the Americas*, 35:6 (2002), 31–5

Valls, Andrew, 'Racial justice as transitional justice', *Polity*, 36:1 (2003), 53–71

Van Boven, Theo, 'The petition system under the International Convention on the Elimination of All Forms of Racial Discrimination: A sobering balance sheet', *Max Planck Yearbook of United Nations Law*, 4 (2000), 271–87

Vinjamuri, Leslie and Snyder, Jack, 'Advocacy and scholarship in the study of international war crime tribunals and transitional justice', *Annual Review of Political Science*, 7:1 (2004), 345–62

Waughray, Annapurna, 'Caste discrimination: A twenty-first century challenge for UK discrimination law?', *Modern Law Review*, 72:2 (2009), 182–219

Waughray, Annapurna, 'India and the paradox of caste discrimination', *European Yearbook of Minority Issues*, 8 (2010), 413–52

Waughray, Annapurna, 'Capturing caste in law: Caste discrimination and the Equality Act 2010', *Human Rights Law Review*, 14:2 (2014), 359–79

Waughray, Annapurna, 'Is caste discrimination in the UK prohibited by the Equality Act 2010?', *International Labor Rights Case Law*, 2 (2016), 70–6

IV. Reports and other sources

Armstrong, David, Davenport, Christian, Pradeep, Manjula and Macwan, Martin, 'Understanding Untouchability: A Comprehensive Study of Practices and Conditions in 1589 Villages' (Navsarjan Trust and Robert F. Kennedy Center for Justice & Human Rights, 2010)

Bunche, Ralph, 'Some Reflections on Peace in Our Time', Nobel Lecture, 11 December 1950, available at: www.nobelprize.org/nobel_prizes/peace/laureates/1950/bunche-lecture.html

Chakma, Suhas and Jensen, Marianne (eds), *Racism against Indigenous Peoples* (Copenhagen: International Work Group for Indigenous Affairs (IWGIA), No. 105, 2001)

Charters, Claire (ed.), *Making the Declaration Work: The United Nations Declaration on the Rights of Indigenous Peoples* (Copenhagen: International Work Group for Indigenous Affairs (IWGIA), 2009)

Council of Europe Human Rights Commissioner, 'Human Rights of Roma and Travellers in Europe' (Strasbourg: Council of Europe, 2011)

De Friedemann, Nina S. and Arocha, Jaime, 'Colombia', in Pedro Pérez Sarduy and Jean Stubbs (eds), *No Longer Invisible: Afro-Latin Americans Today* (London: Minority Rights Group International, 1995), pp. 47–76

Dhanda, Meena, Waughray, Annapurna, Keane, David and Mosse, David, 'Caste in Britain: Socio-legal Review', Equality and Human Rights Commission Research Report 91 (Manchester: Equality and Human Rights Commission, 2014)

Dhanda, Meena, Mosse, David and Waughray, Annapurna, 'Caste in Britain: Experts' Seminar and Stakeholders' Workshop', Equality and Human Rights Commission Research Report 92 (Manchester: Equality and Human Rights Commission, 2014)

Doyle, Cathal and Carino, Jill, 'Making Free Prior and Informed Consent a Reality: Indigenous Peoples and the Extractive Sector' (London: Middlesex University, ECCR, PIPLinks, 2013), available at: http://solutions-network.org/site-fpic/files/2012/09/Making-Free-Prior-Informed-Consent-a-Reality-DoyleCarino.pdf

Foreign Relations of the United States, 1948, Vol. I (Washington, DC: United States Government Printing Office, 1975)

Gagliardone, Ivan, Gal, Danit, Alves, Thiago and Martinez, Gabriela, *Countering Online Hate Speech* (Paris: UNESCO Publishing, 2015)

Human Rights Commission of Malaysia (SUHAKAM), 'The Human Rights Commission of Malaysia calls on the Government to accede to the International Convention on the Elimination of All Forms of Racial Discrimination 1969', 21 March 2015, available at: www.suhakam.org.my/wp-content/uploads/2015/04/Press-Release-ICERD-2015-.pdf

International Movement Against All Forms of Discrimination and Racism (IMADR), *ICERD and CERD: A Guide for Civil Society Actors* (Geneva: IMADR, 2011), available at: www.ohchr.org/Documents/HRBodies/CERD/ICERDManual.pdf

International Movement Against All Forms of Discrimination and Racism (IMADR), 'Written Statement: Best Practices, Achievements and Challenges of the ICERD' (2015), available at: www.ohchr.org/Documents/HRBodies/CERD/50Years/IMADR.pdf

Jacobe-Asperin, J. R., 'Community Perspectives on the Business Responsibility to Respect Human Rights in Countries Affected or Threatened by Conflict'

(Institute for Human Rights and Business, Collaborative Learning Projects, 2010)

Leighton, Kevin, 'The Scandal of Inequality in Latin America and the Caribbean' (Christian Aid, 2012)

McGonagle, Tarlach, 'The Troubled Relationship between Free Speech and Racist Hate Speech: The Ambiguous Roles of the Media and Internet', Expert Paper, Day of Thematic Discussion 'Racist Hate Speech' (28 August 2012), UN Committee on the Elimination of Racial Discrimination, Eighty-first Session, Geneva, 6–31 August 2012

Metcalfe, Hilary and Rolfe, Heather, *Caste Discrimination and Harassment in Great Britain* (London: Government Equalities Office, 2010)

Muman, Satpal, 'Caste in Britain' in Dalits in the New Millennium: Report of the Proceedings of the International Conference on Dalit Human Rights, 16–17 September 2000 (London: Voice of Dalit International, 2000)

N'gome, M'Baré, 'Inclusión, interculturalidad y etnoeducación en el Perú y en América latina', in Centro de Desarrollo Étnico, *Desde Adentro: Etnoeducación E Interculturalidad En El Perú Y América Latina* (Lima: Centro de Desarrollo Étnico – CEDET, 2011), pp. 315–24

Office of the High Commissioner for Human Rights, 'Guiding Principles on Business and Human Rights: Implementing the United Nations "Protect, Respect and Remedy" Framework' (New York and Geneva: United Nations, 2011)

Office of the High Commissioner for Human Rights (OHCHR), 'Selected Decisions of the Committee on the Elimination of Racial Discrimination: Vol.1' (New York and Geneva: United Nations, 2012), available at: www.ohchr.org/Documents/Publications/CERDSelectedDecisionsVolume1.pdf

Office of the High Commissioner for Human Rights (OHCHR), 'International Convention on the Elimination of All Forms of Racial Discrimination: 50 years of fighting racism', 26 November 2015, available at: www.ohchr.org/EN/HRBODIES/CERD/50/Pages/Icerd50.aspx

Pritchard, Sarah, 'Stirrings: Early warning/urgent action decision concerning Australia from the UN Committee on the Elimination of Racial Discrimination', *Indigenous Law Bulletin*, 4:15 (1999), 17

Remedy Australia, 'Hagan v Australia (CERD, 2003)', available at: http://remedy.org.au/cases/15/

Report of the African Commission's Working Group of Experts on Indigenous Populations/Communities, submitted in accordance with 'Resolution on the Rights of Indigenous Populations/Communities in Africa', adopted by the African Commission on Human and Peoples' Rights at its twenty-eighth ordinary session, DOC/OS(XXXIV)/345 (2003)

Sánchez, Margarita and Bryan, Maurice, 'Macro Study: Afro-descendants, Discrimination and Economic Exclusion in Latin America' (London: Minority Rights Group International, 2003)

Sarduy, Pedro Pérez and Stubbs, Jean (eds), *No Longer Invisible: Afro-Latin Americans Today* (London: Minority Rights Group International, 1995)

Simonovic, Dubravka, 'Convention on the Elimination of All Forms of Discrimination against Women: Introductory note', Audiovisual Library of International Law, available at: http://legal.un.org/avl/ha/cedaw/cedaw.html

Skinner, Gwynne, 'Parent Company Accountability: Enhancing Justice for Human Rights Violations' (International Corporate Accountability Roundtable (ICAR), 2015), available at: http://icar.ngo/wp-content/uploads/2015/06/ICAR-Parent-Company-Accountability-Project-Report.pdf

Special Representative of the Secretary-General on Human Rights and Transnational Corporations and Other Business Enterprises, 'Mapping State Obligations for Corporate Acts: An Examination of the UN Human Rights Treaty System Report No. 1: International Convention on the Elimination of All Forms of Racial Discrimination' (2006), available at: www.valoresociale.it/detail.asp?c=1&p=0&id=291

Statement by President of Liberia, Ellen Johnson Sirleaf, at a National Visioning Conference (2012). See further: www.emansion.gov.lr/doc/EJS_National_Constitution_Conference_Liberia_March_30_2015.pdf

Subanon of Mt Canatuan, 'Submission to the CERD regarding Discrimination against the Subanon of Mt Canatuan, Siocon, Zamboanga del Norte, Philippines, in the context of large-scale gold mining on their ancestral domain', CERD Seventy-first Session, 30th July – 17th August (2007)

'Truth and Reconciliation Commission of South Africa Report' (Cape Town, South Africa: Truth and Reconciliation Commission, 1999), available at: www.justice.gov.za/trc/report/index.htm

'Truth and Reconciliation Commission of Liberia Final Report' (Monrovia, Liberia, 2008), available at: http://trcofliberia.org/reports/final-report

TVIRD, 'There is NO Sacred Mountain', Social and Environmental Review, available at: www.tvird.com.ph/stakeholders/nosacredmountain.html

UNDP, 'Visibilidad Estadística: Datos Sobre Población Afrodescendiente En Censos Y Encuestas de Hogares de América Latina' (Panamá: United Nations Development Programme, 2012)

United Nations Secretariat, 'Concept paper on the High Commissioner's proposal for a unified standing treaty body' (2006), HRI/MC/2006/2

UNWomen, *Progress of the World's Women 2015–2016: Transforming Economies, Realising Rights* (New York: UNWomen, 2015)

Index